THE
CABINETMAKERS OF AMERICA

Books by Ethel Hall Bjerkoe

THE CABINETMAKERS OF AMERICA

DECORATING FOR AND WITH ANTIQUES

THE
CABINETMAKERS
OF AMERICA

by

ETHEL HALL BJERKOE

assisted by

JOHN ARTHUR BJERKOE

Foreword by Russell Kettell

ILLUSTRATED WITH PHOTOGRAPHS AND DRAWINGS

BONANZA BOOKS • NEW YORK

To

Those Men and Women

Whose Study, Interpretation, and Enthusiasm

Have Contributed So Much

to Our

Knowledge of

the Cabinetmakers of America

and the

Furniture They Made

LIBRARY OF CONGRESS CATALOG CARD NUMBER 57-7278

COPYRIGHT © MCMLVII BY DOUBLEDAY & COMPANY, INC.

ALL RIGHTS RESERVED

PRINTED IN THE UNITED STATES OF AMERICA

*This edition published by Bonanza Books,
a division of Crown Publishers, Inc., by arrangement
with Doubleday & Company, Inc.*
B C D E F G H

FOREWORD

IN *The Cabinetmakers of America*, Mrs. Bjerkoe has made a real and presently needed contribution toward advancing our knowledge of American furniture.

There were, as early as the 1860s or '70s, a few farsighted people who began to collect or bring down from their attics the good pieces that had been hibernating through the long Victorian winter. But it was not until Mr. Lockwood published his splendid *Colonial Furniture in America* in 1901 that anyone had a chance to sit down with a book and learn about the pieces so long banished from public approval. How Mr. Lockwood was able to produce so knowledgeable and complete a story where he had no predecessor to pick up and expand has always been a source of mystery and admiration to me.

Twenty years or so afterward came another pioneer, Charles Wolsey Lyon, with his *Colonial Furniture of New England*. Then the astonishingly active and successful Wallace Nutting, a clergyman, retired for his health to make a name for himself photographing apple blossoms out of doors and beautiful girls at spinning wheels in Colonial interiors. Soon his interest turned exclusively to furniture, which he collected extensively, and in 1921 he gave a ready public his *Furniture of the Pilgrim Century*. Thereby he established a market into which he sold his own fine collection and everyone was happy.

Nutting's books, like Lockwood's, rank as milestones. Other general treatments of the subject followed, notable among them Miller's *American Antique Furniture* in 1937, valuable for the great weight of evidence in its more than two thousand illustrated pieces.

Today, in Joseph Downs' *American Furniture—Queen Anne and Chippendale Periods*, we have the first of other volumes that are planned to tell the whole general story through examples in the collection of a single museum. It is hard to imagine a better presentation.

At the same time, this is not the only sort of book needed in pushing out the frontiers of our knowledge. Fortunately there have been a considerable number of men and women whose interests have led them to look at American furniture from very special angles. George Francis Dow, in *The Arts and Crafts of New England—1704-1775*, culled Boston newspapers between these dates and grouped for us his produce of references to everything from looking glasses to paint. Fiske Kimball wrote a definitive book on Samuel McIntire, as did Nancy McClelland on Phyfe. Mr. and Mrs. Andrews focused their attention on the quiet simplified taste of a religious community, the Shakers. Dr. Mercer contributed by *Ancient Carpenter's Tools*. Luther told perhaps all there is to be known about *The Hadley Chest*. Albert Sack, in *Fine Points of Furniture*, sharpened our critical observation by a novel Good, Better, Best method of comparison of many pieces. Marion Nicholl Rawson's books, telling how things used to be, are perhaps well summed up by one of her titles, *Handwrought Ancestors*. Bridenbaugh's *The Colonial Craftsman* informs us, after his extensive research, about the men themselves and their place in the social structure. And the arts and crafts of the once busy seaport of Newport, Rhode Island, home of the well-known Townsend and Goddard dynasty of cabinetmakers, are admirably covered by Ralph Carpenter's attractive publication.

v

Unlike Alexander the Great, we still have plenty of areas to conquer. Not only are there good workmen not yet properly written up and many specific designs, like the Brewster chair and the Taunton chest, waiting for closer study, but there is a new scientific approach just beginning to be made use of. Our museums' painting departments have a quarter of a century start on us.

What kind of wood is this? Oak? Red or White? English or American? The older men of a generation ago had ready answers all the way down the line. Then followed a more cautious period, when even after a microscopic examination of the wood structure not everything was plain. Today this sort of scientific study is considered the only reliable hope, and some museum labels are already having to be changed. Furthermore, in identifying the secondary woods used in a piece of furniture it is often possible to determine the region in which it was made.

What a useful book will be developed someday if this identification can be properly explained to the average museum or collector who will be assumed to have only relatively inexpensive equipment.

The X-ray, too, is being experimented with in searching out restorations on furniture that may not be noticeable from the surface, just as the painting departments can discover one painting under another on a canvas. And the spectroscope can probably tell much that we do not yet know about the composition and application of our early paints. About the red, for instance, that holds tenaciously onto the wood against everything but scraping—which heaven forbid!

Is there not plenty of opportunity for research by those who are willing to dig into the faded records?

There is also need for a list of all pieces definitely dated, either as a decoration or through a bill of sale; and likewise one of everything indisputably ascribed to a known craftsman.

In all these projects Mrs. Bjerkoe's list of cabinetmakers is going to be a great help. It will be added to, of course, as time goes on. In many cases, pieces of furniture and the names of their makers will be brought together after a long lapse of years.

To bring the matter right down to an individual usefulness, may I end this foreword by telling of my own experience?

When I was looking hopefully under the K's, there to my great pleasure I found a Jonathan Kettell, 1759-1848, of Charlestown, Massachusetts, "who moved to Newburyport just after the Charlestown fire in 1775."

Now, my father was born in Charlestown in a four-square Salem type of house almost on the top of Bunker Hill and overlooking the Navy Yard. In a nearby graveyard, today completely surrounded by mad commercial traffic, are some twenty or thirty stones that show KETTELL spelled in every possible way—even beginning with a C—and of dates back as far as 1622 (which must, of course, be a date of birth although it does not say so).

The early Kettells were potters by trade, now fairly well recognized in the antique world. This Jonathan, however, seems to have been more interested in cabinetmaking and made a fresh start in Newburyport.

Thanks to Mrs. Bjerkoe's list and notes, I have been alerted to this ancestor; perhaps I can learn more about him and his work.

RUSSELL HAWES KETTELL

Lexington, Massachusetts

CONTENTS

ACKNOWLEDGMENTS

THIS BOOK could never have been written without the help of many, many people and to all I am humbly grateful. Some I shall never know by name—among them, many of those who have been so generous and so patient with their help at museums and libraries. Others have provided data for specific cabinetmakers and this assistance is noted under the individual cabinetmaker. Expressing one's gratitude in this way is, perhaps, a dangerous thing to do, lest one omit to acknowledge the assistance of even one person. I truly trust there will be no such omission. If it should occur, it is due to oversight, not to design.

During the years in which I have been preparing the material in this book, I have traveled thousands of miles, visited many museums, historical societies, collections, and libraries, and have talked with many people. All of this has been pleasant and rewarding. Together with the important information I have acquired many happy memories—pictures, if you will.

It would be impossible to forget last March in Salem, Mass. This was an additional visit to clear up some minor details about the cabinetmakers of this important town. Engrossed in the fascinating collection of Derby papers at the venerable Essex Institute we had not noticed the sudden heavy snowfall until we were asked if we minded if the building were closed since the staff feared difficulty in getting home. We realized the wisdom of the decision when, after leaving by a rear door nearest the parking lot, we waded through deep snow to reach our car. The five mile drive to the President's House at Endicott Junior College, where we were to be overnight guests, was beautiful, precarious, and long. Once there, however, we were comfortably and happily snowbound for several days. This, too, had its compensations. I could sit at my window and watch the lovely snowbound land, the lowering gray sky reflected in the stormy waters of Mingo Bay, and study the history of Salem in its early days.

My remembrance of Richmond presents quite a different picture. Wandering through the lovely little Virginia Museum of Fine Arts, I suddenly came upon a room on the second floor, breath-taking in its dramatic beauty. It was a small room, the walls and ceiling dark—perhaps charcoal gray—the lighting indirect and subdued. On one wall was a large painting by Sargent, the life-size portrait of a woman in a red dress. In the center of the room, back to back, with one facing this painting, was a pair of most gorgeous sofas by the Victorian cabinetmaker of New York City, John Henry Belter. The framework of these was carved and gilded so that it resembled fashioned gold, the upholstery the brilliant red of the painting. There, too, I found an interesting eighteenth-century block-front desk made in Halifax, N. C.

Baltimore remains in my memory as a place of springtime beauty. We left Connecticut with laggard winter dominant, but the next morning we found that lovely spring had invaded the Baltimore countryside, and the drive through a blossom fairyland was a happy prelude to hours of study at the charming Maryland Historical Society headquarters and the imposing Museum of Art.

In Kansas City, Mo., the drive to the William Rockhill Nelson Gallery of Art, to see the eighteenth-century furniture there, was in the heat of a summer day, but I shall always remember the pride of the taxi driver in his town, in his lovely museum, in himself as a citizen of Kansas City. And his pride was akin to that of everyone I met that day.

Not least are my memories of Newport, R. I. Miss Ruth B. Franklin opened the doors of the town to us and everywhere we were welcomed as her friends. At the Historical Society we worked surrounded by furniture made by the Goddards and Townsends. The staff of the Society provided us with fascinating and important account books, documents, and other material from the big vault. With kindness and graciousness they shared their knowledge and affection for Newport with us. Later we found willing assistance and friendship at the Redwood Library, one of the loveliest in the land. We wandered along Washington Street and the old Easton's Point Section where the Quakers had their settlement and where the Goddards and Townsends lived and worked, and we felt closer to them and to their days than we did to the present.

There are memories like these associated with all the places we visited and worked but space will not permit the telling. Other persons and institutions that assisted us in various ways were:

The Albany Institute of History and Art, Albany, N. Y.

The Beverly (Mass.) Historical Society

The Cleveland Museum of Art

The Concord (Mass.) Antiquarian Society

The Connecticut Valley Historical Museum, Springfield, Mass.

The Detroit Institute of Arts

E. Milby Burton, Director, The Charleston Museum, S. C.

Eleanor Offutt O'Lear, Frankfort, Ky.

The Filson Club, Louisville, Ky.

The Forbes Library, Northhampton, Mass.

The Henry Ford Museum, Dearborn, Mich.

The Henry Francis Du Pont Winterthur Museum, Winterthur, Del.

Mrs. Burton N. Gates, Worcester, Mass.

The Ipswich (Mass.) Historical Society

The Maine Historical Society, Portland

The Metropolitan Museum of Art, New York City

The Monmouth County Historical Society, Freehold, N. J.

The Museum of the City of New York
The Museum of Fine Arts, Boston, Mass.
The Museum of Fine Arts, Bowdoin College, Brunswick, Me.
The Newark Museum, Newark, N. J.
The New-York Historical Society, New York City
The Ohio Historical Society, Columbus
The Old Barracks Association, Trenton, N. J.

The Philadelphia Museum of Art
The Rensselaer County Historical Society, Troy, N. Y.
The Rhode Island Historical Society, Providence
The Robert Hull Fleming Museum, University of Vermont, Burlington
The Society for the Preservation of New England Antiquities, Boston
The Troy Public Library, Troy, N. Y.

People all over Connecticut have been helpful with this work. I wish it were possible to say thank you to each one individually, for I have requested a great deal and never has there been lack of gracious and kindly response. Without their help and encouragement, the years of research and writing would have been less happy. I am especially grateful for the assistance that came from:

Mrs. Katharine Prentis Murphy, Westbrook, Conn., and New York City
The Connecticut Historical Society, Hartford
The Connecticut State Library, Hartford

The Wadsworth Atheneum, Hartford
The Wesleyan University Library, Middletown
The Yale University Library and Art Gallery, New Haven

The drawings for this book were made by Lyn Watson and Richard Leach.

CABINETMAKING AS IT
DEVELOPED IN AMERICA

THE STORY of the cabinetmakers of America and the furniture they made is usually said to have begun with the arrival of the *Mayflower* in 1620. In reality, it began long before that date in the mother country, since it was a continuation of the story there—the crafts practiced, the styles of furniture in use, the customs inherent in the life of the people. It is a story filled with mystery, suspense, romance; it contains all the elements of the known and the unknown.

In most instances details concerning the lives of these men and their work lie buried in elusive records—account books, diaries, letters, town records, and histories. Many of the cabinetmakers combined furniture making with other occupations. Many contributed to the history of our country by holding important civic positions and fighting in its wars both as privates and as officers. These men were of many nationalities; the blending of which made the New World great. Their story is an integral part of the story of America.

Much has been discovered about these cabinetmakers, particularly during the past thirty years. Until now, however, there has been no comprehensive compilation. The six years' search that at last made one possible has been stimulating. The finding of considerable new data about some cabinetmakers already known and the discovery of many long forgotten has been rewarding. Much still remains to be discovered. This is a quest that attracts the antiquarian, the true collector, the student of history. An unknown today may be tomorrow's great craftsman. How many knew anything about Benjamin Frothingham of Charlestown, Mass., and his beautiful furniture thirty years ago? Stephen Badlam? The Dunlaps? Who can say today who made the Guilford chests? And who was Benjamin "Burnam," whose cherry blockfront desk made in 1769 may be seen at the Metropolitan Museum of Art, New York City? Some say the son of Benjamin Burnham, the innkeeper of Norwich, Conn. To which others reply, "Impossible." Somewhere hidden away is the clue that will settle the question. Who will be the one to uncover it?

The earliest piece of furniture made in the New World which bears an identifying inscription is the Nicholas Disbrowe carved oak chest made at Hartford, Conn., about 1680. Back of the lower drawer in contemporary script is "Mary Allyns Chistt Cutte and Joyned by Nich: Disbrowe." A group of chests closely related to the Disbrowe in time and design, and attributed to a group of workmen along the Connecticut River in Massachusetts and Connecticut, are the so-called Hadley chests. Many of these of the Hatfield type are believed to have been made by members of the Allis and Belding families of that town. But who constructed those believed to have been made in or near Hartford and at Coventry? Closely related to the Hadley chests are those known as the Connecticut Sunflower chests, which were made at about the same time in the vicinity of Wethersfield (PLATE III, No. 1). In whose shop were these made?

It has been possible to say that some twenty pieces of furniture made between 1650 and 1670 were probably the work of John Alden and/or Kenelm Winslow because the two were capable of making such furniture and were living near Plymouth during those years, and one or more pieces are documented as of Plymouth origin.

A group of chairs, chests, boxes, and cupboards made at Ipswich in the last years of the seventeenth century have been attributed to Thomas Dennis with certainty since at least two of the group stem directly back to his shop by documentary history, and the construction and carving designs of all are so closely akin as to make attribution simple.

When we appraise the Chippendale period with its groups of cabinetmakers in Philadelphia, Newport, R. I., and other sections of the country, there is little, in the absence of a label or other document, to assist in the attribution of specific pieces of furniture. In the early days of our country, few men marked their work or used a label. In fact, few used a label at any time.

One can assert that the Goddard-Townsend group introduced the block-front furniture in America and were the foremost exponents of this style, but, then again, it was adopted by cabinetmakers in other places. One can say that Thomas Affleck of Philadelphia made outstanding highboys and lowboys, elaborately carved and rich in design. But so did half a dozen other men of Philadelphia, and perhaps the same man did the carving for many. And so in the absence of a label or some documentary evidence, we must say that the piece is of the Goddard-Townsend or the Philadelphia school.

During the years the work of a few men showed characteristics so individual as to be almost as significant as a label. Such men, however, were few in comparison with the great army of cabinetmakers in our country from the earliest days. The carving of Samuel McIntire shows in almost every instance motifs used by him alone at the time he was working. Nonetheless, there is some hesitancy about attributing an article of furniture to him in the absence of documentary evidence. In the Mabel Brady Garven Collection at Yale's Art Gallery, there is a mahogany chest-on-chest with carved reclining figures at each end of the pediment and a carved figure of Peace, or Justice, as the central pediment ornament. Experts consider this second only to the chest-on-chest, in the M. and M. Karolik Collection at the Boston Museum

of Fine Arts, constructed by William Lemon of Salem and carved by Mc-
Intire, and called "the masterpiece of Salem." For a long time the piece at
Yale was attributed to McIntire. A handwritten label attached to it says:
"Keep this side up & preserve it from the Sun, from Wet & from bruises. It is
of consequence enough to merit great attention." But one day not so long
ago Mabel Munson Swan of Barrington, R. I., in searching through the many
books of Derby papers at the Essex Institute, Salem, suddenly noticed a bill
to Elias Hasket Derby for a chest-on-chest. This was in the handwriting of
a little-known cabinetmaker, Stephen Badlam of Dorchester Lower Mills. A
comparison of the handwriting on the bill with that on the label at Yale
showed them to be by the same hand, and so attribution of the Yale piece was
definitely made to Stephen Badlam. Further research revealed that the Skillins
of Boston had carved the figural ornaments.

We think of Duncan Phyfe of New York City as having stamped his individuality upon the productions of his workshop. In fact, he did so more
than any other workman of his time. To him have been attributed many
pieces of furniture later found to have been made by such contemporaries
as Charles Honoré Lannuier. Undoubtedly, further research will show that
many pieces both in and out of museums now tentatively attributed to certain
cabinetmakers, by comparison with their labeled or documented furniture,
were actually made by others. Men working in the same locality at any given
time made furniture with similar characteristics, of similar materials.

Thus, one cannot with any degree of certainty attribute pieces of furniture
to a particular man except in those cases where there is a label, some documentary evidence, or individual characteristics so obvious as to make such
attribution realistic. Only the uninitiated would believe it possible to set
down rules by which one could examine a piece of furniture in the block-
front style and say "Ah! a John Goddard." However, by knowing and
recognizing the characteristics of the block-front furniture as designed, constructed, and carved by the various members of the Goddard-Townsend
group working in Newport at the time this furniture was being made, one
can say with a great degree of certainty, "This was made at Newport by
one of the Goddard-Townsend group."
furniture made in the seventeenth, eighteenth, or early nineteenth century;
learning the characteristics of the work produced in the various sections of
And so men and women spend years tracing the lineage of a piece of
the country; studying the history and records of towns and cities to find
details of a cabinetmaker's life and work; attempting to find proof that
a certain man made a certain piece or group of furniture, or that some furniture attributed to one cabinetmaker was doubtless made by another working
at the same time. Through the efforts of these men and women, more and
more details of this fascinating and alluring subject are coming to light.

The furniture produced in any part of America during these two hundred and more years had a direct relationship to the culture and needs of the people in a particular locality at a particular time.

The Pilgrims were simple folk who had spent long years in exile in Holland, and it is quite certain they brought only absolute necessities with them to their new home. Soon, however, colonies were established around Boston, and their Puritan leaders were often persons of higher economic status; moreover, many coming there from the west of England brought with them considerable furniture and other household goods. Before long the settlers were constructing furniture of native woods, including oak, copying the English pieces in the colonies or making others from memory or to fill some new need. Copying, as they did, these early workmen created furniture in the Jacobean tradition with traces of the earlier Tudor-Elizabethan and Gothic,

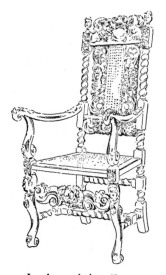

Jacobean chair, 1680–1700   Oak press cupboard, circa 1650–60

with typical carving and paneling. Lunettes, strapwork, arched panels, and molded panels in rectangular and lozenge shapes were usual. The oak they used differed from that in the English-made furniture since the American oak was lighter in color and often quartered to show the grain. In the early days of the colonies it is problematical whether the joiners and cabinetmakers had the tools to attempt elaborate or delicate work. And it is doubtful that many of them had the required skill. In general, then, the furniture constructed by them was sturdy and utilitarian. The turnings, the chamfering and channeling, the moldings and shallow carvings, which they used so successfully, were all possible of execution with a limited number of tools and with no great amount of skill. In New England they made the all-important chest; the impressive but cumbersome court cupboard; wainscot, and turned chairs now called Carver (PLATE VI, NO. 1) and Brewster; various kinds of tables; and other furniture as needed in their simple homes. It must be remembered that even in Europe at this time furniture was not to be found in quantity except in the homes of the great, and according to our standards even those castles were sparsely furnished.

The development of seventeenth-century colonial furniture making must be studied largely in New England. We know that elsewhere much less furniture was produced. Moreover, we find that there are much less data concerning work done by colonial cabinetmakers outside of New England and that fewer pieces of their furniture are in existence today.

Slat-back chair, circa 1700-1730

It is possible to assume that many pieces of simple furniture were constructed in the Dutch colonies of New York during the last half of the seventeenth century and that in design they followed closely those brought from Holland by the settlers, but there are no records of workmen important as furniture makers at that time. The furniture of this period in the Dutch colonies would naturally be identical with that in use in Holland if brought from their old homes by the colonists; if constructed in the settlements, it would be similar in design to the imported pieces, but cruder, less expertly constructed, and of native woods. Records show that in these Dutch colonies there were stools, leather chairs similar to the Cromwellian (which had been introduced into England from Holland), cane chairs, tables, the Dutch *kas* (this was found in none but the Dutch settlements, and served the purposes for which the New England colonists used their oaken cupboards, of which no mention appears in early New York inventories); and the various other types of furniture in general use at that time. The Dutch homes were undoubtedly better equipped at this period than the average New England household.

Although the Dutch colonies fell to England in 1664, the Dutch characteristics were so firmly impressed upon the various settlements that they remained paramount until well into the eighteenth century, not only in the craftsmanship of these colonies themselves but to some extent in that of the artisans and cabinetmakers in the nearby coastal settlements of New Jersey and even adjacent parts of Connecticut.

In 1681 the territory west of the Delaware River between New York and Maryland was assigned to William Penn in payment of a debt owed him by the English Crown, and there began the Anglo-Welsh Quaker settlements founded under his supervision and known as "Penn's Holy Experiment." Many of the settlers in these colonies were comparatively prosperous and brought with them from their homes in England large supplies of household furnishings. Accompanying them were many artisans, and without doubt furniture making began early in these colonies. As yet no records have come to light giving the names of any furniture makers of importance during the last years of the seventeenth century. By 1722, however, there were some one hundred joiners and cabinetmakers in Philadelphia, and by the middle of the century they had reached such a degree of skill that the work they produced in the Chippendale style has never been surpassed in America in beauty of design and richness of carving.

Very early in the eighteenth century, German colonists from the Rhenish Palatinate began coming to the New World in large numbers, populating the settlements around Philadelphia. They brought with them the traditional craftsmanship of their country and continued this tradition in the construction, carving, and painting of their furniture for about one hundred years. These Pennsylvania-German forms and designs had a great influence upon the entire surrounding region; producing a style long misnamed Pennsylvania-Dutch.

Charleston, S. C. (Charles Town until after the Revolution), was an important colony even before its removal to its present location in 1680. By the early 1700s the Carolina low country was the home of a wealthy landed gentry that imported much of its furniture from England and the North. Charleston records reveal cabinetmakers as early as 1720. The number increased rapidly during the late eighteenth and early nineteenth centuries and a large amount of beautiful furniture was made by Thomas Elfe and other cabinetmakers during those years.

Savannah, Ga., became an active center for furniture construction as well as for importation at an early date. Quantities of furniture arrived there from New England, and records show the names of many cabinetmakers, but none earlier than 1700.

Although Lord Baltimore's brother, Leonard Calvert, arrived with two hundred settlers in 1633, Baltimore-Town was too far inland to become important as a colony until after the Revolution.

The Virginia colony—the earliest and most important in the South—had suffered hardships of many kinds for years before it got a permanent start. Many of its colonists who settled on large plantation grants webbing out into the surrounding countryside were men of substance. There were others with little of this world's goods and in addition many adventurers, and even some less desirable. Naturally, it was the plantation owners who set the tone of the royal colony. They kept in close touch with England, and most of their fine furniture was imported from there in exchange for tobacco and other native products. From the earliest days, the inventories of these plantation owners disclose no lack of the very finest furniture. Some pieces have been identified as having been made locally during the seventeenth century, but in no instance is the name of the maker known. Doubtless some furniture was made on the plantations by itinerant craftsmen and some by trained slaves, using imported furniture as their models. As of the present, the earliest cabinetmakers of record are Mardan Vaghn Eventon of Dumfries, who advertised in 1762, and John Clark of Richmond, who advertised in the *Virginia Gazette* in 1776.

Banister-back chair with
carved top, circa 1700–1710

Pine dresser, circa 1740–60

By the end of the seventeenth century, the colonial cabinetmakers knew and used all the methods of construction and joining known to the cabinetmakers of today. Then, however, the toilsome work was done entirely by hand; today much by machinery. Perhaps that is why furniture remaining to us from those days has such an appeal; it helps us to understand the men who built it, the times in which they lived. They had an enviable capacity for hard, painstaking work, a resourcefulness, and a decided independence.

As the years of the seventeenth century gave way to the eighteenth, life became much less of a problem in all the colonies of the New World. Mere existence was no longer the chief concern of the settlers and they thought more of beauty and comfort in their homes. By 1750 the Georgian house was the fashion from north to south (much earlier in the more sophisticated South than in the North), richly furnished and adorned with whatever the colonist desired and could afford to have; that is, whatever was available in the fashion centers of England, the Continent, the Orient. There was constant communication between Europe and the colonies. Soon the colonial artisans were eagerly copying in native woods the beautiful furniture which came from Europe or following the designs in the books on cabinet-making that were finding their way to American shores. Perhaps the introduction of mahogany from the West Indies shortly after 1700 had the greatest effect upon furniture making in America.

In all the colonies of the New World, the first half of the eighteenth century was a time of much prosperity. In New England such towns as Portsmouth, N. H., and Salem and Boston in Massachusetts, competed in beauty and elegance with the royal town of Williamsburg in Virginia. Philadelphia, New York City, and Charleston, S. C., Savannah, Ga., Annapolis, Md., all increased in importance. During these years many small settlements grew into thriving towns, and there were innumerable new ones in all parts of the country along the eastern seaboard. There was, also, a trend of colonization westward, generally along the rivers. The entire period was one of developing trade, of growing industries, and of more comfort and luxury for the colonists. Every settlement had its turners, joiners, and cabinet-makers.

Although many speak of the eighteenth century as though it were a century of artistic sameness, it was one in which there was a gradual change in furniture, from the cumbersome, uncomfortable and somewhat crude style of the seventeenth century to the increased comfort of the William and Mary, the refinement of the Queen Anne, the magnificence and rococo of the Chippendale, and after the Revolution the delicate, classic Hepplewhite and Sheraton.

In considering these various styles as they relate to our American scene, we must keep in mind the time lag; new designs appearing at first in the seaports and centers of fashion, then slowly reaching the inland settlements; always with an overlapping of the different styles. Often a single feature foreshadowed the coming of an important change in furniture design, as it did in house design. Then, too, the workmen in the various sections of the country interpreted the newly introduced styles in somewhat different manners—producing interpretations peculiar to a locality, and in a lesser degree to individual workmen.

Throughout the entire eighteenth century, even during the time of conflict with the mother country, the colonists looked largely to England for their styles in architecture and their fashions in furniture; styles and fashions greatly influenced in England by an influx of workmen and ideas from Holland.

William and Mary came to the throne of England in 1689, but it is doubtful if furniture in the baroque style bearing their names—a direct importation into England from Holland—reached the colonies until shortly before 1700. How it reached them even at that date is a matter of speculation, but doubtless some furniture in this style was brought over by new settlers and then copied by colonial joiners ready for any new idea that would add to the beauty and comfort of their productions. Many artisans from Europe arrived at this time in all the colonies, and they, too, brought with them knowledge of the new fashion.

Although the William and Mary style had considerable effect upon the furniture made in the colonies, it was, after all, short-lived and in many ways a transitional style between the heavy and elaborate Jacobean and the beautiful Queen Anne.

William and Mary highboy with
trumpet turnings, circa 1700–1710

Some of the William and Mary furniture was made of oak, so popular in the preceding periods, but the colonial workmen were finding walnut, maple, pine, applewood, sycamore, and other native woods much easier to use and so this new-style furniture was not only less heavy and bulky because of its design but also because of its construction from lighter-weight wood. Marquetry became an important feature of decoration during these years and frequently took the form of elaborate floral patterns. Veneering was also popular. In England walnut was used almost exclusively for furniture in this style, and the period there is often referred to as "The Age of Walnut."

Anne, a sister of Queen Mary, came to the throne of England in 1702, and during her reign the Dutch style favored by William and Mary continued with certain modifications as the period advanced. There was a gradual modification of the heavy underbraced style of the earlier periods; a step forward in the refinement of design and also in comfort. Straight lines gave place to curved; the use of the cyma curve (a simple double curve similar to the letter S) made possible a beauty of line not present in earlier furniture. The cabriole leg, which had begun to appear in the William and Mary period, was characteristic of the Queen Anne. The elaborate carving used on Tudor-Elizabethan and Jacobean furniture gave way to greater simplicity. In England the Queen Anne furniture was constructed almost exclusively of walnut as in the William and Mary years, although some mahogany was used.

As usual, there was a time lag of many years between style periods in England and their appearance in America, and little of this new furniture called Queen Anne reached the colonies before the Queen's death in 1714.

Queen Anne side chair

Even then, its development proceeded slowly. However, after its acceptance by the colonial cabinetmakers and their clients, it continued to be the major fashion until the advent of the Chippendale style; indeed, the heavy ornate furniture made in England during the years between 1714 and the rise of the Chippendale style had little influence at all. Even after the introduction of Chippendale into America, the colonial craftsmen did not give up the Queen Anne immediately. They liked it; their clients liked it. Although much of this Queen Anne was made of walnut in the colonies, other woods, particularly in New England, were more popular.

During the first half of the eighteenth century, the number of cabinetmakers in all the colonies increased as the various regions of the country became prosperous, and the names of many are becoming known to us today through careful search into contemporary records. Cabinetmakers everywhere, however, were loosely organized, dependent upon the apprenticeship system for the training of new workers. There were guilds in many towns or counties; there were itinerant "joiners" working their way from town to town; and in the South slaves trained in carpentry and cabinetmaking carried on their craft on many of the big plantations, some, indeed, working in the shops of cabinetmakers. By this time, furniture making was divided into many branches, each with its own trained workmen. Many were chairmakers only, and when the Windsor chair became popular around the middle of the century, some devoted their entire energies to the making of this type chair. Other men worked as turners, carvers, or upholsterers. Some combined more than one phase of workmanship in their shops; nevertheless there was a separation between the numerous branches of the trade.

Windsor armchair

About the middle of the eighteenth century an impetus was given to furniture making in the colonies by the appearance of Chippendale's *The Gentleman and Cabinet-Maker's Director*. A first edition of this appeared in England in 1754, but the third edition appeared in 1762 and this seems to have been the popular one in this country. Although the styles shown in Chippendale's *Director* had been common in England for some years, it was not until this catalogue became available to American craftsmen that furniture in the Chippendale style was attempted by them. Many details of the Queen Anne, however, foretold its advent.

Although furniture in this new style was made in all the centers of America, there were two especially important groups that developed it and became famous for their product. One was at Philadelphia; the other at Newport, R. I.

Colonial Philadelphia held an important place in the New World as a city of wealth and fashion, and by the middle of the eighteenth century its cabinetmakers were coming to the fore as the creators of some of the finest furniture ever made in America. We can say without hesitation, I think, that the group of Philadelphia men working at this time from the designs in the *Director* created furniture which has never been surpassed and seldom if ever equaled by any other group of workmen in America, except, perhaps by the Goddard-Townsend group of Rhode Island.

Walnut and mahogany were the favorite woods of the Philadelphia men during this period. Maple was seldom used, although Savery on occasion made some simple piece from it. Carving reached its greatest perfection at the hands of the Philadelphia cabinetmakers and the carvers they employed at this time. Their highboys, lowboys, secretaries, tables, chairs, and other pieces of furniture are the very finest examples of design, construction, and ornamentation. The furniture is sophisticated, rococo with complicated carving, and every part of each piece is masterfully executed. Its perfection of design, careful execution, and unparalleled decoration established a style known today as the "Philadelphia." These cabinetmakers and carvers of Philadelphia used all the motifs and designs illustrated in Chippendale's *Director* to enhance the beauty and richness of their work. They did more. They gave to it an individuality that is entirely their own. It is usually possible to decide even when no label is present whether a piece of Chippendale-style furniture was Philadelphia-made or not; at times to declare with some degree of certainty to which individual cabinetmaker it should be attributed.

Detail of richly carved chair back, probably of New York origin, since tassel and ruffle motif has been found on several chairs made there during the Chippendale period

For some years students believed that William Savery, whose work ranges from simple chairs of maple with rush seats to carved highboys, was the greatest of the Philadelphia group. Then for a while, Benjamin Randolph was given the topmost spot, and in 1929 a wing chair bearing his label brought $33,000 at an auction, the highest price ever paid for an American chair. After this the tide of opinion placed Thomas Affleck at the top, and who can say which man may someday supplant him? It needs but the discovery of a few outstanding pieces bearing the labels of another maker to elevate him to the top. On these little bits of paper, advertising media in their day, depends the reputation of many an individual cabinetmaker. Unfortunately, there are not too many of these "little bits of paper" extant.

In Newport, R. I., during the years of the eighteenth century, there were some twenty Goddards and Townsends all working at the making of furniture, the fathers passing down to their sons the traditions of their craft as well as their shops and their tools. Both families were Quakers, closely associated by friendship, marriage, and religious ties. This group became almost as famous as that of Philadelphia—is considered superior by some. In their earliest work, they followed the Queen Anne tradition. Chairs in this style from their workshops are outstanding; of choice wood, excellent design, at times with shell-carved knees and top rail. The fame of this group of men depends, however, upon their superlative mahogany block-front and shell-carved case furniture in the Chippendale style. Although this block-front furniture was made by cabinetmakers in Massachusetts, Connecticut, and elsewhere, it never reached the beauty and perfection of the Newport furniture. John Goddard and John Townsend have been credited with its development, at times even with its inception. Doubtless, the honor of originating and perfecting it should be shared by others, particularly by Job and Christopher Townsend, the elders of the group.

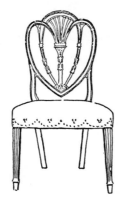

Hepplewhite-style side chair

The influence of these two important centers of furniture making spread to the other colonies—that of Philadelphia to New York on the north and southward to the colonies of Maryland and Virginia. The influence of Philadelphia was felt to a slight degree even in Connecticut, where there were at least two cabinetmakers, Benjamin Burnham and Eliphalet Chapin, who had served their apprenticeships in the Quaker city. Generally, the New England cabinetmakers created furniture no less beautiful, but somewhat simpler, than that of the Philadelphia school. Although mahogany was the choice of many of the New England men for their furniture in this style, cherry was not overlooked and it was the favorite of the Connecticut cabinetmakers. Chippendale was the last great furniture style of the Colonial period, since the influence of Hepplewhite and Sheraton was of little importance until after the Revolution.

When the Revolution was over, the people again turned their minds to fashion, and the styles popular for so long gave way to the lighter, more classic, known as Hepplewhite and Sheraton. At this time innumerable artisans poured into all the centers of America from England, France, and Holland.

In London, Alice Hepplewhite was carrying on the business established by her husband, George Hepplewhite, who had died in 1786. In 1788 she published his *The Cabinet-Maker and Upholsterer's Guide*, a book containing approximately three hundred furniture designs. In this, Hepplewhite borrows freely from both Robert Adam of England and the French. Louis XV of France had died in 1774, and with his death the rococo went out of fashion there and was followed by the classic ideal, as in Adam's England, both countries being influenced by the excavations at Herculaneum and Pompeii. Whereas Chippendale's *Director* was essentially a trade catalogue of what the various cabinetmakers' shops were able to execute, Hepple-

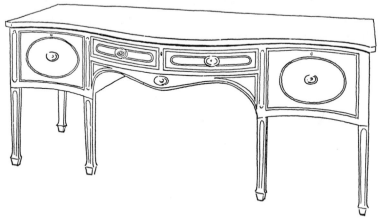

Serpentine-front sideboard showing both
Hepplewhite and Sheraton influence

white's *Guide* was compiled for provincial and colonial craftsmen who were desirous of knowing the latest fashions in London. Unlike the designs in Chippendale's *Director*, those in the *Guide* were practical and technically accurate. In them the traditions of the Chippendale were carried on except in the chairs, which showed a distinct difference; a trend toward lightness and gracefulness. Whereas the Chippendale had been sturdy and robust, the Hepplewhite was light and slender. Whereas the Chippendale was ornate with carving, the new style used flat surfaces with inlay, painting, and veneering. Carving if used was light and classic in feeling. The American interpreters of this new style did not follow Hepplewhite's fondness for carving. They had had sufficient in the rococo Chippendale. Little of the furniture produced at this time in America makes use of carving except, perhaps, the chairs. Many pieces, however, were embellished with a great deal of inlay done with woods used in such a way that they contrasted with the body of the piece itself, accentuating its lightness and gracefulness and drawing attention to its simple lines.

Mahogany continued to be the popular cabinetwood for this new style, but color and contrast were achieved by the extensive use of satinwood, holly, tulipwood, and other light-colored woods for the inlaid panels. Some pieces were decorated with exquisite painted designs. Hepplewhite reached its apogee in those pieces made of satinwood which are entirely decorated with

painted ornamentation in a wide range of beautiful colors. In America, however, few pieces were made entirely of satinwood in this fashion, which was
almost too delicate for a growing colonial people. In New England, particularly, the cabinetmakers created interesting pieces in this style by the
use of mahogany with curly or bird's-eye maple for contrast. As in the case
of Chippendale furniture, the cabinetmakers in various sections of America
made Hepplewhite furniture which differed in some details from that made
in other sections and from that made in England.

It was at this time that the cabinetmakers of Maryland came into their
own. Nowhere did the art of inlay reach greater perfection. Their work
with its drapery festoons, bellflowers, husks, eagles, shells, cross-banding, and
the use of different woods for contrast equaled in workmanship and effect
that of the master French craftsmen of the Louis XV period. Although the

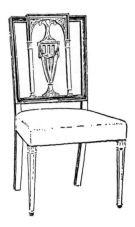 

Sheraton-style side chair   Late Sheraton-style side chair
of the variety called "Fancy"

spread eagle as a design for inlay was used in other cities, it was perhaps used
earliest in Baltimore. Similar work was produced in Annapolis at this same
time. All in all, the furniture made by the Maryland cabinetmakers was a bit
more elaborate than that produced in New York or in New England. At
this same time, however, Samuel McIntire of Salem, Mass., was designing and
carving furniture that equals in every way the furniture made in any other
part of the country. His exquisite and chaste carving, his well-executed designs, show him to be one of the outstanding craftsmen of America.

Thomas Sheraton was the last of the great English furniture designers.
Although he was a well-trained cabinetmaker, his experience—indeed his
very background—was that of the provinces and not of fashionable London,
and unlike Chippendale and Hepplewhite, he never had a London shop. In
1791 he published his *The Cabinet-Maker and Upholsterer's Drawing-Book*.
In making his selections from the designs in vogue at the time and in developing his own designs, Sheraton avoided the curve in favor of straight lines.

Again as in other periods, the chair is the distinctive piece of furniture, the one most characteristic of the style. Sheraton's typical chair is fundamentally rectangular, with a central panel slightly higher than the top rail and with the lower back rail well up from the seat. He used more underbracing than did Hepplewhite. Sheraton showed reeding and fluting, fan-shaped inlays, ornamental disks, the sunburst, leaf carving, the long-popular cockleshell, lattice-work, urns, swags, the lyre, and a small carved rosette to decorate the face of corner blocks. Like Hepplewhite, he used many beautiful woods, including mahogany, with inlay, veneering, and painting.

In America, although there were differences in the interpretation of these two styles—especially in the chairs—there was a definite intermingling of the Hepplewhite and Sheraton. This is doubtless owing to the fact that the *Guide* by Hepplewhite and the *Drawing-Book* by Sheraton reached the American cabinetmakers at about the same time.

As the years advanced the influence of the French Directoire and then of the French Empire was felt in America. These styles were not interpreted in New England in the same way as in New York City and other sections of the Republic because the New England scene was dominated by Samuel McIntire of Salem, Mass., and John Seymour of Boston, to mention but two.

After 1810 the Sheraton influence became less and less noticeable, even in New England. With the increasing prosperity resulting from the development of shipping and new industry, many people having little background, education, or tradition acquired large fortunes, and these were the ones who demanded a more pretentious style than the charming Hepplewhite and Sheraton. In New York City the fashionable Duncan Phyfe was unable to resist the demands of this clientele and his very individualistic furniture in the Sheraton-influenced style changed to that showing the Directoire influence and then that of the French Empire. John Henry Belter followed him as the fashionable cabinetmaker of New York, creating richly carved and designed furniture, but by the time of his death the factories of America were speedily replacing the individual craftsman and furniture was being mass-produced to fill the needs of the fast-growing population.

As the industrial revolution of the mid-nineteenth century advanced, the machine became the dominant factor in the American economy. Soon the fame and prestige of the most fashionable cabinetmakers of the preceding generations became obscured, and little, if anything, remembered of their lives or their work. Possessors of their furniture valued it less than the newly manufactured productions from the factories. And then, some forty or fifty years ago, the pendulum began a slow swing in the other direction, helped largely by the enthusiasm, the understanding, and the research of a few who appreciated the superb work of our great craftsmen. Today this furniture and the men who made it fill a topmost place in the story of the crafts of America. Research has uncovered much information. We know a great deal about some individual men and the work they produced.

Lists have been compiled of cabinetmakers in various towns and sections of our country. Not before, however, has a country-wide compilation been made. This has required careful searching and checking. Everything available, insofar as feasible, has been studied—directories, early newspapers, town histories, wills, inventories, books, magazines, and tradition. Vital statistics in the early days were not as completely kept as they are today. A birth, for instance, might not be recorded but a baptism generally was. Town records contain the data important to the townspeople at that time, and it is apparent that importance depended upon need; so the blacksmith and the shoemaker were of greater significance than the maker of fine furniture. Many of the cabinetmakers, chairmakers, turners, and joiners advertised in local papers as soon as these media became available, but the advertisements often contain very little information. Many of the towns and cities had directories by the time the Revolution was over, and a careful search of these yields much information as to the names of workmen, the location of their shops, and the years they were working. At times tradition, not always trustworthy, produces the name of a workman who can be traced through deeds, newspaper advertisements, and directory listings. And yet, many good cabinetmakers may never be known and much outstanding work remains unidentified.

It is obvious that such a list as this does not contain all cabinetmakers— possibly not even all those of note—during the seventeenth, eighteenth, and early nineteenth centuries. It is believed, however, that it contains the majority of these, although the years will doubtless give us others to add to the list. And it is hoped that the inclusion of many names perhaps unimportant today and with little data may spur others to seek further information regarding them and their work. It is also obvious that in a work of this scope, with data gathered from sources often containing inaccuracies and inconsistencies, a considered selection had to be made with the belief that time would correct any such discrepancies. Interpretation also differs in a subject of this type. As the years advance and facts become better known and more conclusive, these interpretations will become more stable. This may very well mean that furniture attributed to one cabinetmaker today may be attributed to another tomorrow, as was the case with the Stephen Badlam piece in the Mabel Brady Garvan Collection at Yale University. Nevertheless, in spite of possible inaccuracies and inconsistencies of attribution and interpretation, it is hoped that the gathering together of the material presented here for the first time as a unit will be of help to those interested in the cabinetmakers of America and the basis for further research on this interesting subject.

NOTE TO THE READER

THE ENTRIES for individual cabinetmakers, partnerships, and companies are alphabetized throughout the text. However, in the case of family groups, such as the Allises, the Goddards, the Townsends, and others in which several generations are involved, the alphabetized entries for the individual members are preceded by an entry for the entire family giving the chronology.

A few carvers have been included; those who were both carvers and cabinetmakers and those who worked closely with various cabinetmakers.

Name spelling, which is always a problem for the student of history, varied in the material studied. An attempt has been made to include the variants. Occasionally a surname only has been found.

Cross-references appear in the entries wherever they seem pertinent.

The bibliography lists the most important references consulted. When references in this bibliography are repeatedly mentioned in the entries they are abbreviated there.

The section devoted to photographs is arranged to portray the chronological development of furniture styles in America. When a plate illustrates the work of a particular cabinetmaker, a cross-reference to it will be found in his entry.

E. H. B.

CABINETMAKERS:
BIOGRAPHICAL SKETCHES

AARON, John, *Salem, Mass.*
Married Ruth Perkins, May 6, 1832. Living as late as 1864. Belknap says he was a cabinetmaker but doubtless did not have his own shop.

ABBOTT, Daniel, *Newburyport, Mass.*
Listed as cabinetmaker on Middle St. in 1809.

ABBOTT, Levi, *Woburn, Mass.*
Born circa 1821. Married Phebe Lovejoy, Nov. 27, 1845, in Andover. Listed as cabinetmaker.

ABORN, James, *Marblehead, Mass.*
Baptized Dec. 9, 1759. Listed as cabinetmaker and joiner. Still working in 1821.

ACKLEY, John Brientnall, *Philadelphia, Pa.*
Son of Thomas and Elizabeth (Brientnall) Ackley. Was a Windsor chair maker on Front St. as early as 1790. Bamboo-turned balloon-back Windsor with mahogany arms in loan exhibition of Windsors at Old Congress Hall, Philadelphia, May 1952. *See* entry for Taylor & King.

ACKLEY, Thomas, *Philadelphia, Pa.*
Married Elizabeth Brientnall, daughter of the Windsor chair maker John Brientnall, in 1752. Father of John Brientnall Ackley. Learned his trade with Solomon Fussell, who was making rush-bottom chairs as early as 1742. Ackley's shop was on the east side of Fourth St. near Market and the family lived on the floor above the shop. In 1764 he advertised this building for sale. Listed as both turner

and chairmaker. In records of the Assembly under date of Dec. 20, 1759, is the following item: "Paid Thomas Acherly for Chairs for the State House." (Hornor)

ACRES, George, *Boston, Mass.*
Listed on Back St. as cabinetmaker in 1789.

ADAMS, Benjamin, *Salem, Mass.*
Married Sally Leach, April 8, 1804. Partner of Thomas Russell Williams (*q. v.*). (Belknap)

ADAMS, Elisha, *Boston, Mass.*
Had cabinetmaker's shop on Federal St. in 1798.

ADAMS, John, *Savannah, Ga.*
Working in 1807. (Comstock)

ADAMS, Joseph, *Boston, Mass.*
Listed as cabinet- and chairmaker on Center St. in 1789.

ADAMS, Lemuel, *Hartford, Conn.*
In partnership with Samuel Kneeland; for data regarding this, *see* entry for Kneeland & Adams. This partnership was dissolved March 5, 1795. In the archives of the Connecticut State Library a bill, dated May 1796, for the furnishings of the old State House carries Adams' name as the maker of chairs, desks, etc., for which he was paid £105/6. This bill was rendered by Jeremiah Halsey, who was commissioned to supply the furnishings and apparently subcontracted the work. The Hartford Directory for 1799 lists Adams on the south side of Ferry St. In

the *Connecticut Courant* for Feb. 5 and Feb. 19, 1798, Adams had the following advertisement: "Has constantly on hand, all kinds of Cabinet and Cherry tree FURNITURE, made in the neatest and most approved fashions, which he will sell cheap for cash, or well approved notes."

Eight chairs believed to be those made by Adams for the old State House may be seen in the Museum of the Connecticut State Library, and another at the Connecticut Historical Society, Hartford.

(*Connecticut Chairs in the Collection of the Connecticut Historical Society*, 1956)

ADAMS, Moses, *Beverly, Mass.*
Born circa 1759 in Ipswich; died circa 1795. At one time in partnership with Adams Smith. (Belknap)

ADAMS, Nathaniel, *Boston, Mass.*
Record of his death in 1690 lists him as cabinetmaker.

ADAMS, Nathaniel, *Charlestown, Mass.*
Born in Medford, Mass.; moved to Charlestown in 1764. Working in Charlestown in 1775, since on the insurance lists he is listed as a cabinetmaker who suffered loss from the burning of Charlestown by the British.

ADAMS, Nehemiah, *Salem, Mass.*
Baptized April 16, 1769, in Ipswich; died Jan. 24, 1840, in Salem. Married Mehitable Torry of Boston, Aug. 20, 1802. His cabinetmaking shop, on the corner of Newbury and Williams streets, burned April 3, 1798. In 1804 he became a member of the firm of Williams & Adams, the senior partner being Thomas Russell Williams (*q. v.*). Benjamin Adams was also a member of this firm, but it is not known whether he was related to Nehemiah or not. The first work of Adams to become known was a Hepplewhite-style secretary-bookcase found in Cape Town, Africa, with his label attached: "Nehemiah Adams/ Cabinet Maker/ Newbury Street Near the Common /Salem/ Mass." This is now in the Winterthur Museum, Delaware. An interesting feature of this piece is the kneehole. The cupboard doors have a second rectangular band of inlay outside the oval, and the bars of the glazing are curved in a simple segmental pattern.

In *House Beautiful* for March and April 1931 a sofa made in 1810 for Lucy Hill Foster with carving ascribed to Samuel McIntire, as well as a worktable, are described and illustrated.

At the Metropolitan Museum of Art, a worktable in the Bolles Collection and another in the Palmer Collection are attributed to Adams.

Characteristic features of Adams' work are elongated bulb feet and table legs with a long cylindrical neck with a pair of small beads at the top and bottom. These features are also found on furniture made by other Salem cabinetmakers.

ADAMS, Obed, *Newburyport, Mass.*
Born July 12, 1810, in Newbury; died Sept. 27, 1848, in Ipswich. Listed as cabinetmaker.

ADAMS, Oren, *Providence, R. I.*
Listed in directory for 1832 as cabinetmaker at 71 Westminster St.

ADAMS, Richard III, *Newburyport, Mass.*
Born June 10, 1822. Working as cabinetmaker in Newburyport as late as 1854 but disappears from the records at that time.

ADAMS, Samuel, *Charlestown, Mass.*
Married Ruth Waite in 1718. Listed as joiner.

ADAMS, Samuel, *Boston, Mass.*
Listed as cabinetmaker on Cambridge St. in 1796.

ADAMS, Stephen, *Hill, N. H.*
Born 1778 in Lexington, Mass. Made dining-room furniture still extant. A mahogany butler's sideboard with satinwood

and bird's-eye maple is illustrated in *American Collector*, June 1937.

ADAMS, Stephen, *Medway, Mass.*

Born 1829; died 1885. A descendant of Obadiah Adams, who settled in Medway in 1710. Stephen worked at cabinetmaking until 1878, when ailing health compelled him to give up all active labor. His house still stands and is now owned and occupied by Mr. Herbert Hixon. A former president of the Medway Historical Society, Mr. Hixon says that Adams' workshop is now his parlor and that in it is a cherry desk made by Adams for Mr. Hixon's great-grandfather. A bed and a bureau are owned by a great-granddaughter of Adams in Franklin, Mass., and his workbench and sign are still in West Medway, privately owned. (Jameson)

ADAMS, William, *Hartford, Conn.*

In 1737 purchased from Freeman Goss a plot of land and was listed in the deed as a cabinetmaker. He later sold the land to Isaac Tucker (*q. v.*) and again signed as a cabinetmaker. (Love)

ADAMS & NORTH, *Lowell, Mass.*

Privately owned in Pittsburgh, Pa., is a breakfront that has in one of the small drawers the following label:

From
Adams & North
Wholesale and Retail Dealers in
Furniture, Feathers
Carpets, Etc.
Nos. 7 Central, and 28 Merrimack St.,
Wyman's Exchange
Lowell, Mass.

The label was printed by B. H. Penhallow.

AFFLECK, Thomas, *Philadelphia, Pa.*

Born in Aberdeen, Scotland; died 1795. Believed to have received his training in England; arrived in Philadelphia in 1763. His shop was on Second St. at Lowne's Alley.

At the moment Affleck is considered by many as the one who produced the finest furniture in the Philadelphia Chippendale style. Hornor says of him, "Affleck was the paramount figure in the cabinet- and chair-making craft and was by far the leader of the Philadelphia Chippendale School."

Affleck made the beautiful furniture in the Chinese Chippendale style for Governor John Penn (see many plates in Hornor), which caused Joseph Downs

Intricately carved ornament, fretwork, and scroll end of chest-on-chest attributed to Thomas Affleck, circa 1770–80

to say, "He brought an unparalleled urbanity of Chinese Chippendale to Philadelphia work."

He was employed by the wealthy and important of Philadelphia, and many pieces of his furniture have been traced through his account and receipt books. He is known to have owned a copy of Chippendale's *Director*. In 1783 his occupational tax was £250, which was greater than that paid by any of his contemporaries; two and a half times as much as that of Gostelowe, five times as much as that of Savery, Tufft, or Gillingham. But by 1786 it had dropped to about one third the amount. It is understandable, perhaps, that his sympathies during the Revolution were with the Royalists, and on Sept.

2, 1777, he was arrested as a Tory and banished to Virginia for more than seven months. After Thomas' death his son, Lewis G. Affleck, advertised in the Philadelphia paper that he "carries on the cabinet making business in the shop lately occupied by my father in Elmslie's Court." The son was not successful, however, and soon gave up.

So many pieces of furniture have been attributed to Affleck that it is not possible to mention all in this sketch. A sofa (Hornor, pl. 258) with skirt, legs, and Marlborough block feet fully carved is said by Hornor to be "unexcelled by any other of Philadelphia workmanship." A sideboard table made for Levi Hollingsworth is illustrated in *Antiques*, Dec. 1946.

Examples of work attributed to Affleck are at the Philadelphia Museum of Art, the Boston Museum of Fine Arts, the Winterthur Museum, and many others.

At the Metropolitan Museum of Art is a Chippendale butler's secretary possibly made by Affleck (PLATE XIII, No. 1).

Many of these pieces show the Marlborough-style leg which he used so often, and many show the elaborate carving common to the furniture attributed to him. Among the outstanding pieces are the Cadwalader marble-top table at the Metropolitan Museum of Art and the other so like it at the Philadelphia Museum of Art.

At the Boston Museum of Fine Arts there is a mahogany card table, made 1750-75, with folding top and swinging leg to support leaf when open. This has fluted legs of the Marlborough style. Also at this museum are two chairs, one of mahogany, the other of walnut. Both have vase-shaped backs with carved and pierced splat with the top rail richly carved with leafage and shells. Both chairs show cabriole legs with knees richly carved and with claw-and-ball feet. In addition to tables, chairs, and sofas, Affleck also constructed case fur-

niture, particularly highboys and low-lowboys. (Hornor)

AITKEN, John, *Philadelphia, Pa.*

Born in Dulheath, Scotland; came to Philadelphia about the time of the Revolution. Hornor calls him "President Washington's favourite cabinet-maker." At one time in partnership with William Cocks under the name of Cocks & Co. They advertised as "Cabinet-Makers & Upholsterers At the corner of Sixth in Chestnut Street."

In 1797 Aitken made a tambour secretary and bookcase for President Washington upon his retirement to Mount Vernon, for which he billed him $145. This is now at Mount Vernon. At the same date he made for him two sideboard tables, a desk for Martha Washington's granddaughter, Nellie Custis, as well as other pieces. These included a set of twelve chairs in Sheraton style, now at the Smithsonian Institution, part of the collection of Lewis family heirlooms acquired by the government in 1878.

AITON, Thomas, *Baltimore, Md.*

On April 20, 1793, advertised in the *Maryland Journal* and *Baltimore Advertiser* that he was carrying on the "Cabinet-Making Business in all its branches" next door to Mr. William Hammond's Merchant, at the upper end of Market St. Aiton had learned his trade in Europe, from which he had lately arrived.

ALCOCK, John, *Boston, Mass.*

Listed as chairmaker in 1746.

ALDEN, John, *Plymouth, Mass.*

Born 1599 in Southampton, England; died 1687. Came to America on *Mayflower*, 1620. Married Priscilla Mullins about 1622, their romance made famous by Longfellow. Assistant governor of the colony 1633–39 and again 1651–86. In 1632 moved to nearby Duxbury. At his death sole survivor of *Mayflower* passengers. Working alone or with Kenelm Winslow is believed to have constructed chests, cupboards, etc. This group of furniture is known as the Plymouth group and includes the Prince-Howes press cupboard at the Wadsworth Atheneum, Hartford, Conn. (PLATE I), a chest at the Detroit Institute of Arts, and one at the Stone House, Guilford, Conn. They are described more fully under Kenelm Winslow. (Willison)

ALEXANDER, Giles, *Charlestown, Mass.; Boston, Mass.*

Born 1751; died 1816. Arrived in Charlestown from Roxbury in 1792 and married Susannah Fowle. Listed in Boston Directory at 51 Back St. in 1789. In 1816 inventory of his estate showed him to have been prosperous.

ALEXANDER, James, *Boston, Mass.*

Listed in Boston Directory of 1803 as cabinetmaker at 51 Back St.

ALEXANDER, John, *Baltimore, Md.*

Listed in city directories as cabinetmaker from 1800 to 1803.

ALEXANDER, William, *Boston, Mass.*

Listed in Boston Directory of 1789 as cabinetmaker at 51 Back St. In 1796 in partnership with man named Stone. Used a label, "Stone & Alexander," one of the very few who used a label at this time. After 1796, however, the partnership is no longer listed, but the three Alexanders—Giles, William, and James—appear separately, Giles and William in 1789, James in 1803. William served in the Revolution from 1781 and died in a Boston almshouse. *See* entry for Stone & Alexander.

ALFORD, Arba, Jr., *Hitchcocksville, Conn.*

See entry for Lambert Hitchcock.

ALLEN, Amos Denison, *Norwich, Conn.*

Born March 13, 1774, son of Amos Allen, Jr., and Anna Babcock Allen. Shortly after his father's death in 1788, apprenticed to Col. Ebenezer Tracy of Lisbon (*q. v.*). On Aug. 18, 1796, Amos married Lydia, a daughter of Tracy.

Soon after this marriage Amos opened his shop in his home, a custom with many cabinetmakers. Windsor chairs bearing his brand mark "A. D. Allen" are similar in design and workmanship to those bearing Ebenezer Tracy's mark. It is known that he also made chairs of curly maple, the wood stained and embellished with gold. These chairs show the Sheraton influence as well as a slight relationship to the later Hitchcock. Allen also made clock cases and case furniture. It is probable that many pieces of furniture made by Allen were destroyed when his home and barn burned. Allen died Aug. 19, 1855; is buried in Windham cemetery. (*Antiques*, Aug. 1956; Bayles; *Vital Statistics Norwich*)

ALLEN, Arthur S., *Manchester, Mass.*

Born circa 1823; died Nov. 22, 1846, in Rockport. Belknap lists him as cabinetmaker.

ALLEN, Benjamin, *Salem, Mass.*

Born April 26, 1699; still living in 1775. Married Abigail Lowther, Dec. 10, 1724. Joiner. (Perley, *History of Salem*)

ALLEN, Caleb, *Providence, R. I.*

Listed as cabinetmaker at 118 North Main St. in directories from 1828 to 1839.

ALLEN, Forster, *Manchester, Mass.*

Born April 26, 1803; died March 21, 1839. Belknap calls him a cabinetmaker.

ALLEN, Henry P., *Manchester, Mass.*

Born Nov. 15, 1807. Married Mary Elizabeth Potter, Aug. 24, 1844. Cabinetmaker. (Belknap)

ALLEN, Joseph, *Salem, Mass.*

Born circa 1755; died Sept. 21, 1786. Cabinetmaker. (Perley, *History of Salem*, Vol. 3)

ALLEN, Joseph, *Philadelphia, Pa.*

Paid an occupational tax as "joyner" in 1783.

ALLEN, Josiah, *Charleston, S. C.*
In directories for 1809 and 1813 as cabinetmaker.

ALLEN, Luther, *Manchester, Mass.*
Born Feb. 2, 1809. Married Aug. 30, 1829. Cabinetmaker. (Belknap)

ALLEN, Nathan, Jr., *Manchester, Mass.*
Born 1794; died 1826. Cabinetmaker. (Belknap)

ALLEN, Oliver, *Norwich, Conn.*
Working early nineteenth century. Vital statistics for Norwich show "Jane, the Daughter of Oliver Allen and of Jerusha his wife was born January 21st A.D. 1829 and departed this life April 27th A.D. 1831." Maker of a chest, owned in Ohio, made about 1820 with label:

F U R N I T U R E
Oliver Allen

Offers for sale (a few rods North of the Norwich Bank, Shetucket Street) an extensive assortment of Cabinets and Chairs, furniture of the best materials and war'nted workmanship. Looking Glasses, Gilt and Mahogany Frames.
N.B. All orders thankfully received and punctually attended to. Norwich, Conn.

The chest bearing this label is of red walnut with glass knobs; illustrated in *Antiques*, Nov. 1931.

ALLEN, Samuel Prince, *Manchester, Mass.*
Born Oct. 19, 1811. Married Elizabeth Knight, June 2, 1837. Cabinetmaker. (Belknap)

ALLEN, Stephen Baker, *Manchester, Mass.*
Born July 7, 1828. Married Sabra Ann Cross, Nov. 23, 1848. Cabinetmaker. (Belknap)

ALLEN, William H., *Manchester, Mass.*
Born circa 1818. Married Abby D. Pickard of Beverly, Jan. 21, 1846. Cabinetmaker. (Belknap)

ALLEN, William R., *Salem, Mass.*
Born circa 1811 in Gloucester; died March 17, 1847. Working as cabinetmaker for Hill, Henderson & Co., 1837–42. A partner in firm of Henderson, Allen & Co., 38 Washington St., in 1846.

ALLING, David, *Newark, N. J.*
Born 1773; died 1855. Working as early as 1800. A manufacturer of fancy Sheraton and Windsor chairs as well as other furniture. At the New Jersey Historical Society, Newark, there is an oil painting of "David Alling's House and Shop, Newark." This house was built in 1790 and stood on Broad St. opposite William near Fair. In the painting some of his chairs are displayed in front of the shop.

ALLIS FAMILY, *Hatfield, Mass.*
As recorded in the Allis genealogy, William Allis came to America with the Winthrop colonists from London and Essex, England, and is believed to have been one of the thirty-nine men on the third voyage of the *Mayflower*, which landed at Boston, July 1, 1630. This group included the so-called Braintree Company, in which were William Allis, Thomas Graves, and Thomas Meekins. On May 13, 1640, William Allis was made a freeman. At that time only members of the church were made freemen and only freemen could vote and hold office. In 1641 Allis married a woman by the name of Mary, but her family name is unknown. Their son John was born March 5, 1642, and another son, Samuel, Feb. 24, 1647.
In 1658 many of the Braintree group migrated to Wethersfield, Conn., making the trip on foot, taking with them a few needed supplies while the remainder of their possessions followed by boat down the coast and up the Connecticut River. In 1661 one of the many dissensions over

church government developed in Wethersfield, and several of those who had come from Braintree again migrated, to Hadley, Mass. In this group were members of the Allis, Meekins, and Graves families. They settled on the west side of the river at Hadley, and in May 1670 that part of the town became the town of Hatfield. Today in Hatfield the meetinghouse, town hall, and Congregational Church stand on the land assigned to William Allis.

William was not himself a cabinetmaker but was the ancestor of those Allises to whom are attributed many of the Hadley chests. His first wife died in 1677 and on Sept. 6, 1678, he married Mary Bronson Graves, widow of John Graves of Haddam, Conn., and a niece of Nicholas Disbrowe, the cabinetmaker of Hartford. Thus as early as 1678 there was a relationship between the people of Hatfield and Disbrowe. William Allis lived but a short time after this marriage. The cabinetmaking Allises were as follows:

John, eldest son of William; Samuel, son of William; Ichabod, son of John; John, son of John. *See* their entries below. *See* also the entries for Belding, Jr. and Sr., Disbrowe, Hawkes, Pease, and John Taylor.

(References for the Allises include: H. D. Allis, *Genealogy of William Allis and Descendants, 1630-1919*, Hartford, Conn.; Judd; Luther; G. Sheldon, *History of Deerfield*)

ALLIS, John (Captain), *Hatfield, Conn.*

Born 1642; died 1691. John, the eldest son of William Allis, was born at Braintree, Mass., and in 1658, when sixteen years old, accompanied his parents to Wethersfield, Conn., and again in 1661 to Hadley, Mass. On Dec. 14, 1669, he married Mary Meekins Clark, daughter of Thomas Meekins and widow of Nathaniel Clark. They were the parents of twelve children.

In 1669 Thomas Meekins erected a sawmill, and according to town records of Dec. 16, 1670, "Thomas Meekins has liberty of cutting any timber on the common lot that he wishes to saw, during the standing of the mill, and the mill shall be free from town rate, during the first three years of the standing." Thomas Meekins died in 1687 and John Allis and his wife received the lands, housing (this term was used to indicate dwelling and other buildings), and mills. John, in town records, is spoken of as "millwright and carpenter of note," and it is a matter of record that he built several churches. He

Center panel Hadley chest

formed a business partnership with Samuel Belding (Belden) which continued through the next generation, his son Ichabod carrying on the business with Samuel Belding, Jr. It is believed that many of the Hadley chests were made by this firm of Belding & Allis, and it is certain that the making of them ceased with the deaths of Ichabod Allis and Samuel Belding, Jr. It is thought that the fashion for these "hope" chests began among the ladies of these two prominent families and became a fad among many of their friends and relatives. Chests were made for four of John Allis' daughters and two for his wife. When he died, his widow married Samuel Belding, Sr.

A most comprehensive study of the Hadley chests was made by the Rev.

Clair Franklin Luther in 1935. In that study he recorded his findings on 109 located in various parts of the country, and since the publication of this book and Mr. Luther's death other chests have been located and recorded, largely through the efforts of Mr. Newton Brainard of Hartford, Conn., until the number has now reached 118.

The A A chest (Luther's No. 2) is believed to be the first of the Hadley chests of the "Hatfield" type. It follows closely the design of the Mary Allyn chest. (See Disbrowe.) Luther believed it was made for Abigail, daughter of John and Mary Meekins Allis, born in Hatfield Feb. 25, 1672, and married to Ephraim Wells in 1696. He thought this chest was made circa 1680. It is in the John Huntington Collection, Cleveland Museum of Art. (PLATE II, No. 2)

The E A chest (Luther's No. 4) made for Elizabeth, another daughter of John and Mary Meekins Allis, is also attributed to John Allis. This follows closely the design of the Disbrowe chest, especially the vine tracery, although there is wide variation in the treatment of the flower motif. This chest is privately owned.

A third chest attributed to John Allis is the H A chest (Luther's No. 5). This was made for his daughter Hannah and is now at the Wadsworth Atheneum, Hartford, Conn. The R A chest (Luther's No. 8), believed to have been made circa 1680 by John Allis for his daughter Rebecca, is owned by the Pocumtuck Valley Memorial Association, Deerfield, Mass.

Considered the finest of the "Hatfield" type is the L A chest (Luther's No. 6), made for Lydia Allis, another daughter, born Aug. 15, 1680, who died Aug. 31, 1691. It resembles closely the A A and the E A chests of her sisters and was evidently also made by her father. This, too, is privately owned.

In addition to the making of chests, the firm of Belding & Allis constructed buildings. George Sheldon's *History of Deerfield* notes: "John Allis, millwright

and carpenter contracted to build our first corn mill at Mill River, 1690; he died January 1691 before it was finished."

ALLIS, John, *Hatfield, Mass.*

Born 1682. Son of Capt. John Allis and brother of Ichabod. The two brothers worked together at their father's trade in the firm of Belding & Allis.

ALLIS, Ichabod, *Hatfield, Mass.*

Born July 10, 1675; died July 9, 1747. Ichabod, one of John Allis' twelve children, and Samuel Belding, Jr., carried on the partnership organized by Samuel Belding, Sr., and Capt. John Allis under the name of Belding & Allis, where many of the Hadley chests are believed to have been made.

Sometime after Ichabod's widowed mother became the third wife of Samuel Belding, Sr. (about 1691), Ichabod married Mary, a daughter of his partner, Samuel Belding, Jr. Thus the families were very closely tied together by friendship and marriage as well as by business association. When Mary died in 1724, Ichabod within a short time married Sarah, daughter of Benjamin Waite and widow of John Belding.

The L A chest (Luther's No. 7) with molded rails and posts is believed to have been made by Ichabod. This chest bears an inscription (obviously written at a later date): "This dower chest was made for Miss Lydia Allis daughter of Ichabod and Mary Allis. She was born in Hatfield, January 7, 1702. She married Daniel Dickinson. She died January 13, 1737, aged 35."

The A A chest (Luther's No. 3), which is identical with the L A chest, was at one time attributed to Disbrowe by Lockwood. Abigail, for whom it is believed Ichabod made this A A chest, was born in 1700 and the chest is thought to have been made about 1710-20. Abigail married Nathaniel Smith of Sunderland in 1720. The chest is now at the Deerfield, Mass., Museum.

ALLIS, Samuel, *Hatfield, Mass.*

Son of William and brother of Capt. John Allis, Samuel was born at Braintree, Feb. 24, 1647. When he died in 1691, his widow, Alice, married Sgt. John Hawkes of Deerfield, to whom are attributed several of the Hadley chests. Samuel is also referred to in records as a carpenter and builder and doubtless was a member of the firm of Belding & Allis. He inherited half of his father's home lot but sold it to his brother John, who had inherited the other half. John sold the entire lot to the town December 1690 for 100 pounds.

ALLISON, Michael, *New York City*

Working 1800 to 1845, Allison was a contemporary and neighbor of Duncan Phyfe and produced work that showed him to be an excellent cabinetmaker. His earliest label reads: "Vesey St., near the Bear Market, N. York." A later label on an Empire table with paw feet reads: "M. Allison's Cabinet and Upholstery Furniture Warehouse No. 46 & 48 Vesey St., New York, May 1817."

At the Metropolitan Museum of Art there is a chest of drawers in Hepplewhite style with eagle brasses made circa 1810 with the Allison label. Written on the bottom of one of the drawers is "Maria May Scott's chest of drawers given her by her mother, Elizabethtown 1810." Also at the Metropolitan is a mahogany worktable-desk, made in 1823, with Allison's label (PLATE XXIX, No. 2).

Thomas Ormsbee, in the *American Collector* for June, 1935 says, "Similarly a pair of urn-pedestal card tables Phyfe in design and carved decorative detail have been discovered stenciled with the name of Michael Allison. Other labeled pieces show that this craftsman could and did work in a different manner. The Metropolitan Museum has a chest of drawers that is distinctly Hepplewhite in feeling."

ALLWINE, Lawrence, *Philadelphia, Pa.*

Working 1786. Windsor chair maker. Made chairs for Governor John Penn. Name stamped on bottom of a fan-back Windsor. He claimed to make "The best Windsor Chairs, gilt, plain and variously ornamented, being painted with his own patent colours" for which he had secured a United States patent. (Hornor)

ALLYN, Isaac, *Preston, Conn.*

Advertisement in the *New London Gazette*, July 7, 1813, says he sold his cabinet-making shop to Allyn Chapman.

ALWAYS, John and James, *New York City*

Advertisements indicate they were working from 1786 to 1815 as chair makers.

AMES, Daniel, *Rocky Hill, New Britain, Conn.*

Born Feb. 1, 1751; died Nov. 19, 1822. Married Mercy Langdon, Sept. 7, 1780. The son of John Ames. Learned his trade as joiner and cabinetmaker in Rocky Hill with an unknown cabinetmaker. Moved to New Britain, where he built a house on the west side of Main St., a short distance south of the South Green. Shortly sold the place to Aaron Roberts, who had learned his trade in the same shop at Rocky Hill. In 1788 Ames lost an arm when a gun burst, after which he retired from the cabinetmaking business and taught school. (Camp)

ANABLE, John, *Manchester, Mass.*

Born circa 1807. Cabinetmaker. (Belknap)

ANDERSON, Alexander, *New York City*

Listed as a freeman joiner in 1770. Receipted bill of 1786 in Historical Society of Pennsylvania. Cabinetmaker and joiner. (Article by Harold Gillingham, *Bulletin*, New-York Historical Society)

ANDERSON, Elbert, *New York City*

Working in New York City around 1790. *Antiques*, March 1951, shows two chairs with superbly carved shield backs made for the Wanton family of Newport, R. I., and attributed to Elbert Anderson. The two shown belong to a set of eight dining-room chairs consisting of two armchairs and six side chairs, of which two are not contemporary.

At the Metropolitan Museum of Art there is a Hepplewhite-style mahogany shield-back chair, straight across the top, with inlaid and carved back, possibly made by Elbert Anderson. The quality of carving, construction and workmanship generally reveals the maker to have been an expert. (PLATE XXVI, No. 2)

ANDERSON, Francis, *Providence, R. I.*
Listed in the Providence Directory of 1824 as cabinetmaker.

ANDERSON, James, *Savannah, Ga.*
Working circa 1736. Listed as "joyner." Theus lists him as among the earliest settlers and probably the first Georgia cabinetmaker known by name. (*Antiques,* Feb. 1954)

ANDERSON, James, *Savannah, Ga.*
Working circa 1797. Doubtless a descendant of James Anderson above. In 1797 advertised in *Georgia Gazette*: "James Anderson Respectfully informs the public that he has again commenced the Chairmaking business in Broughton Street next door to Mr. John Andrews, Cabinetmaker."

ANDERSON, John, *Annapolis, Md.*
Working circa 1746–59. Advertised in *Maryland Gazette,* 1746: "John Anderson, Cabinetmaker and Carver late from Liverpool, makes Chairs, Tables, Desks, Bureaus, Dressing Tables, Clock-cases, and all kinds of furniture, which is made of Wood, Belonging to a House, in the neatest, cheapest and newest mode." Advertised in same paper, July 11, 1754: "Removed from his late Dwelling house in South East Street to the house facing the Parade where Mr. James Maccubbin lately lived."

ANDERSON, Samuel, *Baltimore, Md.*
Listed in city directory for 1800 as cabinetmaker.

ANDERSON, W. H., *Boston, Mass.*
Listed as cabinetmaker in Boston in 1814.

ANDREW, Jonathan, *Salem, Mass.*
In 1947 Shreve, Crump & Low Company of Boston had a small mahogany secretary inside which was written "Jonathan Andrew brother of John Andrew, Salem, Massachusetts, 1749–1791." This was an expertly constructed and designed piece. The upper section was fitted with pigeon holes and small drawers behind a center cabinet, which was reeded to simulate the sliding tambour on either side. The writing flap was lined with green felt and the lower section inlaid with narrow lines at each end. The drawers were bordered with boxwood. The brasses were diamond-shaped, decorated with a basket of fruit. Research has failed to disclose a cabinetmaker by this name in Salem. Perley (*History of Salem,* Vol. 3) speaks of a John Andrews, a jeweler who married in 1769 and who had two sons named John and Jonathan.

ANDREWS, Gilman D., *Manchester, Mass.*
Born Aug. 22, 1814, in Essex. Married Lucy Ann Nutter of Hamilton in Essex, Aug. 3, 1835. Listed as cabinetmaker in Manchester by Belknap.

ANDREWS, John, *Savannah, Ga.*
Working 1797. Mentioned by James Anderson in his advertisement of Sept. 2, 1797, in the *Georgia Gazette* as "cabinetmaker" on Broughton St.

ANDREWS, Will, *Savannah, Ga.*
Death listed in *Georgia Gazette* in 1734. Cabinetmaker.

APPLEGATE, William, *New York City*
Family tradition says he learned his trade with a Patrick Jackson of New York. Research has failed as yet to discover data regarding a cabinetmaker by this name. Curly maple secretary with broken-arch pediment attributed to Applegate by family tradition shown in *Antiques,* August 1942.

APPLETON, Benjamin, *Gloucester, Mass.*
Married Rebecca Gillingham in Gloucester, May 20, 1758. Died about 1798. Belknap lists him as cabinetmaker.

APPLETON, Daniel, *Haverhill, Mass.*
Belknap says that Daniel was born Feb. 22, 1719/20; worked as cabinetmaker in Haverhill until 1768, when he moved to Chester, N. H.; then moved to Salem, N. H., and finally in 1800 to Ipswich, Mass., where he died April 7, 1807.

APPLETON, John, *Ipswich, Mass.*
Cabinetmaker about 1790. (Waters)

APPLETON, Nathaniel, *Salem, Mass.*
Salem records give no dates for births or deaths of any Appletons by the name of Nathaniel, but Belknap believes there were two or three cabinetmakers bearing this name. According to the shipping lists of the *Welcome Return* in 1803, Nathaniel Appleton was consigning furniture for export at that time. For a while he was a partner in the cabinetmaking firm of Appleton & Ives at Derby and Handy streets, since his advertisement on April 13, 1806 announced that he was continuing the business alone. Who Ives was, how long the partnership was in existence, and why Ives left the firm, is not known at this time. Nathaniel Jr., is listed in the Salem Directory from 1837 to 1859 at 80 Derby St.

Some of the mahogany furniture attributed to the Appletons is not unlike that attributed to Samuel McIntire. It is known that Samuel Field McIntire did carving for the Appletons.

At the Essex Institute, Salem, there is a secretary attributed to one of the Appletons. This is in the Hepplewhite style, veneered but not inlaid. It has curved bracket feet. The doors of the upper case are divided in simple lozenge panes. Above the frieze and the usual cavetto surmounting it, there is a row of dentils. This is somewhat unusual, as dentils of any kind are rare on Salem-made furniture. The center ornament is a carved eagle and may have been carved by Samuel Field McIntire as it is of a type carved by the McIntires.

At the William Rockhill Nelson Gallery of Art, Kansas City, Mo., there is a bed that can be attributed perhaps to Samuel McIntire but more possibly to Nathaniel Appleton; *see* Nutting, Vol. 1, pl. 1513–15.

APPLETON, Thomas, *Salem, Mass.*
Born Oct. 12, 1772, in Ipswich; died April 25, 1855, in Marblehead. Member of firm Harris & Appleton, Salem, which was dissolved July 28, 1815. A Thomas Appleton worked as a cabinetmaker on Milk St., Boston, in 1819; whether the same man not known.

APPLETON, William, *Ipswich, Mass.*
Baptized Jan. 8, 1737/8; died Aug. 9, 1807. Belknap lists him as cabinetmaker.

APPLETON, William, *Salem, Mass.*
Baptized June 30, 1765; died Sept. 23, 1822. Listed in Salem Directory for 1794, his shop a few doors west of Sun Tavern. In July 1794 advertised in Salem paper for "two journeymen at the Cabinet Making Business to whom the highest wages will be given." In 1803 shipped mahogany furniture to Brazil on *Welcome Return.* From 1795 to 1804 on corner of Liberty and Charter streets. A contemporary of McIntire. *Antiques*, Nov. 1949, illustrates inlaid mahogany secretary-desk bearing original label "William Appleton, cabinetmaker, corner of Charter and Liberty Streets, Salem, Massachusetts."

ARCHBALD, Robert, *Charleston, S. C.*
When he became citizen in 1799 stated he was from Scotland and a cabinetmaker. (Burton)

ARCHIBALD, George, *Boston, Mass.*
Listed as cabinetmaker, 1814.

ARMAND, John, *Baltimore, Md.*
Listed in directory for 1802 as cabinetmaker.

ARMINGTON, George, *Providence, R. I.*
Listed in directories from 1824 to 1828 as cabinetmaker on Benevolent St.

ARMINGTON, James, *Providence, R. I.*
Listed in directories from 1824 to 1828 as cabinetmaker on Benevolent St. Doubtless he and George had a shop together.

ARMITT, Joseph, *Philadelphia, Pa.*
Married 1738; died 1747. Listed as cabinet- and chairmaker. Horner says that Joseph, a native of Philadelphia, is credited with making a fully developed Chippendale chair before his death; shows (pl. 23) a walnut Queen Anne side chair attributed to him; believes that he made the Queen Anne bonnet-top walnut chest-on-chest and its accompanying lowboy (pls. 37 and 39) and the "finest Queen Anne Roundabout known" (pl. 71).

ARMITT, Stephen, *Philadelphia, Pa.*
Born 1705; died 1762. Inventory of his stock in 1762 listed "A pr. of fluted corner walnutt draws" and "A pair of plain ditto." Also a "Curled Maple Draws and Table" and "Curld Maple (boards valued) at 5 s 3 d." The use of maple by a Philadelphia cabinetmaker at this time is interesting. (Hornor)

ARMSTRONG, Thomas, *Baltimore, Md.*
Listed in city directory of 1802 as cabinetmaker.

ARNIT, William, *Boston, Mass.*
Listed as cabinetmaker, June 3, 1766, just arrived from Scotland.

ARNOLD, James, *Providence, R. I.*
Listed in city directory for 1832 as cabinetmaker at 68 Broad St.

ARNOLD, John, *Boston, Mass.*
His will was probated in 1784 and he was listed as cabinetmaker.

ARTMAN, John, *Charleston, S. C.*
Listed in directory for 1803 as cabinetmaker at 28 Meeting St. Burton believes him to be the John Artman listed as planter of James Island in letters granted to Peter Artman on Dec. 5, 1817, to administer the estate of John Artman.

ASH, Gilbert, *New York City*
Born 1717; died 1785. Listed as freeman joiner as early as 1748. Advertised regularly in newspapers from 1759 for a number of years. Based upon present knowledge, probably the most outstanding maker of Chippendale-style furniture in New York City. He seems to have been unusually successful in the making of chairs. Downs says: "Among the earliest Chippendale chairs were those inscribed by Gilbert Ash in Wall St., where he was established in 1756 and remained active for seven years."

The *New-York Mercury* for October and November 1759 has the following advertisement:

GILBERT ASH
At the Upper End of Wall-Street, near the City Hall, Carries on the Manufactory of hard Soap-Boiling and has by him a Parcel of very good Soap to dispose of both brown and white; and also a Parcel of Barbary Wax mould Candles. The Shop-Joiner or Cabinet Business is still carried on at the same Place, where may be had all sorts of Work made in that Branch, Tables, Chairs, Desks, &.

To Gilbert Ash is attributed by comparison with a chair bearing his label the handsome set of chairs constructed for Sir William Johnson. These are considered by many to be the finest chairs in the Chippendale style made by any New York craftsman and for many years were considered of Philadelphia origin. They show an interesting scroll back with cupid's-bow top rail, front legs of the cabriole style with elaborately carved knees and claw-and-ball feet unlike those seen on many New York chairs in that they are sinuously curved rather than blocked with square profile at knuckles. The rear legs are of the stump variety and the seat is rounded, reminiscent of the earlier Queen Anne chairs. The chair with Ash's label is almost identical except that its seat is of the usual Chippendale square style. A pair of the chairs made for Johnson is now in the Winterthur Museum, Delaware (Downs, No. 149), and another is in the Garvan Collection, Yale University Art Gallery.

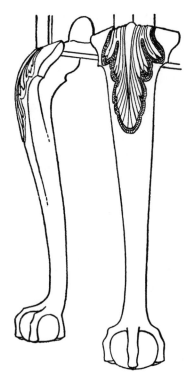

Carving of the type attributed to Gilbert Ash, circa 1760

Ash also made much furniture for the Van Rensselaer family, and the Van Rensselaer chairs at the Metropolitan Museum of Art are attributed to him.

Antiques, March 1951, illustrates a card table attributed to Gilbert Ash around 1760. This is the table owned by the Erskine Hewitt family of New York and included in the collection of the Metropolitan Museum of Art for some ten years.

After 1765 Ash seems to have given up as cabinetmaker but continued his soap- and candlemaking. It is not known why this happened.

ASH, Thomas, *New York City*
    Windsor chair maker. On Feb. 17, 1774, advertised in Rivington's *N. Y. Gazatteer* as follows: "Thomas Ash, Windsor Chair Maker, At the corner below St. Paul's Church in the Broad-Way, Makes and sells all kinds of Windsor chairs, high and low backs, garden and settees ditto. As several hundred pounds have been sent out of this province for this article, he hopes the public will encourage the business, as they can be had as cheap and good, if not superior to any imported; he has now by him, and intends keeping always a large quantity, so that merchants, masters of vessels, and others may be supplied upon the shortest notice. N.B. Shop goods will be taken in pay."

ASH, Thomas and William, *New York City*
    A sample Windsor chair with each of the four legs turned in a different style (owned by Lamplighter Antiques of Hackensack, N. J.) bears the original label "Thomas and William Ash, No. 27 John St., New York, Where Windsor settees and Garden Chairs are made in the Neatest Manner." It is known that Thomas Ash, the Windsor chairmaker listed above, had a son Thomas who was a chairmaker, and it may well be that both this Thomas and William were his sons; it seems more probable, however, that they were the sons of Gilbert Ash, whose will of 1785, filed at the New-York Historical Society, mentions three sons, Thomas, William, and John.

    In the *New York Packet*, March 3, 1785, is the following advertisement; "Thomas and William Ash, Windsor Chair Makers No. 17 John Street, Beg leave to return their sincere thanks to the Gentlemen of this city and state and particularly to the Captains of Vessels, for the many favours they have received and would by the continuance of their commands. They have now ready at the

Ware-House, a great number of very neat Chairs and Settees, some of which is very elegant, being stuffed in the seat and brass nailed, a mode peculiar to themselves and never before executed in America."

ASHTON, H. S., *Philadelphia, Pa.*
Working in the early nineteenth century. At the Old Barracks Association, Trenton, N. J. there is a black painted armchair made by this chairmaker.

ASKEW, William, *Baltimore, Md.*
Cabinet- and chairmaker. Advertised in the *Maryland Journal*, Feb. 22, 1780, that he had "moved from Mr. Gerard Hopkin's over to his own house a few doors from Mr. Griffith's bridge at the sign of 'The Tea Table & Chair.' "

ASTENS, Thomas, *New York City*
Listed in the New York City directories for 1818–21 at 12 Beaver St., for 1822 at 20 Beaver St., and for 1823 at 8 Vesey St. For illustration of a marble-top mahogany table showing Empire features and carrying a label dated 1822, see *Antiques*, March 1935.

ATKINS, Gibbs, *Boston, Mass.*
Born 1739; died 1806. In 1766 listed as cabinetmaker at Prince and Hanover streets. Atkins was a Tory and in 1781 his property was confiscated. He apparently was successful since he owned considerable real estate on Middle St., Black Horse Lane, and Prince St. In 1789 he married Hannah Sanderson and in a few years was able to buy back the confiscated property.

ATKINSON, Parker, *Newburyport, Mass.*
Born Jan. 8, 1780; died 1799. Chairmaker. Estate administered Oct. 9, 1799. (Belknap)

ATWOOD, John Brett, *Newburyport, Mass.*
Born July 16, 1807. Belknap says he was working as late as 1849 as cabinetmaker and until 1860 as ship's joiner.

AUDEBERT, Isaiah, *Boston, Mass.*
Notice of death in 1769 listed him as chairmaker.

AUGUST, Charles, *Charleston, S. C.*
Listed in directory for 1809 as cabinetmaker at 99 Queen St.

AUSTIN, Asa, *Lowell, Mass.*
Listed as cabinetmaker on Lowell St. in 1833.

AUSTIN, James, *Manchester, Mass.*
Born circa 1788. Listed as cabinetmaker in Lynn in 1835 and as late as 1837 in Manchester.

AUSTIN, John, Jr., *Charlestown, Mass.*
Chairmaker. Listed as having moved to Woburn, Mass., after the burning of Charlestown by the British.

AUSTIN, Josiah, *Salem, Mass.*
Born 1740; died 1825. Son of John Austin, the carver. Lived in Charlestown until it was burned by the British in 1775, then in Medford and finally in Salem. In 1782 made a "mahogany swell'd Desk and Low Bookcase" for Elias Hasket Derby at a cost of 24/16/0. Had a partnership with Elijah and Jacob Sanderson in 1799 under name of E. & J. Sanderson Co. Exported furniture from Salem to Charleston, Baltimore, Savannah, South America, Africa, and the West Indies until about 1820. Known as an excellent cabinetmaker.

AUSTIN, Richard, *Suffield, Conn.*
Born 1688; died 1761. Listed in land records of 1746 as "Joyner."

AUSTIN, Richard, *Salem, Mass.*
Born 1744; died 1826. Son of John Austin, carver, and brother of Josiah. Went to Salem from Charlestown after fire of 1775. Listed as chairmaker in 1817. Did much work for the Sandersons— bamboo chairs, fan-back chairs, and others. (Belknap)

AUSTIN, William, *Charlestown, Mass.*

Born 1734. Cabinetmaker working as late as 1807.

AVERILL, James K., *Salem, Mass.*

Married Eliza H. Brown, Nov. 10, 1835. Member of firm of Price & Averill, Vine St., in 1829, at store "formerly occupied by John Jewett." From 1837 to 1857 at 112 Essex St. (Belknap)

AVERY, Oliver, *Norwich, Conn.*

Advertised in *Norwich Packet*, Jan. 23, 1781: "Oliver Avery, Cabinet and Chair Maker, Near Court House, Norwich, etc."

AXSON, William, Jr., *Charleston, S. C.*

Born 1739; died 1800. Formed partnership with Stephen Townsend (*q.v.*) in 1763. Notice in *South Carolina Gazette*, Sept. 28, 1765: "Last Tuesday morning fire broke out in the Workshop of Messrs. Townsend and Axson, Cabinet Makers, n.e. corner Tradd and Old Church Street, which in a short time consumed it, and communicated itself to two adjoining houses, etc., a subscription was the same morning set on foot to make good the loss of Messrs. Townsend & Axson, two industrious young men, who had not long set up their business, which to the honour of the inhabitants was completed the same day." In 1768 the partnership ended and Axson set up shop at White Point.

AYRES, Jacob, *Manchester, Mass.*

Born Jan. 2, 1820. Cabinetmaker. (Belknap)

BABBRIDGE, Christopher J., *Salem, Mass.*

Baptized 1792; still living in 1864. Worked as cabinetmaker until 1850, then as ship's joiner. (Belknap)

BACHMAN, John (*et al.*), *Lampeter Township, Lancaster County, Pa.*

There has been considerable confusion regarding the cabinetmaker by the name of Bachman who made beautiful Chippendale-style furniture, examples of which are at the Winterthur Museum, Delaware, and the Boston Museum of Fine Arts. Research into family records proves that his name was not Jacob as previously thought but John II. The following family data which proves this was kindly supplied by a direct descendant, Mr. Herbert B. Weaver, of Lancaster, Pa.

John Bachman I brought his family to America from Switzerland in 1766, but there is little other information regarding him, although it is believed he is buried in a graveyard on the Senator Amos H. Mylin farm in West Lampeter Township.

Mr. Weaver has carefully examined the tombstones of John II and his wife in the Rohrer family cemetery known as the Big Spring graveyard in West Lampeter Township and of John III and his wife in the Stone Church graveyard near New Danville, Pequea Township. Jacob Bachman is buried in the old Mennonite Cemetery, Strasburg, Pa.

JOHN BACHMAN II, born March 20, 1746, in Switzerland; died April 20, 1829. Married Maria Rohrer: born Jan. 28, 1749; died Aug. 8, 1812.

JOHN BACHMAN III, born Jan. 20, 1775; died April 10, 1849. Married Ester Greider: born Feb. 16, 1780; died Sept. 28, 1870.

JACOB BACHMAN, born Sept. 24, 1798; died July 4, 1869. Married Barbara Kindig: born Nov. 6, 1803; died 1876.

CHRISTIAN BACHMAN, born May 22, 1827; died May 14, 1901. Married Barbara Buckwalter, who died March 22, 1901.

ELLIS BACHMAN, born Aug. 15, 1856; died Feb. 29, 1933.

All five of these men were cabinetmakers and undertakers. The above data indicates that John Bachman II was the first working cabinetmaker in this country, that he arrived in America when twenty years old, that he had already received his training in Europe. In 1771 he married Maria Rohrer, whose ancestors had come from Lorraine. One of their nine children, John III, became a cabinetmaker, as did Jacob, Christian, and finally Ellis, who was the last of this line of cabinetmakers. It would seem from records that the Bachmans were primarily custom cabinetmakers. The first work attributed to one of the Bachmans seems to have been clock cases made for clock-makers in Lancaster County. Carl Dreppard has written that it seems probable that Jacob made clock cases for Christian and Daniel Forrer, who were making clocks during the years 1754–74, and that John the son, and John the grandson, could have made cases for Anthony Baldwin, who was working during the years 1810–40, and for Joseph Bowman, who was making clocks during the years 1820–50. This surmise is doubtless accurate if one changes the name Jacob in the first instance to John and the name of the grandson from John to Jacob.

In addition to clock cases, John II worked during the years of the Revolution making furniture to order for the citizens of Lampeter Township. Since he had been trained in Switzerland, this furniture showed the influences of fashions under Louis XV. John II also made furniture showing the influence of the nearby Philadelphia school, and until recently some of this has been attributed to the cabinetmakers of Philadelphia.

A Chippendale carved walnut tea table with tilting top in the Karolik Collection, Boston Museum of Fine Arts, was at first attributed to the Philadelphia school. This piece was purchased in York, Pa., and is now known to be the work of John II. Mr. Maxim Karolik is quoted as saying that he knew "of no other tea table to be compared with it in terms of individual beauty in spite of the fact that the two other tea tables in the collection display richer carving and ornamentation." (PLATE XX, No. 3) Mr. S. E. Dyke, of Lancaster, Pa., deserves much credit for establishing the identity of John II

and his outstanding work. He says of the same tea table, "It is definitely a Bachman piece and one of the finest there is."

At the Winterthur Museum, Delaware, there is a curly maple tea table and a desk-bookcase tentatively attributed to Bachman.

Descendants of the Bachmans in both Strasburg and Lancaster own clock cases made by the cabinetmakers of their family. Many of the cabinetmaking tools belonging to the Bachmans are also owned by a descendant in Strasburg.

Account books of several of the Bachman cabinetmakers are now in the possession of the Winterthur Museum, Delaware, and further data will undoubtedly be published at some future date. (Downs; Dreppard, *American Collector*, Oct. 1945; Hipkiss)

BACON, Pierpont, *Colchester, Conn.*

Born 1724 in Middletown; died in 1800. According to manuscript of William Kinne, preceptor of Bacon Academy in 1853: "having been bred a house joiner, at the age of 21, says tradition, he [Bacon] betook himself to Colchester on foot with his tools on his back." There he evidently worked as a cabinetmaker and became prosperous. His will dated 1800 left a bequest to found Bacon Academy, which is still functioning.

BACON, Thomas, *Roxbury, Mass.*

Listed as cabinetmaker in 1800.

BADGER, Jonathan, *Charleston, S. C.*

In 1746 purchased land on Tradd St. Apparently engaged in a variety of occupations from cabinetmaking to publishing a collection of psalms and hymns, and acting as an attorney. In 1770 was living in Newport, R. I. (Burton)

BADLAM, Stephen, Sr., *Dorchester Lower Mills, Dorchester, Mass.*

Born 1751; died 1815. Stephen was the son of a tavern-keeper who did cabinetmaking in his spare time. When Stephen was but seven years old both his father and mother died, and little is known of him until he entered the army when nineteen or twenty. He received a commission in the artillery shortly after the outbreak of the Revolution and when obliged to resign because of illness had become a captain. Many years later he was made a general in the Massachusetts militia.

By 1790 he was established in business with a cabinetmaking shop, as well as his house, on old Plymouth Road, now River St. In 1791 he made an extraordinary chest-on-chest for Elias Hasket Derby. This is now in the Garvan Collection, Yale University Art Gallery (PLATE XXI). It bears a written label: "Keep this side up & preserve it from the Sun, from Wet & from bruises. It is of consequence enough to merit great attention." This label identifies the maker since it is in the same handwriting as Badlam's bill to Derby, which is filed with the Derby papers at the Essex Institute, Salem, Mass. This chest-on-chest has elaborate figural finials, carved by the Skillin brothers of Boston, considered the outstanding carvers of their day.

The many bills among the Derby papers at Salem reveal that Badlam did a great deal of work for Derby. The following one indicates the kinds of furniture Badlam made and the prices charged:

Elias Hasket Derby in acc't with
    Stephen Badlam Dr.

To a dresser & Bookcase	22:10:0
To 24 Chairs covered in hair-cloath at 42/	25: 4:0
To 6 Chamber Chairs covered in Russia sheeting at 33/	9:18:0
To 5 cases for the above	1:10:0
To 2 Sofa's covered in Russia Sheeting at £9 each	18: 0:0
To 3 bedsofas with frames for Curtains covered in sheeting	39: 0:0
To 5 cases for do	2:10:0
To a case of Draws exclusive of the carving	19: 0:0
	137:12:0

Cr.

June	
By cash on acc't	48: 0:0
By brasses for the case of Draws purchased by Mr. Derby	1: 2:6
July 22	
By a chest of Bohea	16:20:0
By one of Hyson Tea	26: 8:9
By cash in full	45: 2:9
	137:12:0

Rec'd payment Salem 22 July 1791

It is apparent from his account books that Badlam did a great deal of turning for other cabinetmakers, and as is found true of most cabinetmakers, he combined his craft with a variety of other occupations. On Dec. 8, 1797, he advertised in the *Massachusetts Mercury*, "Stephen Badlam has for Sale at his Store near the Lower Bridge in Dorchester, Elegant Gilt and Burnished moulding and sheet glass for picture Frames and Window Glass of various sizes, also N.B. Glass and picture Framing, Gilding and Cabinet making." When Badlam died an inventory of his estate estimated its value at $24,088.01, a very substantial fortune in those days.

Furniture made during the last years of his life was in the Hepplewhite style and several pieces have been located with "S. Badlam" stamped or burned upon them. At the Metropolitan Museum of Art, New York City, there is a mahogany side chair in Hepplewhite style, with tapered legs, fluted and stop-fluted, made about 1790, attributed to Badlam. (Records at Essex Institute, Salem, Mass.; *Antiques*, May 1954)

BADLAM, Stephen, Jr., *Boston, Mass.*

Born 1779. His name appears in the Boston Selectman's records in 1809 as having made a survey, and he is listed in the Boston Directory in 1820 at Old Court House. His label has been found on a Hepplewhite mahogany shaving mirror with inlay. "Stephen Badlam, junr. No. 42 Cornhill, Boston. A constant supply of fashionable Looking Glasses, Wholesale and Retail." (*Antiques*, May 1954)

BAILEY, Amaziah, *Haverhill, Mass.*
Born Feb. 18, 1797. Belknap says he had a cabinetmaking shop in Haverhill but moved to Hartford, Conn., and then to Aurora, Ia.

BAILEY, Constant, *Newport, R. I.*
Died Oct. 27, 1801. Mason writes of Bailey as "a well known cabinetmaker." The account book of Robert Jenkins, Jr., Newport, R. I., at Rhode Island Historical Society, Providence, shows:

Adventure to West Indies In comp'y
with John Boutin
Dr. To Sundry Accot Ship in Mary Ann
To Constant Bayley
1 Mahogany Table & Caseing   38:
Feb. 20, 1752

The account book of Aaron Lopez, at the Newport Historical Society, shows:

1761 Cr. Constant Baley
by 4 maple tables 4 foot
each at 36   144
by 1 maple desk   80

BAILEY, John, *Rowley, Mass.*
Born Sept. 9, 1741; died 1826. Chairmaker. Married Hannah Dresser. (*Early Settlers of Rowley*, Blodgett & Jewett, 1933)

BAILEY, Jonathan, *Haverhill, Mass.*
Born Aug. 4, 1791. Cabinetmaker at Haverhill but later moved to Cincinnati, Ohio, 1817. (Belknap)

BAILEY, Leonard, *Ipswich, Mass.*
Born circa 1825 in Amherst, N. H. Working in Ipswich as late as 1849 as cabinetmaker.

BAILEY, Richard, *Savannah, Ga.*
Advertised as carpenter and joiner in 1750.

BAILEY, Samuel, *Newbury, Mass.*
Born Nov. 25, 1709; died Aug. 1, 1796. Working as chairmaker in Newbury until 1738, then returned to Rowley, his birthplace.

BAILEY, Thomas, *Newburyport, Mass.*
Born Dec. 5, 1742 at Rowley; died Feb. 16, 1825. Worked as cabinetmaker at Newburyport.

BAILEY, Thomas Jefferson, *Haverhill, Mass.*
Born March 14, 1804. Cabinetmaker. Sometime after 1824 he moved to Aurora, Ia., probably in the company of Amaziah Bailey. (Belknap)

BAILEY, Thomas S., *Newburyport, Mass.*
Married May 5, 1841. Working as cabinetmaker in Newburyport as late as 1852.

BAILY, Nicholas, *New York City*
Listed as freeman cabinetmaker in 1739. Advertised in newspapers in 1739-40.

BAKER, Benjamin, *Newport, R. I.*
Died Jan. 6, 1822. Mason says he sold furniture to New York and West Indies. William Langley's account book, at the Newport Historical Society, lists him as "Benj. Baker, Joyner." Also mentioned in Dr. William Hunter's account book, at the Newport Historical Society, as "Joyner."

BAKER, Ebenezer, *Ipswich and Manchester, Mass.*
Married Feb. 20, 1765. Estate administered Oct. 2, 1797. (Belknap)

BAKER, Seth II, *Providence, R. I.*
Listed in directories for 1832 through 1839 as cabinetmaker working at 57 High St., residing at Stevens St.

BALL, Peter, *New York City*
Subscribed to *Life of Whitefield* in 1774 as cabinetmaker.

BALLARD, Daniel, *Boston, Mass.*
Newspaper notice in 1760 records that fire destroyed his shop with large loss.

BANK, Patrick, *Baltimore, Md.*
Listed in directories for 1807 and 1808 as cabinetmaker.

BANKSON & LAWSON, *Baltimore, Md.*
Advertised as cabinetmakers in *Maryland Journal or Baltimore Advocate,* July 29, 1785. Gordon & Bankson had advertised a "Cabinet Warehouse" in *Maryland Gazette,* July 18, 1750. (Bordley)

BANKSON & WILKINSON, *Baltimore, Md.*
Advertised as cabinetmakers in 1793. The names Wilkinson & Smith listed in 1796; that of Robert Wilkinson in 1799.

BARKER, Benjamin, *Newport, R. I.*
Working before 1775 as joiner. Elected overseer of smallpox, 1794. Obituary notice in *Newport Mercury,* Nov. 8, 1817.

BARKER, James, *Boston, Mass.*
Listed as cabinetmaker in 1814.

BARKER, Thomas, *Charleston, S. C.*
Working as early as 1694. On Feb. 14, 1694, "Thomas Barker, Joyner," administered an estate. Burton believes he died about 1706.

BARKSDALE, Charles, *Charleston, S. C.*
Died 1757. Carried on trade of cabinetmaker in Christ Church parish. Married Mary Wingood in 1741. Inventory of his estate in 1757 showed that he had amassed a considerable amount of property and money. (Burton)

BARNARD, Abner, *Northampton, Mass.*
Not a cabinetmaker by trade but made the wedding furniture for his daughter Anna about 1774. Anna was married to Joseph Hawley Clarke in 1772; died shortly thereafter in 1774. Either just before or after her marriage her father made her a card table, armchair, tip table, and several side chairs; all of cherry wood. The chairs are in the Chippendale style with Cupid's-bow top rail and pierced back splats, some with cabriole legs with claw-and-ball feet, others with straight legs. The tip table has a revolving top with small gallery, and a vase-shaped pedestal. The card table has square, tapered legs and block feet. The furniture has remained in the Barnard family in Northampton ever since.

BARNARD, Julius, *Northampton, Mass.*
Shop on South St. (Licking Water St.). In 1792 advertised "Desks, Secretaries, Bookcases, Chest upon Chest of Drawers, Bureaus, Sideboards, Breakfast, Dining & Tea Tables, Card Table, Bedsteads, Clock cases, Firescreen, Night Stools, Wine Cisterns, Wash hand Stands, Sofas, Easy Chairs, Compass do, framed do, plain do." In August 1796 in building next to R. Breck & Son. Worked in mahogany and cherry. In November 1799 advertised as cabinet- and chairmaker in Tontine, Mass. (Judd)

BARNES, Elizur, *Middletown, Conn.*
Advertised in *Middlesex Gazette,* June 23, 1808: "The subscriber continues to carry on the Cabinet Making Business in all its various branches at the old Stand in the Main Street on the corner of the Street that leads directly to the Ferry where all orders in that line will continue to be thankfully received and punctually attended to."

BARNES, James, *Charleston, S. C.*
In directory for 1801 as cabinetmaker at 132 Church-Street-continued.

BARNES, Nathaniel, *Middletown, Conn.*
Advertised in *Middlesex Gazette,* May 17, 1799: "Barnes, Nathl. & Thos. Sill [*q.v.*] Have Commenced a Copartnership together in carrying on the business of Cabinet Making In all the Several Branches thereof, at their shop in Middletown (lately occupied by Mr. Duc) a little North of the Church."

BARNET, Sampson, *Delaware*
Advertised in *Delaware Gazette,* Oct. 31, 1789. Signed Windsor chairs by him exhibited by Wilmington Society of Fine Arts, 1950.

BARNETT, Alexander, *Barnett's Station, Ky.*

Working about 1789. Came to Kentucky from Virginia. Maker of a walnut desk inlaid with holly. (Whitley)

BARRETT, John M., *Baltimore, Md.*

Listed as cabinetmaker in directories during 1812–17 at 5 York St. His label appears on a gilt Sheraton mirror that is privately owned.

BARRETT, Thomas, *Baltimore, Md.*

Listed in directories for 1799 and 1800 as cabinetmaker.

BARRITE, Gerred E., *Charleston, S. C.*

In 1824 bought property on Church St. On Nov. 16, 1824 advertised in the *Courier*: "G. E. Barrite, Cabinet-Maker. Gratefully acknowledges the goodness and liberality of the citizens of Charleston and its vicinity and begs leave to inform them that he has re-commenced his business at No. 107 Church street in front of Concert Hall . . . LaFayette Bedsteads, the most elegant pattern offered in this city, price $55 a 65: Bureaus $16 a 25; Ladies Work Tables, large size $18 a 20; . . . Two Journeymen will find steady employment. N.B. A colored Boy of Proper age, will be taken as an Apprentice." Apparently his business did not prosper, for in directory of 1829 he is listed as grocer. In 1833 property he had purchased in 1824 was sold. (Burton)

BARRY, J. B., *Philadelphia Pa.; Savannah, Ga.*

Barry learned his trade in London. He came to Philadelphia, where he became a well-known cabinetmaker. Like so many other Philadelphians he left the city to escape the yellow fever epidemic of 1773. He went to Savannah and took space there with Meins & Mackay at 1 Commerce Row. In the Savannah newspaper, Oct. 5, 1798, he advertised: "A most compleat assortment of elegant and warrented well finished mahogany furniture." On Nov. 28, 1798 he advertised again in the Savannah paper that he was returning to Philadelphia.

A Sheraton-style breakfront bookcase with Barry's elaborate label is illustrated in *Antiques*, March 1954.

BARTLETT, Joseph, *Newburyport, Mass.*

Born April 17, 1765; died 1810. Listed by Belknap as cabinetmaker.

BARTLETT, Levi, *Concord, Mass.*

In 1809 advertised for four journeymen cabinetmakers and guaranteed to make furniture as stylish and fine as could be bought in Boston. In 1810, however, his business was taken over by Porter Blanchard, who made churns.

BASS, Benjamin, *Boston, Mass.*

Listed as cabinetmaker on Orange St. in 1798.

BASS, Elisha, *Hanover, Mass.*

Known as maker of a Sheraton-type sideboard made about 1800.

BATCHELDER, George, *Salem, Mass.*

Born circa 1768. Listed as cabinetmaker as late as 1795.

BATCHELDER (or BACHELLER), Theophilus, *Lynn, Mass.*

Born 1751; died 1833. Cabinetmaker. (Belknap)

BAYLEY, Moses, *Newburyport, Mass.*

Born 1744; died 1838. Listed as cabinetmaker and house joiner.

BEACH, Moses Y., *Springfield, Mass.*

Born Wallingford, Conn., 1800; died 1868. Served his apprenticeship under Daniel Dewey of Hartford, Conn. Dewey (*q.v.*) advertised in 1826 and 1830. Beach worked as cabinetmaker in Springfield for ten years, then became a journalist and one of the founders of the *New York Sun*. Represented at show at the Springfield Museum of Art, 1936, by an Empire sideboard and chair.

BEADLE, Lemmon, *Salem, Mass.*

Born July 30, 1680; died Nov. 17, 1717. Son of Samuel. Married Rebecca Atwater, Jan. 4, 1709. Carver and joiner. (Belknap)

BEADLE, Samuel J., *Salem, Mass.*

Died 1706. Came with his father from Charlestown in 1661. Married Hannah Lemmon, June 10, 1668. Worked as turner. Wounded in King Philip's War, after which he became an innkeeper on St. Peters St. (Perley, *History of Salem,* Vol. 2)

BEALL, Gustavus, *George-Town, Md.* (*now part of Washington*)

A table of Duncan Phyfe style with Beall's label is illustrated in *Antiques,* May 1944.

BEAMER, James, *Charleston, S. C.*

Died 1693/4. Working as early as 1687. Inventory of estate showed items used in making furniture although he is listed as joiner. (Burton)

BEARD, James M., *Reading, Mass.*

Born circa 1826. Married 1849. Listed as cabinetmaker by Belknap.

BECAISE (or BECAISSE), Claude, *Charleston, S. C.*

Born 1763. A Frenchman who arrived in Charleston at unknown date. In directory for first time in 1806. Became a citizen in 1815, at which time he stated he came from Provence, France. (Burton)

BECK, Frederick, *Salem, N. C.*

Master joiner. *See* entry for Wohlfahrt.

BECKE, Manasses, *Boston, Mass.*

Listed as cabinetmaker in 1686.

BELCHER, Benjamin, *Newport, R. I.*

Working in 1706 as joiner. (Richardson)

BELCHER, Edward, *Newport, R. I.*

Working 1770 as joiner and housewright. (Richardson)

BELDING (or BELDEN), Samuel, Sr., *Hatfield, Mass.*

Born circa 1633 in Staffordshire, England; died 1713. His father and mother brought the family to Wethersfield, Conn., about 1640. In 1654 he married Mary ——, and in 1661 moved to Hadley with the Allises, Meekins, Graves, and others. In 1678 purchased lots 9 and 10 along the main street, on the west side of the river. William Allis had lot 8, John Allis lot 10, and John Hawkes lot 13. His wife was killed by Indians who attacked Hatfield in September 1677. On June 25, 1678 he married Mary, widow of Thomas Wells. She died Sept. 29, 1691. For his third wife he married Mary Meekins Allis, widow of John Allis, and after her death on April 10, 1705, Sarah, widow of John Wells. In November 1699 it was voted by the town that "the present meeting house is insufficient and that a new one be built 45 feet square with gable windows upon each square of the roof." Samuel Belding was among those chosen to build this new meetinghouse. He was the senior member of the firm of Belding & Allis, to which are attributed many of the Hadley chests.

See entries for: Allis, Hawkes, Pease, John Taylor.

(Judd; Charles C. Whitney, *Belding Genealogy,* 1896.)

BELDING, Samuel, Jr., *Hatfield, Mass.*

Born April 1657; died circa 1737. Samuel Jr. and Ichabod Allis carried on the partnership of Belding & Allis after the death of their fathers (*q.v.*). The making of Hadley chests continued during the years of their ownership but ceased with their deaths. Samuel Jr. was the father of six daughters but had no sons. One daughter became the wife of his partner Ichabod Allis. Town records for Jan. 7, 1688/89, show that the selectman authorized "Samuel Belding, Jr. & John White to make 3 additional seats in the gallery on South side 'for fornicators' and 3 on north side—and an east-west window in the roof with four lights each

—rail the stairways and shut up [one word illegible] windows now there. They to receive 53/." (Judd) The younger Samuel's will was made in 1727. He probably died in 1737 as he was living in 1736 and the will was presented in February 1738.

BELL, Thomas, *Salem, Mass.*

Married Mrs. Elizabeth Butman, July 27, 1834. His will was administered in May 1837 and listed his cabinetmaker's shop at 199 Essex St.

BELT, Charles, *Anne Arundel County, Md.*

Advertised as cabinetmaker in the *Maryland Gazette*, Baltimore, Nov. 30, 1775.

BELTER, John Henry, *New York City*

As the long popularity of Duncan Phyfe waned, his place in the fashionable world of New York City was filled by another cabinetmaker whose name was as much a household word during the years 1844–67 as Phyfe's had been during the previous half century. This man was John Henry Belter.

Belter was born in Germany in 1804 and served his apprenticeship in Württemberg, where he learned both cabinetmaking and carving. He appeared on the New York scene in 1844 at 40½ Chatham Square, the fashionable cabinetmaking center of that day. In the same year he married Louisa Springmeyer, whose brothers became his business partners. Belter occupied at least two different shops on Broadway (no. 552 and then 722), and in 1858 opened a large five-story factory at 1222 Third Ave., corner of 76th St., where he employed as many as forty apprentices. From 1856 on, his company was called J. H. Belter & Co., his several brothers-in-law joining with him. Many of his carvers had been trained in Alsace-Lorraine or the Black Forest of Germany, Belter preferring them to any others for the expert carving he demanded.

Belter died in 1863 and is known to have destroyed most of his patterns and pattern molds before his death. Although the business was continued under the company name, it became bankrupt in December 1867.

Much of the furniture produced by Belter was of rosewood. The curved backs so characteristic of his chairs and sofas were achieved by means of a laminated method of construction, a process developed by him to lessen shrinkage, to secure strength, and to permit curving. When Belter applied for a patent for this method in 1856 he described it in this manner:

"I take sufficiently long strips of veneer and covering the whole of one side with glue, apply to it the short piece and compress the whole either between plain or slightly dished cawls until cold, then laying a sufficient number of these . . . together between the clamps I turn the screws and confine them while I apply the peculiar plane and reduce the edges . . . Having properly heated the heavy inside cawl . . . , and provided suitable means for clamping the whole . . . together, I apply the glue to the exterior face of an inner stave. . . . This process being repeated with all the inner staves, it follows that . . . [they] are held ready to be forced into . . . position as soon as the pressure is applied from outside. The staves of the middle series are next immediately applied. . . . I repeat this process for any number of layers of staves, working rapidly to prevent the glue from becoming cold. . . . When all are in position the outer heated cawls are applied and compressed. . . . On removal . . . some 24 hours later . . . the pressed work envelops the interior cawl. (Downs, *Antiques*, Sept. 1948)

Thus, several thin layers of rosewood were glued together, the layers so arranged that the grain ran at right angles. The number of layers varied from three to sixteen, although the average was from six to eight, the width measuring about one inch. Today's plywood is an example of this method of lamination.

The sofas and chairs made at the Belter workshops are highly individual and show his most ornate designs. The finest have the backs skillfully carved at the top in intricate lacy scrolls and floral patterns in high relief. At times the elaborate carving was gilded, giving the rich appearance of carved or fashioned metal. Again the backs were deeply carved but without pierced lacework, while those made at a later period have only flat serpentine bands to support the upholstered seats and backs. The elaborately carved chairs and sofas were usually upholstered in gorgeous brocades or damasks. As good as a Belter label was the use of finished wood to face the backs of chairs and settees, a feature used by no other cabinetmaker. Rosewood, the favorite of Belter for the construction of his fashionable Victorian furniture, was never plentiful and was not easy to carve. By experimentation, American cabinetmakers of the period discovered that black walnut—found in quantity in the forests of America—when properly treated with certain chemicals resembled the imported rosewood, and so black walnut eventually supplanted rosewood for the making of Victorian furniture. While Belter did not overlook black walnut for his cabinetwork, it appears that he used rosewood whenever possible for his finest work. At times he stained oak and other hard wood to resemble ebony. During the early 1860s Belter's designs changed somewhat from the rococo of his earlier years to the rectilinear of the Gothic, but they still remained ornamentally complex except in a few instances. Belter also made other pieces of furniture besides chairs and sofas at his factory. He was an excellent cabinetmaker, carver, and craftsman. His careful workmanship is shown in the use of maple—plain or figured—for lining drawers. At times in addition to the rich carving, pieces of solid wood were used in relief as additional ornamentation. Naturally Belter had many competitors but none achieved the richness of carving and design shown in his work. By the time of his death in 1863, furniture was being produced in factories, where cheap reproductions of his carefully constructed and carved furniture were turned out. Ere long the name of John Henry Belter was forgotten except in a few households where pieces of his furniture were carefully cherished. Some years ago, he was brought back to a permanent place among the cabinetmakers of America by the careful research of Thomas Hamilton Ormsbee.

At the Virginia Museum of Fine Arts, Richmond, there is a superb pair of sofas made by John Henry Belter about 1850. They are of carved and gilded rosewood, and were reupholstered in 1954 in red silk damask (PLATE XXX).

Works by Belter at the Metropolitan Museum of Art, New York City, include: (1) a rosewood table with white marble top, part of a parlor set made for George Henry Bissell of New York City; the inside frame signed "J. H. Belter & Co." in black ink, and (2) a rosewood side chair, upholstered in damask; made for Mrs. Elliot, 27 West 33rd St., New York City, 1864.

At the Museum of the City of New York are: (1) several other pieces, including side chairs and armchairs, and (2) a rosewood sofa covered with two-color silk damask. This sofa displays Belter's carving at its finest. It was part of a large parlor set made for Mrs. Carl Vietor of New York City.

At the Theodore Roosevelt Birthplace, 28 East 20th St., New York City, many other examples of Belter's work may be seen.

(*Antiques*, Sept. 1948; *Catalogue Loan Exhibition New York State Furniture*; Downs)

BEMAN (or BEEMAN), Reuben, *Kent, Conn.*

It seems possible that there was a family relationship, and perhaps a professional contact, between Reuben Beman of Kent and Col. Ebenezer Tracy the cabinetmaker of Lisbon, Conn. Reuben's forebears in the Tracy line run as follows:

Jonathan Tracy (Preston, Conn., part of Norwich, Conn.)

  Married July 11, 1672

Mary Griswold (daughter of Francis Griswold, one of the proprietors of Norwich)

David Tracy (son of Jonathan; born Sept. 24, 1687)

  Married Oct. 6, 1709

Sarah Parrish

Rachel Tracy (daughter of David; born Nov. 29, 1724)

  Married Feb. 25, 1741

Ebenezer Beeman (Preston, Conn.)

Reuben Beeman, the son of Rachel Tracy and Ebenezer Beeman, was born Dec. 14, 1742, and is registered in *Kent Land Records* (Vol. 1–10) as Rubeen Beeman. He is listed in Kent town records in 1785 as a cabinetmaker.

In the Winterthur Museum, Delaware, there is a double chest with the chalk inscription "Reuben Beman, Junr" and another inscription which says "Bought Dec. 1801." This double chest is of cherry with soft pine for the drawer sides tapered from ⅝ inch at the bottom to 5/16 inch at the top. The backs of the drawers are ⅞ inch thick, which is heavy even for Connecticut furniture. The roof is of very thin ash. The sides are chamfered and fluted at both top and bottom. There is a pinwheel on the center top drawer, and this is repeated on each inner end of the scroll top. There is gadrooning along the lower edge of bottom section. (PLATE XIX, No. 1) (*Kent Land Records; Vital Statistics* for Kent, Preston, and Norwich)

BENJAMIN, Samuel, *Winthrop, Me.*

Born Sept. 7, 1786, at Livermore, Me.; died April 27, 1871. Son of Lt. Samuel Benjamin. In 1806, preferring to be a mechanic rather than go to college, he entered the shop of Deacon Joseph Metcalf of Winthrop to learn the trade of cabinet- and chairmaker. In 1809 bought a small plot of ground in the village on the west side of the stream, built a shop, and began the business of cabinetmaking. Served nine years as town clerk. Became captain in the militia after serving as lieutenant at Wiscasset in the War of 1812. On Jan. 11, 1816, married Olivia, daughter of Calvin and Eunice Metcalf of Winthrop. Pictures of Capt. Samuel Benjamin, his wife, and their home appear in *The History of Winthrop, Maine*, by E. S. Stackpole, 1925.

BENNETT, Aaron Lee, *Manchester, Mass.*

Born March 27, 1817. Married April 14, 1845. Listed as cabinetmaker by Belknap.

BENNETT, Colton, *Beverly, Mass.*

Born in New Market, N. H. Listed as cabinetmaker in 1817. Married Mary Ann Allen at Beverly, July 20, 1820. Belknap says Bennett was living in 1849.

BENT, Thomas, *Boston, Mass.*

Had cabinetmaking shop on Washington St. in 1811.

BERNARD, Nicholas, *New York City*

In 1769 advertised in both New York and Boston newspapers. Carver.

BERRY, Ferdinand and Robert, *Baltimore, Md.*

In directory for 1796 as cabinetmakers.

BERSON, John Baptiste, *Baltimore, Md.*

In directory for 1810 as cabinetmaker.

BERTINE, James, *New York City*

Working 1790–97. With revocation of Edict of Nantes, 1685, Bertine's Huguenot ancestors fled to England and then to America, settling in New Rochelle, N. Y. Not known when or where James was born, nor where he served his apprenticeship. Listed in New York directories during 1790–97 at Pearl and Queen streets as Windsor chairmaker. Apparently did no advertising. Chairs made by him New England in type. One owned by Roland M. Howard, Blue Hill, Me., is branded on underside of seat "J.Bertine N.York."

BESSELEU, Lewis, *Charleston, S. C.*
Probably born March 26, 1779. In directories for 1806 and 1807 as cabinetmaker at 29 Beaufain St. (Burton)

BETTS, John, *New York City*
Made a freeman in 1774. Listed as cabinetmaker.

BEUWISE, Richard, *Baltimore, Md.*
In directory for 1799 as cabinetmaker.

BIGGARD, John, *Charleston, S. C.*
Primarily a turner. Arrived in Charleston from Philadelphia about 1767. Advertised in *South Carolina Gazette; And Country Journal*, March 23, 1767, that he had opened a shop on Queen St., "where gentlemen may be supplied with windsor and garden chairs, walking sticks and many other kinds of turnery ware, as neatly finished and cheaper than can be imported."

BIGWOOD, John, *Manchester, Mass.*
Born circa 1822, in Frome, England. Married in Manchester, 1846, when he was listed as cabinetmaker.

BINGHAM, Henry Lee Tuck, *Manchester, Mass.*
Born May 8, 1805. Married Oct. 22, 1838. Cabinetmaker. (Belknap)

BIRD, Jonathan, *Charleston, S. C.*
Born 1777. Death announced in *City Gazette*, Sept. 22, 1807: "Died, on Sullivan's Island, on Saturday morning last, Mr. Jonathan Bird, Cabinetmaker, aged 30 years, a native of Yorkshire, England. The pleasing manners and disposition of this young man had endeared him to his friends and acquaintances who will long deplore the loss of so valuable a friend and member of society."

BISHOP, Lemuel, *Charlotte, N. C.*
A Hepplewhite side table sold at the King Hooper sale at National Art Galleries, New York City, December 1931, No. 325, bore handwritten label: "Made by Lemuel Bishop Charlotte 1815."

BLACKFORD, Thomas, *Boston, Mass.*
Chairmaker in 1784.

BLACKMAN, James, *Boston, Mass.*
Listed as cabinetmaker in 1814.

BLAIR, John, *Boston, Mass.*
In directory for 1807 as chairmaker.

BLAKE, Benjamin S., *Andover, Mass.*
Born circa 1822. Married in Salisbury, 1846. Cabinetmaker. (Belknap)

BLAKE, James, *Boston, Mass.*
In directory for 1806 as cabinetmaker at the Neck.

BLAKE, John, *Boston, Mass.*
Listed as cabinetmaker. In 1680 owned land on both sides of Hogg Alley.

BLAKE, Judson, *Providence, R. I.*
In directory for 1824 as cabinetmaker on President St.; during 1832–37 at 9 President St.

BLAKE, Samuel, *Stratford, N. H.*
"Mr. Blake settled in Northumberland on the outskirts of the town, so near the border that in theory, if not in fact, he might be reckoned one of Stratford's citizens. He was a skilled artisan and specimens of 'Uncle Sammy's' craft are treasured in Stratford homes today." (Thompson)

BLAKE, William, *Boston, Mass.*
Listed as cabinetmaker in 1800.

BLANCHARD, Rufus, *Providence, R. I.*
Listed in directory for 1832 as cabinetmaker at 68 Broad St.

BLANCHARD, Simon, *Boston, Mass.*
Listed in 1807 as cabinetmaker in Wilson's Lane.

BLANEY, Jonathan C., *Marblehead, Mass.*
Born circa 1777; died March 10, 1844. Listed as cabinetmaker.

BLANVELT, Harmon, *Providence, R. I.*
Listed in directory for 1832 as chairmaker at 100 Broad St.

BLASDELL, Abner, *Chester, N. H.*
Born April 18, 1771; died in the War of 1812. Listed as cabinetmaker. (Belknap)

BLISS, Ebenezer, *Newport, R. I.*
Chairmaker. Married Martha D. Boss, March 7, 1821. Death notice in *Rhode Island Republican,* Sept. 23, 1824.

BLISS, Elijah, *Newburyport, Mass.*
Had cabinetmaker shop on Middle St. in 1809.

BLISS, Pelatiah, *Springfield, Mass.*
Working circa 1800–10. Advertised in *Hampshire Federalist*: "Pelatiah Bliss, Cabinetmaker, Informs his friends & the public in general that he still carries on the cabinetmaking business at his old stand one fourth mile north of Bridge Lane, where he keeps constantly for sale, all kinds of mahogany and cherry furniture. Also an assortment of chairs. Any kind of joiner work done at the shortest notice. Country produce taken in payment, or a reasonable credit given if desired. Springfield, February 10, 1810."

BLOCK, Nathaniel, *Charleston, S. C.*
Listed in directory for 1809 as cabinetmaker on Wentworth St.

BLOUNT, Stephen, *Savannah, Ga.*
Born 1761; died 1804. Chairmaker who migrated to Georgia from South Carolina. At his death his estate was appraised at $11,000. (*Antiques,* Feb. 1954)

BLYTHE, Thomas, *"Winyaw," S. C.*
Arrived in South Carolina before April 9, 1733. Inventory of his estate was made in 1762 but not recorded until seven years later (Charles Town, South Carolina, Probate Court Book, Y 1769). Made a mahogany chest-on-chest with cypress as secondary wood; the name Blythe written in pencil is now obliterated. (*Antiques,* March 1955)

BOARDMAN, Langley, *Portsmouth, N. H.*
Born circa 1760; died 1829. Langley, son of Thomas and Sarah Langley Boardman, is thought to have been born in Stratham, N. H., where his father had moved from Ipswich, Mass. Originally the family name had been spelled Boreman and the immigrant ancestor had arrived in Ipswich as early as 1635.

It is believed that Langley served his apprenticeship in Portsmouth shortly after the close of the Revolution, since by 1800 he was well established in his own building at 3 Congress Street, where he had a store and a cabinetmaking shop. It is thought that he designed the furniture made in his workshop but that he employed workmen and apprentices to do much of the actual work. He also designed his own home, which was built about 1815 and which is one of the beautiful houses in Portsmouth today. At the time this house was sold, the buyer purchased with it several pieces of furniture which apparently had been made in the Boardman workshop. These included several sets of chairs, a mahogany sofa, and an early Empire sideboard. Other documented pieces are in the Hepplewhite and Sheraton styles. No labeled piece has as yet been found. Boardman accumulated a fortune. He held several public offices as well as that of State Senator.

(*American Collector,* May 1937; *Newtown Bee,* Newtown, Conn., Jan. 4, 1952)

BOARDMAN, Leonard C., *Amesbury, Mass.*
Born circa 1821. Married in Salisbury in 1845. Listed as cabinetmaker by Belknap.

BOARDMAN, Timothy, *Middletown, Conn.*
Born Jan. 20, 1754. Son of Timothy and Jemima Johnson Boardman, who were married Nov. 14, 1751. Listed as a joiner on Main St., between Parsonage St. and Episcopal Church, 1770–75. (Barber)

BOGUE, John, *Alexandria, Va.*
Advertised in Alexandria papers in 1795 as a house builder, ship's joiner, and cabinetmaker.

BOHONON, Moses, *Salisbury, N. H.*
Working about 1800. Maker of several marked pieces in existence. At one time had as many as eight workmen. (*American Collector*, June 1937)

BOLCOM, Seth, *Salisbury, Vt.*
Working as chairmaker in Salisbury, 1815. (Weeks)

BOND, Oliver, *Lowell, Mass.*
Listed in directory for 1834 as cabinetmaker.

BONNER, John, *Charleston, S. C.*
Listed in directories during 1822–55.

BOOKER, Richard, *Williamsburg, Va.*
Advertised in *Virginia Gazette* more or less regularly during 1773–76 as cabinetmaker.

BOOTH FAMILY, *Newtown and Southbury, Conn.*
Since there has never been any published data on the three cabinetmakers with the name Booth, it is important to register them in their proper places within the Booth family, one of the prominent families of Connecticut, particularly in early Stratford.
Richard Booth was one of the early settlers of Stratford. His grandson, Ebenezer, born there March 11, 1685, migrated to Newtown, where he died Feb. 11, 1726/27. His son, also named Ebenezer, was born at Newtown, April 1, 1718; married Rachel Sanford, Newtown, Dec. 5, 1739; and died Jan. 7, 1803. It is not known whether he was a cabinetmaker but two of his sons—his third child, Ebenezer, and fourth, Elijah— were both cabinetmakers, as was his grandson (Ebenezer's son) Joel. (D. L. Jacobus, *Genealogy of the Booth Family*, published by Eden C. Booth, Pleasant Hill, Mo., 1952; *Vital Statistics*, Connecticut State Library, Hartford)

BOOTH, Ebenezer, *Newtown, Conn.*
Ebenezer was born at Newtown, Aug. 16, 1743. He married Olive Sanford of Woodbury (daughter of Jonathan and Phebe [Platt] Sanford), Nov. 20, 1766. As yet no piece of furniture has been directly attributed to him but it is reasonable to believe that furniture made by him would have many features in common with that made by Elijah and by Joel. It is not known with whom they learned their trade. It would seem probable that Ebenezer and his brother Elijah were apprenticed to the same cabinetmaker and that Joel learned his trade from his father. Ebenezer died in 1790. His will, dated March 14, 1789, and proved July 5, 1790, left his son Joel "two-thirds of the property and the Joiner's Shop." In addition, "I give & bequeath to my son Joel Booth forty shillings to be paid out of my Joyner tools in consideration of his being my eldest son." The inventory of Ebenezer's estate showed considerable lumber and furniture in the shop; among other things it listed:

202 chair parts	154 Do round
1 Stole, 1 Desk & Drawers	
1 Chest and Draws	
one round fall table	6 round top chairs
one large Do	5 fiddle backs
8 plain Chairs	1 plain Chest
150 feet Chery bords, 400 feet of oak bord	
800 feet Whitewood Do, 340 feet pine	
350 feet Maple, 464 feet white pine	
100½ of Birch do	

The inventory also contained a great many tools—chisels, gouges, planes, "one set of patterns," chest locks, etc.

BOOTH, Elijah, *Southbury, Conn.*
Elijah was born at Newtown, Oct. 26, 1745. On Oct. 14, 1772, he married Anna Hinman, daughter of Deacon Noah Hinman of Southbury (part of Woodbury at that time) and they were the parents

of eight children. Anna died April 15, 1804, and Elijah married Anna Deming, Oct. 23, 1805.

Elijah was in Southbury as early as 1770, when he bought property from Noah Dudley in the parish of Roxbury. Over the years Booth did a great deal of buying and deeded the same property over and over again, the deed given as security for a loan, upon payment of which the deed was invalidated.

In 1771 he bought a plot of ground from Edward Hinman (*Woodbury Land Records*, Vol. 18, p. 75), and that was the land upon which were his dwelling house and cabinetmaking shop. The deed reads in part: "In Consideration of One Hundred and twenty-three Pound, Twelve Shillings, Lawfull money in hand Recd. of Elijah Booth of Woodbury . . . one Certain Tract of Land lying in said Woodbury, in the Parish of Southbury, being one half acre at the North west corner of the said Edward Hinman Home Lot, and described as follows: Beginning at the northwest corner where the two highways or streets meet, thence East by highway 10 rods to a heap of stone, then South 8 rods to a heap of stone, westward 10 rods to a heap of stones by the street, North by the street 8 rods to first mentioned bounds. Contains one-half acre more or less with a dwellinghouse standing thereon and a well dug thereon." Elijah died Sept. 24, 1823, at the age of seventy-eight, and it is apparent that he was not well enough to carry on his cabinetmaking work for some years prior to his death. On March 15, 1806, he sold to Eli Hall (*Woodbury Land Records*, Vol. 4, p. 193) for 160 pounds "Lawful money . . . A certain piece of land lying in Southbury containing about half an acre of Land with a Dwelling House, a *Joiner's Shop* [author's italics] and a Barn thereon." This was the property he had bought from Edward Hinman in 1771, where he and his family had lived and where he had carried on his work, but between the time of its purchase in 1771 and its sale in 1806 a joiner's

shop had been added and the value had gone up from 123 pounds to 160 pounds. It is possible that any joiner's tools owned by Elijah were included in the sale because the inventory of his estate, Oct. 20, 1823, revealed few possessions and no tools. There were several pieces of furniture: 1 cherry stand, 1 chest with drawers, 1 chest, 1 candlestand, 1 bedstead, 4 chairs, a "Winsor" chair, 1 case "Draws," 8 kitchen chairs. All of this was left to his second wife. However, shortly before his death there had been deeds conveying several pieces of property to various members of the family, and since at the time of the signing of his will he was apparently unable to write his name, it is evident that he was very ill and had been trying to get his affairs in order.

Many pieces of furniture owned by families living in and near Southbury are attributed to Elijah Booth's cabinetmaking shop by very definite tradition. His memory is kept alive in the minds of many still living in Southbury. They say he employed several apprentices, that he bought tracts of timber, which he cut down and used for his furniture, much of which is made of native cherry wood. Pieces attributed to him indicate that he was a well-trained cabinetmaker, working in a style some years earlier than that in vogue elsewhere, but this was often true in the case of workmen at a distance from the larger cities.

Elijah made tables, highboys, lowboys, secretaries, desks, chairs, and chests-on-chest, all in the Chippendale style. Almost as good as a signature is the beading along the edge of cabriole legs, high or low. Unlike the beading used by the Rhode Island men, which ends in a curl, that used by Booth ends in a simple dart. With his short cabriole leg he used a claw-and-ball foot, the claw firmly grasping the ball; or his version of a Spanish foot. On highboys, the front legs generally have claw-and-ball feet; the rear legs, pad feet. Again all four legs may have pad feet. Fluting and stop-fluting are found at corners topped by a well carved rosette. Finials are of the cone variety. His carved shell is individualistic.

In July 1935 *Antiques* advertised and illustrated a cherry secretary from the collection of the late Dr. J. Milton Coburn, who at one period of his life lived in Danbury. Its present whereabouts is unknown. This piece was attributed to E. Booth of Woodbury and was given a date of 1760, which, of course, was much too early. The secretary had a brass eagle centered in the pediment, star inlay on the paneled doors, a deeply carved shell on the middle drawer identical to those on pieces now in Southbury, and the characteristic Spanish feet on short cabriole legs. While this was at the time attributed to E. Booth of Woodbury, it could possibly have been made by Ebenezer. Further study of the history of this piece is required.

In the Three Centuries of Connecticut Furniture exhibition at the Morgan Memorial, Hartford, 1935, was a mahogany highboy with scroll top, carved rosettes, cone finials, fluted columns with square rosettes above, square drawer in upper and lower sections with shell, cabriole legs with pad feet, the characteristic beading along the upper legs, and an interesting snakeskin carving on the leg top. (PLATE XIX, No. 2) This was attributed to an unknown cabinetmaker of Woodbury, Conn. This highboy has an interesting history. It was purchased by the late Samuel A. Griswold of Branford from an undertaker in Woodbury by the name of Swan, some fifty years ago for $65. Swan had gotten it from the Stiles Russell family for less than that. Like so many pieces attributed to Booth, this had been made for a member of the Stiles family, Stiles Russell's mother having been a Stiles and this piece evidently a wedding present. The highboy was willed to the Society for the Preservation of New England Antiquities by Mr. Griswold and is now in the Lt. Pratt House in Essex, Conn.

Still told in Southbury is the following tale about Elijah. His several young apprentices were obliged to work in the shop until sundown, when it was the chore of one of the lads to go to the back lot and bring in the cows. Like all normal boys, the apprentices resented this extra duty, so one night they all ran off and it was necessary for Elijah to search out the cows himself. Shortly after leaving home Elijah returned, somewhat breathless and without the cows. His wife could see he was flustered, perhaps aided by a long draught of homemade apple brandy.

"Anna, do bull frogs talk?" asked Elijah. "You know bull frogs don't talk," said Anna. "Well," replied Elijah, "I was down to the back lot by the pond and I heard a bull frog say, ' 'lijah Booth, 'lijah Booth, 'lijah Booth.' " "And then," added Elijah, still breathless, "a little peeper said, 'Damn him, damn him, damn him!' " After pausing a moment, Elijah added, "When bull frogs and peepers begin to talk, it's time for an honest man to stay at home!" It leaked out later that the mischievous apprentices hidden near the footbridge had been highly successful in getting even with their master.

(Mr. and Mrs. Clarence G. Stiles of Southbury have kindly provided much of the information concerning Elijah Booth.)

BOOTH, Joel, *Newtown, Conn.*

Joel, the eldest son of Ebenezer, and nephew of Elijah, was born in Newtown, June 17, 1769, when his father was twenty-six and his uncle twenty-four. One year after Joel's birth, Elijah was in Woodbury. Thus it would seem probable that Joel learned his trade with his father. Joel was only twenty-one when his father died and he lived but four years longer. In those days, however, lads of fourteen began to learn their trade, and at his death in 1794 an inventory of his estate showed an enormous stock of material, finished and unfinished furniture, and joiner's tools. Evidently his death was very sudden for he had borrowed money from many people. It was apparently invested in his business, for when the estate was inventoried, large as it was, it had to be sold to pay an indebtedness amounting to £466:3:9½, a very large sum. Much of it was due members of his family and those of his wife's, but some of it was probably owing for supplies. Administration of his estate was granted Nov. 6, 1794, and among other things the inventory included:

Joiner's Shop including Benches,
    Laythes   35/0/0
Work in Shop Part Done
  One finished case of Drawers at 180/
  One Cest of Drawers & 20 two
    Bed chests   12/
  One half of a Case of Drawers at 12/
  One Cherry Desk begun   /7
  One Table Frame at   3/6
  One Clock Case part done   /8
  One Mahogany frame for a desk
    at   12/
  One three Square Candle Stand at 2/6
  One fall stand at   12/
  One Mahogany Card Table   30/
  One Spinnet at   12/
    pillars and Loge for stand   1/6
  One trundle bedstead   6/
  Six plain Chairs red   3/
  Two black chares at   4/

A great deal of furniture was listed in the house, including dining chairs, "Winsor" chairs, a huge red chest, "Leather back and Botom Chare," a case of drawers, a double leaf square table, "One Desk case of Drawers at 100/" etc.

Stock in the shop included: "Four Hundred and Forty-three feet of Mahogany Boards, Thirteen Hundred Cherry, Seventy-five of Whitewood, Two Hundred of Pine, Nine Hundred Feet of Cherry Boards."

His joiner's tools were in large numbers and of every kind: "Twenty-five molding tools, Three Rabit plains, four smoothing Do, two Jack Do, three Jointers, One plough, two Coars Saws, three Brass Back Do, one Steel back do, Four Compass Do, Five gouges, Chizzels, Turning Chizzels," etc.

BOUTON, John, *Norwalk, Conn.*
    Working about 1830. *See* entry for Rufus H. Pickett.

BOWEN, Nathan, *Marblehead, Mass.*
    Born Oct. 5, 1752; died Aug. 9, 1837. At the Detroit Institute of Arts there is a bonnet-top chest-on-chest attributed to Bowen. This has "NB 1774" marked on the back. The chest was made for the wedding linen of Mary Ann Hidden and was purchased from her descendant of the fifth generation in Marblehead. The piece is of mahogany, the lower chest block-front supported on cabriole legs with claw-and-ball feet. The broken pediment at top supports an elaborate overhanging scroll molding which terminates in carved rosettes. The three finials are spiral twist. A writing tablet separates the two sections. (PLATE XVII, No. 1)
    At the Boston Museum of Fine Arts there is an unattributed chest-on-chest almost identical with the one described above.

BOWEN, William, *Philadelphia, Pa.*
    In 1786 paid an occupational tax as a cabinet- and chairmaker. In 1794 listed as a Windsor chair maker. Shop taken over by sons George and Thomas in 1797.

BOWEN, William, *Baltimore, Md.*
    Listed as cabinetmaker in city directory for 1799.

BOWERS, John, *Baltimore, Md.*
    Listed as cabinetmaker in city directory for 1799.

BOWLES, Joshua, *Boston, Mass.*
    Working as a carver in 1768. Since it is probable that he worked with Simeon Skillin, he is listed here; for while it is not the intent to publish names of carvers in this book, a few of very real importance such as the Skillins and Rush have been included.

BRADFORD, Thomas, *Charleston, S. C.*
In March 1792 formed a partnership with Henry Clements (*q.v.*), at which time he is called an upholsterer. In Probate Court records at time of death, 1799, he is called a cabinetmaker. (Burton)

BRADLEY, Harrison, *Alexandria, Va.*
Advertised in *Alexandria Gazette*, June 16, 1835, as chairmaker.

BRADSHIRE, William, *Baltimore, Md.*
Listed as cabinetmaker in city directory for 1803.

BRANCH, William L., *Providence, R. I.*
Listed in directory of 1832 as cabinetmaker working at 103 Westminster St. and residing at 17 Market St.

BREED, Ebenezer, *Charlestown, Mass.*
Listed in Charlestown at time of burning in 1775. One year later listed as cabinetmaker in Boston.

BREED, Ephraim, *Lynn, Mass.*
Born May 26, 1736; died April 4, 1812. Listed as chairmaker by Belknap.

BREED, Joseph, *Weston, Mass.*
In Charlestown at time of burning in 1775 but then moved to Weston. Listed as cabinetmaker.

BRETT, John, *Newburyport, Mass.*
Born circa 1756; died Sept. 13, 1839. Belknap lists him as cabinetmaker.

BRIDGE, John, *Boston, Mass.*
Listed as cabinet- and chairmaker at Burditt's Wharf in 1807.

BRIDGE & FESSENDEN, *Boston, Mass.*
Listed as cabinetmakers at 15 Ann St. in 1807.

BRIENTNALL, John, *Philadelphia, Pa.*
Windsor chair maker whose daughter Elizabeth married Thomas Ackley in 1752. Inventory of his estate in 1747 showed "high Chest Drawers, Cur'l Maple."

BRIGGS, Cornelius, *Boston, Mass.*
Listed as cabinet- and chairmaker in 1817. Lived at 2 Temple Place.

BRIGGS, Moses, *Boston, Mass.*
Born circa 1824. Married in Marblehead in 1848. Listed as cabinetmaker by Belknap.

BRIGGS, William, *Providence, R. I.*
Listed in directory for 1832 as cabinetmaker on Cranston St.

BRIGHT, George, *Boston, Mass.*
Born 1726; died 1805. The earliest of a number of cabinetmakers with the name of Bright. His shop and house were both on Fish St. The Assessors Taking Book of 1780 reveals him as one of the largest taxpayers in Boston at that time, one of the few who had survived the failures due to the depression following the Revolution. A bill dated Dec. 28, 1763 indicates that he made furniture for export. He also made furniture for John Hancock and chairs for the new State House. Inventory of his estate showed many joiner's tools, much mahogany, and many pieces of completed and unfinished furniture.

BRIGHT, John, *Boston, Mass.*
Listed in directory for 1789 at Marlborough St.

BRIGHT, John and William, *Boston, Mass.*
Listed in directory for 1797 at 44 Marlborough St.

BRIGHT, Joseph, *Boston, Mass.*
Listed in directory for 1797 as chairmaker, cabinetmaker, and upholsterer at Vincents Lane.

BRIGHT, Richard, *Boston, Mass.*
Listed in directory for 1789 as cabinetmaker at 44 Marlborough St.

BRIGHT, Thomas, *Boston, Mass.*
Listed in directory for 1796 as cabinet-maker at Spring Lane.

BRIMBLECOME, Thomas, *Marblehead, Mass.*
Born May 17, 1719; died Sept. 17, 1765. Listed as chairmaker.

BRIMMER, Andrew, *Boston, Mass.*
A serpentine-front desk taken to Waldoboro, Me., by Col. Isaac Reed in 1789 and bearing Brimmer's label, "52 Cornhill, Boston," was sold at Creamer Auction, May 1930, at Waldoboro.

BRINNER, John, *New York City*
Advertised in New York City newspapers in 1762 and again in 1763: "John Brinner, Cabinet and Chair Maker from London at the Sign of the Chair opposite Flatten Barrack Hill, in the Broad-Way, New York, where every article in the Cabinet, Chair-making, Carving and Gilding Business is enacted on the most reasonable Terms with the Utmost Neatness and Punctuality. He carves all Sorts of Architectural, Gothic, and Chinese Chimney-pieces, Glass and Picture Frames, Slab Frames, Girondels, Chandaliers, and all Kinds of Mouldings and Frontispieces, etc. etc., Desk and Book Cases, Library Book Cases, Writing and Reading Tables, Study Tables, China Shelves and Cases, Commode and Plain Chests of Drawers, Sofa Settees, Couch and Easy Chairs, Frames, all Kinds of Field Bedsteads, etc. etc. N.B. He has brought over from London six Artificers, well-skilled in the above branches."

BROCAS, John, *Boston, Mass.*
Working as cabinetmaker in 1736 and 1737 at his shop on Union St.

BRODERICK, Ephraim, *Newport, R. I.*
Working in 1725 as joiner. (Richardson)

BROESING, Andreas, *Salem, N. C.*
Joiner. *See* entry for Wohlfahrt.

BROOKS, Jonathan, *New London, Conn.*
Advertised as cabinetmaker in *New London Gazette*, April 22, 1768. Married Mercy, daughter of James Chapman. At his death in 1808, Brooks' cabinetmaking shop on Second St. was given to his son Nathan, and two dwellings were given to his son John.

In *Antiques*, November 1949, there is illustrated and offered for sale a highboy of cherry with the inscription behind one of the drawers "Made by John Brooks, 1769." It could have been by this man.

BROOKS, Thomas, *Brooklyn, N. Y.*
Born 1811. Maintained a "Cabinet Warehouse" at 127–129 Fulton St., corner of Sands St., Brooklyn, as early as 1856. Listed in directories until 1876 under name of Thomas Brooks & Co. Died in Dalton, Mass., July 6, 1887.

BROOMHEAD & BLYTHE, *New-Market Plantation, S. C. (about one mile from Charleston)*
Advertised in the *South Carolina Gazette* in 1732: "At New-Market Plantation, about a mile from Charleston, will continue to be sold all sorts of Cabinet Work, chests of Drawers, and Mahogany Tables and Chairs made after the best manner; as also all sorts of peer Glasses, Sconces, and dressing Glasses. Where all sorts of bespoke Work is made and mended at the lowest Price." (Burton; Rose)

BROWN, Alexander, *Baltimore, Md.*
Listed in directory for 1796 as cabinetmaker on Harrison St.

BROWN, Benjamin, *Charlestown, Mass.*
Born 1680; died 1720. Married Mary Frothingham before 1702. Cabinetmaker.

BROWN, Benjamin, *Salem, Mass.*
Born Sept. 30, 1819. Cabinetmaker at various addresses before 1864. In 1864 at 30 Lafayette St.

BROWN, Benjamin, *Providence, R. I.*
In directories during 1828–32 as cabinetmaker working at 101 Westminster St., residing on John St.

BROWN, Benjamin, *Boston, Mass.*
Listed in directory for 1831 as chairmaker.

BROWN, Daniel, *Charleston, S. C.*
Listed in directory for 1801 as cabinetmaker on King St.

BROWN, David A., *Providence, R. I.*
Listed in directories for 1836 and 1837 as cabinetmaker working on Fulton St., living at 23 Westminster St.

BROWN, Eben, *Boston, Mass.*
Listed in directory for 1766 as cabinetmaker.

BROWN, Eleazer, *Salem, Mass.*
Born Feb. 16, 1690/1; died 1750. Married Sarah Putnam, Dec. 7, 1716. Listed as joiner. (Perley, *History of Salem*, Vol. 3)

BROWN, James, *Newport, R. I.*
Joiner, working in 1714. (Richardson)

BROWN, James, *Hamilton, Mass.*
Born 1753; died Oct. 4, 1844. Cabinetmaker. (Belknap)

BROWN, James, *Newburyport, Mass.*
Working as cabinetmaker 1851–58.

BROWN, John, *Philadelphia, Pa.*
Paid occupation tax as cabinetmaker of £40 in 1783, and £25 in 1786. (Hornor) Attended meeting of cabinetmakers in Philadelphia, July 4, 1788. (Nutting, Vol. 3)

BROWN, John, *Ipswich, Mass.*
Turner about 1790. (Waters)

BROWN, John S., *Providence, R. I.*
Listed in directory for 1828 as cabinetmaker at 245 North Main St.; in those during 1832–37 on Davis St.

BROWN, Joseph, *Charlestown, Mass.*
Married in 1723, at which time called a turner.

BROWN, Joseph, *Newbury, Mass.*
At Essex Institute, Salem, his account book states: "Joseph Brown cabinetmaker Newbury His Book bought July 7, 1725." Business taken over by Stephen Emery at Brown's death in 1742.

BROWN, Joseph, *Boston, Mass.*
Listed in directory for 1800 as cabinetmaker.

BROWN, Joseph, *Baltimore, Md.*
Listed in directories for 1803 and 1804 as cabinetmaker.

BROWN, Michael, *Charleston, S. C.*
Listed in directory for 1809 as cabinetmaker at 99 Queen St.

BROWN, Nathaniel, *Savannah, Ga.*
Windsor chair maker, working about 1777–1803, who went to Savannah from Philadelphia. (Theus, *Antiques*, Feb. 1954)

BROWN, Nathaniel, *Litchfield, Conn.*
In 1797 advertised in *Litchfield Monitor*: "Windsor and fiddle-back chairs. Shop near that of John Mattocks just west of the center of town." Again advertised he made: "Windsor, fiddleback, dining room, parlor, kitchen, and children's chairs." (White)

BROWN, Nicholas, *Hartford, Conn.*
Chair-, chaise-, and harness-maker, just north of Col. Jeremiah Wadsworth on Main St. in 1769. In 1771 advertised he was building a stagecoach for the accommodation of passengers from Hartford to New Haven. When the war broke out he advertised his place for sale and apparently went to Shelburne, Nova Scotia. (Love)

BROWN, Samuel, *Ipswich, Mass.*
Born circa 1708; died Nov. 7, 1775. Listed as chairmaker by Belknap.

BROWN, Samuel, *Newburyport, Mass.*
Born circa 1720; died 1798. Listed as chairmaker and turner by Belknap.

BROWN, Samuel, *Newburyport, Mass.*
Born Dec. 23, 1752, at Newbury; died 1815. Listed as cabinetmaker by Belknap.

BROWN, Samuel, *Boston, Mass.*
Working as cabinetmaker in 1766.

BROWN, Samuel, *Greensburg, Pa.*
Advertised in *Farmers' Register* (published in Greensburg, Westmoreland County) on April 11, 1801: "Samuel Brown, Cabinet-maker informs the people of Westmoreland that he carries on the cabinet-making business in all its branches at the place whereon he now lives, about two miles from Dennistons town and one from Irvines Mill (Loyalhannah Creek). Having had experience in the above business in different parts of the United States and practiced with European workmen, he is enabled to supply those who will favour him with their custom in any fashion of Walnut or Cherry furniture, either ornamental or plain. N.B. an apprentice is wanted."

BROWN, Samuel F., *Hamburg (Lyme), Conn.*
Advertised in the *New London Gazette*, Jan. 12, 1831 and April 11, 1832.

BROWN, William, *Charlestown, Mass.*
Joiner. Moved from Charlestown to Boston in 1737.

BROWN, William, *Baltimore, Md.*
Advertised in *Maryland Gazette*, Oct. 18, 1753, as joiner and cabinetmaker "at London Town where Mr. West deceased formerly dwelt." Listed in directory of 1796 as cabinetmaker and in that of 1800 at 109 North High St. A privately owned solid-door secretary bears his label.

BROWN, William F., *Montville, Conn.*
Advertised as cabinetmaker in the *New London Gazette*, May 29, 1805.

BROWN & COOK, *Baltimore, Md.*
Listed as cabinetmakers in directory for 1796.

BROWN & KENNEDY, *Baltimore, Md.*
Advertised as cabinetmakers in 1795.

BRUCE, Luther, *Charlestown, Mass.*
Listed as cabinetmaker in 1737. From Sudbury.

BRUEN, Battheas, *Newark, N. J.*
Working 1780–1800. (*Antiques*, Sept. 1952)

BRUMLEY, Joseph, *Georgetown, Va.*
Advertised in 1800 as cabinetmaker. (Comstock)

BRYANT, Nathaniel, *Charlestown, Mass.*
Born 1784; died 1868. Worked as apprentice of Charles Forster. In 1813 was member of firm of Loud & Bryant on Court St., Boston, cabinetmakers and chairmakers.

BUCHANNON & ROBB, *Baltimore, Md.*
Advertised as cabinetmakers in 1784.

BUCKINGHAM, John, *Pittsburgh, Pa.*
Advertised in the *Pittsburgh Gazette*, Dec. 28, 1793, as cabinetmaker. *See* entry for William Earl.

BUCKLAND & MUIR, *Alexandria, Va.*
Advertised in newspapers in 1794 as cabinet- and chairmakers, house and ship's joiners. (Comstock)

BUCKTROUT, Benjamin, *Williamsburg, Va.*
Working circa 1766–1812. Arrived from London in 1766. Advertisements in *Virginia Gazette* brought him much work and he soon became the leading cabinetmaker of his time in Williamsburg. In 1769 advertised in same paper for journeyman cabinetmakers and apprentices. In his shop on Francis St. maintained a store of general merchandise in addition to his cabinetmaking. Sold store in 1779.

His shop has been restored in Colonial Williamsburg.

BUCKTROUT, Richard M., *Williamsburg, Va.*

Son of Benjamin. Carried on the business of cabinetmaking until about 1820.

BUDD, Edward, *Boston, Mass.*

Listed as chairmaker in 1670.

BUDD, John, *New York City*

Apparently exported furniture to the South. A Sheraton card table bears the label "John Budd / Cabinet Maker / No. 118 Fulton Street / Between William & Nassau / New-York" and the date May 1817. He is listed in the New York Directory until 1840. His label also carried this information: "Has constantly for sale a general assortment of Cabinet Ware, on the most reasonable terms. Orders from southern ports immediately attended to." His work is similar to that of Phyfe and Lannuier. (*American Collector*, Oct. 1936)

BULKLEY, David, *Litchfield, Conn.*

In partnership with George Dewey two doors west of County House. They became famous for their carving beyond limits of township. In 1839 company became Bulkley & Cooke. (White)

BULKLEY, Thomas, *Farmington, Conn.*

At his death circa 1798, Samuel Kneeland (*q.v.*) took over his shop.

BULL, Charles, *Boston, Mass.*

Arrived in Boston from North Carolina, 1716. Listed as cabinetmaker.

BULL, Henry, *Newport, R. I.*

Working as joiner in 1709. (Richardson)

BULL, Joshua, *Baltimore, Md.*

Listed in directory for 1803 as cabinetmaker.

BULLITSCHEK, Joseph, *Salem, N. C.*

Moravian cabinetmaker. Moved to Salem from Pennsylvania. Also an experienced organ builder. (Fries, *Records of the Moravians in North Carolina*)

BUMSTEAD, Jeremiah, *Boston, Mass.*

Listed as joiner in 1710.

BUNER, Jo, *Savannah, Ga.*

Advertised in 1735 as joiner. (Comstock)

BURBANK, Joseph King, *Suffield, Conn.*

Born 1772. In town records as joiner.

BURCHKISS, Lewis, *Boston, Mass.*

Listed in directory for 1821 as cabinetmaker.

BURDEN, Joseph, *Philadelphia, Pa.*

In 1796 in partnership with Francis Trumble.

BURDON, Reuben, *Providence, R. I.*

Listed in directories from 1824 to 1832 as cabinetmaker on Middle St.

BURGESS, Joseph, *Baltimore, Md.*

Advertised in *Maryland Gazette or Baltimore General Advertiser*, Nov. 1, 1785, as cabinetmaker.

BURK, E., *Alexandria, Va.*

Advertised in 1815 that he "had served his apprenticeship in New York."

BURKE, Patrick, *Charleston, S. C.*

Listed in directories from 1801 to 1803 at various addresses on Queen St.

BURLESSON, Ebenezer, *Suffield, Conn.*

Born circa 1710. Son of Fearnot Burlesson (*q.v.*). Listed in land records of 1734 as joiner. Apparently left Suffield about 1745.

BURLESSON, Fearnot, *Suffield, Conn.*

Born 1679; died 1732. Inventory of estate, on file at Northampton, Mass., shows carpenter's and joiner's tools.

BURLING, Thomas, *New York City*

It is believed he learned his trade with Samuel Prince (*q.v.*). When made a freeman in 1769, listed as cabinetmaker. Advertised in *New York Gazette*, Feb. 17, 1772, that he was working as cabinetmaker "at the Sign of the Chair" in Beekman Street, "commonly called Chapel Street." He explains here that the partnership with his brother, John Burling, is being dissolved. Listed in New York directories during 1773–93 at 36 Beekman St., in that of 1797 at 25 Beekman St. Announced in *New York Packet*, March 16, 1786, that he was opening a new shop. In this advertisement he mentions his early association with Prince. Burling made a "writing desk and apparatus" for George Washington when he was living on Cherry St., New York City; this is now owned by the Historical Society of Pennsylvania. A mahogany wardrobe in Chippendale style with Burling's label is at the New-York Historical Society. According to tradition this was given by Judge David A. Ogden of New York City to his wife as a wedding present in 1797. Illustrated in *Antiques*, May 1936, are two pieces of furniture with Burling's label: a slant-top mahogany desk with claw-and-ball feet in front, rectangular bracket feet behind, carved gadrooned skirting in front, made circa 1790; and a secretary-bookcase made about the same time. (*American Collector*, June 1935 and March 1946; *Antiques*, Jan. 1934)

BURN, James, *Charleston, S. C.*

Listed in directory for 1790 as cabinetmaker at 285 King St., in that of 1802 at 39 Church-Street-continued.

BURNHAM, Benjamin, *Norwich, Conn.*

Married Mary Kinsman. Father of Benjamin Burnham (*q.v.*). At his death in 1737, the inventory of his estate showed him to be at least a chairmaker, if not a cabinetmaker, in addition to being an innkeeper. The inventory listed: "4 augurs, a frow, 2 bits, 3 pair of chisels, gouges, 723 foot pine boards, 100 pine planks, 45 dozen chair rounds." Also "1 table, 8 chairs, 3 chests, 3 chests and cupboard, 2 chests and a box, 2 chests."

BURNHAM (or BURNAM), Benjamin, *Norwich, Conn.*

Born 1729. Son of Benjamin and Mary (Kinsman) Burnham. Married Jemima (Leonard) Perkins in 1750. Had several children: a daughter who married a Tracy, undoubtedly a relative of Col. Ebenezer Tracy the cabinetmaker (*q.v.*); Benjamin, who was tax collector at the time of Ebenezer Tracy's death in 1803 and who owed Tracy's estate money; Elisha (?), who married Tracy's daughter Sarah; and Jedediah, who died in 1828, at which time the inventory of his estate included "two high cases of drawers, old desk, long table, etc."

Like his father, Burnham was an innkeeper, and a picture of Burnham's Inn is shown on page 63 of H. F. Bishop's *Historical Sketch of Lisbon*. Where he learned cabinetmaking is a matter for conjecture. At the Metropolitan Museum of Art, New York City, there is a cherry desk attributed to Benjamin Burnam. (PLATE XVIII, No. 1) It has a slant top with inlaid stars, four shallow blocked drawers in the lower section, and small drawers in the desk section, ornamented with carved shells in the manner of the Newport cabinetmakers but less graceful. On the base there is gadrooning, a feature found on Connecticut furniture. There are ball-and-claw feet in front, curved bracket feet in the rear. The inscription reads: "This desk was maid in the year 1769 buy Benj^m Burnam that sarvfed his time in Felledlfey." If the desk was made by Benjamin Burnham of Norwich as many believe, it is not known when he went to Philadelphia; possibly he went there at an early age and served his apprenticeship, returning home in 1750, the year he was married. The desk was made before John Townsend was in Norwich. However it is apparent that the maker of the desk was acquainted with the work of the Newport cabinetmakers since his own work is closer to their designs than to the desks of Philadelphia cabinetmakers. This is the only piece with the "Burnam" signature or label, but on the basis of similarities to it other pieces have been attributed to Benjamin Burnham. Altogether too few details of this cabinetmaker's life are known, and it may very well be that further research will disclose that it was a presently unknown "Benj. Burnam" who constructed the cherry desk at the Metropolitan Museum of Art.

There is record that Burnham served in the Revolution; in 1775 he signed the muster roll as captain. At the time of his death in 1799 his estate was small and his debts of a size to make it necessary to sell everything to pay his liabilities. Few tools remained and this leads one to surmise that he had not been working at his trade for some years before his death. His will was written April 1, 1799, just two months before his death in June 1799. In beginning this will he says: "Although Labouring At Present under Some indisposition of body, yet being of Sound Disposing mind and memory and understanding. . . ." The inventory of the estate is dated June 4, 1799, and shows considerable furniture but very few tools, far fewer in number than those in his father's estate in 1737, which leads one to the conclusion they had been disposed of before his death.

(Bishop; *Connecticut Muster Rolls, 1775; Lisbon Vital Statistics; Town Records of Lisbon*)

BURNSTEAD, Josiah, *Boston, Mass.*
Listed in directory for 1796 as cabinetmaker.

BURR, William W., *Providence, R. I.*
Listed in directory for 1828 as cabinetmaker at 249 North Main St.

BURRAGE, Thomas, *Charlestown, Mass.*
Listed as cabinetmaker in 1788.

BURRILL, George, *Boston, Mass.*
Notice of his death in 1721 listed him as chairmaker.

BURROUGHS, Ezekiel, *Newport, R. I.*
Working as joiner in 1763. (Richardson)

BUTLER, Gamaliel, *Annapolis, Md.*
Cabinetmaker. Advertised in *Maryland Gazette*, April 4, 1754, as "near the dock."

BUTTRICK, Nathan, Jr., *Carlisle, Mass.*
Born Feb. 19, 1811. Working as late as 1842 as turner and cabinetmaker. (Belknap)

BYRNES, Caleb, *Stanton, Del.*
A secretary attributed to him, made circa 1771, was exhibited at the Wilmington Society of Fine Arts, 1950. (*Antiques*, Aug. 1950)

CADE, G., *New England*
A mahogany bombé desk made about 1760 is illustrated in *Antiques*, January 1941. Stamped on the back is the name G. Cade, which might be that of the maker or original owner.

CADY, Milton, *Providence, R. I.*
Listed in directories from 1824 to 1837 as cabinetmaker on Mill St.

CAHOON, Ebenezer, *Newport, R. I.*
Working as joiner in 1733. (Richardson)

CAHOON, John, *Newport, R. I.*
Working as early as 1748 (Richardson). Married Betsy Hudson, June 1, 1782. His ledger is in the possession of the Newport Historical Society. It spans the years 1749–60 and shows that he sold various merchandise as well as furniture, which he bought in large quantities from various workmen. Cedar chests, desks, etc., were made in great quantity in Newport, apparently for export to the West Indies.

In the Isaac Stelle (merchant) account book (No. 496, p. 74), at the Newport Historical Society, there appears the following:

> to John Cahoone, Joyner
> Contra By 2 Seader Desks
>   By 1 Tea Table
>   By 1 Mahogany table
>   By 1 Desk Seder
>   By 1 Desk Sedar

Notice of his death appeared in the *Newport Mercury*, Aug. 13, 1792.

CAHOONE, John Spear, *Newport, R. I.*
Chairmaker. Working in 1775 on Back St. (Richardson)

CAHOONE, Jonathan, *Newport, R. I.*
Chairmaker, 1781. (Richardson)

CAINE, Isaac, *Charleston, S. C.*
In his will, dated March 28, 1786, he speaks of himself as a cabinetmaker. (Burton)

CALDELUGH, Andrew, *Philadelphia, Pa.*
Working during the Chippendale era on Arch St. In 1773 worked for David Evans. (Hornor)

CALDER, Alexander, *Charleston, S. C.*
Born 1773; died 1849. On Dec. 10, 1796 advertised in *City Gazette and Advertiser*: "Alexander Calder, Cabinetmaker opposite to the Scots Church, Meeting-Street, Begs to inform the Public in general, that he has on hand a Variety of elegant and useful Cabinet Work, consisting of Secretaries and Wardrobes—Secretaries and Book Cases of different forms, Card and Breakfast Tables, do, do. Elegant Sideboards, do, Sets of Dressing Tables, A variety of handsome Chairs and Sofas of the newest fashion."
He married a Mrs. Scott, Feb. 15, 1797. Became a citizen in 1803, at which time he stated he was thirty years old, a cabinetmaker, and a native of Edinburgh, Scotland. About 1807 gave up cabinetmaking and apparently went into the hotel business. (Burton)

CALDER, James, *Charleston, S. C.*
Born 1790. Nephew of Alexander Calder. Came to Charleston at an early age. In 1809 had a shop at 38 Meeting St. Became a citizen in 1813, at which time he stated his age as twenty-three, his profession as that of cabinetmaker, his home as Glasgow, Scotland. Died Nov. 21, 1855. (Burton)

CALDWELL, Josiah, *Salem, Mass.*
Cabinetmaker on Essex St., "next to Dr. Barnard's," in 1810. (Belknap)

CALEF, Ebenezer, *Nantucket, Mass.*
Baptized July 22, 1739; died Oct. 18, 1807. Made a labeled bureau described in *American Collector*, Sept. 1937. (*Vital Statistics Nantucket*)

CALL, Thomas, *Charlestown, Mass.*
Born 1689; died 1781. Joiner.

CALL, Timothy, *Charlestown, Mass.*
Listed as chairmaker in 1720.

CALLENDER, William, *Boston, Mass.*
Listed as cabinetmaker and turner in 1789.

CAMP, William, *Baltimore, Md.*
From 1802 to 1819 listed in city directories or advertising as cabinetmaker. His name not associated with any furniture as yet, but he used a large label bearing his name and "Cabinet & Upholsterer, 25 Water Street, Baltimore." (*Baltimore Furniture*)

CAMPBELL, James, *Harrodsburg, Ky.*
Working 1795–1805. (Comstock)

CAMPBELL, James, *Boston, Mass.*
Died 1809. Cabinetmaker and chairmaker on Spring Lane. In 1791 had a partnership with Moses Ward under name of Campbell & Ward. Mrs. Burton N. Gates of Worcester, Mass., owns a wingchair with the name "J. Campbell" on frame of upper part of wing. Possibly it refers to this man.

CAMPBELL & WARD, *Boston, Mass.*
See entries for James Campbell and
Moses Ward.

CANTER, Benjamin, *Charleston, S. C.*
Appears in 1813 directory as cabinet-
maker at 64 Broad St. Burton believes he
is the same man mentioned in *Jews of
South Carolina* by Elzas as being in
Charleston in 1802.

CANTERBURY, Ira, *Providence, R. I.*
Listed in directory for 1832 as cabi-
netmaker on Middle St. and 124 Broad
St.

CARGILL, John M., *Providence, R. I.*
Listed in directories from 1832 to 1837
as cabinetmaker at 50 and 57 High St.

CARLILE, John, *Providence, R. I.*
His grandfather emigrated to this country in the company of a relative who was
the father of Paul Revere. John was born
in Boston in 1762. At an early age, as
was the custom, he was apprenticed to a
cabinetmaker, probably in Boston. At
some unknown date he arrived in Providence and with his brother Samuel had a
lumber business at 113 South Main St.
He was an original member of the Providence Association of Mechanics and
Manufacturers and was chosen its president in 1817, an office which he held
until 1823. He represented Providence in
the General Assembly in 1801–02. He
was a member of the Town Council from
1818 to 1824. In 1824 he was listed in the
city directory at 93 South Main St.
and was living at 16 George St. in a house
which he built. He married Nancy Dana
(daughter of Nathaniel) and they had
thirteen children. He died in Providence
in 1832 and was buried in St. John's
churchyard.
A copy of a picture of him painted by
Gilbert Stuart is at the Rhode Island Historical Society, Providence. The original
was destroyed by fire. Also at the Rhode
Island Historical Society is a side chair
attributed to him, of good design and

workmanship. At the Rhode Island
School of Design, Providence, there are
chairs and a table attributed to him. These
are of mahogany with bird's-eye maple
inlay. (*Mechanics' Festival and Historical
Sketches;* other data at Rhode Island Historical Society)

CARMAN, Andrew, *Charleston, S. C.*
Born 1785. His death notice in the
Courier, Nov. 7, 1806, listed him as
cabinetmaker.

CARMER, Henry, *New York City*
Advertised in the *New York Gazette*
in 1774 as cabinetmaker.

CARNE, John, *Charleston, S. C.*
In 1764 had partnership with Edward
Weyman (*q.v.*) on Queen St. under the
name Weyman & Carne. Early in 1764
announced in *South Carolina Gazette*
that he had opened a shop next door to
Capt. John Stevenson's, where he was
carrying on the cabinet- and coffin-
maker's business. (Rose; Burton)

CARR, Alexander, Jr., *Trenton, N. J.*
Chairmaker before the Revolution.
(*Catalogue State Museum,* Trenton, N. J.,
1953)

CARR, John, *Pittsburgh, Pa.*
On Oct. 16, 1805, advertised in the
Pittsburgh Commonwealth that he was
"lately arrived from Philadelphia." At
that time his shop was on the corner of
Ferry and Front streets. On June 18, 1806,
he advertised "a handsome assortment of
Cherry and Walnut furniture." On July
30, 1806, he advertised that he had moved
to the "three story frame house next
door to the corner of Front in Market."
He advised that he was equipped to do
turning and that he had in his employ
journeymen from Philadelphia. Evidently
he retired from business in 1807, as on
December second of that year he advertised his shop, tools, and house for sale.

CARR, Nicholas, *Providence, R. I.*
Listed in directories for 1836 and 1837 as cabinetmaker working at 101 Westminister St., residing at corner of Aborn and Sabin streets.

CARRINGTON, Edward, *Charlestown, Mass.*
Born 1613; died 1684. Listed as turner. (Wyman)

CARTER, John, *Charlestown, Mass.*
Born 1719; died 1804. Listed as joiner.

CARTER, Ralph, *Boston, Mass.*
Notice of death in 1699 listed him as cabinetmaker and turner.

CARTER, Thomas, *Boston, Mass.*
Listed in directory for 1789 as cabinetmaker.

CARWITHEN, William, *Charleston, S. C.*
Born 1704. Advertised in *South Carolina Gazette*, April 21, 1733: "Whereas I have been informed by People thro' several Parts of the Country, that there has been a Malicious Report, persuading my Customers that I have left off Trade; These are to satisfy all people as shall want Desk and Book-Cases, Chests of Drawers, Clock Cases, Tables of all Sorts, Peer-Glass Frames, Swinging Frames, and all other sorts of Cabinet Ware, made as neat as ever, and Cheap." Apparently he continued in business for many years, although it would seem as though he became so prosperous as to give up cabinetmaking some years before his death, since no mention of it appears in the following notice of Sept. 3, 1770, in the *South Carolina & American General Gazette*: "Last Sunday died, aged 66 (41 of which he had resided in the province) Mr. William Carwithen, Librarian of the Charles Town Library Society."

CARY, Edward, *Boston, Mass.*
Listed as cabinetmaker on North St. in 1796.

CARY, Peleg, *Newport, R. I.*
Joiner in 1750. (Richardson)

CHALLEN, William, *New York City*
In 1797 advertised: "Fancy Chairmaker from London manufactures all sorts of dyed, jappanned, wangee and bamboo chairs, settees, etc., and every article in the fancy chair line executed in the neatest manner, and after the newest and most approved London patterns."

CHAMBERLAIN, Wilson, *Charlestown, Mass.*
Born 1724; died 1791. *Antiques,* January, 1956, illustrates a mahogany ladderback chair with carved back and crest. It is signed "Chamberlain" and is attributed to this man.

CHAMBERS, Alexander, *Trenton, N. J.*
Chairmaker before the Revolution. (*Catalogue State Museum,* Trenton, N. J., 1953)

CHANLER, Samuel, *Boston, Mass.*
Working as joiner as early as 1687.

CHAPIN, Aaron, *Hartford, Conn.*
Born 1753, in Chicopee, Mass. Son of Deacon Edward and Eunice (Colton) Chapin. Aaron was twelve years younger than his second cousin Eliphalet, the cabinetmaker of East Windsor. In the fall of 1774, he entered Eliphalet's shop as an apprentice. In 1777 he married Mary King of East Windsor. It is probable that he and his wife lived with the widowed Eliphalet until June 1778, when Eliphalet remarried, because at that time Aaron bought a building lot adjoining that of Eliphalet and on it built a home. It was in this house that his son Laertes was born in August 1778. It is also probable that he worked in Eliphalet's shop, and that, working together, they constructed many pieces of furniture. In addition each must have worked on various items alone, for Aaron's advertisement of Dec. 9, 1783, suggests that each

had his own clients. In 1787 Aaron sold his home in East Windsor to a member of the Stoughton family from whom he had purchased the land in 1778. He had already moved to Hartford.

In the *Connecticut Courant* of Dec. 9, 1783, Aaron advertised: "Begs leave to acquaint the public, as well as his former customers, that he has lately removed from East Windsor to Hartford, and now improves the shop opposite Mr. Samuel Burr's where he now carries on the Cabinet and Chair making business, in as great variety perhaps as is done in any shop in the State, in both Mahogany and Cherry Tree, of which he has now a good stock. Any Gentlemen or Ladies disposed to encourage him with their favours, may depend on being served with fidelity, and as great dispatch as his present accommodations will admit of. He has now on hand a few good Tea and Kitchen Tables, a variety of Tea and Wine Servers to dispose of on reasonable terms for good pay in hand."

On Dec. 17, 1798, he advertised: "Watches, Cabinet Furniture &c. Aaron Chapin Having had 20 years successful practice in Watch Cleaning, repairing &c. offers his service to such persons as have unfaithful Watches, whether foul or otherwise disordered, at his Shop sixty or eighty rods north of the Court-House. Customers may rely on a careful attention to their orders and reasonable dispatch. And for a reasonable fee, work warranted, or not, as may be most agreeable. Now ready for sale cheap and good, various articles of Mahogany and Cherry tree furniture; sundry Bass Viols, complete for use; Pitch Pipes; Fifes: Watches do. Seals, keys, chaines, &c." Thus we see yet another cabinetmaker combining his cabinetmaking business with some other occupation.

On Jan. 1, 1807 Aaron took his son Laertes into partnership and thereafter the business was conducted under the name of Aaron Chapin & Son, Cabinet Makers. On Aug. 11, 1808, the *American Mercury*, Hartford, published the following advertisement: "House Furniture, Aaron Chapin & Son. At their shop seventy rods north of the Court-House Have on hand a general assortment of mahogany and cherry House Furniture, both plain and elegant, Among which are sideboards, secretarys, desks, bookcases, bureaus, tables, bedsteads, washstands, candle-stands, sofas, easy-chairs, swinging cradles &c. &c., which they offer for sale on liberal terms. Also for sale New English and French watches, pitch pipes, fifes, furniture varnish, &c. &c."

Of all the furniture made by the Chapins there are only two documented pieces, although much is attributed to them by tradition and by comparison. Both documented pieces are by Aaron. One is a simple cherry piece at the Connecticut Historical Society, Hartford; the other a beautiful Hepplewhite-style serpentine-front eight-legged sideboard at the Wadsworth Atheneum, Hartford. Although the Chapins made much of their furniture of cherry, this sideboard is of mahogany with inlay and was made in 1804 for Frederic Robbins. The bill is dated Nov. 22, 1804. (PLATE XXVIII, No. 1.) Aaron died in Hartford on Dec. 25, 1838. The business was carried on by his son.

See references under Eliphalet Chapin.

CHAPIN, Eliphalet, *East Windsor, Conn.*

Church and town records of Somers, Conn., show Eliphalet Chapin, son of Ebenezer Chapin and Elizabeth, his wife, born Sept. 18, 1741. Elizabeth was the daughter of Jonathan Pease of Enfield, Conn., son of John Pease, Sr. (*q.v.*), and brother of John Pease, Jr. (*q.v.*), the maker of a Hadley chest. John Pease, Jr., had a son John who married Elizabeth Spencer of Hartford, a member of the cabinetmaking family of that name closely associated with Nicholas Disbrowe, thus Eliphalet had close contact with the cabinetmaking craft.

Eliphalet's father and mother did not remain in Somers long after his birth but returned to Enfield to live with the

Detail of pediment of cherry highboy attributed to Eliphalet Chapin, circa 1780-85

father, Jonathan Pease. In 1750, when Eliphalet was nine years old, his father died. Five years later his mother remarried.

In his *History of Enfield* Allen records the following: "Peletiah Pease (Pees) of Enfield made guardian of Eliphalet Chapin, age 14 years, son of Ebenezer Chapens late of Enfield, dec'd. 5 Aug. 1755." There are various records that show Eliphalet to have been in East Windsor on several occasions between 1762 and 1771. The following item is recorded in Allen's *History of Enfield*:

Detail of pediment of chest-on-chest attributed to Eliphalet Chapin, circa 1780

"Elce Chapin daughter of Eliphalet Chapin age 12 years made choice of her grandfather Jonathan Bartlett of East Windsor to be her guardian. March 23d 1779." This would seem to indicate that Eliphalet was the acknowledged father of an illegitimate child born in East Windsor in 1767.

In the spring of 1771, however, he established himself in the First Society in East Windsor, in the County of Hartford. By this time he had served his apprenticeship, undoubtedly in Enfield, and had furthered his training by some four years spent in Philadelphia. He purchased a home from John Loomis—a half-acre home site bounded on the south by land of William Stoughton the blacksmith, near the present town hall in South Windsor. In November 1773 he married Mary Darling, who died only a few weeks after the birth of their daughter Sophia in August 1776. Her grave and that of Sophia are in the old cemetery in South Windsor. In 1778 Eliphalet married for his second wife Anne White Reed of Canterbury, widow of Abijah Reed.

Furniture attributed to Eliphalet Chapin shows evidences of his training in Connecticut and in Philadelphia. Every piece attributed to him has been found in South Windsor or East Windsor Hill, although there are many references to work by him in the account book of Joseph Pease from July 1789 to November 1792. Eliphalet worked largely in cherry, and produced distinctive and beautiful furniture. His period of greatest productivity seems to have been the years 1780 to 1795, and it is doubtful if any of the furniture attributed to him was made before 1771. While his work shows the Philadelphia influence, it is smaller in size and lighter in feeling. Characteristic of his furniture are the spiraled rosettes which terminate the broken arch of his secretaries, chest-on-chests, and highboys; fluted quarter columns at corners, occasionally brass-stopped and in one instance, at least, ending in brass capitals and bases; and a distinctive cabriole leg and claw-and-ball foot. He often used a simplified pierced-center ornament similar to but simpler than those found on Philadelphia work of the period. He used a variety of finials. At times he employed a pierced quatrefoil or other pierced scrolls in the pediment. Occasionally he used inlay. In

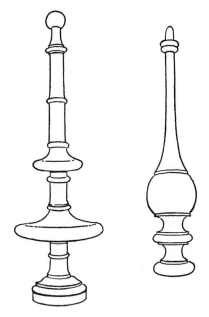

Two of the various types of finials found on case furniture attributed to the Chapins

the Garvan Collection at the Yale University Art Gallery there is a cherry highboy attributed to Chapin. This has a scroll top, carved rosettes, latticework under the scrolls, a center ornament in Chippendale style, quarter fluted columns, cabriole legs, and claw-and-ball feet. It is thought that this piece was made circa 1780-90. In the same collection is a chair which is considered a key piece to Chapin's work.

In the Charles M. Davenport Collection at Williams College there is a bonnet-top maple highboy with broken-arch pediment attributed to Eliphalet Chapin. The date of 1760 ascribed to this piece is evidently too early. This piece has three

flame finials and a carved sunburst on the center top and center bottom drawers. The apron is scrolled and there are two turned drops. The cabriole legs have pad feet.

In *Antiques*, May 1945, there is illustrated an exceptionally fine cherry secretary-desk attributed to Eliphalet Chapin that has a latticework cornice and elaborate inlay.

Antiques, October 1951, pictures a cherry block-front secretary also attributed to Eliphalet by tradition. It was made in 1785 for a family in Windsor, Conn., and is the only known block front by him.

Also illustrated in *Antiques*, February 1941, is a late mahogany bureau-desk with the following inscription written in ink on the bottom of one of the smaller drawers: "This desk was made by Eliphalet Chapin in the year of our Lord 1802 in the State of Connecticut for Pontius Winslowe." The writing is definitely not that of Chapin.

Antiques, March 1949, shows a pair of slipper chairs described as follows: "possibly unique examples of an excessively rare form of chair-making in this country—known as the 'Slipper Chair.' These beautifully designed, carved, cabriole leg, ball and claw foot chairs, made of cherry are of New England origin. In all probability the work of Eliphalet Chapin of Connecticut."

About 1795 Eliphalet evidently thought of retiring or of moving his business to New York State. In the *Connecticut Courant*, Oct. 5, 1795, appeared the following advertisement:

For Sale by the Subscriber:
A brick dwelling house, cabinet-maker's shop, barn, wood-house, chaise-house, and half an acre of land with a good well of water, garden, fruit trees, etc. beautifully and pleasantly situated in East Windsor, 80 rods south of the meeting house in first society.
ELIPHALET CHAPIN
East Windsor, September 28

N.B. Said Chapin has for sale bureaus, and book cases with china doors, chest on chest swel'd, and chairs with a variety of other cabinet furniture, tea and wine sarvers, etc.

Also fifes, gauging rods, log rules with tables, vice and cramp screws, various sizes, a second hand chaise, a one horse wagon and two sets of stone stoves.

Said Chapin continues the cabinet business at present in all its branches but as he proposes to remove into New York State the beginning of next summer he desires to have all those that have accounts with him to bring them for settlement.

Evidently he did not find a buyer for his place, as two years later the same advertisement appeared in the *Courant*. So far as is now known, Eliphalet was still living in East Windsor when he died Jan. 8, 1807.

(*Account book of Joseph Pease* [lists supplies sold to Eliphalet Chapin in East Windsor and furniture bought from him; at Kent Memorial Library, Suffield, Conn.]; Allen; G. W. Chapin, *Chapin Book of Genealogical Data* [Hartford, 1924]; W. R. Cutter, *Genealogical and Family History of the State of Connecticut* [New York, 1911]; *East Hartford Vital Statistics* [at Connecticut State Library, Hartford]; *East Windsor Land Records* [at Connecticut State Library]; *East Windsor Vital Statistics* [at Connecticut State Library]; *Somers Vital Records;* Stiles)

CHAPIN, Laertes, *Hartford, Conn.*
Born 1778 in East Windsor. Son of Aaron and Mary King Chapin. Probably working with his father as early as 1804, when he receipted bill for sideboard made for Frederic Robbins. On Jan. 1, 1807 he and his father formed a partnership and the business was thereafter called Aaron Chapin & Son, Cabinet Makers. Carried on the business until 1845, then moved to East Hartford, where he died in 1847.

CHAPIN, Silas, *Big Flats, Tioga County, N. Y.*
Born 1793; died 1828. A distant cousin of Aaron Chapin. Used the label "Silas Chapin of Big Flats, Tioga County, New York." A table of his in late Sheraton style was shown in *Antiques*, June 1930.

CHAPLEN, John, *Newport, R. I.*
Working as joiner and cabinetmaker from 1709 to 1727. "Kept tables for sale." (Richardson)

CHAPMAN, Allyn, *Preston, Conn.*
Married Betsey Kimball, Aug. 7, 1814. Advertised in the *New London Gazette*, July 7, 1813, that he was now located in former shop of Isaac Allyn.

CHAPMAN, Israel, *Newport, R. I.*
Working as joiner in 1750. (Richardson)

CHARNOCK, Thomas, *Charleston, S. C.*
A free Negro cabinetmaker. In 1810 sold property. Appears in 1819 directory as cabinetmaker at 16 Magazine St., in 1822 directory at 37 Anson St. (Burton)

CHEEVER, Joseph, *Boston, Mass.*
Listed as cabinetmaker in 1775.

CHEEVER, Samuel, *Salem, Mass.*
Born circa 1759. Grandson of the Reverend Cheever of Manchester. Had a cabinetmaking shop near end of Court St. Died May 14, 1818. (Belknap)

CHENEY, Benjamin, *East Hartford, Conn.*
On Aug. 18, 1721, he bought a quarter interest in a sawmill at East Hartford, and a few months later acquired a second quarter. In the deeds he is described as a carpenter, joiner, and wheelwright. It is thought that he and his sons—Timothy, who was also a joiner, and Silas, who was the operator of the sawmill—had come to East Hartford just before the purchase of the mill from Newbury, Mass. Benjamin died in 1760. Timothy and Silas were his heirs. The inventory of his estate, May 1760, showed him equipped to do all kinds of fine work,

and listed: "one Inch orger, half inch orger, 1/3 ditto, hand saw, Shave, a frow, Small broad ax, a groving plow, a harving plow, 2 rabbit plaines, 3 oges, a quarter Round and half orger, a Gouge, five old chisels, a foot wheel, old ax, holing ax, chisels broad, narrow and mortising, one jointer, a set of mach plains, Iron Square." Also "one case Draw," several tables, chests, one desk, two square tables, one with a "draw," a clock, several chairs including one "Great Chair."

CHENEY, Silas E., *Litchfield, Conn.*

Silas was born in Manchester, Conn., Feb. 12, 1776, the son of Silas and grandson of Benjamin (*q.v.*). His father and his uncle Timothy had inherited their father's estate. Records indicate that the father was not a cabinetmaker and there is no record of where the son received his training as one. In 1799 when he arrived in Litchfield he was a well-trained cabinetmaker and he worked there for twenty-two years. He kept very carefully his account books—five in number—covering the years from 1799 until his death in 1821. These are still in Litchfield. Although he did not use a label, it has been possible to identify pieces from his careful records. Judge Tapping Reeve, founder of the first law school in America at Litchfield, was a customer of Cheney. In Cheney's account book under date of September 1800, there is listed for Judge Reeve "to a Sideboard 20 pounds." This is a finely made piece in the Hepplewhite style and may still be seen in the Judge Tapping Reeve House, in Litchfield, which is open to the public. Cheney seems to have specialized in sideboards and several are in existence, privately owned.

(*American Collector*, Nov. 1937; *Antiques*, Dec. 1928)

CHESSMAN, Edmund, *Boston, Mass.*

Listed as cabinetmaker on Back St. in 1807.

CHESTNUT, *Wilmington, Del.*

Working in the early nineteenth century. Chair by him exhibited at Wilmington Society of Fine Arts, 1950.

CHILD, VIALL & WOOD, *Providence, R. I.*

Listed in directories of 1836 and 1837 as chairmakers at 51 South Water St.

CHIPMAN, John, *Salem, Mass.*

Born circa 1746; died Dec. 26, 1819. Shop on southeast corner of Liberty St. Later moved to entrance to Salem Turnpike. (Belknap)

CHIPMAN, Wondley, *Newport, R. I.*

Working as joiner in 1752. (Richardson)

CHISHOLM (Archibald) & WATERS (William), *Annapolis, Md.*

Working as cabinetmakers in 1793.

CHOAT, J., *Hartford, Conn.*

Advertised in the *American Mercury*, Hartford, April 11, 1820:

ATTENTION ECOMISTS

'A penny sav'd by prudence, is as good as a penny earned by labour'

This maxim holds good also on the score of DOLLARS. Embrace then, the golden season, wherin you may if you will, procure for your-selves, or children a very useful article of household furniture by calling at

J. CHOAT'S

about 15 rods south of the Brick Meetinghouse, who has in store, and is constantly manufacturing a variety of

FANCY and COMMON
CHAIRS

comprising most of the kinds now in use. In point of beauty and durability they will equal (to say the least) those of any other manufactory, as he is determined to accommodate his prices and terms of sale, to the pressure of the times, thus making it advantageous to both parties. He feels an assurance that he shall receive such a share of the public patronage, as will enable him to prosecute his business both with benefit to the public and profit to himself. *Hartford*—Apr. 10

CHRISFIELD, Absalom, *Baltimore, Md.*
Listed in city directories of 1807 and 1808.

CHURCHILL, Lemuel, *Boston, Mass.*
Listed as cabinet- and chairmaker at 26 Orange St. in 1805.

CLAP, John, *Boston, Mass.*
Listed as cabinet- and chairmaker in 1818.

CLAPHAMSON, Samuel, *Philadelphia, Pa.*
Advertised in newspaper, Jan. 8, 1785, as being "late from London." In 1786 paid occupational tax of £100 as "Joyner." In 1794 one of a committee advertising for "From Thirty to Forty Journeymen Cabinet-makers." (*Bulletin, Pennsylvania Museum*, Jan. 1925; Hornor)

CLAPP, Zebulon, *Lowell, Mass.*
Listed as cabinetmaker during 1833–37.

CLARK, Job, *Newport, R. I.*
Working 1751–54. In his ledger, John Cahoon lists payment to Clark for much furniture. This included many "Seeder Desks" at £12 to £14, maple desks, an elm desk, mahogany and walnut desks, bedsteads, one mahogany case of drawers. Clark's specialty, however, seems to have been desks. In four years Cahoon paid him some £1380. Doubtless much of this furniture, particularly that made of cedar, was for export to the South and to the West Indies. (*John Cahoon's ledger*, Newport Historical Society; Richardson)

CLARK, John, *Richmond, Va.*
Richmond's first cabinetmaker. Advertised in *Virginia Gazette* in 1776. Listed in census of 1782.

CLARK, Joseph C. & Co., *Middletown, Conn.*
Advertised in the *Middletown Gazette*, May 12, 1797: "Joseph C. Clark & Co. Most respectfully inform their Friends and the Public in general, that they have commenced Business at the shop a few rods north of the Crossway Bridge where they intend carrying on the above Business in all its various Branches, in the neatest manner. Those who please to favor them with their commands may depend on their being Dispatched with Justice and Every Favour Gratefully acknowledged. Cabinet Work."

CLARK, Josiah, *Hartford, Conn.*
Chairmaker. Working in 1774. (Love)

CLARK, Oliver, *Litchfield, Conn.*
Born Feb. 8, 1774. Son of Ebenezer and Deborah Clark. In 1797 Oliver and Ebenezer Plumb, Jr., advertised: "Have taken the shop lately occupied by Mr. Ozias Lewis, in the main South Street, a few rods below Mr. Kirby's where they intend (if properly encouraged) to furnish every description of cabinet work, elegant and common to fancy on agreeable terms. They make Heart-back Cherry Chairs from 7 to 9 dollars each; Windsor ditto from 8s to 15s each. Pungs and sleighs; of any model on short notice. All kind of stuff fit for Cabinet or Shop work, received in payment."
In 1799 Oliver was at work at the same shop but his partnership with Plumb dissolved. He advertised "swell'd and straight sideboards, bureaus, chairs, etc. of mahogany, cherry and other stuff highly finished." (White)

CLARK, Robert, *Newburyport, Mass.*
Born 1775; died 1846. Cabinetmaker. Advertised in 1817 for an apprentice. At that time located on Middle St.

CLARK, Samuel, *Newburyport, Mass.*
Born July 13, 1805. Listed in directories for 1849 and 1853 as cabinetmaker.

CLARK, Samuel, *Baltimore, Md.*
Listed as cabinetmaker in city directories for 1807 and 1808.

CLARK, William C., *Providence, R. I.*

Listed in directory for 1828 as cabinetmaker on Union St.

CLARKE, Christopher Thomas, *New York City*

Announced in the *New York Mercury* in 1766: "Intending to follow the Cabinet and Upholsterers Business will sell at publick Sale all his remaining Store of Dry Goods and Jewellery."

CLARKE, Daniel, *Salem, Mass.*

Born March 14, 1768; died March 1830. Came to Salem in October 1794 to work for the Sandersons. Married Mary Sanderson. In 1796 his shop was on Essex St. In March 1799 sent out a shipment of his own furniture to the South, on the *Fanny*. In 1780 advertised in the *Salem Gazette* that he "respectfully acquaints his friends and the public that he has removed to his new shop in Chestnut Street near Summer and Norman where he continues the Cabinet Business in its several branches & hopes for the opportunity to manifest his gratitude for past favors by strict attention to the future." According to records in the McIntire papers at the Essex Institute, Salem, Clarke not only designed and made furniture in the Hepplewhite style but also carved it.

CLARKE, John, *Boston, Mass.*

Cabinetmaker who arrived in Boston in 1681.

CLARKE, John, *New York City*

Made a freeman in 1768, when he was listed as chairmaker and turner. Advertised in 1774 as shagreen and mahogany case-maker; at this time he spelled his name "Clark," but in those days name spelling was often erratic.

CLAY, Daniel, *Greenfield, Mass.*

Born 1770. Son of Stephen Clay and Patience Bolles Clay, who migrated by stages from New London, Conn., to Greenfield, Mass. In 1785 they were in Middletown, Conn. Daniel is believed to have been apprenticed in Windham, Conn., to either Jabez Gilbert, a Windsor chair maker, or Orrin Ormsby, a joiner. He arrived in Greenfield shortly before his marriage to Lucinda Smead, Nov. 22, 1795. In the spring of 1796 bought property on Federal St. and built a home. From 1813 to 1815 had partnership with Alexander Morgan conducting a retail business in general merchandise. In 1818 forced to sell his house to pay debts. Then entered a partnership with D. Munger and later with R. E. Field. Shop destroyed in a fire which burned the lower section of Federal St. but was reopened later. Business partnership dissolved in 1829.

In *Antiques*, April 1934, there is shown a labeled chest of drawers made by Clay. This is of black cherry, with reverse serpentine front, ogee bracket feet, slightly overhanging top, and cock beading applied directly to drawers. The secondary wood is pine. (*Antiques*, Sept. 1956)

CLAY, Porter, *Whitehall, Ky.*

Brother of Henry Clay. The *Kentucky Gazette* for March 15, 1803 states that the "cabinetmaking shop of Porter Clay . . . was destroyed by fire." He was listed in Charles Directory of 1806 as a cabinetmaker on Mill St. A cherry chair attributed to him was shown at the Exhibition of Southern Furniture, Virginia Museum of Fine Arts, Richmond, 1952.

CLAYPOOLE, George, *Philadelphia, Pa.*

Born 1730; died 1793. Cabinetmaker "with whom Gostelowe learned his trade." (Hornor) In 1783 paid the large sum of £200 as occupational tax and a property tax of £810. In 1786 his tax was only £50.

CLAYPOOLE, James, *Philadelphia, Pa.*

Hornor says he was the ancestor of at least four cabinetmakers and that he came to Philadelphia by way of the West Indies. He is mentioned in Benjamin Randolph's receipt book for 1763–77.

CLAYPOOLE, Joseph, *Philadelphia, Pa.*

Father of Josiah (*q.v.*) and George (*q.v.*). Hornor says he arrived in Philadelphia in 1683, and was in business for himself as early as 1708, as indicated by the following advertisement in 1733 for: "the largest and oldest Stock of Timber— some of which have been in piles near 25 years." Hornor believed he learned his trade with Charles Plumley. In May 1738 Joseph advertised in the *Pennsylvania Gazette* the sale of his cabinet woods, "both local and of West Indian extraction particularly a parcel of choice curl'd maple." At that time he gave up his business and presented his son Josiah with remaining stock and tools.

CLAYPOOLE, Josiah, *Philadelphia, Pa.; Charleston, S. C.*

In May 1738, advertised in the *Pennsylvania Gazette* that he had moved his shop from Walnut St. to the "Joyners Arms" in Second St. near the "Proprietor's" and that he had not only "all sorts of Furniture of the best Fashions" but also "the largest and oldest stock of Timber of the Produce of this Country and the West Indies."

Less than two years later he was in Charleston, S. C. On March 22, 1740 advertised in *South Carolina Gazette*: "Notice is hereby given, that all Persons may be supplied with all sorts of Joyner's and Cabinet-Maker's Work, as Desk and Book Cases, with arch'd, Pediment or O G Heads, common Desks of all sorts, Chests of Drawers of all Fashions fluited or plain; all sorts of Tea Tables, Side-Boards and Waiters, Rule joint Skeleton Tables, Frames for Marble Tables, all after the newest and best Fashions and with the greatest neatness and Accuracy by Josiah Claypoole from Philadelphia, who may be spoke with at Capt. Crosthwaite's in King-street, or at his Shop next Door to Mr. Lormier's near the Market Square, he has Coffin Furniture of all sorts, either flour'd, silver'd or plain. N.B. He will warrant his Work for 7 years, the ill Usage of careless Servants only excepted."

On April 9, 1741 he advertised: "this is further to give Notice, that in a short Time, I shall have two good workmen from London, and shall then be in a Capacity to suit any Person who shall favor me with their Employ." In 1748 he was in financial difficulties. He died circa 1757. One month earlier than his first advertisement in March 1740 there appeared in the same paper an advertisement by Joseph Claypoole "at the Sign of the Cabinet & Coffin in the Market Square in Broad St." Was this Joseph the father of Josiah? Had he gone to Charleston and re-established himself in business, and had the son followed him to what seemed a better location? (Burton; Hornor; Rose)

CLEMENT, Thomas, *Boston, Mass.*

Working as cabinetmaker in 1768.

CLEMENTS, Henry, *Charleston, S. C.*

In March 1792 formed a partnership with Thomas Bradford (*q.v.*). On June 28, 1792 they advertised they were moving from King St. to 30 Broad St.

CLEMENTS, Moses, *New York City*

Made a freeman in 1757, at which time listed as cabinetmaker.

CLEMMONS, James P., *Baltimore, Md.*

"Continues to manufacture and keep on hand at his establishment, near the intersection of Paca & Fayette streets, a large and general assortment of all kinds of furniture." (Varley)

CLEVELAND, Cyrus, *Providence, R. I.*

From 1824 to 1832 listed in directories as cabinetmaker at 245 North Main St.

CLEVELAND, George E., *Providence, R. I.*

From 1828 to 1832 listed in directories as cabinetmaker at 245 North Main St. Doubtless in association with Cyrus Cleveland.

CLEVELAND, Samuel, *Charlestown, Mass.*
Born 1704. Listed as joiner when married in 1732 at Boston.

CLIFFORD, James, *Newburyport, Mass.*
Listed in directories from 1848 to 1852 as cabinetmaker.

CLIFTON, Henry, *Philadelphia, Pa.*
Died 1771. Before 1761 in partnership with James Gillingham (*q.v.*). When this partnership was dissolved in 1768, he moved to Arch St. opposite Friends Burying Ground. In 1750 sold a clock case to John Wood. (Hornor)

CLOUGH, Ebenezer, *Boston, Mass.*
Working as cabinetmaker in 1710.

COATES, J., *Savannah, Ga.*
Listed as turner when he died in 1739.

COATS, Joshua F., *Boston, Mass.*
Died 1819. In 1806 member of Vose & Coats (*q.v.*). In 1817 on Roxbury St.

COE, Adam S., *Newport, R. I.*
Born 1782; died 1862. The only known documented work of this man is a mahogany sofa in the Chippendale style in the Winterthur Museum, Delaware. (Downs, Pl. 276) The inscription, in red chalk, reads: "Made by Adam S. Coe April 1812 for Edward W. Lawton." In 1820 Coe was in partnership with Robert Lee on Long Wharf. (Carpenter; Downs; Records at the Newport Historical Society)

COFFIN, William, *Boston, Mass.*
Cabinetmaker. In 1731 listed as keeper of the "Bunch of Grapes Tavern."

COGGESHALL, Nathaniel, *Newport, R. I.*
Working as joiner before 1775. Died 1826. Notice of his death in the *Newport Mercury*, Oct. 28, 1826, and the *R. I. Republican*, Nov. 9, 1826.

COGSWELL, James, *Boston, Mass.*
Son of John. During 1809–12 was in partnership with Thomas Seymour (*q.v.*). Then joined the Roxbury group of artisans as a partner of Thomas Emmons but this partnership was dissolved in 1813. At 42 Orange St. in 1813 and on Eliot St. in 1820.

COGSWELL, John, *Boston, Mass.*
It is not known where or when John Cogswell was born. He married Abigail Goodwin in Boston in 1762 and twenty years later Abiel Page. He was established as a cabinetmaker by 1769 and was still

Detail of pediment of bombé desk-bookcase, Massachusetts, 1760–80

active in 1789. He held various town offices in Boston from 1778 to 1809. When he died in 1818 an inventory listed his estate at $4,218.65.

John Cogswell is credited with the construction of some of the most beautiful furniture in the bombé, or kettle, shape made in this country. This exotic bombé furniture requires a competent cabinetmaker to shape a solid plank of mahogany into its bulging form. The secondary wood is generally white or soft pine. Sometimes the sides of the drawers, made from this soft wood, conform to the curve of the body; at other times they are straight. The customary foot on this rocaille furniture is either bracket or claw-and-ball. The claw-and-ball as executed by Cogswell shows the claws curved backward, similar to those on furniture made by Benjamin Frothingham. Desks, secretaries, chests of drawers, and double chests were all made in the bombé style but in no great number. A chest and bookcase, privately owned, bears the label "Made by John Cogswell in midle Street, Boston, 1782." In the Winterthur Museum, Delaware, there is a very fine bombé desk and bookcase made 1770–85 that is attributed to Cogswell (Downs, No. 228).

COIT, Job, *Boston, Mass.*
Born 1692; died 1741. Cabinetmaker. In 1731 was living on Ann St.

COKER, Thomas, *Charleston, S. C.*
During 1772–75 Thomas Elfe, Sr. (*q.v.*) recorded in his account book payments for work done by Coker.

COLBY, Nathaniel, *Manchester, Mass.*
Born Oct. 17, 1802. Married Nov. 29, 1832. Belknap lists him as cabinetmaker.

COLE, George, *Baltimore, Md.*
Listed in city directory for 1810 as cabinetmaker.

COLE, Jacob, *Baltimore, Md.*
Chairmaker. Listed in directory for 1796 at Old Town, 73 Front St.

COLE, John, *Baltimore, Md.*
Listed in directory for 1796 at Old Town, Pitt St.

COLE, John, *Salem, Mass.*
Born circa 1811 in Boston; died Nov. 3, 1840. Listed as cabinetmaker and carver at 199 Essex St., Salem, in 1837. In Boston when he died.

COLE, Joseph, *Providence, R. I.*
Listed in 1824 as cabinetmaker on Union St.

COLE, Weedon, *Beverly, Mass.*
Baptized June 29, 1800 in Gloucester. First marriage on June 15, 1825; second

marriage on May 17, 1848. Listed as cabinetmaker.

COLE & BROTHER, *Baltimore, Md.*
Listed in Baltimore Town & Fell's Point Directory for 1796 as Windsor chair makers at Old Town.

COLES, W., *Springfield, Ohio*
Working circa 1835. Maker of a set of eight side chairs similar to Hitchcock chairs, painted and stenciled, and with his name stenciled on the back edge of each seat; one is in the Ohio State Museum at Columbus, the others at the McCook House in Carrollton. (Data supplied by Ohio State Museum)

COLLIER, Isaac W., *Providence, R. I.*
Listed in directory for 1824 as cabinetmaker on President St.

COLLINS, Benjamin, *Newport, R. I.*
Working as joiner in 1733. (Richardson)

COLLINS, Daniel, *Boston, Mass.*
Notice of his death in 1758 listed him as cabinetmaker.

COLLINS, George, *Newburyport, Mass.*
Born Sept. 14, 1822. Listed in the 1848 and 1850 directories as cabinetmaker.

COLLINS, William, *Newburyport, Mass.*
Born March 7, 1814. Elder brother of George. Working as cabinetmaker in 1852 and 1860.

COLLISTER, Thomas, *New York City*
Made a freeman in 1769, at which time listed as cabinetmaker.

COLTON, Aaron, *Hartford, Conn.*
Born 1758 at Longmeadow, Mass.; died June 3, 1840. Settled in Hartford sometime before his marriage to Elizabeth Olmstead on April 5, 1787. Cabinetmaker by trade, but withdrew from general business and during the last twenty-five years of his life worked by himself in

certain specialties, particularly the making of washing machines. At the Connecticut Historical Society, Hartford, there is a clipping (year not given) which reads: "Aaron Colton, Cabinetmaker, near the theatre, Hartford. Has for sale a good assortment of Mahogany and Cherry-Tree Furniture Made in the Newest Manner. He also makes the best kinds of Washing Machines, Apr. 1."

On Aug. 1, 1792 the many cabinetmakers of Hartford held a meeting to form a society for the purpose of regulating the prices of their work. Colton was instrumental in organizing this group. A pamphlet was issued including the resolutions of the society and the prices to be charged, and this was signed by all the members. Much of the pamphlet is quoted in the appendix of Lyon's *Colonial Furniture of New England* (1891). Lyon says that the last part of the pamphlet containing the names of the members was missing. Although various writers list the members, so far as it is possible to ascertain, no authentic list is available.

On Aug. 27, 1792, the following advertisement appeared in the *American Mercury*: "The members of the Society of Cabinet makers in Hartford, and its vicinity, are requested to meet at the home of Mr. Aron Colton in this city on Monday next at 3 o'clock P.M. Hart. August 27, 1792."

COLVIN, Benjamin, *near Clay's Mills, Ky.*
Working circa 1800. "Made high post beds with finials, signed spinning wheels decorated with scrimshaw, desk-bookcases." (Whitley)

CONNELLY, Henry, *Philadelphia, Pa.*
Born 1770. Connelly occupies a position in Philadelphia cabinetmaking comparable to that of Duncan Phyfe in New York City, his early furniture being in the Sheraton style, the later in the early American Empire style. His family had come from Europe with an influx of artisans during the latter part of the eighteenth century. About 1800 Con-

nelly was established at 16 Chestnut St.; then at 44 Spruce St.; then South Fourth St.; and finally in 1824 at 8 Library St. (now Sansom). He died in 1826 at Mill Creek Hundred near Newark, Del.

The furniture of Connelly has much in common with that of Ephraim Haines, a contemporary, and there has for this reason been some difficulty in attributing pieces made by them since both worked for the fashionable of Philadelphia, particularly Stephen Girard and Henry Hol-

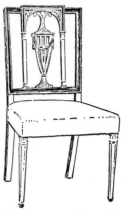

Sheraton side chair attributed to Henry Connelly

lingsworth. Considered typical of Connelly's work is the round spade foot as distinguished from the bulb above a long turned terminal used by Haines.

At the Philadelphia Museum of Art there is a labeled kidney-shaped sideboard made by Connelly about 1806. Other pieces of his are included in collections in and around Philadelphia.

Owned by the Ohio Historical Society is a mahogany secretary in the Hepplewhite style made about 1805 and attributed to him (PLATE XXVIII, No. 2), as well as a mahogany armchair in the Sheraton style made about 1805, and a pair of Sheraton-style side chairs made at the same time. These are all at Adena, in Chillicothe, Ohio, the former home of Thomas Worthington and now the property of the Ohio Historical Society.

(Hornor, *International Studio*, May 1929)

CONNOR, Simon, *Savannah, Ga.*
Advertised as chairmaker in 1786.

COOK, Caleb C., *Providence, R. I.*
Listed in directories during 1828–32 as cabinetmaker at 107 Westminster St.

COOK, Columbus S., *Baltimore, Md.*
"Cabinetmaker at corner of Baltimore & Harrison Sts. in 1833." (Varley)

COOK (or COOKE), Ebenezer C., *Providence, R. I.*
Listed in directories during 1832–37 as cabinetmaker at 99 Westminster St. Member of Shepard & Cook (*q.v.*).

COOK, Elijah, *Savannah, Ga.*
Born 1784; died 1817. Worked as chairmaker. (Comstock)

COOK, James P., *Salem, Mass.*
Born Nov. 4, 1821. Married Nov. 25, 1841. Cabinetmaker at 36 Pleasant St. in 1846; at 18 Andrew St. in 1853.

COOK, Leonard O., *Alexandria, Va.*
On Jan. 8, 1834, advertised in *Alexandria Gazette*: "Cabinet, Chair and Sofa Manufactory on King Street, next door to Washington Street."

COOK, Silas, *Newport, R. I.*
The account book of Robert Jenkins, Jr. (at Rhode Island Historical Society, Providence), records that on Feb. 20, 1752, Cook shipped in *Mary Ann* to West Indies "12 Frames for Chairs, 2 Frames for Arm Chairs and 3 Baggamon Tables valued at £150."

COOK, Silas Adams, *Newburyport, Mass.*
Born April 2, 1825. Working as cabinetmaker in 1850.

COOK, Thomas, *Charleston, S. C.*
Mentioned in Elfe's account book in September 1774; in various documents from 1784 to 1786; in directory for 1790 as cabinetmaker at 12 Meeting St. (Burton)

COOK, Thomas, Jr., *Newburyport, Mass.*
Born July 2, 1808. Belknap says he was a cabinetmaker in Newburyport but moved to Sterling, Mass., where he was listed in 1848.

COOK, William, *Baltimore, Md.*
Listed in directories during 1802–04 as cabinetmaker.

COOKE, James H. & Co., *Litchfield, Conn.*
Cabinetmaker who took over shop of Silas Cheney upon his death. Advertised in *Connecticut Courant*, Oct. 1, 1822.

COOLEY, William, *Charleston, S. C.*
Listed in directory for 1819 as cabinetmaker residing on King St.

COOMBS, Thomas, *Baltimore, Md.*
Listed in directories for 1803 and 1804 as cabinetmaker.

COOPER, John, *Savannah, Ga.*
Born 1763; died 1808. Chairmaker from Massachusetts. (*Antiques*, Feb. 1954)

COOPER, Vincent, *Baltimore, Md.*
Listed in directory for 1803 as cabinetmaker.

COQUEREAU, Charles, *Charleston, S. C.*
From Rochelle, France. Took out his citizenship papers April 2, 1798. In 1816 in directory as cabinetmaker at 196 King St. One of the founders of the Société Française of Charleston. (Burton)

CORNTHWAIT, John, *Baltimore, Md.*
Working as cabinetmaker in 1782.

CORNTHWAIT, William, *Baltimore, Md.*
Listed as cabinetmaker during 1810–18.

COURTENAY, Hercules, *Baltimore, Md.*
Since Courtenay was an important carver and since one or two men with the same name were active in Baltimore and Philadelphia at the same time, he is listed here. Bordley describes him as "A

Carver and Gilder from London" who arrived in Baltimore in 1771. He became active in Baltimore during the Revolution and became a town commissioner. He is also mentioned as an important person in town affairs by Thomas G. Scharf in *Chronicles of Baltimore*, published 1874. In 1772 he was listed in Philadelphia as "late from London," and Hornor says that in this year he did much carving for John Dickinson, but that after the Revolution he became an innkeeper. In 1783 he paid an occupational tax as a tavern keeper. It is probable that there was one Hercules Courtenay and that he worked in both Baltimore and Philadelphia. (Bordley; *Bulletin of the Pennsylvania Museum of Art*, Jan. 1925; Hornor)

COVENHOVEN, John, *New York City*
Listed as freeman cabinetmaker in 1740.

COVERT, Isaac, *Philadelphia, Pa.*
Apprenticed to Joseph Henzey in 1772. Paid occupation tax as chairmaker of £30 in 1783 and of £25 in 1786. Hornor records the sale in 1802 of "One large green Windsor chair for $1.33."

COWAN, John, *Charleston, S. C.*
Born 1790; died Nov. 24, 1850. Arrived in Charleston from Scotland at an unknown date. In 1819 directory as cabinetmaker at 68 Meeting St. Last appears in directory in 1849, when living at 5 Philadelphia Alley. (Burton)

COX, Joseph, *New York City*
First advertised in 1756 as an upholsterer when his shop was on Hanover Square. In May 1757 moved to Dock St. Probably not a cabinetmaker himself, but it is believed he employed cabinetmakers or shared his workshop with independent cabinetmakers on a co-operative basis. In 1760 moved to Wall St. In 1773 in Rivington's *N. Y. Gazatteer* he advertised: "all sorts of canopy, festoon, field and tent bedsteads and furniture; also every sort of drapery. Window curtains; likewise sopha, settees, couches, burgairs, French elbow, easy and corner chairs; back stools, mewses, ribband back, gothic and rail back chairs; ladies and gentlemens desk and book cases, cabinets, chest of drawers, Commode dressing and toilet tables; writing, reading, side board, card, and night ditto; cloth presses, and chest China shelves, etc. etc."

At the Metropolitan Museum of Art, New York City, there is a sofa made about 1760—one of the few pieces of pre-Revolutionary New York furniture—with the label of Joseph Cox on the linen undercover. This says: "Joseph Cox, Upholsterer / From London / At the Sign of / the Royal-Bed. / In Dock-Street, near Countjies- / Market New York."

COX, William, *Philadelphia, Pa.*
Moved from New Castle, Del., to Philadelphia, where he was established from 1767 to 1796 on Second St., just below Christ Church. In 1784 made eighteen dining chairs for Joseph Carson, who mentions them in his receipt book. In 1783 paid tax as a turner of £200 and in 1786 as a chairmaker on shop rented from John Reynolds. (Hornor)

COY, Josiah, *West Suffield, Conn.*
Born 1796; died 1823. Carpenter and joiner. "Made chests." (Bissell)

CRABTREE, John, *Boston, Mass.*
Working as cabinetmaker as early as 1639.

CRANE, James H., *Newark, N. J.*
A cabinetmaker with whom John Jelliff was apprenticed from 1830 to 1836.

CRANSTON, Samuel, *Newport, R. I.*
Working as joiner in 1778. (Richardson)

CRAWFORD, Jacob, *Philadelphia, Pa.*
Became an apprentice of Gostelowe on Nov. 19, 1772 for about twelve years. (Hornor)

CREHORES, *Dorchester Lower Mills, Mass.*

Several men with this name produced piano cases, clock cases, chairs, and general cabinetwork during the last part of the eighteenth century and the early part of the nineteenth. One by the name of Samuel married a daughter of Stephen Badlam.

CRESSON, James, *Philadelphia, Pa.*

Born 1709. Son of Solomon. Chairmaker.

CRESSON, Jeremiah, *Philadelphia, Pa.*

Working during middle of the eighteenth century. Hornor lists him as "Joyner & Chairmaker" and says that he advertised tools including "two picture frame planes."

CRESSON, Solomon, *Philadelphia, Pa.*

Chairmaker and turner who arrived in Philadelphia in 1696. (Hornor)

CRESSY, Henry, *Beverly, Mass.*

Born Jan. 4, 1809. Married Oct. 19, 1828. Working as cabinetmaker at 261 Essex St. in 1837.

CRISP, William, *Philadelphia, Pa.*

Advertised in *Pennsylvania Chronicle,* June 26, 1769: "At his house in Archstreet, between Front and Second street, Philadelphia, Choice MAHOGANY, of all sorts, from the thickness of 5 inches to an half inch; The said CRISP follows the business of Carving in all its branches, where Cabinet-Makers, and others, may have their business done with care and dispatch, and have four months credit allowed them. Also follows the business of Cabinet-making, where town and country may be supplied at the most reasonable rates."

CRITTENDEN, Richard, *Salem, N. C.*

Born 1764 in New Kent County, Va. "Journeyman cabinetmaker." Learned his trade in Baltimore, Md. From there went to Lancaster, Pa. In 1786 moved to Salem to work in the Moravian Brothers House. (Fries, *Records of the Moravians in North Carolina*)

CROCKETT, Thomas, *Piscataway, N. H.*

Working 1633. (*American Collector,* June 1937)

CROMBIE, Samuel B., *Manchester, Mass.*

Born May 6, 1818. In 1848 listed as cabinetmaker in Beverly.

CROMWELL, Thomas, *Baltimore, Md.*

Varley states that Cromwell "Continues to manufacture at his stand 12, Thames street, near Fell's Point Market, fashionable furniture, and keeps on hand a general assortment."

CROOK, Walter, *Baltimore, Md.*

Advertised in 1795 as cabinetmaker.

CROSMAN, Robert, *Taunton, Mass.*

Born 1707; died 1799. His ancestor John Crosman, the first of the name in New England, came from England with his wife and probably a son by the name of Robert as early as 1634. It is believed this family settled first in Dedham, Mass. In 1635, however, John is listed as one of the forty purchasers of land in Taunton. The *History of Taunton* says his son Robert "learned the trade of a carpenter for which he had a taste." He had a son Samuel who was a carpenter and a son Robert who was a millwright. Robert Jr.'s son Nathaniel married Sarah Marack in 1703 and their eldest son, also called Robert, was born in 1707. His painted chests are quite unlike those found in other sections of New England. His designs are delicate, and his favorite was a tree or trailing vine springing from one or more wavy lines representing the ground. Instead of leaf forms, he used C-curves at the end of which were a cluster of dots or sometimes a single dot. In some of the later chests a bird was added to the design. Many of the chests were dated and initialed. A blanket chest dated 1729 is in Historical Hall, Taunton.

Another attributed to him is at the Detroit Institute of Arts. (PLATE VII, No. 2). His grandfather had been a maker of drums, and between the years 1739 and 1745 Robert called himself a drum maker. There are three drums that have his label: one says "Made by Robt. Crosman of Taunton, Drum maker in New England, Anno Domino 1739"; another has the date 1740; and the date 1745 appears on the third.

CROSS, George O., *Methuen, Mass.*
Born May 14, 1825. Married Nov. 29, 1849. Belknap lists him as cabinetmaker.

CROSS, Thomas, *Bradford, Mass.*
Born circa 1695; died Nov. 22, 1772. Worked as chairmaker.

CROWELL, Charles, *Manchester, Mass.*
Born circa 1815 in Hopkinton, N. H. Married Oct. 20, 1845 in Manchester, where he was listed as cabinetmaker.

CROWNINSHIELD, Abraham, *Charlestown, Mass.*
Cabinetmaker; partner of Forster, Lawrence & Co. in the 1790s. (Sawyer)

CULLIATT, Adam, *Charleston, S. C.*
Died 1768. Married Mary Campbell, July 16, 1751. On April 14, 1757 his first advertisement appeared in the *South Carolina Gazette*: "Being removed to Jacksonborough, Pon-pon, gives notice to all gentlemen and ladies who may want any kind of Cabinet, Joiners or Carpenter's work done that they be served by him to their satisfaction . . . and that he is willing to take two Apprentices to learn the Carpenter's & Joiner's Trade." He purchased considerable property. His will, probated Sept. 13, 1768, left land and buildings in Jacksonborough to his wife and five children. (Burton; Rose)

CUNNABEL, John, *Boston, Mass.*
Notice of death in 1724 listed him as cabinetmaker.

CUNNABELL, Samuel, *Charlestown, Mass.*
Joiner. Married in 1710. Later moved to Boston or at least had his shop there.

CURRIE, Robert, *Hartford, Conn.*
In 1768 rented a small shop on lot of John Haynes Lord, just north of Mookler's Barber Shop. (Love)

CURRIE, William, *Annapolis, Md.*
Advertised as cabinetmaker in 1769.

CURRIER, Amos M., *Amesbury, Mass.*
Born Sept. 13, 1825. Married July 4, 1848. Belknap lists him as cabinetmaker.

CURRIER, Jacob Bayley, *Salisbury, Mass.*
Died June 10, 1814. Cabinetmaker. Married Mrs. Elizabeth Johnson, Aug. 18, 1776, in Amesbury.

CURRIER, Seth S., *Salem, Mass.*
Born 1816. Cabinetmaker. Partner of Benjamin R. Millett at 261 Essex St. during 1857–64.

CURTIS & HUBBARD, *Boston, Mass.*
Advertised "Fancy & Bamboo chairs" in 1828.

CUSHING, Josiah, *Boston, Mass.*
Cabinetmaker on Fish St. in 1807.

CYRUS, Joseph, *Charleston, S. C.*
Advertised in 1744 as cabinetmaker. (Rose)

CYRUS, Joseph, *Louisville, Ky.*
Working 1779–89 at 12th and Main streets. Made furniture, boats, and houses. (Whitley)

CYRUS, Richard, *Charleston, S. C.*
Listed in directory for 1809 as cabinetmaker at 29 King St.

DAILEY, Jacob & Son, *Baltimore, Md.*
The father listed in directory for 1804. Varley lists the firm in 1833 "at Baltimore

St. adjoining the Bridge, Chair manufacturer in all its varieties, by wholesale
and retail, and proprietor of the bazaar."

DAM (or DAME), William, *Portsmouth,
N. H.*
Died 1755. *See* entry for Gaines,
John III.

DANE, John, *Beverly, Mass.*
Born Nov. 18, 1749; died 1829. Belknap
lists him as cabinetmaker.

DANE, Samuel, *Beverly, Mass.*
Died before Oct. 6, 1777. Cabinet-
maker. Married Mrs. Hannah Ellinwood,
Nov. 26, 1771.

DANFORTH, George Girdler, *Manchester, Mass.*
Born April 19, 1818; died July 24,
1849. Cabinetmaker. Married Sarah Ann
Bacon.

DANFORTH, Jeremiah, *Manchester, Mass.*
Born Sept. 12, 1809. Cabinetmaker. First
married to Sally Hassam, May 24, 1832;
then to Mary Ann Allen, Nov. 3, 1838.
(Belknap)

DANFORTH, Stephen, Jr., *Manchester,
Mass.*
Born Sept. 25, 1799. Cabinetmaker.
Married Rebecca Miller, Sept. 3, 1848.

DANIEL, Ursual M., *Halifax, N. C.*
An eighteenth-century block-front
desk at the Virginia Museum of Fine
Arts, Richmond, is attributed to him. The
primary wood is mahogany; the secondary wood, southern yellow pine. A label
inscribed "Ursual M. Daniel/Halifax, N.
C." is pasted inside a secret drawer.
(PLATE XX, No. 1)

DANIELS, Eleazar (Captain), *Medway,
Mass.*
Born 1788; died 1858. Doubtless learned
his craft in shop of Luther Metcalf,
with whom he made the chairs and communion table for new meetinghouse in

1816. For some years in East Medway.
(Jameson)

DARLING, Carlos C., *Lowell, Mass.*
"Cabinetmaker at 'Dyars' in Lowell
1834–5 and as Charles C. Darling in 1837."
(Belknap)

DARLINGTON, Amos, *near West Chester, Pa.*
Began working 1796. He and his son,
Amos Jr., kept account books. The
father's covers the years to 1828; the son's
to 1853. (Stockwell, *American Collector,*
April 1939)

DARLINGTON, Amos, Jr., *near West
Chester, Pa.*
Born 1792. In 1813 advertised in *Village Record*: "Amos Darlington, Jun.
Respectfully informs his friends and the
public generally, that he intends carrying
on the CABINET making business, at the
old stand of Amos Darlington, senior,
near West Chester. Coffins made and funerals attended to upon the shortest notice." (Stockwell, *American Collector,*
April 1939)

DARRAGH, John, *Pittsburgh, Pa.*
Advertised in *Pittsburgh Gazette*, July
16, 1802, for runaway apprentice.

DAVANT, John, *Savannah, Ga.*
Death notice in 1733 listed him as cabinetmaker.

DAVENPORT, Adam & Ebenezer, *Dorchester Lower Mills, Mass.*
In 1797 Adam made chairs for the new
State House. Ebenezer is listed as chairmaker in 1802. Together had large chair
factory.

DAVENPORT, John, *Newburyport, Mass.*
Born 1791; died 1842. Cabinetmaker.

DAVENPORT, Thomas, *Newport, R. I.*
Died 1745. Will probated Sept. 3, 1745.
(Newport Town Council Records)
Had married Mary Pitman in 1737.

Her estate administered in 1782. On Dec. 13, 1786, their daughter Susanna sold her right to a tract of land in Newport "that I now have as my share as one of the heirs at law to the estate of Mary Davenport, late of Newport, widow of Thomas Davenport, late of Newport, cabinetmaker, deceased." (*Newport Land Evidence*)

DAVEY, Henry, *Baltimore, Md.*
Listed in directory for 1796 as cabinetmaker on King George St.

DAVEY, John, *Philadelphia, Pa.*
Listed in directory for 1802 at 12 Christian St. First work attributed to him is a satinwood and mahogany secretary in Sheraton style which has a label. Illustrated in *Antiques*, April 1953.

DAVIDSON, David, *New York City*
In business with James Strachan, carver and cabinetmaker, who advertised in 1768 that his partner had died.

DAVIDSON, James, *Baltimore, Md.*
Listed in directories from 1796 to 1806 as cabinetmaker at 1 Baltimore St. On Sept. 6, 1785 advertised in *Maryland Journal or the Baltimore Advertiser* as chair- and cabinetmaker at "next house above the Stone-Cuters in Market Street, Baltimore."

DAVIES, John, *Boston, Mass.*
"Furniture maker." Nutting says he arrived in Boston on the *Increase* in 1635.

DAVIES, Samuel, *Boston, Mass.*
Cabinetmaker with furniture warehouse at 57 Newbury St. in 1792.

DAVIS, Benjamin, *Boston, Mass.*
Death notice in 1718 listed him as chairmaker.

DAVIS, Jacob, *Newburyport, Mass.*
Died 1786. Death notice listed him as joiner.

DAVIS, Jermyn, *near Athens, Ga.*
An itinerant worker to whom a secretary of inlaid walnut with interior of southern yellow pine is attributed. Shown at Loan Exhibition of Southern Furniture, 1640–1820, at the Virginia Museum of Fine Arts, Richmond, 1952. Illustrated in *Antiques*, January 1937.

DAVIS, Joseph, *Newburyport, Mass.*
Chairmaker with shop at Milk and Lime streets. Married Hannah Acres of Newbury, May 28, 1774. Died Aug. 9, 1803.

DAVIS, William, *Newport, R. I.*
The Aaron Lopez account book, at the Newport Historical Society, has an entry for the year 1772 which reads: "Cr. Wm. Davis Joyner/By 1 red cedar desk £144."

DAVISON, Samuel, *Savannah, Ga.*
Advertised in 1736 as chairmaker.

DAY, Isaac Sewell, *Gloucester, Mass.*
Born March 1813. Listed as cabinetmaker. Married Elizabeth Ann Allen of Beverly, Dec. 16, 1838.

DEANS, Robert, *Charleston, S. C.*
Advertised in 1750 as a cabinetmaker "from Scotland." His advertisement in the *South Carolina Gazette*, Jan. 22, 1750, states: "all kinds of cabinet and joiners work are done after the best manner, and at as low rates as any where in town." Apparently discontinued cabinetmaking later and devoted himself to house-building. As a British citizen had his lands confiscated during the Revolution. After the war was over, his heirs attempted to regain them. (Burton)

DECKER, Jefford M., *Manchester, Mass.*
Belknap states it probable that this man was born in Wiscasset, Me., and came from there to Manchester, where he married Harriet Lee, Sept. 2, 1838.

DECKER, Robert M., *Manchester, Mass.*
Born circa 1824. Belknap lists him as cabinetmaker. Married Lydia A. Osborn, July 13, 1845.

DECKER, William, *Manchester, Mass.*
Belknap thinks he and Robert were brothers, probably working together. Married Louisa L. Marsters, June 16, 1839.

DELAGRAND, Samuel, *Baltimore, Md.*
Listed in directory for 1799 as cabinetmaker.

DELAPLAIN, Joshua, *New York City*
Advertised in *N. Y. Gazette* on July 30 and August 6, 1739: "Ran away the 4th of this instant August from Joshua Delaplain, Joyner, an apprentice lad about 18 years of age. His name is James Howard, is a well fed lad, of a sandy Complexion, has short hair, and had on a full Trim'd Drugger Coat and Breeches, a New Tufted Fustian Waistcoat, a good Hat, Shoes and Trousers. He can work pretty well at the Joyners Trade." Again advertised as "Joyner" in 1754.

DELEVEAU, Joseph, *Philadelphia, Pa.*
Working from 1774. Made a bonnet-top highboy with matching lowboy. Typical Philadelphia style, cabriole legs, carved cartouche and skirt, scrolled cornice. (Hornor, pls. 141, 145)

DEMANGEN, Charles, *Baltimore, Md.*
Listed in directories from 1800 to 1817 as cabinetmaker.

DEMELT, Anthony, *New York City*
Advertised in newspapers as chairmaker in 1758.

DEMING, Simeon, *New York City*
See entry for Mills & Deming.

DENHAM, Daniel, *Newport, R. I.*
Working as chairmaker in 1726. (Richardson)

DENMEAD, John, *Baltimore, Md.*
Listed in directories during 1803–10 as cabinetmaker.

DENNIS, John, *Ipswich, Mass.*
Born Sept. 22, 1672; died 1757. Son of Thomas (*q.v.*). Joiner. Inherited the bulk of his father's estate.

DENNIS, Richard C., *Manchester, Mass.*
Listed as cabinetmaker by Belknap. Married Henrietta Story, May 8, 1832.

DENNIS (or DENNES), Thomas, *Ipswich, Mass.*
Thomas Dennis was doubtless born in England, circa 1638, and served his apprenticeship there. On Sept. 26, 1663, he was a resident of Portsmouth, N. H., at which time he purchased a house and lot on the north side of County St. in Ipswich from a William Searle. He did not move to Ipswich at that time. On April 26, 1664, he purchased land in Portsmouth in the section known as Strawberry Bank. On June 19, 1665, he was chosen a constable of Portsmouth. On March 8, 1666/7 he was a juryman, but after that date his name no longer appears in the records of Portsmouth.

On Oct. 26, 1668 he was married at Ipswich to Grace Searle, widow of William Searle, from whom he had purchased the house and land in 1663. From that time he lived in Ipswich until his death on May 23, 1706. He was constable and collector in Ipswich from 1685 to 1692 and in 1691 his taxes were £1.6.0.

He had two sons, Thomas and John (*q. v.*). His wife died Oct. 24, 1686, and although he married again, he and his first wife are buried side by side in the Ipswich cemetery.

John inherited the bulk of his father's estate, and when he died in 1757 inventory of his estate showed a carved sideboard, two carved chairs, a carved chest, a carved box, and a carved salt box in addition to many other pieces of furniture. On a deed dated Sept. 4, 1685 Thomas Dennis is listed as a "joyner," and in a court record of March 28, 1682 one reads that "Thomas Dennis deposed that Grace (Stout) bought a carved box with a drawer in it of him in 1679." These two

PLATE I
Prince-Howes oak press cupboard, Plymouth, Mass., 1660–70. Attributed to Kenelm
Winslow and/or John Alden. Wadsworth Atheneum, Hartford, Conn.

PLATE II, NO. I

The earliest marked piece of American-made furniture; the Mary Allyn chest made by Nicholas Disbrowe of Hartford, Conn., circa 1680. Inscription on back of lower drawer reads: "Mary Allyns Chistt Cutte and Joyned by Nich: Disbrowe."

PLATE II, NO. 2

Hadley chest, Hadley, Mass., circa 1680. Probably the first of the Hatfield type. Attributed to John Allis. John Huntington Collection, The Cleveland Museum of Art.

Connecticut Sunflower oaken chest, circa 1685. Some sixty examples have been traced to the Wethersfield section. Closely related to the Hadley chest. Maker or makers unknown. Courtesy Parke-Bernet Galleries, Inc., New York City.

Chest attributed to Thomas Dennis, Ipswich, Mass., circa 1675. The Metropolitan Museum of Art, New York City.

President's chair, Bowdoin College, Brunswick, Me. Attributed to Thomas Dennis, circa
1675. Bowdoin College Museum of Fine Arts.

PLATE V, NO. 1
Trestle stand, 1770-90. Maple frame;
top made from one pine board.
Found in Connecticut. Wadsworth
Atheneum, Hartford, Conn.

PLATE V, NO. 2
Chippendale Virginia walnut corner
cabinet, Pennsylvania, circa 1760.
Upper section has molded cornice
over double glazed doors with mold-
ed and latticed astragals. Two pan-
eled cupboard doors in underbody.
Scrolled ogee-bracket feet. Courtesy
Parke-Bernet Galleries, Inc., New
York City.

PLATE VII, NO. I
Tulipwood dower chest made by Christian Selzer, Jonestown, Pa., 1785. Signed and dated. The Metropolitan Museum of Art, New York City.

PLATE VII, NO. 2
Painted chest attributed to Robert Crosman, Taunton, Mass., circa 1730. Detroit Institute of Arts.

PLATE VIII, NO. 1
Painted tulipwood flat-top highboy of the "Guilford type."
Henry Francis Du Pont Winterthur Museum, Winterthur, Del.

PLATE VIII, NO. 2
Painted tulipwood chest of the "Guilford type." Henry Francis Du Pont
Winterthur Museum, Winterthur, Del.

PLATE IX, NO. I

A page from the Gaines Account Book presented by Katharine Prentis Murphy to the Joseph Downs Manuscript Collection at Henry Francis Du Pont Winterthur Museum, Winterthur, Del.

PLATE IX, NO. 2

Open armchair, 1710–50, with urn-splat back, pierced-scroll top rail, spool- and block-turned legs, Spanish feet, and rush seat. Of the style attributed to John Gaines III of Portsmouth, N. H. The Metropolitan Museum of Art, New York City.

Maple high chest of drawers attributed to the Dunlaps of Salisbury, N. H. Henry Francis Du Pont Winterthur Museum, Winterthur, Del.

Chippendale wing chair, Philadelphia, circa 1770. Attributed to Benjamin Randolph. Considered the outstanding American-made wing chair. Carved on front, sides, arms, and legs. Even the rear feet are carved. Carved effigy at center of skirt is thought to be that of Benjamin Franklin. Diamond-cut background on three sides of skirt with dots in corner of each diamond. Feet of paw type. Philadelphia Museum of Art.

PLATE XI, NO. I

Chippendale side chair, Philadelphia, circa 1770. Attributed to Benjamin Randolph. One of his famous sample chairs. Philadelphia Museum of Art.

PLATE XI, NO. 2

Chippendale side chair, Philadelphia, circa 1760–75, with label of Benjamin Randolph. M. and M. Karolik Collection, Museum of Fine Arts, Boston.

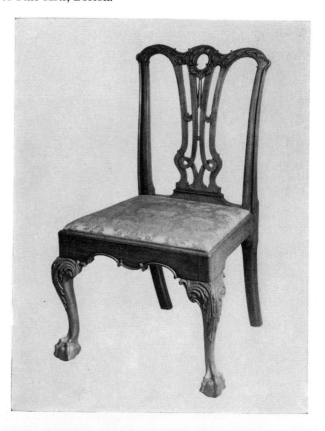

PLATE XII, NO. 1
Chippendale lowboy, Philadelphia, circa 1770, with label of Thomas Tufft. Philadelphia Museum of Art.

PLATE XII, NO. 2
Mahogany Philadelphia Chippendale ladder-back side chair, late eighteenth century. Attributed to either Daniel Trotter or Ephraim Haines. The Metropolitan Museum of Art, New York City.

PLATE XIII, NO. I
Mahogany Chippendale butler's secretary, Philadelphia, circa 1770. Possibly by Thomas Affleck. The Metropolitan Museum of Art, New York City.

PLATE XIII, NO. 2
Chippendale chest of drawers, Philadelphia, circa 1790, with label of Jonathan Gostelowe. Philadelphia Museum of Art.

PLATE XIV, NO. 1

Highboy with Newport closed
bonnet. Attributed to Job Townsend, Newport, R. I. Courtesy
Newport Historical Society.

PLATE XIV, NO. 2

Tray or silver table, 1725–50.
Queen Anne style with slip-
per foot on cabriole leg. Prob-
ably made by Job Townsend.
Came to Newport Historical
Society from Miss Ellen
Townsend, a descendant.

Mahogany desk-bookcase attributed to John Goddard, Newport, R. I., 1760–75. One of
the ten known Newport shell-carved desk-bookcases. M. and M. Karolik Collection,
Museum of Fine Arts, Boston.

PLATE XVI, NO. 1
Mahogany kneehole bureau with label of Edmund Townsend, Newport, R. I. M. and M. Karolik Collection, Museum of Fine Arts, Boston.

PLATE XVI, NO. 2
Block-front shell-carved chest of drawers with John Townsend's label, 1765. The Metropolitan Museum of Art, New York City.

records establish him as a joiner-carver.

Many items of furniture—chairs, chests, desk-boxes, boxes, and cupboards—have been attributed to Dennis; some by family history and tradition, others by comparison with the former. All such pieces show him to have been a meticulous craftsman, apparently English-trained, with a love for the elaborate. His furniture is carefully constructed and well proportioned. His spindles and columns are expertly turned. In his carved pieces, except those with a polychromed background, the pattern completely fills the entire space. His carving designs are rich and he achieves an elaborate effect by the interweaving of motifs. On rails, drawer fronts, and stiles of chests, as well as on the fronts of boxes and desk-boxes, he used a running band of S scrolls with one S impinging upon the next, at times their curves almost overlapping. Often on the front of boxes, this S scroll is used in couplets to form a design and this couplet-design is then arranged in a series to form a running band. Although the carved designs have similarities, they are never identical.

All carved panel decoration is developed around a conventionalized arch or diamond. When the conventionalized arch is used, the usual form of decoration is a drooping willow-like foliage, springing from a formalized base. This design is almost a signature. Floral motifs are either conventionalized roses or tulips. At times Dennis also used as accessory motifs the fleur-de-lis, the trefoil, and the lunette. Designs used on rails, stiles, and drawer fronts are generally intersecting foliated lunettes, foliation, foliated scrolls, guilloches, cartouches, and a characteristic arabesque strapwork found also on the chairs attributed to him.

Some chests, cupboards, and small chest-on-frames have narrow panels, varying in length, placed end to end, usually horizontally, and then arranged in rows. A single boss is applied to the block between the panels and columns and split spindles are used. The split spindles are generally columnar, drumstick, or complex. The first two vary little from type while the third shows a wide range of variation. The turned columns are either vase- or barrel-shaped and are superbly turned. Many of this group of chests, cupboards, and chest-on-frames are initialed and dated (as are some of the carved chests). The dates run from 1678 to 1694, years when Thomas Dennis was living and working in Ipswich.

Many of the chests attributed to Dennis show a wooden cleat-pin hinge, a primitive form in which a wooden pin is passed through a hole of the cleat at each end of the lid to serve as a hinge. This is rarely found on American-made furniture except that attributed to Dennis. White oak was the wood favored by Dennis for his furniture, with pine and maple occasionally used for secondary parts. Occasionally the backgrounds are polychromed with the split spindles and columns painted black.

At the Metropolitan Museum of Art, New York City, there are three three-panel chests (PLATE III, No. 2) a press cupboard, dated 1699, and a box with the initials S P.

In the Robert Hull Fleming Museum, University of Vermont, Burlington, there is a chest of carved oak with hinged cover. The front has elaborate carving with the center panel showing birds and flowers. This chest is attributed to Thomas Dennis.

At the Boston Museum of Fine Arts there is a three-panel chest of oak with the original one-board pine lid. The corner brackets of this piece show the initials M I. The lateral panels have the conventionalized arch design with diamond design in center panel. Panel backgrounds show evidences of original red and black coloring.

At the Essex Institute, Salem, Mass., there are two carved three-panel chests and a press cupboard attributed to Dennis. Of particular interest at the Institute is a wainscot chair. According to its history on file at the Institute, this was given to the Historical Society of Salem (which was later merged with the Essex Institute) by Robert Brookhouse of Salem. He had obtained it with a similar chair and other furniture through his first wife, Martha Farley, whose mother was Sarah Dennis of Ipswich, a descendant of Thomas Dennis.

Almost identical to this chair is one in the Boyd Gallery of the Walker Art Building, at Bowdoin College. It is marked with a silver tablet which states: "This Chair made in 1630, was brought from England probably in 1635 by the ancestors of the Dennis Family of Ipswich. Presented to Bowdoin College by E. W. Farley, of Newcastle, Maine, June, 1872." Since the chair is of American oak, the reference to its English origin is, of course, incorrect. The Bowdoin chair shows a foliated design springing from a vase. The upper rail of the panel, like that of the chair at the Essex Institute, is carved in an arabesque design, and the stiles in a foliated scroll design. The carved design of the lower rails differs from that on the chair at the Essex Institute, while that below the seat in front is almost identical to that of the Institute chair. On either side of the stiles of both chairs are similar applied carvings. The top rail of each chair is set inside the stiles. The cresting on both chairs is composed of two S scrolls with foliations between and three turned finials. (PLATE IV)

At the Winterthur Museum, Delaware, the following pieces are attributed to Dennis: a court cupboard, dated 1684, with the initials of Ephraim and Hannah Foster, for whom it was originally made; a chest of drawers of the small-panel type, marked 1678/s/IM for John and Margaret Staniford of Ipswich, who were married in 1678; a small chest-on-frame marked P 1690 B, believed to have been made for Henry and Mary (Bush) Bartlette, who were married in Marlborough, Dec. 6, 1682; and a spice chest marked T H 1679, believed to have been made for Thomas Hart.

In the Sanford Collection at the Chicago Art Institute there are a small-panel oak chest-on-frame with the initials A/SH, and a box with elaborate carving in a foliated design and the initials A H.

(*Antiques*, Nov. and Dec., 1937, Feb., April, June, and Aug., 1938, and June 1949 [these issues contain definitive study of Dennis by I. F. Lyon]; Downs; *Essex County Massachusetts Court Records*; *Essex County Probate Court Records*; Little; Lockwood)

DENNIS, Thomas, Jr., *Ipswich, Mass.*
Born Nov. 30, 1669; died Jan. 23, 1702/3. Son of Thomas Dennis, with whom he worked.

DENNIS, Thomas, *Ipswich, Mass.*
Cabinetmaker. Born Nov. 25, 1733; died Jan. 25, 1760. Son of John and grandson of Thomas (*q.v.*). When John died in 1757 he left his estate to his sons, Thomas and John. Thomas bought John's interest, Nov. 15, 1757.

DENNIS, William, *Newport, R. I.*
His will (filed at City Hall, Probate Court) was probated April 3, 1826 and calls him cabinetmaker.

DE NOIELLE, Peter, *Providence, R. I.*
Listed in directory for 1824 as cabinetmaker.

DENSLER, William, *Savannah, Ga.*
Died 1811. Advertised in 1806 as chairmaker. (Comstock)

DESEL, Charles, *Charleston, S. C.*
Born 1749; died Oct. 24, 1807. Doubtless arrived from Germany before Revolution. On April 11, 1777 purchased house and lot on Colleton Square from John Fyfe, cabinetmaker (*q.v.*). In 1783 bought another lot on Church St. Listed in directory of 1790 at 15 Maiden Lane and at 44 Church St., the latter his shop. In directories during 1801-7 as cabinetmaker at 50 Broad St. During years bought more property. (Burton)

DESEL, Samuel, *Charleston, S. C.*

Died 1814. Son of Charles. In 1813 listed as cabinetmaker, at 53 Broad St., under name of Charles, which Burton believes to have been an error. He had a brother Charles who was a physician. His will dated Sept. 30, 1814 directs "that my tools, furniture of every kind; Boards, Benches and so forth be sold." On Jan. 3, 1815 the following notice appeared in the *City Gazette and Commercial Advertiser*: "Will be sold Mahogany Boards and Slabs, Cedar Boards, with Benches, Cabinet Makers Tools . . . Finished and unfinished Furniture, being the property of Mr. Samuel Desel, deceased." (Burton)

DESHON, Moses, *Boston, Mass.*

Carver. Carved the Faneuil coat of arms and the Arms of the Colony for House of Representatives in 1752.

DEVENS, Richard, *Charlestown, Mass.*

Lost shop, joiner's tools, and two stores in fire of 1775.

DEWEY, Daniel, *Hartford, Conn.*

Advertised as cabinetmaker in *American Mercury*, Hartford, on March 21, 1826 and March 9, 1830. At one time had partner by name of Olmstead. Two chairs and Empire sideboard from their shop in loan exhibition at Springfield Museum of Art, Mass., 1936. Moses Y. Beach (*q.v.*) served apprenticeship under Dewey.

DEWEY, George, *Litchfield, Conn.*

See entry for David Bulkley.

DEWEY, John, *Suffield, Conn.*

Born 1747; died 1807. Made "6 dining chears" for Elijah and Martin Sheldon in 1790. In 1791 made other furniture and turned bedposts. His account book is at the Kent Memorial Library, Suffield. (Bissell)

DEWING, Francis, *Boston, Mass.*

Cabinetmaker. Arrived from London in 1716.

DE WITT, John, *New York City*

Listed in New York City Directory in 1794 as a "turner" at 38 Whitehall St.; in 1795 as a "chairmaker" at same address. In 1795 moved to 225 William St. but in 1796 and 1797 was at 47 Water St. On Jan. 22, 1798 advertised in *Mercantile Diary and Advertiser*: "John De Witt, Windsor Chair Maker, begs leave to inform his friends and the public in general that he continues to carry on the above business in all its branches at No. 47 Water-street near Coenties-Slip, New York. Likewise, Garden Settees made in the neatest manner. Masters of Vessels may be supplied with either of the above articles in large or small quantities, at shortest notice. Punctuality may be depended on." In that same year, 1798, apparently moved to 442 Pearl St., where he was located for the next three years.

It is a matter of record that De Witt was commissioned by the committee in charge of remodeling Federal Hall in New York to make Windsor chairs for the Senate and Assembly rooms, for which the city paid him £29.14 on Nov. 14, 1796. While at 47 Water St., De Witt made a set of chairs for Killian K. Van Rensselaer of Claverack, N. Y. These chairs were upholstered. De Witt's label is still attached to three of them, and one bears the label "William W. Galatian, Upholsterer & Paper Hanger . . . No. 10 Wall-Street, New York" and the date 1797. The custom of upholstering Windsor chairs was evidently not limited to New York and Philadelphia. A set at the Stone House, Guilford, Conn., with a history of Connecticut provenance, is also upholstered, and examination of a still unpainted seat beneath the leather revealed that this was so originally.

(*Antiques*, May 1938 and July 1952)

DEXTER, Dana, *Newburyport, Mass.*

Cabinetmaker at 9 State St. in 1849.

DICKINSON, Edmund, *Williamsburg, Va.*

Advertised in *Virginia Gazette* in 1770.

DISBROWE, Nicholas, *Hartford, Conn.*

Disbrowe, whose father was a joiner, was born at Walden, Essex, England, in 1612/13. There is no record of his arrival in America. It is known, however, that he came to Hartford with Thomas Hooker and his "living church," a group of about one hundred men, women, and children, which left the "New Towne" (Cambridge), Mass., on May 31, 1636, arriving at the new settlement in Connecticut about two weeks later. Disbrowe shared in the allotment of land given these early families "by courtesie of ye town," which was recorded on Jan. 7, 1639. He fought in the Pequot War of 1637 near the settlement and was voted fifty acres of land by the town on May 11, 1671 for this service. His shop was in his house at the north end of Burr St., now Main. Evidently his cabinetmaking did not occupy his entire time in those early years because for various periods from 1647 to 1669 he was elected "chimney viewer." In 1660 he was "surveyor of highways." In 1640 Disbrowe married Mary Bronson. In 1660 he was voted permission by the town to build a shop "on ye highway next his fence 16 Foote square." He died in 1683. The inventory of his estate, on file at the State Library, Hartford, is dated Aug. 31, 1683, and shows the following: "Plan stacke and Iorns, Seven chessells, passer bitts and gimblets; a parsell of small tools & two payer compasses & five hand saws, two fros, a payer of plyers, two rasps, a file and a saw, two parser stake, a shave, two hammers and fower axes, two bettells and fower wedges, a bitt and five augers, two tropes, two payer of joynts & a payer of hooks and Ringes, an adys, a warming pan, two smoothing Iorns, grin stone."

Nicholas Disbrowe made a carved oak chest which is the earliest piece of American furniture that can definitely be assigned to a maker because it is marked. (PLATE II, No. 1) On the back of the lower drawer is the inscription "Mary Allyns Chistt Cutte and Joyned by Nich: Disbrowe." Mary Allyn, for whom the chest was made, was the daughter of Col. John Allyn, Secretary of the Colony. She was born in Hartford in 1657 and died in 1724. Disbrowe died in 1683 and it is believed that this chest was made shortly before his death, probably about 1680. This chest was in the collection of Mr. and Mrs. Luke Vincent Lockwood of Greenwich, Conn., but was sold at auction at the Parke-Bernet Galleries, New York City, May 15, 1954, for $4,000.

The decorative treatment of this oaken chest—the front stiles and rails are profusely carved with a continuous undulating vine bearing clusters of tulips and curving leafage—is quite unlike anything found before this time; and even though it differs in several particulars from the standard Hadley chests (by Allis, Belding, Hawkes, Pease, and Taylor) it was believed to have furnished the decorative motif for the other Hadley chests until the discovery near Boston in 1931 of the R E B chest (Luther's No. 15). This chest by its structure and history seems to be somewhat older than the Disbrowe. It has four panels with grooved stiles and dentiled posts and lower rail. The tulip and leaf decoration, the leaves with rounded stems as on the chests of the Hartford group of Hadleys, and the initials common to the Hadley chests are present. Structurally this four-panel chest is closer to the earlier Jacobean models than are the other Hadleys and it is the only one with four panels. A possible date of 1650 has been assigned to it, some thirty years earlier than the date of the Mary Allyn chest, and it is deemed possible that it was constructed by one of the very earliest cabinetmakers, Phineas Pratt (*q. v.*), who was in Weymouth, Mass., as early as 1622.

In considering the origin of the manner in which the decorative motif of tulip and leaf is used on the Hadley chests and whether the Pratt or Disbrowe chest is the one from which they stemmed, is it not feasible to suggest at least an acquaintanceship between Phineas Pratt and Nicholas Disbrowe? In 1623

Pratt fled from Weymouth to Plymouth, where he married Mary Priest in 1626. He died in 1680 in Charlestown (very near to Cambridge, where Disbrowe had lived). If there was an acquaintanceship, it could mean that Disbrowe had seen work by Pratt which used the not uncommon tulip motif in this unusual way, and that, remembering it, he had used it when carving the Mary Allyn chest. The inspiration for the design then could have reached the various makers of the other Hadley chests directly from Disbrowe.

Whatever the source of inspiration, it is of interest that most of the chests known as Hadley were made for the daughters or wives of a small group in a localized section of the country (Hadley, Hatfield, and Deerfield, Mass.; Enfield, Hartford, and Coventry, Conn.) during a very limited period of time.

Some have questioned the authenticity of the inscription on the Mary Allyn chest since Nicholas Disbrowe could not write. Any known documents signed by him bear his mark rather than a signature. It has been noted, however, that the lettering on the chest corresponds closely to the handwriting of Mary's father, a most methodical man. In accordance with our knowledge of his habits, it would have been entirely in character for him to mark the chest made for his daughter in this manner. Until it has been proved that the inscription is not authentic, we can but accept it as indicating that the chest was made by Disbrowe.

There was close friendship between the Disbrowe and Spencer families and it is possible that the turned ornaments used by Disbrowe (his inventory lists no turning equipment) came from the wood-turning shop of the Spencers. Obadiah Spencer, Jr., grandson of Thomas (who had also come to Hartford with the Hooker group), married Disbrowe's daughter sometime after Disbrowe's death.

At the Yale University Art Gallery, at the Rhode Island School of Design, Providence, and at the Metropolitan Museum of Art, New York City, are chests attributed to Disbrowe. These were shown at the Wadsworth Atheneum, Hartford, in 1935 (*see* catalogue, *Three Centuries of Connecticut Furniture, 1635–1935*, Nos. 17, 18, 19).

Also attributed to Disbrowe is the so-called Wesleyan Wainscot Chair in the Olin Memorial Library, Middletown, Conn. This chair is believed to have been made about 1662 and is of American oak. It is said to have been used by Gov. John Winthrop, Jr., of Connecticut, and it is

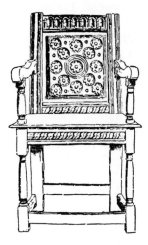

Oaken chair at Wesleyan University, Middletown, Conn., believed to have been made by Nicholas Disbrowe circa 1662

thought this chair may have been made for the ceremonies accompanying the reception of the Connecticut Charter, which Winthrop brought from England in 1662. It has been owned by Wesleyan University since 1836. The *Alumni Record* of Aug. 26, 1836 states: "About this time the Governor's Chair of Connecticut, made of carved oak, brought from England in 1629 and used in the inauguration of the younger Winthrop, came into possession of the College." Since this was written, it has been discovered that the chair is of American oak. Lockwood said of it: "Across the top of the back is a series of gouges, so finished as to resemble an arcade. The lower rail of the back and the upper rail of the under part are cut in a rope design. Originally there were a cresting and finials at the top now missing." He continues: "The rabbets of this chair (on the stiles at the back and upon all four stretchers) and those on the Mary Allyn chest are cut by a rabbet plane. . . . The workmanship of Hadley chests shows that these workmen did not own such planes. Therefore, it seems logical that the same cabinetmaker that made the Mary Allyn chest made this chair." (*Antiques*, Jan. 1930; Collections of the Connecticut Historical Society, Hartford, Vol. 14; Lockwood; Luther; Willison)

DIVINE, WILLIAM, *Waterford and Leesburg, Va.*

His label appears on chest of drawers dated 1816, privately owned. (Comstock)

DIX, Samuel, *Boston, Mass.*

Arrived in Boston in 1637 with two apprentices, William Storey and Daniel Linsey. (Nutting, Vol. 3)

DIXON & ALLYN, *Alexandria, Va.*

Advertised in newspapers in 1787 as coach- and chairmakers.

DIXSON, Robert, *New York City*

Advertised in newspaper in 1763 as cabinetmaker.

D'LAMATER, Abraham, *Savannah, Ga.*

Advertised from 1803 to 1827 as cabinetmaker.

DOAK, William, *Boston, Mass.*

Cabinet and Windsor chair maker on Back St., 1789.

DOBBINS, John, *Charleston, S. C.*

On Aug. 12, 1768 advertised in *South Carolina Gazette* that he "intended to depart the province for some time." He did not leave immediately, however, for on Nov. 27, 1770 he advertised again in *South Carolina Gazette; And Country Journal*: "John Dobbins. The subscriber, departing the Province in the Spring, will sell . . . a neat assortment of Cabinet Work, consisting of Chairs and Tables of all kinds, Chinese Tables, carved & plain mahogany bedsteads, neat double and half chests of drawers; French chairs; brass nailed ditto." In this advertisement he stated that he had sold the business to John Forthet. It appears that Dobbins returned to England, where he died, although his wife apparently remained in Charleston. (Burton)

DOBBINS & M'ELHINNY, *Pittsburgh, Pa.*

In 1802 advertised in *Pittsburgh Gazette* as follows: "Cabinet-Makers and Upholsterers Respectfully inform the Ladies and Gentlemen of Pittsburgh and the Public in general that they carry on the above business at their home in Market Street, corner of Front-street in all its various branches, and of a superior quality to any made here or imported." This partnership dissolved on Jan. 28, 1803; Dobbins continued by himself.

DODGE, Cyrus, *Manchester, Mass.*

Born June 4, 1814. Cabinetmaker. Married Julia E. Coes of Kennebunkport, Me., Dec. 20, 1846.

DODGE, David, *Beverly, Mass.*

Born June 11, 1813; died Feb. 6, 1837. Cabinetmaker. (Belknap)

DODGE, Ephraim, *Salem, Mass.*

Cabinetmaker at 2 Monroe St. in 1850.

DODGE, Jonathan Stanwood, *Manchester, Mass.*

Born May 20, 1821. Married Charlotte Procter Allen, Nov. 13, 1846.

DODGE, Moses, *Manchester, Mass.*

Born circa 1739; died May 4, 1776. Cabinetmaker. (Belknap)

DODGE, William (Deacon), *Beverly, Mass.*

Died Dec. 13, 1810. Cabinetmaker.

DOGGETT, John, *Roxbury, Mass.*

Born 1780; died 1857. Cabinetmaker, carver, gilder. Made chairs for Burpee Chair Co. and for the Sandersons. Had learned carving as a boy but in addition to carving and gilding, carried on furniture-making at his factory in Roxbury. Cornices of bed in one of the McIntire rooms at the Boston Museum of Fine Arts were made by William Lemon and gilded by Doggett. Employed cabinetmakers and carvers.

DOGGETT, William, *Roxbury, Mass.*

Working as cabinetmaker in 1789. Doubtless related to John.

DOLE, Ebenezer, *Newburyport, Mass.*

Had cabinetmaking shop on Middle St. in 1809.

DOLE, Elam, *Methuen, Mass.*

Cabinetmaker. Married Elizabeth H. Fry, Oct. 7, 1830. Still working in 1847. (Belknap)

DORSEY, John, *Baltimore, Md.*

Listed in directory for 1810 as cabinetmaker.

DOUD, George, *Providence, R. I.*

Listed in directory for 1832 as cabinetmaker at 208 South Main St.

DOUGHERTY, John, *Baltimore, Md.*

Listed in directories from 1796 to 1808 as cabinetmaker at back of 148 Baltimore St.

DOUGLAS, James, *Charleston, S. C.*

Listed in directories during 1802-9 as turner. In 1816, the year he died, listed as cabinetmaker.

DOUGLAS, John, *Charleston, S. C.*

Born 1773. Purchased lot on Meeting St. in 1799. Listed in directory for 1801 as cabinetmaker at 138 Meeting St. In 1802 took out citizenship papers, at which time he declared he was twenty-nine, a native of Edinburgh, Scotland, and a cabinetmaker. Inventory of his estate, Dec. 31, 1805, listed five sideboards, two secretaries, and a quantity of mahogany, cedar, and pine. (Burton)

DOUGLASS, William N., *Providence, R. I.*

Listed in directory for 1832 as cabinetmaker at 101 Westminster St.

DOW, Thomas, Jr., *Manchester, Mass.*

Born July 4, 1820. Cabinetmaker. (Belknap)

DOWDNEY, Nathaniel, *Hopewell Township, Cumberland County, N. J.*

Born circa 1736; died after 1793. Advertised in Philadelphia newspaper, July 16, 1764, that "Nathaniel Dowdney, Joyner" had bought from "Thos. Willing of Philadelphia" property on the north side of Third St., between Race and Vine streets. In this section were many of the smaller shops in which cabinetmakers were established. By this time Dowdney had apparently served his apprenticeship and was beginning his own business. He remained at this address for six years and then sold the property, having already moved back to his old home in New Jersey. The deed of sale reads "Nathaniel Dowdney, cabinetmaker, late of the City of Philadelphia, now of Cumberland Co., N. J." In this deed, dated Jan. 21, 1770, he calls himself a "cabinetmaker" instead of "Joyner." No examples of his work are known except a clock case of excellent workmanship, bearing the written label "Nathaniel Dowdney, No. 24." His sister Mary married John Wood, a well-known clockmaker of Philadelphia. (*American Collector*, Oct. 1937)

DOWN, Thomas, *Boston, Mass.*

Listed as cabinetmaker in 1796.

DOWSE, Jonathan, *Charlestown, Mass.*

Working as joiner in 1694.

DRAPER, Richard, *Boston, Mass.*

Working as joiner in 1690.

DRUMMOND, John, *Andover, Mass.*
Belknap lists him as cabinetmaker in 1843.

DUBOIS, Aime, *Baltimore, Md.*
Listed in directories during 1810–16 as cabinetmaker.

DUDDELL, James, *Charleston, S. C.*
Listed in directory for 1801 as residing at 251 Meeting St. In 1802 at 209 Meeting St. In 1806 listed as cabinetmaker.

DUDLEY, Joseph, *Guilford, Conn.*
In 1691 the town chose him "for the making of coffins." (*Proceedings at the Celebration of the 250th Anniversary Settlement of Guilford*, 1889)

DUGLAS, Thomas, *New York City*
Subscribed to *Life of Whitefield* in 1774 as chairmaker.

DUHY, John, *Georgetown, Va.*
Advertised in 1800 as chairmaker.

DUKEHART, Henry, *Baltimore, Md.*
Cabinetmaker at 58 Baltimore St. in 1833. (Varley)

DUNARGEIN, William, *Baltimore, Md.*
Listed in directory for 1802 as cabinetmaker.

DUNHAM, David, *Newport, R. I.*
Working as chairmaker in 1726. (Richardson)

DUNLAP FAMILY, *Chester and Salisbury, N. H.*
Time may clear up many details regarding this family of cabinetmakers. It is thought that Samuel I came from Ireland to America and settled in Chester, N. H., where he married Martha Neal in 1741. At the moment it is not believed he was a cabinetmaker. Samuel II served his apprenticeship to a carpenter in Chester but after his marriage to Nancy Cockran moved to Henniker and in 1797 to Salisbury, where he lived until his death in

1830. In 1783 he helped build the steeple of the First Congregational Church in Concord. Samuel III, born Dec. 15, 1783, learned the cabinetmaker's trade. He moved to Andover, Me., in 1834, where he lived until his death some fifteen years later. There were also a John Dunlap (1754–92) and a John Dunlap, Jr., (born 1784). P. H. Burroughs made a study of the John Dunlaps and his findings were published in the *American Collector*, June 1937. Some of these differ from those in *A History of Salisbury, New Hampshire* by J. J. Dearborn, 1890. Burroughs places John in Bedford, N. H., in 1771; it was there that John Jr. was born in 1784. This could mean that John was responsible for the paneling in the room at the Winterthur Museum that is discussed below. Burroughs also says that John Jr. moved to Antrim, N. H., about 1806, where he remained until his death.

It was Burrough's conclusion that the finer pieces of maple furniture attributed to the Dunlaps were made by Samuel II and that certain cherry pieces with inlay were made by John Jr. When Samuel II moved to Salisbury in 1797 he purchased the Elkins property and lived in that house until his death in 1830. Later the house was moved to New Boston, N. H.

At the Winterthur Museum, Delaware, there is a room from the Thomas Chandler house at Bedford, N. H. The woodwork is now in the original brick red and blue found under many coats of paint. The cornice shows a stylized egg-and-dart molding which matches that on a high chest of drawers in the room (PLATE x, No. 1) which is attributed to the Dunlaps, as is the paneling of the room. The same style of molding is found on many of the pieces attributed to the Dunlaps. In the Chandler room there is also a maple chair, painted blue, with a carved shell in its cresting similar to those in the pediment of the chest. Here, too, is a maple desk attributed to a member of this family, made 1770–90. This has an intaglio fan, unusually large, and other characteristic carvings. The feet are bracket.

All furniture attributed to the Dunlaps is decidedly individualistic. The chest-on-chests, the highboys, desks, and chairs all show an interesting combination of scrolls, open interlaced pediments, and peculiar carved intaglio fans. Some of the case pieces have a gallery about the top with a small central broken arch above a sunburst or fan, with a similar sunburst or fan at each corner. Between these ornaments there is basketwork. The apron, which is longer than that used by most cabinetmakers, has a carved central motif in the form of Flemish scrolls, often flanked by an intaglio fan. Legs are generally short with claw-and-ball or bun feet. All Dunlap furniture is described as having a "low center of gravity"; this quality is quite unmistakable. At the Metropolitan Museum of Art, New York City, there are several pieces attributed to Dunlap.

(*American Collector*, June 1937; *Antiques*, Dec. 1944 and Feb. 1955)

DUNTON, Ebenezer, *Newport, R. I.*
Listed in Dr. William Hunter's account book as joiner in 1780. (Richardson)

DURGIN, Alvah, *Lowell, Mass.*
Belknap says he was a cabinetmaker in 1834 but after 1835 was called a machinist.

DURKEE, Stephen, *Baltimore, Md.*
Varley lists him as cabinetmaker and undertaker at Harrison St. near North Gay St. in 1833.

DUTCH, Nathaniel, *Ipswich, Mass.*
Born May 30, 1714; died Aug. 28, 1795. Cabinetmaker.

EANERAGY & Co., *Baltimore, Md.*
Listed in directory for 1803 as cabinetmakers.

EARL, William, *Pittsburgh, Pa.*
Advertised in *Pittsburgh Gazette*, Dec. 28, 1793, as cabinetmaker. In partnership with John Buckingham.

EARMAN, John, *Baltimore, Md.*
Listed in directory for 1796 as chairmaker in French Alley, between Charles and Sharp streets.

EASTMAN, Abiel, *Salem, Mass.*
Cabinetmaker at 13 Franklin St., 1837.

EATON, William, *Providence, R. I.*
Listed in directories during 1832–37 as cabinetmaker at rear of 77 Westminster St.

EDEN, Joshua, *Charleston, S. C.*
Born 1731. Advertised in *South Carolina Gazette*, Jan. 19, 1767, that he did turning "in its several branches, such as banisters, column bedposts, table frames. . . . In the meantime he continues to make straw bottom chairs which he will sell very reasonable." Listed in directory of 1790 as turner at 15 Beresford Alley. In 1801 listed as chairmaker on Church St. Died March 26, 1802. (Burton)

EDES, Edmond, *Boston, Mass.*
Working as joiner in 1709.

EDGE, Walter, *Gilmanton, N. H.*
Maker of curly maple secretary-desk (1760–70) with name inscribed on back in contemporary script. Lower section has reverse serpentine curve and an unusual carved pendant shell on base. Corkscrew finials. Formerly in Francis P. Garvan Collection. Illustrated in Nutting, Vol. 1, pl. 689.

EDGERTON, William, *Haddonfield, N. J.*
Working about 1775. (*Catalogue, State Museum*, Trenton, N. J., 1953)

EDMANDS, Jonathan, *Charlestown, Mass.*
Born 1705; died 1760. Joiner.

EDWARDS, Alexander, *Boston, Mass.*
In 1765 had shop on lane leading to Mill Pond. Warehouse and contents destroyed by fire in 1773. After Revolution had shop in Back Bay.

EDWARDS, Benjamin, *Northampton, Mass.*

Windsor chair maker working about 1800. Appointed administrator of Ansel Goodrich's estate in 1803.

EDWARDS, Thomas, *Boston, Mass.*

Cabinetmaker in 1687.

EGAN, A. & D., *Baltimore, Md.*

Cabinetmakers and undertakers at 68 West Pratt St. in 1833. (Varley)

EGERTON, Matthew, Sr., *New Brunswick, N. J.*

Matthew Sr. was the founder of the Egerton family of cabinetmakers who for three generations made beautiful furniture for the people of New Brunswick and the surrounding countryside during the last half of the eighteenth century and the first third of the nineteenth. Egerton, of English ancestry, married Catelyna Voorhees, or Van Voorhees, of Dutch lineage. He seems to have been a prosperous and prominent citizen. On May 20, 1793 he sold a lot on Burnet St., adjoining that on which his own dwelling and shop were located, to his son, Matthew Jr. At his death in 1802 he left a widow, five children, and twelve grandchildren. His executors sold his house, shop, stock of cabinet wood, and tools. Various pieces of furniture bearing his label have been found, and this has made it possible to attribute to him many unlabeled items. His printed oval label reads: "Matthew Egerton, Cabinetmaker in Burnet Street, New Brunswick (N. J.)." Egerton worked with veneers and inlays in the manner of Hepplewhite and Sheraton. He made innumerable secretaries, bureaus, chests, clock cases, tables, and bedsteads, but evidence would indicate that he did not make chairs. He chose his woods with care. Although the exteriors of his furniture were always of the highest workmanship, the interiors at times seem to have had somewhat less care.

At an exhibition at the New Jersey State Museum, Trenton, 1953, there was a mahogany secretary in the Hepplewhite style bearing his label. This had line and oval inlay. The interior was fitted with inlaid small drawers and cupboard. The door was inlaid with an unusual lily-of-the-valley motif.

Attributed to Egerton by comparison with a labeled sideboard is an outstandingly beautiful sideboard of mahogany with satinwood inlay at the Boston Museum of Fine Arts. This is six feet long, has six legs, and is in the Hepplewhite style. It has a serpentine front with veneering of crotch-grained mahogany. The decorative lines and motifs are of satinwood. The top is of solid mahogany faced to appear thicker. The ring handles have blue and white enamel plaques, probably Battersea. (PLATE XXVII, No. 1) (*Antiquarian*, Dec. 1930; *Antiques*, Sept. and Nov. 1928)

EGERTON, Matthew, Jr., *New Brunswick, N. J.*

Matthew Jr. was the only one of Matthew Sr.'s sons to follow his father's trade. It is believed that he owned his own shop as early as 1785, some years before he purchased land for a house and shop on Burnet St. from his father. He married Maria Bergan and there were three sons. Matthew Jr., like his father, became a prosperous and important citizen of his town. The earliest marked example of his work is a very tall grandfather's clock with his label inside the door: "MADE and SOLD by Matthew Egerton, Junior, Joiner and Cabinetmaker, New Brunswick, NEW JERSEY—No.—" He used two styles of label; the earlier one octagonal in shape, the later one with a scalloped edge. Several other clock cases made by him have been located. All have French feet and fans and circular inlays of satinwood on the long door and base; also mahogany insets and feathered edges. The work of the son is similar in many ways to that of the father, so much so that it is safe to assume he learned his trade in his father's shop. In some cases, it is even difficult—says Hornor—to determine whether an unlabeled piece was made by the father or the son. In addition to clock cases Matthew Jr. made other pieces of furniture similar to those constructed by Matthew Sr.

Matthew Jr. had two sons, John Bergan and Evert, who apparently learned the cabinetmaking trade in their father's workshop. Evert was for a time in partnership with his father under the trade name of "Matthew Egerton (Jr.) & Son." It is believed the elder son had his own business. Within one year of Matthew Jr.'s death in 1837, both of his cabinetmaking sons had died.

(References: *see* Matthew Sr.)

EHRENMAN, J., *Baltimore, Md.*

Listed in directories during 1804–10 as cabinetmaker.

EHRENPFORD, John Godfrey, *Charleston, S. C.*

Born 1786 in Germany. Listed in directory for 1809 at 28 Meeting St., in that for 1813 as cabinetmaker at 27 Broad St.

ELFE, Thomas, Sr., *Charleston, S. C.*

It is probable that Thomas Elfe was born circa 1719 in London and there served his apprenticeship. It is not known when he arrived in Charleston, but that he was there before 1747 is indicated by an advertisement in the *South Carolina Gazette*, Sept. 28, 1747, which locates his shop "near Doct. Martini's." In 1748 he married a widow, Mary Hancock, but she died within a few months and in 1755 he married Rachel Prideau. There were several children from this marriage. It would appear that Elfe had little difficulty getting established in Charleston since he did not do much advertising at any time and his customers included the fashionable of South Carolina. On Jan. 7, 1751, however, the following appeared in the *South Carolina Gazette*: "Thomas Elfe, Cabinet-Maker, having now a very good upholsterer from London, does all kinds of upholsterer's work, in the best and newest manner and at the most reasonable rates, viz: tapestry, damask, stuff, chints, or paper hangings for rooms: beds after the newest fashion, and so they may be taken off to be washed without inconvenience or damage; all sorts of festoons and window curtains to draw up, and pully rod curtains; chairs stuff covered, tight or loose cases for ditto; All kinds of Machine Chairs are likewise made, stuffed and covered for sickly or weak people and all sorts of cabinet work done in the best manner, by the said Thomas Elfe."

There was a partnership of some kind between Elfe and Thomas Hutchinson (*q. v.*) as early as 1756, since at that time they were working together on balusters for the steeple of St. Michael's Church. In 1758 they made chairs and tables for the Council Chamber, and in 1763 were engaged to make a mahogany communion table for St. Michael's. There is no data regarding dissolution of the partnership. The men remained good friends, and Hutchinson was the godfather of Thomas Elfe, Jr.

Elfe's account book for the years 1768–75 has been recovered and is in the archives of the Charleston Library Society. This book, kept with care, contains not only the names of customers, the prices they paid, and descriptions of the various kinds of furniture made at the Elfe workshop but many interesting details regarding apprentices, workmen, and shop practices. It shows that Elfe had many apprentices and a large number of slaves, among whom were several trained as joiners and cabinetmakers, that he employed many competent men for carving and upholstering, and that turners and other workmen in their own shops in Charleston also did work for him. During the eight years covered by the account book, some fifteen hundred pieces of furniture were made at Elfe's shop. Since the period covered by the book is a small portion of the years spent by Elfe in the cabinetmaking business, the quantity of furniture made at his shop must have been tremendous. And yet not a single piece with his label has been found. Because of the data in the account book, however, it has been possible to trace a few pieces through family histories. The book shows that Elfe made many double chests-of-drawers, tables of all kinds, mahogany beds, bookcases, secretary-bookcases, chairs, a few wardrobes, and a number of desks. He made simple furniture as well as elaborate. Among the latter are bedsteads of mahogany with eagle's claws, carved knees, brass caps and casters; and easy chairs with eagle's claws for feet. All furniture attributed to Elfe either by family history or on stylistic grounds is of excellent design and workmanship, in the Chippendale style, usually of mahogany with cypress as the secondary wood. Some beds were of tulipwood. The account book shows the purchase of much "poplar plank" as well as cypress, cedar, ash, pine, and walnut.

A feature of Elfe's work is an applied fret used so consistently as to be almost as distinguishing as a label. This is found on case furniture such as bookcases, double chests of drawers, and secretaries. Entries in the book indicate that an extra charge was made for this detail and that Elfe also made similar frets to order for chimney pieces. Another feature of his work is the use of a cross member running from front to rear in the center of the large drawers.

It is not known just when Thomas Elfe entered into a partnership with John Fisher (q.v.), but an advertisement in the *South Carolina and American General Gazette*, May 27, 1771, announced its dissolution: "The co-partnership of Elfe and Fisher being dissolved some time, and all debts due to them assigned unto Thomas Elfe, he hopes all indebted to them will pay off the same or settle as soon as possible. I am much obliged to all Friends for their Favours, and hope for a continuance of them, as I shall carry on the Business of Cabinet- and Chair-making as usual, at my old Shop

in Broad-Street, and am their humble servant, Thomas Elfe."

Thomas Elfe died Nov. 28, 1775. The inventory of his estate showed him to have accumulated much wealth in the years he had worked as a cabinetmaker in Charleston. He owned much property, many slaves, and considerable money in addition to the contents of his cabinet-making shop. These were divided among his wife and four children, but to Thomas Jr. were also given his father's tools, workbenches, and "three negro fellows brought up to my Business named Joe, Jack and Paul."

(Burton; *South Carolina Historical and Genealogical Magazine*, Vol. 35–42, gives details of Elfe's account book)

ELFE, Thomas, Jr., *Charleston, S. C.*

Born 1759; died Nov. 12, 1825. Only son of Thomas Elfe to become a cabinet-maker. Godson of Thomas Hutchinson (*q.v.*). In 1778 married Mary Padgett. During the British occupation of Charleston became a British subject. When war was over he was ordered banished and his property confiscated. This order was not carried out but apparently he was forced to give up some of the property. In 1784 he moved to Savannah but in 1801 was back in Charleston and listed in the directory at 2 West St. and in 1802 at 17 Wentworth St. It is apparent that he did not possess the skill of his father either in cabinetmaking or in managing his possessions. In the directory he is listed simply as a carpenter. (Burton)

ELFRETH, Jeremiah III, *Haddonfield, N. J.*

Working circa 1775. (*Catalogue, State Museum*, Trenton, N. J., 1953)

ELFRETH, Josiah, *Philadelphia, Pa.*

Died 1794. Paid an occupational tax as cabinetmaker in 1783 of £4, but in 1786 of £110. Had partnership with a Joseph Clark but this was dissolved in 1786. A member of the Library Company of Philadelphia in 1790. (Hornor)

ELHORS, William, *Salem, Mass.*
Cabinetmaker at 11 Gedney Court in 1853.

ELLIOT, Andrew, *Beverly, Mass.*
Born Sept. 22, 1821. Cabinetmaker. (Belknap)

ELLIOTT, John, Sr., *Philadelphia, Pa.*
Born June 1713 at Bolton, Lancashire, England; died 1791. Came to America in 1753. First advertised in *Pennsylvania Gazette*: "John Elliott, Cabinetmaker, in Chestnut-street, the corner of Fourth-street. . . ." Nutting says that since Elliott also imported glasses, on which his name as dealer was probably pasted, one cannot know whether an example is English or American, but Downs states there is evidence that some of his labeled mirrors were Philadelphia-made. (*See* Downs, No. 254.) While located on Chestnut St., circa 1755–56, Elliott sold the following articles to Charles Norris for the dining room in his home at Fifth and Chestnut streets: six side chairs "with Shell at the top front knee" at £8.2.0, and matching stools "covered with damask to match window curtains." In 1762 Elliott moved to Third and Walnut streets. In that year he billed Edward Shippen, Jr., for dining room furniture. Between 1753 and 1761 he used a label printed in both English and Pennsylvania-German. He used a second type of label between 1762 and 1767 (Downs, No. 395), and a third type during 1768–76 (Downs, No. 397). In 1781 he was a member of the Library Company of Philadelphia. In 1784 he signed a deed as cabinetmaker. In 1784 his son (*q.v.*) joined him in the cabinetmaking business. In 1786 he paid a tax as cabinetmaker and looking-glass manufacturer of £300.
At the Winterthur Museum, Delaware, there is a set of four walnut stools made by Elliott with shell carving typical of Philadelphia work but with pad feet (Downs, No. 294); also a walnut side chair made in 1755–65 (Downs, No. 122) tentatively attributed to Elliott since it is similar to chairs made for Charles Norris. (Cescinsky; Downs; Hornor; Nutting; Miller)

ELLIOTT, John, Jr., *Philadelphia, Pa.*
Carried on the business of John Sr. (*q.v.*). Used a label from about 1784 to 1803. In 1804 was joined by his two sons. They used the label "John Elliott & Sons" from 1804 to 1809.

ELLIS, Matthew, *Charleston, S. C.*
In 1803, when administrator of an estate, referred to as a cabinetmaker. Listed in 1806 directory. (Burton)

ELSWORTH, Ashuerus, *New York City*
Signed as chairmaker when witness to a will in 1757.

ELSWORTH, George, *New York City*
Listed as chairmaker when made a freeman in 1739. Witness to a will in 1752 and again in 1757.

ELVVES, William, *Baltimore, Md.*
Listed in directory for 1796 as cabinetmaker at 7 North Liberty St.

ELWELL, Henry Jr., *Manchester, Mass.*
Cabinetmaker. Married Elizabeth Ann Lynn, July 20, 1843. (Belknap)

EMERY, Calvin, *West Newbury, Mass.*
Born Nov. 15, 1821. Cabinetmaker. Married Waita Todd of Raymond, N. H., Oct. 29, 1846.

EMERY, Stephen, *Newburyport, Mass.*
When Joseph Brown died in 1742, Emery took over his business. (*Brown's account book*, at Essex Institute, Salem)

EMMONS, Thomas, *Roxbury, Mass.*
James Cogswell (*q.v.*) moved to Roxbury from Boston and entered into a partnership with Emmons. Partnership dissolved in 1813, at which time Emmons was at 39 Orange St.

ENGLISH, William, *Boston, Mass.*
Working as cabinetmaker in 1809.

EUSTIS, Ebenezer, *Salem, Mass.*
Cabinetmaker with shop on North St., June 13, 1824. Moved to Essex St. near Buffums Corner, Jan. 14, 1825. At 402 Essex St. in 1837.

EVANS, David, *Philadelphia, Pa.*
Three account books of Evans, covering 1774–1811, are now at the Historical Society of Pennsylvania. They show that Evans made furniture for many of the prominent people of Philadelphia, including beds, card tables, and Pembroke and breakfast tables. Had shop on north side of Arch St. above Third St. His books show that in 1774 he employed Andrew Caldelugh and Jesse Williams, a journeyman cabinetmaker. In 1776 made tent poles, camp chairs, and coffins. In 1777 made "a Large Chest with Square head" for Richard Peters, and in 1785 a "Walnut Bearou table with Cullum corners." In 1786 shipped furniture to Virginia on the sloop *Betsey*. Under date of June 26, 1790, his books record that six chairs were made for his relative Edward Garrigues, and there are various other entries relating to furniture made for the Garrigues family.
On May 8, 1780 he rented a house located on Elfreth's Alley from Thomas Tufft. Later moved to Cherry St. and finally into his own building on Arch St. west of Sixth St. Listed in Philadelphia directories until 1814.
(*Evans' account books;* Hornor)

EVANS, Ephraim, *Alexandria, Va.*
Advertised in Alexandria newspaper in 1786 that he was a Windsor chair maker "Lately from Philadelphia."

EVENTON, Mardan Vaghn (or EVENG-TON, Mardum V.), *Dumfries, Va.*
On June 2, 1762 advertised in *Maryland Gazette* for journeyman cabinetmaker and mahogany plank. At that time he was at Dumfries, not far from Mount Vernon. On Aug. 15, 1777 advertised in the *Virginia Gazette*: "Mardum V. Evengton, at Capt. Richard Baugh's in Chesterfield County being now at leisure, would be glad to be employed as a master workman in the various branches of architecture, either in public or private building, from the most elegant and superb, down to the gentleman's plain country seat. He understands the various branches of architecture, both ancient and modern. He has an excellent assortment of tools and books for his business and will take charge of any number of hands in the mechanic way." On the same date he advertised as being "A Master workman in the various branches of the Cabinet Business, Chinese, Gothick, carving, turning, etc." Illustrated and described in *Antiques*, February 1954, is a secretary made by Eventon. It is of walnut with southern yellow pine as secondary wood.

FAIRCHILD, Robert, *Charleston, S. C.*
Born 1729; died 1775. In deed of 1750 conveying property from James Taylor to his daughter, who was Fairchild's wife, Fairchild is spoken of as "cabinetmaker and joiner of James Island." His first wife died in 1754. His second wife, Sarah Wigg, died Sept. 20, 1770. At the time of his second marriage, he moved to Beaufort, S. C., where he carried on his cabinetmaking business. (Burton)

FAIREN, Joseph, *Baltimore, Md.*
Listed in directory for 1799 as cabinetmaker.

FARIS, George G., *Savannah, Ga.*
Advertised in 1823 as cabinetmaker.

FARIS, William, *Baltimore, Md.*
Listed in directories during 1799–1802 as cabinetmaker.

FARLEY, John, *Savannah, Ga.*
Died 1781. (Comstock)

FARNHAM, John, *Boston, Mass.*
Listed in a deed of 1669 as joiner.

FARROW, Charles, *Chestertown, Md.*
Bordley in his manuscript at the Maryland Historical Society mentions having seen Farrow's label in a most intricate secret drawer of a slant-top desk now destroyed by fire. A lantern slide (no. 56) showing this desk is on file at the Baltimore Museum of Art. There is also a slide (no. 31) of the label, which shows eagle holding two arrows and olive branch. (Bordley)

FARSON, John, *Baltimore, Md.*
Cabinetmaker at 6 North Gay St. in 1833. (Varley)

FAULKNER, John, *New York City*
Advertised in newspaper in 1770 as successor to James Strachan.

FAULKNER, John, *Andover, Mass.*
Born March 7, 1785; died June 27, 1823. Cabinetmaker.

FEARFERVIS, Robert J., *Boston, Mass.*
Working as chairmaker in 1780.

FELKER, John C., *Amesbury, Mass.*
Cabinetmaker. Married Caroline F. Allen, Aug. 6, 1843, in Manchester.

FELL, Isaac, *Savannah, Ga.*
Born 1759; died 1818. Came from England. Advertised in *Georgia Gazette* in 1789: "all kinds of Cabinetmaking & upholstery work will be done in the most fashionable and elegant and masterly manner."

FELLOWS, Israel, *Salem, Mass.*
Born Aug. 28, 1816. In cabinetmaking business in 1837. In 1846 had partnership with John Whipple at 199 Essex St. Still located there in 1864.

FELT, Nathaniel, Jr., *Salem, Mass.*
Baptized Oct. 6, 1751. Died April 20, 1792. Cabinetmaker on Front St. (Perley, *History of Salem*, Vol. 3)

FELT, Samuel, *Somers, Conn.*
Baptized June 5, 1698 in Salem, Mass. Died March 23, 1788 in Somers. "Joiner." (Perley, *History of Salem*, Vol. 3)

FELTON, Benjamin, *Salem, Mass.*
Born circa 1613; died 1688. Turner. (Perley, *History of Salem*, Vol. 1)

FERGUSON, Stephen, *Manchester, Mass.*
Born May 18, 1808; died after 1847. Cabinetmaker. Married Mary Elizabeth Mann, Jan. 4, 1835. (Belknap)

FERNSIDE, Jacob, *Boston, Mass.*
Listed as cabinetmaker in notice of death in 1716.

FETTER, Jacob, *Salem, N. C.*
Working in 1797. Moravian cabinetmaker. (Fries, *Records of the Moravians in North Carolina*)

FIEDER, Louis, *Springfield, Mass.*
Had shop on Main and Bliss streets, 1831–54. Three chairs and table in loan exhibition at Springfield Museum of Art, Mass., 1936.

FIELD, Benjamin, *Providence, R. I.*
Listed in directory for 1824 as chairmaker at 16 Pawtuxet St.

FINLAY, John and Hugh, *Baltimore, Md.*
Working 1799–1833. John listed in directories of 1799–1802 on South Frederick St. John and Hugh listed from 1803. In 1808 they moved to North Gay St. Varley lists them at 32 North Gay St. in 1833. These men have been known largely as makers of painted furniture. In 1803 and 1804, however, they made sets consisting of two marble-topped corner tables, a marble-top pier table, and a pier glass, and Bordley believes these pieces were copies of those in the Music Salon at Fontainebleau. Of particular interest is Bordley's statement that "Mr. Ferdinand Latrobe tells me on the authority of papers and designs of his distinguished

ancestor, the architect, Benj. Latrobe, that John and Hugh Finlay, after the designs of Latrobe, built the furniture for completely furnishing the President's House during the administration of President Madison."

Owned by the direct descendants of John B. Morris, for whom the set was made, but on indefinite loan to the Baltimore Museum of Art, is a set of ten chairs, two settees, and a pier table. On the backs of the chairs and settees are depicted the homes of distinguished Baltimoreans of the period. Three of these homes are in existence today—Montclare, Homewood, and Willow Brook (now the Home of the Good Shepherd). According to family tradition, the paintings on these pieces were done by a "gifted English painter." Bordley says, however, that Hugh Finlay, the younger of the two brothers, was spoken of by his contemporaries as a "gifted painter," and it might well be that he did the paintings. In addition to the Finlay pieces at the Baltimore Museum of Art, there is a corner table at the Maryland Historical Society with marble top, French Provincial legs, inlay, and gold-painted glass panel. (Bordley)

FINLAYSON & FAIRLEY, *Charleston, S. C.*

Mungo Graeme Finlayson was the son of Mungo Finlayson, a cabinetmaker and friend of Thomas Elfe, Sr. The father died Nov. 29, 1793. The son was baptized on Aug. 25, 1776 and undoubtedly learned cabinetmaking in his father's shop. Hance Fairley was born in Ireland in 1771. He took out citizenship papers in Charleston in 1799. He is listed in various issues of the directory as a cabinetmaker on Meeting St. On Feb. 9, 1795 the following appeared in the *South Carolina Gazette*: "The subscribers having entered into Copartnership under the firm of Finlayson & Fairley, Intend to carry on the Cabinet-Making Business in all its branches, and in the most fashionable and approved taste, the knowledge of

which H. Fairley is perfectly acquainted with, being lately from London. Any order that they may be favoured with, will be executed on the most reasonable Terms, and at the same time in such a manner as they flatter themselves will give satisfaction to their employers. The above business will be carried on at the shop formerly occupied by Mr. Mungo Finlayson, deceased, in Queen-street, where the upholsterer's business likewise be conducted by Mr. Henry Campbell, from Boston, who through this means offers his best services to the public in said line, with assurances of his best endeavours to merit their favours." Finlayson died in 1799, just four years later.

FISHER, John, *Charleston, S. C.*

Advertised in *South Carolina Gazette; And Country Journal*, May 5, 1767: "John Fisher, Cabinet-maker from London, Takes this method to acquaint the Publick, That he has taken part of the house in Tradd-Street, where Mr. Wise formerly lived, and intends carrying on the Cabinet Business in all its branches. Those Gentlemen and Ladies who please to favour him with their commands may depend upon having their orders well executed, and on the shortest notice. N.B. Venetian Blinds made as in London." Fisher was in partnership with Thomas Elfe (*q.v.*) from some unknown date until 1771, at which time Fisher purchased the stock and negroes from Stephen Townsend (*q.v.*) as well as Townsend's house on Meeting St. In 1778 and 1781 he made large purchases of real estate. He was restored to the status of a British subject when Charleston was occupied by the British during the Revolution. He left Charleston when the British departed. (Burton; Rose)

FISHER, Robert, *Baltimore, Md.*

Listed in directories during 1807–12 as "fancy chair" maker. Used paintings on several pieces. Labeled some furniture. (Miller)

FISHER, William, *Baltimore, Md.*
Listed in directories for 1803 and 1804 as cabinetmaker.

FISK, Ansel, *Lowell, Mass.*
Working as cabinetmaker in 1835. (Belknap)

FISKE, William, *Salem and Roxbury, Mass.*
Son of Deacon Samuel Fiske, who also was a cabinetmaker. Father and son in partnership on Washington St., Salem, until the former's death in 1797. William then worked for the Sandersons for a short time. After 1800 went to Roxbury and joined the colony of craftsmen centered around the Willard clock works. Became one of the most prosperous of the group. In 1837 was still working, and at that time showed four portable rosewood desks at the exhibition of the Massachusetts Charitable Mechanics Association, Boston.

FITHIAN, Josiah, *Bridgeton, N. J.*
Advertisement dated Jan. 25, 1823 in loan exhibition at State Museum, Trenton, N. J., 1953. Cabinetmaker.

FLAGG, William, *Hartford, Conn.*
Advertised in the *American Mercury,* July 4, 1796: "Cherry Furniture. William Flagg Most respectfully informs his Friends and the Public in general, that he has taken a Shop, two doors North of Mr. Elisha Babcock's Printing Office, —where he makes all kinds of Mahogany or Cherry Furniture—such as side-boards, selection of straight Fronts, Easy chairs, Sofas, Secritaries, Bureaus, Oval Breakfast, circular Card Tables, Chairs of different patterns, all made in the neatest N. York fashions."

FLANAGIN, James, *near Greenwich, N. J.*
Advertisement dated March 25, 1824 in loan exhibition at State Museum, Trenton, N. J., 1953. Cabinetmaker.

FLANDERS, John, *Newburyport, Mass.*
Born circa 1787; died April 4, 1840.

Cabinetmaker. Married Elizabeth Greenleaf on Dec. 30, 1804, and Esther Park of Newbury on March 28, 1830. (Belknap)

FLEMING, Stein, *Baltimore, Md.*
Listed in directory for 1803 as cabinetmaker.

FLINT, Archelaus, *Charlestown, Mass.*
Listed as cabinetmaker when he married in 1803.

FLINT, David, *Marblehead, Mass.*
Baptized Oct. 11, 1795; died after 1835. Cabinetmaker. Married Ruth Bridges, May 11, 1820. (Belknap)

FLINT, Erastus, *Hartford, Conn.*
Advertised in the *Connecticut Courant,* July 2, 1806: "Erastus Flint, Cabinet Maker, At the corner 12 rods north of the Court House Offers for Sale, Cabinet Furniture in all its variety, made in the newest and most approved fashion, Also Sofas, Chairs, Bedsteads, etc. made to order with neatness and dispatch." Formed a partnership with John I. Wells under name of Wells & Flint (*q.v.*). This was dissolved in 1812. It is evident that in addition to the furniture mentioned in the above advertisement Flint also made fancy chairs, since on Jan. 22, 1812 he advertised in the *Connecticut Courant*: "Erastus Flint, Main St., Hartford, WANTED IMMEDIATELY, two smart active LADS, from 14 to 16 years of age as apprentices to Chair Making, Painting and Gilding Business."

FLINT & AMES, *Hancock, N. H.*
In 1811 advertised in the *Patriot:*

All kinds of Cabinet Furniture made at the shortest notice on reasonable terms, for cash, country produce or approved credit and delivered within thirty miles of our shop free of expense if purchased to the amount of fifty dollars.
WILLIAM B. FLINT
JACOB AMES

FLOWERS, William H., *Salem, Mass.*

Born Aug. 2, 1813. Cabinetmaker at 62 Broad St. in 1834; at 324 Essex St. in 1842 and 1846.

FOLEY, John, *Baltimore, Md.*

Listed in directories during 1799–1800 as cabinetmaker.

FOLEY, Timothy, *Baltimore, Md.*

Listed in directories during 1807–20 as cabinetmaker.

FOLWELL, John, *Philadelphia, Pa.*

Hornor calls him "the Thomas Chippendale of America." In 1775 Folwell, who was then on Front St., proposed to publish an American counterpart of Chippendale's work to be called "The Gentleman and Cabinet-maker's Assistant, Containing A great Variety of Useful and Ornamental Household Furniture." He sought the co-operation of men in New York, Baltimore, Annapolis and Charleston in this project, but the publication never materialized. Hornor believes Folwell was a competent designer as well as a maker of furniture, and that he was also a carver. To him is attributed the Speaker's Chair made for the State House in 1779 and called "John Hancock's Chair"; this is now at Independence Hall. He also made in 1771 the University of Pennsylvania orrery. (*Bulletin*, Pennsylvania Museum of Art, Jan. 1932; Hornor)

FOOT, Thomas, *Boston, Mass.*

Cabinetmaker on Creek Square in 1796.

FOREST, John, *Boston, Mass.*

Listed in 1796 as cabinetmaker.

FORSTER (or FOSTER), Charles, *Charlestown, Mass.*

Son of Jacob (*q.v.*). Partner in Forster & Lawrence, and Forster, Lawrence & Co.

FORSTER, Jacob, *Charlestown, Mass.*

Born 1764; died 1838. Arrived in Charlestown in 1781 from Berwick, Me., and is believed to have served his apprenticeship in Watertown, Mass. He used a label which reads: "Jacob Forster, Cabinet Maker, Charlestown, Massachusetts, Where are Made Tables of all kinds in the newest and best mode. Desks, Book Cases, Mahogany Chairs, Sofas, Lolling & Easy Chairs, Clock Cases, etc."

Sawyer has written that Jacob "purchased of John Harris in 1793 the lot of land on the west corner of Main and Union Streets, on which he erected the large wooden building now standing there, which has been used in part as a furniture store ever since. His own calling was that of a cabinetmaker and he originated and established here the business afterwards successfully carried on by his son Charles Forster (1798–1866) and Edward Lawrence under the style of Forster and Lawrence, and when Abraham Crowninshield was joined, Forster, Lawrence and Company. Mr. Forster occupied the rear of the premises and a portion of the front building as a home for his family and apprentices and under the roof of this old mansion a good many young men were made contented and comfortable who afterwards became prominent among furniture dealers in Boston."

Nutting says he made a serpentine chest of drawers with claw-and-ball feet that is of a type belonging to an earlier period, and has the label "J. Forster, Charlestown, Massa. 179/."

On July 13, 1803 Jacob advertised in the *Columbian Sentinel*: "For Sale by Jacob Forster Charlestown 1400 field and high Maple bedposts, all turned of the best wood and in the newest mode for less than the turning will cost."

A circular table made by him about 1790–1800, of mahogany with inlay and with Hepplewhite legs, was shown in *Antiques*, December 1929.

FORSTER & LAWRENCE, *Charlestown, Mass.*

See entry for Jacob Forster.

FORTHET, John, *Charleston, S. C.*
Bought business of John Dobbins on Tradd St. in 1770. (Rose)

FOSS, Leonard C., *Salisbury, Mass.*
Baptized 1823. Cabinetmaker. Married Caroline Marsters of Salem, Nov. 28, 1844. (Belknap)

FOSS & ROWLES, *Baltimore, Md.*
Cabinetmakers and undertakers on Saratoga St. one door from corner of Howard St. in 1833. (Varley)

FOSTER, Abraham, *Charlestown, Mass.*
Name may have been spelt Forster. Baptized 1744. "Probably the cabinetmaker of Boston, Ward 3, 1780." (Wyman)

FOSTER, Benjamin, *Beverly, Mass.*
Probably died March 11, 1844. Cabinetmaker. Married Anstiss Day of Ipswich, June 16, 1796. (Belknap)

FOSTER, David Calvin, *Ipswich, Mass.*
Cabinetmaker. Married Nancy H. Lamson, Oct. 30, 1831. In Ipswich as late as 1846; in Beverly in 1849.

FOSTER, JESSE, *Boston, Mass.*
Cabinet and Windsor chair maker in 1796.

FOSTER, Joseph Ropes, *Salem, Mass.*
Baptized March 20, 1806. Cabinetmaker. At 12 North St. in 1846.

FOULDS (FOWLES?), William, *Charleston, S. C.*
A William Fowles is listed in directory for 1813 as cabinetmaker at 62 Meeting St. Burton thinks him the same man as Foulds, who was a partner of John McIntosh (*q.v.*); both listed in directory for 1809.

FOWLE, Jonathan, *Boston, Mass.*
Working as chairmaker in 1784.

FOWLE FAMILY, *Boston, Mass.*
Several generations by this name were noted primarily for their expert carving. The first known Isaac Fowle (1648-1718) was recorded as a joiner when he became a member of the church in Charlestown in 1676. Another Isaac Fowle and Edmund Raymond who had been apprentices with the Skillins advertised on July 20, 1806 that they had "commenced business at the Shop formerly occupied by the late Mr. Skillin where they intend to carry on House and Ship ornamental carving in its various branches." In 1833 John and William Fowle and Spencer Beatley were taken into the firm in partnership, Raymond having retired in 1822.

FOWLER, Nathaniel, *Marblehead, Mass.*
Died 1792. Cabinetmaker. Married Hannah Stevens in Danvers, Oct. 6, 1774. Also had a shop in Danvers. (Belknap)

FOX, Walter, *Savannah, Ga.*
Listed as turner when he died in 1741. (Comstock)

FRANCIS, Abraham, *Boston, Mass.*
Cabinetmaker. Died in 1720. Inventory showed he left an exceedingly large estate.

FRANCIS, Joseph, *Boston, Mass.*
Listed as cabinet- and chairmaker in 1789.

FRANCIS, Simon, *Boston, Mass.*
Cabinetmaker at 40 Middle St. in 1800.

FREELOVE, James, *Boston, Mass.*
Listed as cabinetmaker in 1800.

FREEMAN, William, *Baltimore, Md.*
Listed in directories during 1802–12 as cabinetmaker.

FREEMAN & SAVERIN, *Pittsburgh, Pa.*
Advertised in *Pittsburgh Gazette*, Nov. 17, 1786: "Freeman & Saverin, Cabinet Makers & Upholsterers, makes in the

newest fashion and neatest manner, all kinds of Cabinet work; also they do the business of upholsterers in the different branches." In January 1787 William Freeman advertised that the firm was dissolved.

FRENCH, John, *New London, Conn.*

Born Sept. 17, 1762. Advertised as cabinetmaker in *New London Gazette,* May 29, 1820.

FRENCH, John & Son, *New London, Conn.*

Advertised as cabinetmakers in *New London Gazette,* Jan. 27, 1823.

FRENCH, John 2d., *New London, Conn.*

Married Betsey Rogers, daughter of Benjamin Rogers, Oct. 13, 1807. Advertised in the *Connecticut Gazette,* Feb. 18, 1807: "WINDSOR CHAIRS of all qualities and fashions made in the neatest manner for sale by JOHN FRENCH, 2d."

FRENCH & WAY, *Wilmington, Del.*

Cabinetmakers. Listed in directory for 1814 at 99–101 Market St.

FREW, John, *Charleston, S. C.*

Born 1776. Advertised in *State Gazette of South Carolina,* Sept. 25, 1795, that he "Informed his friends in particular and the Public in general, that he has commenced business for himself at his Shop No. 124 Queen-street and executes in all its various branches every article of the Cabinet Making business." Also added that he wanted two or three journeymen and one or two apprentices. Died Nov. 10, 1799 at the age of twenty-three.

FREY, Jacob, *Milton, Pa.*

Antiques, March 1933, shows a walnut chest-on-frame that bears the date 1795 and the initials J F in middle upper drawer. On bottom of lower drawer appears the written inscription "Jacob Frey, 1795."

FROST, James, *Boston, Mass.*

Cabinetmaker on Cambridge St. in 1807. *See* entry for William Seaver.

FROTHINGHAM, Benjamin, Sr., *Boston, Mass.*

Born 1708; died 1765. Married in 1733. Father of Benjamin Jr., the famous cabinetmaker (*q.v.*). His shop, near Milk St., burned in 1760.

FROTHINGHAM, Benjamin, Jr. (Major), *Charlestown, Mass.*

Born in Boston, Mass., April 6, 1734; died in 1809. Pieces of furniture bearing the label "Benj[n] Frothingham / Cabbinet Maker / in / Charlestown, N. E" are of great value today. This was the early label of Benjamin Frothingham. His father, also named Benjamin, was a cabinetmaker with a shop near Milk St., Boston. This burned in 1760.

Doubtless the son learned his trade in his father's shop. It is believed he was already established as a cabinetmaker in Charlestown by 1756, when he enlisted in Richard Gridley's Artillery Company. He took part in the expedition to capture

Shell carving on front of interior drawer in block-front secretary attributed to Benjamin Frothingham, circa 1750–80

Quebec and during the Revolution served in the colonial army in several different positions, finally becoming a major of artillery. When the war was over, he returned to Charlestown and rebuilt his house and shop, which had been destroyed June 17, 1775 when the British General Gage burned the town. Here Frothingham resumed his cabinetmaking business. At some earlier date he had married Mary Deland, and they were the parents of six daughters and a son. Benjamin, the son, was born in 1774. He also became a cabinetmaker, but has not, as yet, been deemed of the same importance as his father. New evidence, however, is coming to light constantly and time may prove that he, too, was a fine cabinetmaker.

Major Frothingham (as he was always called after the Revolution) became a member of the Society of the Cincinnati. He was also a friend of George Washington. In 1789 Washington called upon him at his home in Charlestown, the only private call he ever made in that town.

Frothingham constructed outstanding block-front furniture which compares favorably with that made by the Goddard-Townsend group of Newport, R. I. The blocking of the Massachusetts-made furniture, however, has a somewhat rounder quality than that of the Newport furniture. The Massachusetts pieces are simpler in adornment, and the bird's claws of the claw-and-ball feet turn backward in a diagonal line, the claw holding the ball somewhat lightly—in a manner quite unlike those on the Goddard-Townsend

Pediment of secretary attributed to Benjamin Frothingham showing interior carving

pieces. In addition the Massachusetts work does not show the undercut talon, a detail attempted nowhere in America except at Newport.

Frothingham also made reverse-serpentine-front chests and desks while some of his latest work was in the Hepplewhite style. A feature of his reverse-serpentine-front furniture is the shaping of the top drawer front, which is cut from a solid piece of wood and is round-blocked. He also used a delicate ogival bracket foot

and for corner finials a crisp corkscrew rising from an urn.

Some eight pieces of furniture bearing Frothingham's label have been located and many more have been attributed to him by comparison with the labeled pieces. Although he worked chiefly in mahogany, one simple secretary bearing his label is of cherry. He used a label engraved by Nathaniel Hurd, a member of the famous family of Boston silver-

Detail of corkscrew finial of type used by Benjamin Frothingham

smiths. The early labels read "Benjn Frothingham / Cabbinet Maker / in / Charlestown, N.E". The later labels omitted the "N.E".

At the dispersal sale of the Luke Vincent Lockwood Collection at the Parke-Bernet Galleries, New York City, on May 15, 1954, a Chippendale carved and parcel-gilded, mahogany bonnet-top block-front chest-on-chest with kneehole sold for $15,000. A matching dressing table, or bureau, sold for $10,000. While these two pieces were not attributed to Frothingham in the listing, it seems probable that he constructed them. The catalogue states: "Mr. Lockwood remarks that a chest-on-chest, the exact duplicate of the present one, is in the Warner House, Portsmouth, N. H., and that both pieces bear every earmark of having been executed by the same maker as the chest-on-chest originally belonging to Smith & Beck of Philadelphia." At the time the Smith & Beck chest-on-chest was advertised for sale the description said: "To our knowledge there are only three pieces of this type in existence . . . in all probability the work of Benjamin Frothingham of Charlestown, Mass., circa 1760."

In the Ashley House, Deerfield, Mass., there is a block-front mahogany secretary attributed to Frothingham. This originally belonged to the Rev. John Marsh of Boston. Longfellow used it at Cambridge, and at his death it became the property of his daughter who was the wife of the younger Richard Henry Dana.

Frothingham's signature has been found on the seat rail of a Hepplewhite-style side chair with carving attributed to Samuel McIntire of Salem. This piece is privately owned.

At the Detroit Institute of Arts there is a mahogany card table attributed to Frothingham.

At the William Rockhill Nelson Gallery of Art, Kansas City, Mo., there is a block-front secretary attributed to Frothingham. (PLATE XVII, No. 2) This was made for Commander Thomas Dawes of Boston, State Councilor and a member of the Academy of Arts and Sciences. For a full discussion of this piece, see *Connoisseur*, January 1932.

(Downs; Lockwood; Morse; Nutting, Vol. 1; Parke-Bernet Galleries Inc., *Sale Catalogue*, May 13–15, 1954; Sawyer; Wyman)

FROTHINGHAM, Benjamin III, *Charlestown, Mass.*
Born 1774; died 1832. Son of Benjamin Frothingham, Jr. (*q.v.*). Cabinetmaker.

FROTHINGHAM, Joseph, *Charlestown, Mass.*
Born 1677. Joiner. Married 1701.

FROTHINGHAM, Nathaniel, *Charlestown, Mass.*
Born 1671; died 1730. Joiner.

FROTHINGHAM, Samuel, *Salem, Mass.*
Partner of James Pulcifer in firm of Pulcifer & Frothingham on Church St.

On June 1, 1795 moved to Court St. Firm dissolved Dec. 14, 1795.

FROTHINGHAM, Thomas, *Charlestown, Mass.*
Born 1713; died 1775. Joiner. Went to Woburn after the fire of 1775 and died there.

FROTHINGHAM, Walter, *Charlestown, Mass.*
Antiques, June 1953, illustrates a mahogany chest of drawers on which his name is written.

FRYE, Nathaniel, *Andover, Mass.*
Born 1786; died 1822. Cabinetmaker. (Belknap)

FULLERTON, William, *Boston, Mass.*
Working as chairmaker as early as 1742. Notice of death in 1750.

FUSSELL, Solomon, *Philadelphia, Pa.*
Working as chairmaker in middle of eighteenth century. In 1754 owned "1 pr. old Cheretree Draws Chest of Chest." Hornor says he made chairs for Benjamin Franklin and rush-bottomed chairs.

FYFE, John, *Charleston, S. C.*
Cabinetmaker. Married Sarah Dott, a widow, July 2, 1775. In 1777 sold a house and lot on Colleton Square to Charles Desel (*q.v.*). Died before 1779, when his widow remarried.

GAINES, George, *Portsmouth, N. H.*
Born 1736; died 1808. (For information on his background, *see* first the entries below for his grandfather John Gaines II and his father John Gaines III.) George was the only son of John Gaines III. He developed a large business not only as a cabinetmaker but as a house-builder. He doubtless learned his trade in his father's shop from whomever it had been rented to by his mother.

Although no work is definitely attributed to George Gaines, it is deemed possible that he made a set of cherry ladder-back side chairs in the Chippendale style for Capt. Tobias Lear (father of Col. Tobias Lear, George Washington's secretary). The chairs were made in Portsmouth about 1760. It is known that Lear and Gaines were friends. Moreover, Gaines was the most prominent cabinetmaker in Portsmouth at the time, and it would seem feasible that he received the order for these chairs. It is also deemed possible that he made a pair of Chippendale chairs for his friend Capt. William Rice of Portsmouth; these chairs were made at about the same time as those for Lear, have a Gothic splat, and are branded with Rice's name.

GAINES, John II, *Ipswich, Mass.*

Born 1677; died circa 1750. Son of John Gaines I and Mary Tredwell. Father of John and Thomas. It is possible that John Gaines I was also a chairmaker but as yet there is no data regarding him. John Gaines II did turning as early as 1707, and made "great chairs" as early as 1711, banister-backs in 1717, and crown-back and painted chairs before 1724. The discovery of the account book of John and Thomas Gaines at Ipswich has thrown much new light on the family. Until 1738 the accounts are those of John II, afterwards those of Thomas. They reveal that John II, like his son John III, made "great chairs" with ram's horn arms.

This account book is now in the Joseph Downs Manuscript Collection at the Winterthur Museum, Delaware, and was the gift of Mrs. Katharine Prentis Murphy. (PLATE IX, No. 1)

GAINES, John, III, *Portsmouth, N. H.*

Born Nov. 17, 1704 in Ipswich. Undoubtedly learned his trade in his father's shop. Moved to Portsmouth in 1724 and opened his own shop. Married Ruth Waterhouse, member of an old Portsmouth family, Jan. 28, 1728. In that same year built a house on what was then the outskirts of the town (now Congress St. near Market), next door to the Bell Tavern. Died in 1743 when he was but thirty-nine years old, leaving a seven-year-old son George (*q.v.*). While George was growing up, his mother rented the cabinetmaking shop to one of Portsmouth's chairmakers — doubtless William Dam (Dame), who died in 1755, or George Banfield, who died in 1751.

Attributed to John Gaines III by family tradition are four side chairs which he made for himself in 1728 and which are still owned by his descendants. These chairs have the carved Spanish foot, elliptical bosses of the turned front stretcher, pierced cresting of the back, and rush seats. They are made of native hardwood, painted brown and grained to resemble walnut. In his *Rambles about Portsmouth* (1858), Brewster says, "That Mr. Gaines made his own furniture not only handsomely but faithfully, we have seen evidence in the now daily use of his first parlor chairs, which have passed down in the family for a hundred and thirty years, and are yet as good as new. They never had a price put upon them." Brewster was a descendant of John Gaines and the chairs were in his possession when he wrote the *Rambles*. They still remain in the Brewster family. A maple side chair at the Winterthur Museum, Delaware, and another at the Metropolitan Museum of Art, New York City, so closely resemble the chairs described above that they, too, are attributed to John III. A maple armchair at the Metropolitan Museum of Art, which has the Gaines-type back, feet, stretchers, and seat rail was doubtless also made by him. (PLATE IX, No. 2)

Practically every outstanding house built in Portsmouth between 1730 and 1785 has what is known as the Portsmouth type of balusters in the main staircase. These are identical in every house in which they appear; three to a step, one turned, one spiraled, and one fluted. It is believed these were designed by John Gaines III and made in his workshop, and that the design and tradition were carried on in his workshop after his death. They may be seen today in the

Sir William Pepperell House, the Tobias Lear House, and the Wentworth-Gardner Mansion.

GAINES, Thomas, *Ipswich, Mass.*

Son of John II and brother of John III. Apparently worked with his father and carried on the business after his father's death. Entries in his handwriting appear in the father's account book as early as 1735, and in 1738 he took part of the book as his own, marking it "Thomas Gaines, his Book of Accounts, from ye 150th page." (*American Collector*, Nov. 1938; *Antiques*, Sept. 1954; Brewster, *Rambles about Portsmouth*, 1858)

GAINOR, William, *Baltimore, Md.*

Listed in directory for 1810 as cabinetmaker.

GALER, Adam, *New York City*

On Sept. 2, 1774 advertised in Rivington's *N. Y. Gazatteer* as follows: "Adam Galer, Windsor Chair-Maker (Lately from Philadelphia) in Little Queen Street, next door to the corner of Great George Street, opposite Hull's tavern, Makes and sells all kinds of Windsor Chairs. Any gentlemen or masters of vessels may be supplied with a neat assortment upon reasonable terms."

GALUSHA, Elijah, *Troy, N. Y.*

Born 1804 in Shaftsbury, Vt.; died July 27, 1871 in Troy, N. Y. Son of Capt. Amos Galusha. Grandson of Jacob Galusha and Lydia Huntington Galusha of Norwich, Conn., where his father was born. Family first moved to Salisbury, Conn., and then to Shaftsbury, Vt. Amos grew up in Shaftsbury, where he married Mary Clark, formerly of Preston, Conn. He moved to Troy, N. Y., about 1830 and opened a cabinetmaking establishment. He was considered the city's "master cabinetmaker." He made a great deal of fine furniture, much of which is still cherished in the old homes of Troy. In many cases there are receipted bills to attest to the authenticity of these pieces.

The style of his furniture changed with the demands of fashion from Sheraton to Empire, from Empire to Victorian. He worked in mahogany and rosewood. At the Rensselaer County Historical Society House in Troy, there is a set of Galusha furniture consisting of a sofa, two side chairs, and a secretary-bookcase.

(*American Collector*, Dec. 1936; Col. H. B. Britton, President, Rensselaer County Historical Society, Troy, letters to the author; Miss Fanny C. Howe, Librarian, Troy Public Library, letters to the author; C. Reynolds, ed., *Hudson-Mohawk Genealogist and Family Memoirs*, 1911)

GANT, Thomas, *Philadelphia, Pa.*

In 1748 listed as "Joyner." In 1745 owned "A Pine Cupboard with Sash Doors" and in 1748 had a "Pine Cupboard with Lach Door." In 1748 made a "Pillar & Claw Tea Table." Hornor says that he stocked wild cherry along with other woods.

GARDINER, Samuel, *Genesco, N. Y.*

Working circa 1825. Found on a sewing table is his label "CABINET FURNITURE IN ALL ITS VARIETY, Made and sold by SAMUEL GARDINER (Two doors south of E. Hill's drug store)." (*Antiques*, Oct. 1923)

GARDNER, Charles, *Salem, Mass.*

Baptized Jan. 2, 1803. Cabinetmaker at 37 Mill St., Salem, in 1837. Moved to South Carolina in 1853. Died 1862/3 in North Carolina. (Perley, *History of Salem*, Vol. 3)

GARIOS, William, *Baltimore, Md.*

Listed as cabinetmaker in 1799.

GARNIER, Jean, *Baltimore, Md.*

French cabinetmaker in someone's employ from 1792 to 1800, when he opened a shop of his own. (Bordley) Listed in the directory for 1796 as a cabinetmaker at 17 Light St. is a Jean Gainnier—possibly the same man.

GARRISH, Francis B., *Baltimore, Md.*
Listed as cabinetmaker in 1803.

GAUTIER, Andrew, *New York City*
Listed as freeman joiner in 1746. In the Minutes of the Common Council of New York City his name appears at various times from 1748 through 1776. Advertised in newspapers during the early 1760s as a maker of Windsor chairs. In the *New York Journal*, Feb. 13, 1766, advertised (in part): "To be Sold by Andrew Gautier—A large and neat Assortment of Windsor Chairs, made in the best and neatest Manner, and well painted,—fit for Piazza or Garden . . . Children's dining and low chairs, etc." This advertisement was illustrated with a woodcut of a Windsor chair. Advertised in the *New York Gazette* at intervals throughout 1765 and 1766. In Weyman's *New York Gazette*, 1767, he listed the types of Windsor Chairs, "Viz; High-back'd, low back'd, and Sack back'd Chairs and Settees, or double seated fit for Piazza or Gardens."

GAUTIER, Daniell, *New York City*
Made freeman in 1731; listed as joiner. Mentioned in the Minutes of the Common Council of New York City in 1734. In 1739 records show he was paid one pound four shillings and three pence "for making a table for the Assembly at Greenwich, and for fitting and fixing it afterwards at Mr. Rutger's."

GAVET, Jonathan, *Salem, Mass.*
Born 1761; died 1806. Working in 1801 as a turner for the Sandersons. About 1784 made a walnut tip-top table. Beneath the top is a paper which says, "This stand was bought of Jonathan Gavet December 15, 1784 by my Grandfather Thomas Holmes. Cost 1/8/.0 Joseph Ropes, Salem." (Perley, *History of Salem,* Vol. 3)

GAVET, Joseph, *Salem, Mass.*
Baptized March 5, 1699. Died 1765. Married Mary Williams, May 20, 1725. Joiner. (*Perley, History of Salem,* No. 3)

GAVET, William, *Salem, Mass.*
Born 1766; died Jan. 8, 1856. Married Martha Richardson, 1799. Turner. (Perley, *History of Salem*, Vol. 3)

GAW, Gilbert, *Philadelphia, Pa.*
Windsor chair maker. Used the label "All Kinds of / Windsor Chairs and Settees / Made and Sold By / Gilbert Gaw / No. 90 North Front, twelve doors above Mulberry or Arch St / Philadelphia / Where Merchants, Masters of vessels, and others, may be supplied at the shortest notice, at the current prices, for cash or approved notes. / N.B. Orders from the West-Indies or any part of the continent will be punctually attended to." Hornor says that for the first time documentary evidence now indicates that twenty-four "ovel Back Chairs" (Hornor, pl. 484) were sold by Gilbert and Robert Gaw for forty-four dollars on May 14, 1796 to President Washington and that on May seventeenth three more Windsors were sold to him at a cost of four dollars.

GERSHOM, Thomas, *Boston, Mass.*
Cabinetmaker on Back St. in 1789.

GHISELIN, Reverdy, *Baltimore, Md.*
Early nineteenth-century chairs by him at St. John's College, Annapolis, Md.

GIBBON, Peter, *Boston, Mass.*
His death notice in 1729 listed him as cabinetmaker.

GIBBONS, Thomas, *Boston, Mass.*
In 1739 in partnership with Lenier Kenn (*q.v.*). (Nutting, Vol. 3)

GIBBS, John, *Newport, R. I.*
Working as joiner in 1742. (Richardson)

GIFFIN (Robert) & THORN (William), *Pittsburgh, Pa.*
Advertised in *Pittsburgh Gazette,* April 15, 1797 and March 24, 1798, and in the *Pittsburgh Tree of Liberty,* Feb. 28, 1801.

GIFFORD & SCOTLAND, *New York City*
Advertised in *New York and General Advertiser*, Dec. 21, 1799, as cabinetmakers.

GILBERT, Ignatius, *Gloucester, Mass.*
Born Nov. 8, 1819; died Sept. 12, 1848. Married Sarah E. Dolliver, Dec. 8, 1844. Cabinetmaker. (Belknap)

GILBERT, Jabez, *Windham, Conn.*
Windsor chair maker. Married Mary Read, June 8, 1769. (Bayles)

GILES, Alfred, *Gloucester, Mass.*
Born July 31, 1820. In 1846 married Eliza Jane Torrey in Rockport. Working there as chairmaker as late as 1849. (Belknap)

GILES, George B., *Providence, R. I.*
Listed in directory for 1832 as cabinetmaker at 57 and 149 High St.

GILES, James, *Gloucester, Mass.*
Born June 16, 1817. Cabinetmaker. Doubtless brother of Alfred. Married Hannah E. Long of Whitefield, Me., in Rockport. (Belknap)

GILES, Samuel, *Salem, Mass.*
Born Sept. 17, 1694. Married Susannah Palfrey, Sept. 10, 1719. Still living in 1754. Joiner and cabinetmaker. (Perley, *History of Salem*, Vol. 1)

GILLAM, Charles, *Old Saybrook, Conn.*
The study of this cabinetmaker is interesting not only for what it produces but for what it leaves undiscovered. It begins with a deed, a birth record, and an inventory.
On Nov. 17, 1703 a piece of land was sold to Cartret Gyllam "Mariner" by Capt. John Clark; in *Saybrook Land Records* (Vol. 2) it is described as follows: "One Dwelling House with house-Lott and Orchard, Lieing in and being in Say-Brook aforesaid, Lately in the possession of Mr. William Wilson of Say-Brook, merchant, and is Bounded on the East with the Land of Daniell Buckingham and on the south with the said Daniell Buckingham's land, on the West and North with highways Leading to the coave; containing by estimation two acres, be it more or less."
Saybrook Vital Statistics record on March 1, 1707/8 the birth of Charles Gillam, son of Cartret and Mary Gillam.
Probate Court Records on file at Guilford, Conn., show the inventory of the estate of Charles Gillam, cabinetmaker, Aug. 23, 1727. Since the son, Charles, would have been but twenty years old at this time, since there is no record of other children of Cartret and Mary, and since the estate was left to a nephew, James Gillam, of Hebron, one is led to the deduction that Cartret Gyllam was known as Charles and that the inventory was of his estate. It would further appear, although there are no records to show this, that at the time of his death neither his wife nor son was living.
The inventory of his estate includes among other things: "a book of architecture, a book of Mechanical Exercise, 8 draw locks, a case of drawers not finished, frame for a chest of drawers, one carved chair, a painted chest with drawers, a frame saw, a fine back saw, a new saw, a hand saw, an iron frame saw, a small saw, 5 pr. of moulding plains, 2 square rabits, 2 pr. match plains, a screw plain, a mitre plain, a hand plain, a box saw, 2 match plain, joynter, a pareing chisel, 2 carpenter's chisels, 3 gouges, 3 hammers, 2 hold fasts, one ½ inch angle, a tap borer, 2 Cornish gouge, mortising chisel, a small anvil, 3 bench hooks, 4 squares, one brace, 3 bits . . . a glue pot, 7 turning chisels, 2 benches, lignum vita dust, a parcel of collours, boxes, brushes & gums, &c, glue 109 lbs., oaker, a levell, umber, a French testament."
This inventory indicates several things about Gillam. First of all, it would seem that he was from some part of Europe where French was spoken and that he had received excellent training either

there or in England as a cabinetmaker, carver, and painter. Although he had several books in English relating to his work, his Bible was in French. Secondly, although Gillam did not purchase land until Nov. 17, 1703 an earlier arrival is not ruled out, but if he had been in the town any length of time working as a cabinetmaker he would not have been called "Mariner" in the deed. Thirdly, few workmen of that day had such an elaborate assortment of tools. This indicates the funds to purchase them and the experience to use them, so undoubtedly Gillam was financially successful in his work. Lastly, the "painted chest," "oaker," "parcel of collours," and so on would certainly signify that he painted some of his furniture.

Daniel Buckingham, mentioned in the deed to Gillam's land, died on May 11, 1725, two years before the death of Gillam. He was the son of the Rev. Thomas Buckingham in whose house the trustees met to organize and to discuss a site and a rector for The Collegiate School—later to be known as Yale University. In April 1702, the Reverend Abraham Pierson of Killingworth (now Clinton) accepted the position of rector and Saybrook was chosen as the location for the college. From 1707 until 1716 the sessions of the school were held at Saybrook. Yale University possesses a chair which was made for the Rev. Abraham Pierson, the first rector, and it has been attributed to Gillam. This is a wainscot chair with a two-panel back, with scrolling beneath the seat frame. Mr. Pierson died in 1707 and the chair was among his possessions, so a date of 1703–7 is given to it.

An inventory of Daniel Buckingham's estate showed several carved chests, a "Great Chair," and considerable other furniture. With a joiner and carver next door, would it not be probable that some of this furniture was made by him?

Moreover, is it not at least possible that some or all of the painted chests arbitrarily called "Guilford" were also made by Gillam? The dates of his working years and the location of his shop would fit in. So far as the author has been able to ascertain, these painted chests have been found east of Guilford toward Saybrook rather than on the west of Guilford or in Guilford itself. There was close relationship between these settlements and at that time they were all within the same probate court district.

The first settlers of Guilford were farmers. As Steiner says, they were not traders or manufacturers; "they had not a merchant among them and scarcely a mechanic." A John Hill, carpenter, was on the second list of freemen in 1659 but he died in 1689. Joseph Dudley was chosen as "coffin maker" in 1691 by the town but there are no data as to his having made furniture. About 1715 Nathaniel and Thomas Allis of Hatfield, Mass. (of the Allis family that made Hadley chests) moved to Guilford but family history says they were not joiners. Robert Griffing, a grandson of Jasper Griffing, an emigrant from Wales to Southold, L. I., learned the joiner's trade and moved to Guilford about 1735, but that date is too late.

Of equal significance is the fact that in the exhibition of some five hundred items connected with the history of Guilford to celebrate its 300th anniversary held in 1939 *not one* painted chest was shown. The exhibition included everything and anything to do with Guilford, from mittens to a plowshare, from a spinning wheel to furniture. If one of the Guilford craftsmen had made painted chests, there would have been one in the exhibit. No trace has been found of James Gillam of Hebron or of the chest he inherited. If this could be located, it might solve the problem.

NOTE: As this goes to press, the author has found what may tie the so-called Guilford chests to Old Saybrook and establish Charles Gillam as the maker. At the Acton Library, Old Saybrook, is a chest similar to the Guilford chest

shown on PLATE VIII, No. 2. The one at
the library has lost its feet, has had the
old hinges replaced, but otherwise is in
good condition. It has a long history in
Saybrook, and in future an attempt will
be made to trace its history back to the
date of its construction. The painted design is its interesting feature. It is closely
related to that on another piece at the
Winterthur Museum (PLATE VIII, No. 1).
Here are the roses, the thistles, and the
crown, and the style of the design is the
same.

(*Births, Marriages, Deaths,* Barbour
Collection at Connecticut State Library,
Hartford; Mrs. Harriet Chesebrough, ed.,
Saybrook, Connecticut, Genealogies, State
Library, Hartford; D. D. Field, *A Sta-
tistical Account of the County of Middlesex,* Clark and Lyman, 1819; G. C. Gates,
*Saybrook at the Mouth of the Connecti-
cut,* William H. Lee Press, Orange and
New Haven, 1935; *Proceedings at the
Celebration of the 250th Anniversary of
the Settlement of Guilford, Connecticut,*
1889, Stafford Printing Co., New Haven,
1889; *Saybrook Town Acts,* manuscript
copy by I. L'Hommedieu at State Library, Hartford; Steiner)

GILLINGHAM, James, *Philadelphia, Pa.*

Born 1736 in Bucks County, Pa. It is
not known where he learned his trade.
His uncle John was a joiner and cabinetmaker in Philadelphia as early as 1735,
and through the marriage of a cousin to
William Wayne, James was related to
this family of cabinetmakers. Apparently
he was in partnership with Henry Clifton
by 1761, since in that year they made a
mahogany chest of drawers for Mrs. S.
P. Moore. This partnership dissolved in
1768. On Nov. 5, 1768, Gillingham advertised in the *Pennsylvania Chronicle* as a
cabinet- and chairmaker who had "taken
shop, lately occupied by Samuel Matthews in Second Street, a little below Dr.
Thomas Bond." Hornor thinks that Jonathan Kinsey and William Matthews may
have been apprenticed to Gillingham. In
1763 he married Phoebe Hallowell at the

Philadelphia Friends Meeting. In 1773
Thomas Tufft (*q.v.*) took over his shop.
After the Revolution Gillingham discon-
tinued cabinetmaking. He died in 1781.

Gillingham made excellent furniture in
the Chippendale style but is particularly
known for the distinctive trefoil pattern
of his chair backs. In 1930 at the Flayderman auction a carved mahogany armchair
made circa 1765 brought $8,500 because
of its similarity to a chair with Gillingham's label. Two mahogany side chairs
made by Gillingham 1770–80 are at the
Metropolitan Museum of Art, New York
City (PLATE XXVI, No. 1); at the Winterthur Museum, Delaware, are several
chairs attributed to him. In the Karolik
Collection, Boston Museum of Fine Arts,
there is a mahogany chair made 1760–75
attributed to Gillingham; there is also one
at the Detroit Institute of Arts. Although
Gillingham is best known for his chairs,
it is evident he made other furniture. *Antiques,* May 1936, shows a mahogany pie-
crust table atrributed to him, owned by
a direct descendant of the one for whom
it was made.

GILLINGHAM, John, *Philadelphia, Pa.*

Born 1710. Established in Philadelphia
as a joiner in 1735. In that year married
Ann Jacob at the Philadelphia Friends
Meeting. Had four daughters but no son.
His oldest daughter, Sarah, married William Wayne (*q.v.*). In directory for 1785
he is listed on Arch St. between Front
and Second as a cabinetmaker. In 1791 he
is listed as a joiner at 27 Mulberry St. and
two years later as a cabinetmaker. (The
terms joiner and cabinetmaker were used
indiscriminately by lay people.) He died
Aug. 11, 1793 of yellow fever, and is
buried in the Friends' burying ground on
Arch St.

When his estate was administered in
1794 the inventory showed: a lot of lumber in the loft, one walnut desk, three
walnut bureaus unfinished, one walnut
breakfast table, six walnut chairs and a
bedstead, five rush-bottom chairs.

He was patronized by Benjamin Franklin and in 1740 made him a desk.
(*Antiques*, June and Oct. 1931; Hornor)

GILSON, Isaac C., *Manchester, Mass.*
Working as cabinetmaker 1835–45.

GILSON, Richard C., *Roxbury, Mass.*
Worked largely in Manchester. Married Mary Frances Lynn of Chester, N. H., July 25, 1841. (Belknap)

GILTNER, Daniel, *near Fayette-Bourbon County Line, Ky.*
Born 1800. Probably an apprentice of Joseph Green. Pieces extant. (Whitley)

GLADDING, George G., *Providence, R. I.*
Listed in directories for 1836 and 1837 as cabinetmaker at 35 Chestnut St.

GLADDING, Jonathan, *Newport, R. I.*
Working as chairmaker in 1770. (Richardson)

GLADDING, Robert, *New Britain, Conn.*
May have learned his trade in Aaron Roberts' shop. (Camp)

GLIDDEN, John, *Beverly, Mass.*
Born Sept. 12, 1794; died Feb. 13, 1846. Cabinetmaker.

GLOVER, Ichabod, *Salem, Mass.*
Baptized March 13, 1747/8. Died Aug. 14, 1801. Perley (*History of Salem*, Vol. 3) calls him a chairmaker. On June 19, 1798 advertised in *Salem Gazette*: "Ichabod Glover Respectfully informs the merchants of Salem and its vicinity, that he makes Ships, Wooden Guns, and Carriages of all sizes, with all the Implements and Furniture belonging to them. He solicits their employment in that line and engages to attend to their commands with punctuality, to do their work faithfully, and to charge it moderately. Said Glover does all kinds of Turning in Wood, and makes chairs and other Furniture on reasonable terms."

GLOVER, John, *New York City*
In 1763 witnessed a will as cabinetmaker. Appears in the Minutes of the Common Council of New York City in 1769.

GLOVER, Joseph, *Salem, Mass.*
Born Feb. 3, 1771; died March 23, 1808. Chairmaker. (Perley, *History of Salem*, Vol. 3)

GLOVER, Samuel Newhall, *Salem, Mass.*
Baptized Dec. 20, 1807. Died March 18, 1845. Cabinetmaker at 319 Essex St.

GLOVER, William, *Boston, Mass.*
Cabinetmaker on Batterymarch St. in 1807.

GODDARD FAMILY, *Newport, R. I.*
The Goddards, with the Townsends, comprise one of the outstanding groups of cabinetmakers in America. Both families were Quakers, closely related by marriage and friendship, both working and living in Newport during the eighteenth and early nineteenth centuries. This group is known variously as the Goddard-Townsend, the Newport, and the Rhode Island.

In much of their work, which must be considered on a group basis, they followed the styles current during the years in which they were active. But it was within this group that the outstandingly beautiful block-front shell-carved furniture was originally made in America. No longer is it believed that John Goddard was the originator of this style. Rather is it thought that many of the group took part in its development.

Few pieces are in existence today bearing labels of individual members of the group, but many pieces have been attributed by comparison with those having labels, by some document, or by tradition. Some of their work shows characteristics not seen on furniture made elsewhere but since these were used by several in the group, they are not in themselves sufficient to make attribution to any one man possible.

Many examples of the Goddard-Townsend furniture are privately owned and many are in museums all over our country. A great deal is undoubtedly still in the homes of descendants of those for whom it was originally made but without label, tradition, or specific characteristic upon which attribution can be made.

A great deal of material relating to the Goddard-Townsend families is at the Newport Historical Society and the Rhode Island Historical Society at Providence. At the Newport Historical Society are the Quaker Records, files of important letters, many interesting account books, and photostatic copies of the *Newport Mercury* and Probate Court Records.

In the Goddard family there were several bearing the name John but only two of them were cabinetmakers. John I was the important cabinetmaker. John II was his grandson, but his work in no way equaled that of his famous grandfather.

FIRST GENERATION

Daniel Goddard was the patriarch of the Goddard family of cabinetmakers in Newport, R. I. He was a housewright. His two sons, John and James, became cabinetmakers, as did three of his grandsons and one great-grandson. It is not known at what date the family moved to Newport. The *Newport Mercury*, on the dates given below, carried the following items about Daniel: May 28, 1764, "Daniel Goddard, Housewright, Killed in S. Kingston while repairing a house"; July 9, 1764, "Goddard, Daniel, Newport, dec'd. Executor John Goddard"; April 7, 1766, "Goddard, Daniel, Newport, dec'd. 2/3 of south half of Rose Island to be sold by John Goddard, executor of his estate"; July 23, 1770, "Goddard, Daniel, Newport, dec'd. Dwelling house, near Liberty Pole to be sold."

SECOND GENERATION

John I (1723–85) and James (1727–?), sons of Daniel. Cabinetmakers. *See* their entries below.

THIRD GENERATION

There were sixteen children born to John I. No data is available concerning three of them; presumably they were girls. The other thirteen were:

Daniel. Born 1747.

Solomon. Born 1748.

Townsend. Born 1750; died 1790. Cabinetmaker. *See* his entry below.

John. Born 1755; died in infancy.

Catherine. Born 1757. Married Perry Weaver of Middletown, R. I., who was born May 5, 1755 and died June 27, 1827.

John. Born 1758.

Job. Born 1760.

Henry. Born 1761; died in infancy.

Henry. Born 1762.

Stephen. Born 1764; died 1804. Cabinetmaker. *See* his entry below.

Thomas. Born 1765; died 1858. Cabinetmaker. *See* his entry below.

Benjamin. Born 1766.

Edmond. Born 1767.

FOURTH GENERATION

Of the children born to Stephen Goddard, there is information concerning only two—Stephen and John II. Stephen (1786–1853) married Susan S. Simmons, daughter of Edward Simmons, Newport, Dec. 3, 1820. John II (1789–1843) was a cabinetmaker; *see* his entry below.

Thomas and Susan were the children of Thomas Goddard. They are mentioned in their father's will, dated July 13, 1853 and probated Sept. 16, 1858. Susan married Theophilus Topham.

GODDARD, James, *Newport, R. I.*

Born 1727. Cabinetmaker. Married Susanna Townsend, daughter of Job Townsend.

GODDARD, John I, *Newport, R. I.*

Born Jan. 20, 1723 at Dartmouth, Mass. (near New Bedford). Dartmouth was an early center of Quakerism, and the Goddards, like the Townsends, were all Quakers. Apparently the family had been established in Newport some years before Daniel Goddard's death in 1764 since he owned considerable real estate. In Newport the Goddards were among friends because a large and prosperous colony of Quakers lived on Easton's Point. At an early age John I was apprenticed to Job Townsend, who, with his brother Christopher, was already well established as a cabinetmaker at Easton's Point. On Aug. 6, 1746 John I married Hannah, his employer's daughter. Some sixteen children are said to have been born of this union (Friends Records, Newport Historical Society), all but the two oldest in the large house with gambrel roof which stood on a hill at Easton's Point—now Washington St. It is probable that John I established his own business shortly after his marriage. Three of his sons—Townsend, Stephen, and Thomas—became cabinetmakers. Doubtless, others of the sons were employed at various times in their father's shop, but there is no record of any specific work accomplished by them.

According to records (either at the Newport Historical Society or the Rhode Island Historical Society at Providence), John I did much work for Moses Brown. Carpenter quotes a letter from him to Moses Brown under date of Oct. 4, 1763 and Brown's reply of Oct. 10. It would appear that Brown was very angry because his order had been delayed while John made some furniture for Governor Hopkins of Rhode Island. Goddard answered, in part: "Thou must have expected I should have Engag'd work to keep my Boys Imployed if it should a little Retard thy work for we must do so or we should be out of Imployment."

All furniture by Goddard is attributed on the basis of tradition or some record such as a letter or bill of sale, with the exception of three pieces which have inscriptions. The first is a block-front, shell-carved desk-bookcase. This is privately owned but is described and pictured by Carpenter; as it is in *Antiques*, April 1929. The inscription, on the rear of one of the cabinet drawers, says, "Made

By John Goddard / 1761 & repeard By / Thomas Goddard 1813." This piece was shown at the loan exhibition at the Nichols-Wanton-Hunter House in Newport, 1953. Nine other desks and bookcases similar to this are in existence, and are attributed to John I by comparison. This is the only one of the ten, however, with leaf carving on the two front feet. The second piece with an inscription is a desk privately owned, that was described and pictured in *Antiques*, Sept. 1936. The third piece is also a desk and is privately owned.

In addition to the shop in Newport, it is probable that Goddard had business connections in Providence, since in 1782 the following advertisement appeared in the Providence newspaper: "Goddard & Engs, Cabinetmakers from Newport at their Shop on the wharf of Mr. Moses Brown . . ." This may very well have been a sales warehouse.

When John I died in 1785 his assets were less than his liabilities. The Quakers had suffered during the Revolution—as had cabinetmakers in all the colonies—and Goddard's business had declined because of both the war and his religious beliefs. He willed his cabinetmaking tools and the use of his shop to his sons Stephen and Thomas. His will, dated June 30, 1785, and probated at City Hall Aug. 15, 1785, reads: "I give and bequeath to my two sons Stephen and Thomas the use and benefit of my Shop where I used to work so long as their Mother shall live in consideration of their working up the Stock of Mahogany in such Furniture as will be most profitable and when worked up to be appropriated as aforesaid."

At the Boston Museum of Fine Arts, there is a mahogany bonnet-top desk-bookcase attributed to John I. (PLATE XV) This has blocking of triple doors in cabinet, of desk lid, and lower case, with six carved shells. The convex shells and blocking are all applied. The bottoms and sides of the large drawers are of chestnut, which was very popular with the Newport men for this purpose, while pine and cherry are used for the secondary wood of the small cabinet drawers.

In the same museum there is a tea table attributed to John I. The top is one piece of San Domingan mahogany with molded

Newport, R. I., side chair, circa 1745-55

edge. The pedestal is a cluster of columns similar to the quarter columns found on many pieces made at Newport. In 1929 Duncan A. Hazard wrote: "The table was made by John Goddard and presented to his daughter Catherine who married Perry Weaver. I purchased it of the estate of Miss Susan J. Weaver" (their great-granddaughter). (Hipkiss)

At the Newport Historical Society there are several pieces attributed to the Goddard-Townsends; one especially interesting piece is a tea table of mahogany made circa 1770–80. This originally belonged to Solomon Southwick, the editor of the *Newport Mercury*. Tradition says it was buried during the British occupation.

There is a tea table attributed to John I by letter at the Winterthur Museum, Delaware; a bonnet-top block-front desk-bookcase and a chair with Queen Anne back with shell and claw-and-ball feet attributed to John I at the Metropolitan Museum of Art, New York City; and other pieces attributed to him are in Providence at the Rhode Island School of Design and the Historical Society.

Because of the similarity in the work done by the various members of the so-called Newport school at any period, it is quite impossible to definitely attribute a piece to a certain man without documentary evidence, close comparison, or solid tradition. In considering the work of this group of men, it is apparent that in their earliest pieces, they followed the Queen Anne tradition. Chairs attributed to them in this style are of choice wood and excellent design, at times having shell-carved knees and top rail, and flat stretchers somewhat thicker than those found on Philadelphia chairs of the same type. However, the fame of the Goddard-Townsend group depends largely upon their block-front and shell-carved furniture in the Chippendale style. Although furniture of this type was made by cabinetmakers in Massachusetts, in Connecticut, and occasionally in other parts of the country, that of the Newport group is foremost in design and workmanship. Cescinsky has said, "Although these Philadelphia high-boys and low-boys bring enormous prices at public auctions, if I were asked to select the finest examples of American furniture in the last half of

Detail of back of mahogany Chippendale-style side chair, Newport, R. I., circa 1760–70

the eighteenth century, my choice would fall on the block-fronted bureaux from Newport, Rhode Island. To my mind they are at once the best and the most logical of all the American pieces, with the exception of similar, and plainer pieces, made on the banks of the Delaware at about the same period, in which the walnut of the locality was substituted for the imported mahogany."

At one time all block-front, shell-carved pieces were attributed to John I but time has shown the folly of this. Un-

Carved shell motif on legs of card table attributed to Goddard-Townsends

doubtedly the honor of originating and perfecting this block-front and shell-carved furniture in America should be shared by John I and John Townsend, and also by Job and Christopher Townsend, the elders of the group. Experts set the years during which this furniture was made in Newport as 1750–85.

Blocking is one of three methods used by cabinetmakers to break up the flat surface of furniture; the other two are the serpentine and the reversed serpentine, called oxbow. Blocking in this country seems to have begun in Newport in the shops of the Goddard-Townsend cabinetmakers. A block front is cut in such a manner as to form a raised surface at either end with a depressed surface in the center; that is, there is a sunken central portion flanked on either side by raised block panels. Occasionally the center portion is not depressed but blocked like the other two, giving three raised panels on a surface. It was the custom of the Newport men to cut the raised block panels on a drawer front or door from a

single piece of wood, although they, as well as cabinetmakers in other parts of the country (a relatively small group, for most block-front furniture was made in New England), sometimes cut the blocks from separate pieces and applied them with glue so skillfully that they seldom came off. An outstanding feature of the block-front furniture is the carved shells. At times the convex shells at the top or bottom of raised block panels were cut from the thick piece of wood, an extremely difficult thing to do, since one slip of the carving tool could easily damage the piece beyond repair. Again, they were cut from separate pieces of wood and applied. The concave or depressed shells at the top or bottom of depressed surfaces were almost always cut from the same piece of wood and were not applied. At times the center of the shell was left plain; at other times there was a combination of fluting and crosshatching. The carving of the shell on all Goddard-Townsend furniture is so distinctive and so alike as to suggest it was done by one

Newport, R. I., carved shell

Newport, R. I., carved shell

person. Records show that James Townsend, a son of Job, and thus a contemporary of John I and John and Edmund Townsend, had at the time of his death a large number of planes and many chisels. This might indicate that he was a carver rather than a joiner and that he was employed by the other cabinetmakers to do their carving; a custom followed by cabinetmakers in all parts of the country.

The blocking of the drawer fronts was generally carried through the heavy bottom molding; often onto the bracket feet. Quite distinctive of Goddard-Townsend furniture are feet of the ogee-bracket

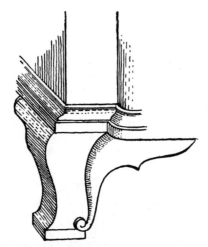

Goddard-Townsend bracket foot with scroll found nowhere else

type. Carpenter says, "The bottom of the foot has a vertical surface from the top of which the cyma curve commences, first flowing in and then out and then in to meet the bottom of the case. The vertical surface at the bottom and the point at which the cyma curve reaches its maximum outward position are in a vertical line." Often used with these ogee-bracket feet was a decorative scroll, another characteristic of Goddard-Townsend furniture. This consists of a narrow beading on the inside edge of the foot, ending in a scroll at the bottom of the foot where the cyma curve and the vertical surface meet. Drawers are usually flush, with a

bead molding on the framework around the drawers but not on the drawers themselves.

Although other wood was occasionally used by the Goddard-Townsend workmen, fine mahogany was their choice for their beautiful furniture. Secondary wood varied from pine to cedar and chestnut, and of the last they used a great deal; at times two different woods were used in the same drawer, one for the bottom, another for the unusually thin sides. Dovetailing in all Newport furniture is of high quality and the dowels are unusually small.

It is believed that the chest of drawers was the first type of furniture to which the Newport cabinetmakers applied blocking. The greater number will be found without the shell carving. The number of drawers varies; somethimes there are three, sometimes four. These are generally flush with a bead molding on the framework around the drawers. The ogee-bracket foot with tiny spiral scroll is used on the chest of drawers as on other pieces of Rhode Island block-front furniture and is a sure sign of its origin since this particular feature is used nowhere else. The base moldings are heavy and shaped to correspond with the drawer above. The chest top is generally straight, the front edge not following the line of blocking on the piece below.

Most examples of the kneehole writing or dressing tables are in the block-front form, although rare examples without blocking have been found. In the block-front type the recessed section in the middle enables a person to sit close to the top. This piece of furniture stands on six feet, four across the front and two at the back. Above the kneehole there is a full-width drawer and at each side a tier of three drawers. Often a small cupboard is at the back of the kneehole. The earliest of these kneehole writing or dressing tables appeared before 1760 with rounded blocking and without shell carving. In the finest of the Newport examples, however, there is a full-width drawer above the kneehole with the characteristic three carved shells. At times there is a fourth shell on the panel or cupboard door at the back of the kneehole. Occasionally the front of the top full-width drawer lets down on hinges to form a writing surface.

The block-front desk constructed by the Rhode Island cabinetmakers has, as a rule, four drawers, although when the

Finial peculiar to Goddard-Townsends

shell carving is used, there may be three. These desks are of the finest mahogany, and the design and workmanship of the highest quality. Shell carving is not usual on the desk drawers although it is occasionally found. Generally, the blocks on the upper drawer are rounded at the top, terminating below the drawer edge, which is straight. The drop lid is sometimes plain, but when it is blocked, the blocks usually terminate in shell carving. While both the claw-and-ball and the ogee-bracket foot are found on block-front desks, the straight bracket foot rarely occurs. A feature found on Rhode Island desks and desk-bookcases and nowhere else is a wooden bolt on the inside of the top drawer, reached from within

the desk well. This was used by the elders of the Goddard-Townsend group since it is found on the labeled Job Townsend desk-bookcase at the Rhode Island School of Design, Providence.

The desk-bookcases made at Newport in the block-front and shell-carved style are of the rich mahogany so popular with the cabinetmakers everywhere during the Chippendale period and are among the finest pieces made by the Goddard-Townsend men. The top—as is that of the chest-on-chest—is of the scroll or hooded type with a carved rosette that is somewhat geometric, in a style peculiar to Newport; at other times a returned molding is used at the inner edge of the scroll. The usual pediment finial is also individualistic. It consists of a shallow, rounded, fluted urn with several flutings omitted at the back, and with a flame of a peculiar corkscrew type. The lower section of the desk-bookcase usually has four drawers with block fronts ending in plain rounded corners on the topmost. Occasionally there may be three drawers only. Except in the finest examples, shell carving is not present on the lower section. The desk lid is usually blocked and shell-carved. Often the doors of the upper section are only blocked; at other times the shell carving is present. In some of the most elaborate desk-bookcases, there are three doors in the upper section instead of the customary two—as is the case of the one at the Boston Museum of Fine Arts. (PLATE xv) When three doors are present, two are hinged and the blocking and carving follows that of the desk lid. Pilasters of fluting or stopped fluting are the general rule on block-front desk-bookcases, although on occasion fluted quarter columns will be found at the corners. As on all Newport case furniture, the brasses are large and handsome. Often a large brass handle is added on either side of the desk, desk-bookcase, or chest-on-chest to aid in moving.

The top of the block-front chest-on-chest is, as stated above, similar to that of the desk-bookcase. Although straight

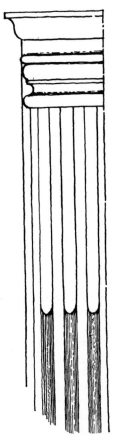

Stopped fluting as used by Newport, R. I., cabinetmakers

in the lower section are the rare and beautiful nine-shell pieces. Again, the shells will be seen at the top and bottom of the blocks in the upper section only. You will search vainly for a block-front and shell-carved highboy or lowboy.

It should be remembered that in addition to the distinctive block-front and shell-carved furniture the Goddard-Townsend men constructed other pieces that differ little from furniture made by cabinetmakers elsewhere during this same period. Much of this simpler type of furniture was made for export. It should also be noted that among the features peculiar to the Newport men was the paw foot used on some pieces such as screens, tea tables, and washstands, and the straight knee and turned leg with pad foot on tables with porringer top. Especially noteworthy is the undercut talon, which was attempted by no other cabinetmakers in America except those of the Newport School. This feature is a somewhat elongated webless claw, revealing openings between the inner ends of the talons and the ball, which the claw lightly grasps. The shape of both the claw and ball may

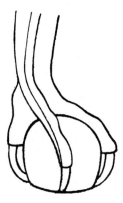

Undercut talons, attempted nowhere else in America except at Newport, R. I.

and ogee-bracket feet and claw-and-ball are all used on block-front double chests, the ogee-bracket with the tiny Newport scroll is generally found in conjunction with the carved shells. Four drawers are the rule in the lower section and four in the upper with three small drawers on top. At times in the shell-carved pieces, three drawers only will be found in the lower section. In some simple pieces, the blocking is present in the lower section only, without the shell carving, the blocking ending on the top drawer with simple rounded corners. On the finest chest-on-chests, however, there is blocking on both sections with shell carving; and those on which shells appear at the top and bottom of the blocks in the upper section and at the top of the blocks

vary from piece to piece. Also used on many pieces of case furniture made at Newport is a vertical reinforcing strip on the inside of the back with chamfered reinforcing blocks. On Goddard-Townsend wall furniture pad feet on rear legs were generally combined with claw-and-ball feet on front legs.

(*Antiques*, Dec. 1947; Downs; Hipkiss; Lockwood; Lyon; Miller; Nutting; Swan, *Antiques*, March and April 1946)

GODDARD, John II, *Newport, R. I.*

Born 1789; died 1843. This John, son of Stephen, and grandson of John I, had a two-story cabinetmaker's shop and warehouse at the northeast corner of Bridge and Second streets. In the collection of the Newport Historical Society there is a trade card which reads "John Goddard Cabinetmaker No. Bridge Street on the Point Newport." This came to light in 1927. On it is pictured a sideboard and two chests in the Hepplewhite style. At the Newport Historical Society there is a mahogany cabinet attributed to John II, made toward the end of his life. (PLATE XXXII)

GODDARD, Stephen, *Newport, R. I.*

Born 1764. Son of John I. Stephen and his brother Thomas were left their father's cabinetmaking tools and shop. Until his death Stephen worked in the shop with Thomas. A labeled card table made by them is described in the entry for Thomas (*q.v.*). One of Stephen's sons, John II, became a cabinetmaker. Another son, Stephen, married Susan S. Simmons, Dec. 3, 1820. In the *Newport Mercury* for June 16, 1804 and in the *Rhode Island Republic* for June 21, 1804 appeared the following: "Stephen Goddard, d. June 11, 1804, age 40, after a long and lingering illness."

GODDARD, Thomas, *Newport, R. I.*

Born 1765. Son of John I. Thomas and his brother Stephen carried on their father's business for many years, the type of furniture produced in their shop following the fashion trend of the period from Chippendale to Hepplewhite to Sheraton. After Stephen's death in 1804, Thomas carried on alone until his death in 1858. In 1789 he married Frances Weaver and sometime during the next two or three years built the house in which they lived on the northwest corner of Church and School streets. The demand for his tables and chairs, in which he seems to have specialized toward the end of his life, became less and less as the years advanced and at times he was forced to turn to the building of small boats to earn a livelihood.

At the Newport Historical Society there are two doll's chairs—side and arm —made for his granddaughter, Mrs. John O. Peckham (Matilda Allen). These were made about 1846, are similar to Hitchcock chairs, have two arrow-type verticals, and are painted black with a stripe of yellow. At the Metropolitan Museum of Art, New York City, there is a half-round card table of mahogany with satinwood inlay, made about 1790 in the Hepplewhite style, which has the label "Stephen and Thomas Goddard Cabinetmakers Carries on Said Business, . . . in Newport." (PLATE XXV, No. 2) Stephen had already died when Thomas did the repair work on the desk-bookcase described above (*see* entry for John I) which has the inscription "Made By John Goddard/1761 & repeard By Thomas Goddard 1813."

Thomas' will, dated July 13, 1853 and probated Sept. 16, 1858, mentions a son Thomas and a daughter Susan married to Theophilus Topham. Cherished at the Newport Historical Society is a clipping from the *Newport Mercury*, written by Henry E. Turner, which reads: "Died in Newport, July 24th, 1858, Mr. Thomas Goddard. The last of his generation has departed from among us. Thomas Goddard, Esq., died on Saturday last, at the ripe age of 93 years and 4 months. His attributes and history were such as entitle him to something more than the ordinary tributes of respect for the dead. During almost a century, he has been well known to this community, and particularly to his immediate neighborhood he was known as the kindest of neighbors and firmest of friends. No man, probably in this or any other community, (whose subsistence depended on the labor of his hands) ever devoted more hours to gratuitous attendance on the sick than Mr. Goddard. In rain or shine, in sickness or in health, the call of suffering humanity never failed to strike the answering chord in his bosom, or to be attended to with promptitude and alacrity; and had he not outlived in great measure the generations who best knew and most benefited by his self-sacrificing benevolence of spirit, it would be idle to recall them by this publication. . . ."

GODDARD, Townsend, *Newport, R. I.*
Born 1750; died 1790. Son of John I. Apparently Townsend was already established in his own shop on Town's Land, Newport, at the time of his father's death. It is probable his father had helped him get started in business since he left Townsend nothing in his will although he was the executor. He lived but five years after his father's death. No authenticated pieces made by him have been discovered to date. It is possible, however, that certain pieces resembling in details the work of the Goddard-Townsend furniture and found in the vicinity of Kingston may have been constructed by him. The author found at the Rhode Island Historical Society, Providence, the following letter by Townsend:

Newport, Rhodeisland December 21, 1777
Friend Ward

I wrote to you by the last conveiance to acquaint you that Joseph Avery was gone on the woodfleet to Longisland, which fleet has since returned, and I find by Enquireing that he left the fleet at Longisland, and it is thought he has gone home, which if he had not he would have been Sent according to my Perole, and Since there has been a general Permission for People to go from this Place, I think that my Return may be Discharged, if you should not be of the same Oppinion you will Point out another under the like Circumstance and I will Endeavor to Procure his Permission.

TOWNSEND GODDARD

P.S. When I left Providence I had not time to fetch my Tools which where at North Kingstown, and if you will be so kind as to grant liberty for them to be sent Down you will much Oblige your Friend

TOWNSEND GODDARD.
Henry Ward Esq.
Providence

GODSOE, William, *Manchester, Mass.*
Born in Kittery, Me. Married Lydia Richardson, May 30, 1841, in Manchester where he was a cabinetmaker. (Belknap)

GOLDSMITH, Jeremiah, *New York City*
Signed subscription list for *Life of Whitefield* in 1774 as cabinetmaker.

GOODALL, Edward, *Glasgow, Ky.*
Brother of Peter, with whom he had a shop.

GOODALL, Peter C., *Glasgow, Ky.*
Working 1812–20. Cabinetmaker. (Whitley)

GOODHUE, Francis, *Ipswich, Mass.*
The account book of John Gaines II and his son Thomas shows that they turned many table frames and bedposts for Goodhue between 1745 and 1761.

GOODHUE, Jonathan, *Gloucester, Mass.*
Died circa 1770. Married Deborah Fellows of Ipswich in 1758. Cabinetmaker. (Belknap)

GOODMAN, John, *Lexington and Frankfort, Ky.*
Working 1790–1810. Advertised in *Kentucky Gazette*, Jan. 10, 1799: "A fine quantity of cabinet work, desks, tables, chairs, etc. at John Coon's or at my factory on Cross Street opposite Colonel Hart's nail factory." At the J. B. Speed Art Museum, Louisville, Ky., there is a Sheraton-style mahogany veneer sideboard with block ends. This was made in Bourbon County circa 1810 and is attributed to John Goodman. (illustrated in the museum's *Bulletin*, February 1954). This was acquired by the museum in 1953. Goodman was the maker of the only known piece of labeled furniture by

a Frankfort, Ky., cabinetmaker. This is a piano made in 1801 for Governor Garrard's daughter. It is now owned by the Society of Colonial Dames and is on exhibition at the Kentucky Historical Society. (Offutt)

GOODRICH, Ansel, *Northampton, Mass.*
Born circa 1773; died July 31, 1803. At age of twenty-three advertised in *Gazette* for a journeyman or apprentice. Again advertised in *Hampshire Gazette* of Northampton: "Ansel Goodrich Has on Hand and keeps constantly for sale a quantity of warranted Chairs, a few rods North of the Court-House, Northampton." He was living at this location in a combination house and shop at time of death. At least two chairs are in existence with his label—Windsors, one bowback, the other fanback. (*Antiques,* July 1930)

GOODWIN, George F. and James, *Providence, R. I.*
Listed in directory for 1832 as cabinetmakers at 69 Westminster St. In 1836–37 James P. Goodwin at 47 Westminster St.

GOODWIN, Joseph, *Charlestown, Mass.*
Chair- and cabinetmaker. In 1771 moved to Salem, where he advertised as cabinetmaker.

GOODWIN, Timothy, *Charlestown, Mass.*
Listed as joiner at time of marriage in Boston in 1708.

GORDON, John H., *Baltimore, Md.*
Windsor chair maker at 41 Water St., southeast corner of South, in 1833. (Varley)

GORDON & BANKSON, *Baltimore, Md.*
Advertised in *Maryland Gazette,* July 18, 1750, cabinet warehouse. (Bordley)

GORET, Peter, *Baltimore, Md.*
Listed in directories during 1807–10 as cabinetmaker.

GOSS, Ezekiel, *Salem, Mass.*
Born Nov. 18, 1814. Shop at 261 Essex St. in 1837. Still working as cabinetmaker in 1861.

GOSS, George, *Salem, Mass.*
Cabinetmaker associated with Ezekiel, who probably was a brother.

GOSTELOWE, Jonathan, *Philadelphia, Pa.*
Born at Passyunk, Pa., in 1745. His father, George, was Swedish; his mother English. Learned his trade in the shop of George Claypoole (*q.v.*). On June 16,

Gostelowe chest of drawers, having serpentine front, chamfered corners, card-cut canted stiles, molded base, ogee-bracket feet

1768 married Mary Duffield, niece of Edward Duffield, clockmaker. She died two years later, leaving him a comparatively wealthy man. He remained a widower for many years but on April 19, 1789 married Elizabeth Tower, daughter of his old friend Robert Tower, the druggist at 66 Market St. (High St.). One month after his marriage he reopened his shop in Church Alley, having sold his stock before leaving to serve in the Revolution. Here he continued his cabinetmaking business for a year, at which time Elizabeth's father died, leaving her and her sister the store at 66 Market St., so the Gostelowes moved the cabinetmaking business there. It is apparent that he retired in 1793. In that year the following appeared in the newspaper: "Having declined business, Will sell at Public Auction, On Monday, the 20th inst. at 10 o'clock in the forenoon, At his Cabinet Shop No. 66 Market Street, A Quantity of Mahogany and other Furniture, Consisting of 10 neat Mahogany chairs . . . fan backs, covered with sattin hair cloth and brass nail'd, Dining tables, End Tables for ditto, Circular Card tables, Square ditto, Pembroke or Breakfast ditto, Washhand stands, Mahogany bedsteads, Button wood ditto, Likewise . . . work benches, tools and The remaining Stock on hand." He died Feb. 3, 1795.

The first labeled piece of his to come to light is in the Philadelphia Museum of Art and was made circa 1790. This is a Chippendale-style walnut chest of drawers with serpentine front and cockbead molding on the drawers which is more delicate than that usually found on furniture of this period. The top and base project an inch beyond the body of the piece on either end. The corners are canted with five flutes each. There are molded bracket feet. The top drawer is divided by a partition lengthwise in the center and these two sections are again divided into five equal compartments. Gostelowe's label is inside this drawer. (PLATE XIII, No. 2)

Attributed to Gostelowe by tradition is the so-called "Wedding Bureau" with dressing glass made by Gostelowe for Elizabeth Tower as a wedding gift. This is considered his masterpiece. The details of construction and workmanship are identical with those of the piece in the Philadelphia Museum but the Wedding Bureau is larger. The mirror frame was originally gilded to match the finials on the walnut support.

On April 23, 1794, Gostelowe, as executor of Robert Tower's will, applied for and received the guardianship of his nephews, the children of Sarah Tower Evans. The eldest of these was Robert Tower Evans and documented furniture has come down through his descendants. Gostelowe made a communion table in 1788 or 1789 and a baptismal font which were presented to Christ Church in Philadelphia. A baptismal font in St. Paul's

Church, Philadelphia, is so like the one in Christ Church that it is also believed to have been made by Gostelowe.

In the northeast bedroom of the Palace at Williamsburg is a serpentine-front mahogany chest of drawers with fluted chamfered corners and Gostelowe's characteristic ogee-bracket feet. This is attributed to him and is given a date of about 1775. In *Antiques*, January 1954, there is an illustration of a Chippendale mahogany highboy attributed to Gostelowe. (Cescinsky; Hornor; Nutting)

GOULD, John, Jr., *New Ipswich, N. H.*
Maker of several labeled pieces, early nineteenth century. Jonas Chickering of piano fame learned his trade with him. Employed other workmen. (*Antiquarian*, Feb. 1930)

GOULD, Nathaniel, *Salem, Mass.*
Baptized Nov. 17, 1734; died circa 1781. Cabinetmaker. (Perley, *History of Salem*, Vol. 3)

GOULD, Nathaniel, *Salem, Mass.*
Joiner and cabinetmaker. Married 1784. Moved about 1785 to St. Pierre Island, Martinique, W. I. (Perley, *History of Salem*, Vol. 3)

GOVER, Samuel H., *Baltimore, Md.*
Cabinetmaker. At corner of Frederick and Second streets in 1833. (Varley)

GRAHAM, Frederick, *Baltimore, Md.*
Listed in directories for 1800–1802 as cabinetmaker.

GRANGER, Abner, *Suffield, Conn.*
Born 1735. Account book at the Kent Memorial Library, Suffield, shows he made furniture.

GRANGER, Bildad, *Suffield, Conn.*
Born 1741; died 1780. Account book, at the Kent Memorial Library, Suffield, shows he made furniture.

GRANT, Erastus, *Westfield, Mass.*
At exhibition at Springfield Museum of Art in 1936 represented by labeled clock

case, chest of drawers, candle stand, and mirror.

GRANT, Henry, *Salem, Mass.*
Chairmaker at Buffums Corner, Essex St. Retired from business in 1809.

GRANT, Henry, *Marblehead, Mass.*
Listed in 1823 as chairmaker.

GRANT, Jesse, *Little Rock, Ky.*
Working 1778–1825. Made a sideboard that is now at Duncan Tavern, Paris, Ky. (Whitley)

GRANT, John C., *Salem, Mass.*
Cabinetmaker at 8 North St. in 1837; at 30 Federal St. in 1846; at 14 Lafayette St. from 1853. Still working in 1864.

GRANT, Moses, *Boston, Mass.*
Listed in 1789 as cabinetmaker.

GRAVES, John (Jr.?), *Ipswich, Mass.*
Born Sept. 11, 1766 (?); died March 7, 1804. Cabinetmaker. (Belknap)

GRAY, Benjamin, *Salem, Mass.*
Born Oct. 3, 1700; died 1761. Chairmaker. Married Sarah Cash, Nov. 15, 1722. (Perley, *History of Salem*, Vol. 3)

GRAY, Benjamin, Jr., *Salem, Mass.*
Born March 29, 1724; died before 1761. Chairmaker. (Belknap)

GREEN, Daniel, *Newport, R. I.*
Working 1743. Mentioned in Dr. William Hunter's account book, at the Newport Historical Society, as a joiner.

GREEN, J. Crawford, *Troy, N. Y.*
Learned his trade with Galusha (*q.v.*), to whom he was apprenticed at the age of fourteen in 1836. When Galusha retired, Green took over the business in partnership with another.

GREEN, John, *Baltimore, Md.*
Listed as cabinetmaker in 1804.

GREEN, Joseph, *Lexington, Ky.*
Working 1795–1810. Employed several apprentices in a large shop near Lexington. (Whitley)

GREEN, William, *Alexandria, Va.*
Advertised in *Alexandria Gazette & Advertiser*, March 22, 1823: "William Green, Cabinet Maker, Royal Street, nearly opposite the Market." Apparently had the shop with his brother James. In 1831 James was head of the shop and had another in Washington, D. C., at Tenth and Pennsylvania Avenue. In 1834 James bought a three-story brick building and lot at corner of Fairfax and Prince streets. Upon William's death business was continued by his three sons as Green & Bros. Firm dissolved in 1880s. (*Antiques*, Feb. 1945)

GREENLAND, Walter, *Charleston, S. C.*
Advertised Oct. 29, 1763 in the *South Carolina Gazette*: "WALTER GREENLAND, Cabinet-Maker and Joiner, Begs leave to acquaint his friends and customers that he has taken a shop on Queen-street."

GREENLEAF, Jonathan, *Newport, R. I.*
Working as joiner in 1735. (Richardson)

GREGG, Samuel, *Boston, Mass.*
Had a "fancy chair" factory in 1808.

GRIDLEY & BLAKE, *Boston, Mass.*
Cabinetmakers at 28 Cornhill in 1820.

GRIFFIN, Jonathan, *Beverly, Mass.*
Born 1767 at Essex; died Sept. 21, 1843. Cabinetmaker. (Belknap)

GRIGG (perhaps GRIGGS), Thomas Sr. and Jr., *New York City*
Advertised as early as 1754. Advertised in the *New York Mercury* in 1768 as joiners and cabinetmakers carrying on the business in all its branches.

GROFF, Henry, *Baltimore, Md.*
Listed in directories during 1800–1807 as cabinetmaker.

GROS, John, *Charleston, S. C.*
Born 1780; died 1853. Not known with whom he served his apprenticeship. In 1804 he and Thomas Lee (*q.v.*) formed a partnership under the name of Gros and Lee. This lasted until 1814, when Lee died and Gros continued by himself. Married Elizabeth Catherine Love, 1807. (Burton)

GROSE, Henry, *Baltimore, Md.*
Listed in directory for 1799 as cabinetmaker.

GROVER, Charles Ellis, *Gloucester, Mass.*
Born Aug. 24, 1820. Cabinetmaker. Married Ann Friend, Feb. 2, 1843. (Belknap)

GRUEZ, John, *New York City*
Born in France. Came to America and was employed by Lannuier as shop foreman. Took over the business on Lannuier's death. His name does not appear in the directories and he did not advertise in the newspapers before this time. His first advertisement, Nov. 8, 1819, in the *New York Evening Post*, stated: "Mr. J. Gruez from Paris has the honor of informing the ladies and gentlemen of this city and the public in general that he has taken the establishment of the late Mr. Lannuier, No. 60 Broad Street, where he continues to make all kinds of furniture and fancy work for which said establishment was so well known throughout the United States.

"Mr. J. Gruez begs also to observe, that having for several years superintended the interior part of Mr. Lannuier's business, he flatters himself that those ladies and gentlemen who were pleased to favor Mr. Lannuier with their patronage, will continue the same toward him, pledging himself to make use of every endeavor in his power to give general satisfaction."

Evidently did not succeed in carrying on the business and by 1822 had moved to 69 Broad St. and two years later was listed on Broad north of Garden St. By 1827 his whereabouts unknown. In Longworth's New York Directory, 1820-21,

Gruez's advertisement was in both English and French:

JOHN GRUEZ
Successor to H. Lannuier
CABINET-MAKER
From Paris
Keeps His Warehouse of
New-fashioned Furniture
At No. 60 Broad Street
New York

———

JOHN GRUEZ
Successeur d'H. Lannuier
EBENISTE DE PARIS, &c
Tient
Fabrique & Magazin de Meubles
Les plus a la Mode
New-York

GUILD, Abner, *Boston, Mass.*
Cabinetmaker listed in 1800.

GUILD, Nathaniel, *Savannah, Ga.*
Working 1778–1805. Cabinetmaker. (Comstock)

GUILD & ADAMS, *Boston, Mass.*
Cabinetmakers on Orange St. in 1796.

GULLIFER, Charles, *New York City*
Advertised in 1768 as cabinetmaker.

GURNEE, Daniel, *Providence, R. I.*
Listed in directory for 1824 as cabinetmaker at Union and Westminster streets.

HADDICK, Gabriel, *Baltimore, Md.*
Listed in directory for 1803 as cabinetmaker.

HADDOCK, Charles, *Haverhill, Mass.*
Died May 1796. Cabinetmaker. (Belknap)

HADDOCK, James, *Haverhill, Mass.*
Born Nov. 29, 1770; died May 10, 1823. Son of Charles. Cabinetmaker.

HADING, Mark, *Boston, Mass.*
Arrived from London in 1716; listed as joiner.

HAINES, Ephraim, *Philadelphia, Pa.*

Born in Burlington, Pa., Oct. 23, 1775; died after 1811. In 1791 apprenticed to Daniel Trotter of Philadelphia (*q.v.*). In 1799 became Trotter's partner and son-in-law. Mentioned in Benjamin Randolph's receipt book for 1763–77. Original bills have made it possible to identify work of Trotter and Haines from 1786 for almost twenty years. (PLATE XII, No. 2). Both were makers of so-called "pretzel-back" chair, a ladder-back type. A feature of Haines' work is the swelled bulb foot, although his earliest work was in a simple Chippendale style with claw-and-ball foot. Until 1811 did much work for the Stephen Girards: in 1806 a field bedstead (Hornor, pl. 247); in 1807 a set of black ebony furniture—chair-back settee, ten matching chairs, and two arm-chairs—at a cost of $500. Assisting him with this set were John R. Morris, who carved the oak leaves on knees and splats; George Bridenhart, who upholstered the set in crimson velvet; Robert Pullen, who applied the brass-head nails. In 1811 gave up cabinetmaking business to operate a mahogany yard. The exhibition at the Philadelphia Museum of Art, 1953, contained examples of his work. There is a Sheraton mahogany side chair attributed to Haines, made late eighteenth century, now at Adena, in Chillicothe, Ohio, owned by the Ohio Historical Society (PLATE XXVIII, No. 2). (*Antiques,* April 1953; Connelly; Downs, No. 48; Hornor)

HAINS, Adam, *Philadelphia, Pa.*

Born Feb. 9, 1768. Son of the proprietor of the Spread Eagle Tavern. Baptized Heinrich Adam Hahns. In 1789 discontinued this form of his name. Not known to whom he was apprenticed. About 1788 established his shop. Married Margareta Baish, Sept. 8, 1791. In the *Pennsylvania Journal,* July 25, 1792, a news item reads that an attempt had been made "to set fire to the house of Mr. Hains Cabinet Maker in Third near Vine Street." On May 18, 1797 moved to 261 Market St. Apparently moved to Berks County about 1803. A carved mahogany table by him (Downs, No. 314) is at the Winterthur Museum, Delaware. Downs remarks that Hains was known for his shapely gadrooned breakfast tables. Hains used the incised or branded mark "A. Hains Phil. fecit."

(*Antiques,* May 1947; Downs)

HAINSNEY, Robert, *Annapolis, Md.*

Working as cabinetmaker in 1762.

HALL, Edward, *Boston, Mass.*

Listed as cabinet- and chairmaker in 1796.

HALL, Edward, *Baltimore, Md.*

Listed in directory for 1804 as cabinetmaker.

HALL, James S., *Providence, R. I.*

Listed in directory for 1828 as cabinetmaker at Hospital St. In 1836–37 at 71–73 Westminster St.

HALL, John B., *Baltimore, Md.*

Listed in directories during 1805–10 as cabinetmaker.

HALL, Paul, *Exeter, N. H.*

Working as turner circa 1725.

HALL, Perley, *Providence, R. I.*

Listed in directory for 1824 as cabinetmaker on Middle St.

HALL, Peter, *Charleston, S. C.*

Advertised in *South Carolina Gazette,* Dec. 19, 1761, as a cabinetmaker from London: "gentlemen and ladies of taste may have made and be supplied with Chinese tables of all sorts, shelves, trays, chimney pieces, etc." Returned to England in 1768. Elfe's account book showed that he did some work for Hall. (Rose)

HALL, Sewell, *Boston, Mass.*

Cabinetmaker on Back St. in 1796.

HALL, Simon, *Boston, Mass.*
Advertised in 1780 "Desks with Bookcases and without, Bureaus, Tables, Chairs, and Tea Boards." Shop on Batterymarch St. In 1796 in partnership on Washington St. under name of Hall & Bisbe.

HALL, William, *Salem, N. C.*
Working in 1793. Moravian cabinetmaker. (Fries, *Records of the Moravians in North Carolina*)

HALL & ALLING, *Newark, N. J.*
In Newark City Directory for 1837 and 1838 as "Wholesale & Retail Fancy and Common Chair Manufacturers."

HALL & HUGHES, *Paris, Ky.*
Working in 1818. (Whitley)

HALLIDAY, Francis, *Newburyport, Mass.*
Died 1776. Cabinetmaker.

HALLOWAY, Jacob, *Boston, Mass.*
Working as cabinetmaker in 1690. On tax list of 1688 as Holloway, joiner.

HAMILTON, George, *Baltimore, Md.*
Listed in directory for 1800 as cabinetmaker.

HAMMET, William, *Charleston, S. C.*
Chairmaker with shop called Sign of the Coffin and Chair. Inventory of estate, Jan. 8, 1738, lists "14 Mahogany chairs about a forth part done £30; also about 160 feet of Mahogany and about 150 feet of Red Bay." (Burton)

HAMMETT, Thomas, *Charleston, S. C.*
Advertised in *South Carolina Gazette*, Oct. 9, 1755, that he "intends to remove from Charles-Town to Jackson-Borough in about a month, and has a house and lot well situated on King-street" to sell. Cabinetmaker.

HAMMOND, Benjamin, *Newport, R. I.*
His will (at Newport Historical Society), probated Jan. 6, 1806, lists him as cabinetmaker.

HAMPTON, Jonathan, *New York City*
Advertised in 1768–69. Name in Minutes of the Common Council, 1770.

HAMPTON, William, *Charleston, S. C.*
Listed in directory for 1790 as cabinetmaker.

HANCOCK, George, *Charleston, S. C.*
Born 1789. Listed in directory for 1813 as cabinetmaker at 3 Hard Alley. Became a citizen in 1814, at which time he said he was from London, twenty-five years old, and a cabinetmaker.

HANCOCK, Henry, *Boston, Mass.*
Working as cabinetmaker in 1818.

HANCOCK, William, *Boston, Mass.*
Chairmaker on Congress St. in 1796.

HAND, Richard, *Bridgeton, N. J.*
Advertisement dated March 25, 1826 was exhibited at State Museum, Trenton, N. J., 1953. Windsor chair maker.

HANNAH, Caleb, *Baltimore, Md.*
Listed in directory for 1796 as Windsor chair maker at two addresses—7 Cheapside and 32 Wilkes St., Fells Point.

HARBISON, William, *Wilmington, Del.*
Listed in Porter's Register, 1814, as Windsor chair maker at 46 King St.

HARDWICK, James, *Lexington, Ky.*
Advertised in *Kentucky Gazette*, March 4, 1794, "Makes Windsor chairs next door to Mr. White's, the coppersmith."

HARDY, Joshua, *Boston, Mass.*
Listed in directory for 1807 as chairmaker in Rainsfords Lane.

HARMON, Joseph, *Suffield, Conn.*
Born 1715; died 1762. Inventory of his estate showed turning tools. (Bissell)

HARRINGTON, Jonathan, *Lexington, Mass.*
Working 1770–80. Last survivor of the Battle of Lexington. A desk attributed to

him sold in the Flayderman auction in New York City, 1930. *Antiques*, March 1953, illustrates a mahogany Chippendale block-front desk attributed to him.

HARRIS, Daniel, *Newburyport, Mass.*
Born circa 1699; died June 28, 1752. Cabinetmaker. (Belknap)

HARRIS, Edward, *Newburyport, Mass.*
As cabinetmaker signed deed of land sold to Oliver Putnam circa 1775.

HARRIS, John, *Newbury, Mass.*
Died before July 1767. Married Martha Fowler of Ipswich, Sept. 15, 1744. Cabinetmaker.

HARRIS, John, *Newburyport, Mass.*
Died 1775. Working as joiner 1750–75.

HARRIS, John B., *Providence, R. I.*
Listed in directories as cabinetmaker on Union St. in 1824 and on Job St. in 1832.

HARRIS, John L., *Marblehead, Mass.*
Born circa 1772. Member of firm of Harris & Appleton, which dissolved July 28, 1815. Harris continued the business.

HARRIS, Robert, *Baltimore, Md.*
Listed in directory for 1799 as cabinetmaker.

HARRIS, Samuel, *Salem, Mass.*
See entry for Caleb Manning.

HARRIS, William, *Baltimore, Md.*
Listed in directories during 1796–99 as cabinetmaker at 8 North Frederick St.

HARRIS, William, Jr., *New London, Conn.*
Advertised in *New London Gazette*, Nov. 14, 1788, as Windsor chair maker.

HARRIS, William W., *Providence, R. I.*
Listed in directory for 1824 as cabinetmaker at 115½ South Main St. and over No. 82.

HARRIS & APPLETON, *Salem, Mass.*
See entries for John L. Harris and Thomas Appleton.

HART, Daniel, *Portsmouth, N. H.*
Working as cabinetmaker in 1790. (*American Collector*, June 1937)

HART, R., *Newburyport, Mass.*
A Pembroke table in Chippendale style, made circa 1760–80, is at the Henry Ford Museum, Dearborn, Mich.

HART, Samuel, *Portsmouth, N. H.*
Working as cabinetmaker in 1745. (*American Collector*, June 1937)

HARTSHORN, Jonathan, *Salem, Mass.*
Born circa 1773; died Nov. 15, 1803. Cabinetmaker.

HASKELL, William, *Salem, Mass.*
Born Nov. 8, 1791; died after 1837. Listed as cabinetmaker in 1817. At 379 Essex St. in 1837.

HASTINGS, Joseph (Reverend), *Suffield, Conn.*
Died 1785. In Suffield as early as 1725. Pastor of the first Baptist church to be established in Hartford County. A "Joyner" by trade. A highboy in Suffield attributed to him. Doubtless other pieces in existence. (Bissell)

HATFIELD, Samuel, *Boston, Mass.*
Chairmaker on Lane's Wharf in 1807.

HAWES, William, *Boston, Mass.*
Chairmaker in Quaker Lane in 1795.

HAWKES, John (Sergeant), *Hatfield and Deerfield, Mass.*
Born 1643 in Windsor, Conn. Probable maker of six so-called Hadley chests. A carpenter and joiner. When he was seventeen years of age, his family moved from Windsor to Hadley and settled on west side of river in that section known as Hatfield, near the Allises and Beldings. Worked for Belding & Allis. Since young

men were generally apprenticed at fourteen, it is interesting to speculate that
Hawkes may have served some of his
apprenticeship in shop of Disbrowe or the
Spencers of Hartford. Records show that
in 1696 he was on the committee to build
the meetinghouse in Deerfield; John and
his brother had moved to Deerfield when
it became a township in 1673. His wife
and some of his children were killed in
the second Deerfield massacre in 1704.
(This was his second wife, Alice Allis,
widow of Samuel Allis, whom he had
married in 1696.) One of his daughters
had married and was living in Waterbury, Conn., and sometime before 1721
John went there to live with her.

Luther attributes the following six
chests to Hawkes on the basis of tradition and workmanship:

1. The A W (Luther's No. 87), made
   for Abigail Wells, daughter of John
   and Sarah Wells of Hatfield. Abigail
   married Eliezer Hawkes, Jr., nephew
   of John Hawkes, Nov. 24, 1714. Chest
   remained in family in same house in
   Deerfield until 1927, and is still in
   possession of a descendant.
2. The S H (Luther's No. 41), made
   for Sarah Hawkes, daughter of Eliezer
   and Judith Smead Hawkes. Sarah was
   their eighth child, born July 26, 1701.
   This is one of the two very rare three-
   drawer chests. Owned by the Pocumtuck Valley Memorial Association,
   Deerfield, Mass.
3. The other three-drawer chest, the
   T S (Luther's No. 84); privately
   owned. It is believed this was made
   for Thankful Smead, daughter of William and Elizabeth Lawrence Smead,
   born May 13, 1677. She married John
   Hawkes, son of Sgt. John Hawkes in
   1695. Both were killed in the Indian
   Massacre of 1704. This chest probably made before the S H chest mentioned above.
4. The two-drawer H H chest (Luther's
   No. 38), made for Hannah Hawkes.
   Although Sgt. John Hawkes had a

daughter Hannah, who married Jonathan Scott of Waterbury, Conn., he
also had a niece Hannah, born July
7, 1703. She married Samuel Allen,
Nov. 3, 1727. Since this chest was
found at Conway, a town near Deerfield, it is believed it belonged to the
niece Hannah, and that Sgt. John
made it.
5. The W A (Luther's No. 9), a one-
   drawer chest in the Museum at Deerfield. This is also tentatively attributed
   to Hawkes.
6. The I E N chest (Luther's No. 59),
   made for John and Elizabeth Nims.
   The probable date is circa 1710. One
   of six chests with initials of both
   bride and groom.

HAWLEY, Samuel, *Ridgefield, Conn.*
    Son of Hezekiah Hawley. Undoubt-
edly learned his trade with his uncle,
Deacon Elisha Hawley, a cabinetmaker.
About 1820 in partnership with Rufus H.
Pickett (*q.v.*). Lived in Brick House situated near northeast corner of Main St.
and King Lane.

HAY, Anthony, *Williamsburg, Va.*
    Advertised in *Virginia Gazette*, 1766.
Later became proprietor of Raleigh
Tavern. (Comstock)

HAY, Edmund, *Boston, Mass.*
    Cabinetmaker on Congress St. in 1807.

HAY, William, *Boston, Mass.*
    Cabinetmaker in 1807, probably work-
ing with Edmund.

HAYES, William, *Annapolis, Md.*
    Advertised as cabinetmaker in 1747.

HAYS, Solomon, *New York City*
    In 1754 advertised in newspapers; had
shop at Beaver and Broad streets.

HAYWARD, Abraham, *Boston, Mass.*
    Member of Hayward & Blake, cabinet-
makers, Ann St., 1789.

HAYWARD, John, *Boston, Mass.*
Listed as cabinetmaker on Ann St., 1770–1813. Probably member of Hayward & Blake also.

HAYWARD, Thomas Cotton, *Charlestown, Mass.*
Married in 1800. Seven spindle "chicken coop" Windsor side chairs in the collection of Mrs. Burton N. Gates, Worcester, Mass., are marked "T. C. Hayward."

HEAD, Jesse (Reverend), *Harrodsburg, Ky.*
Advertised in *Kentucky Gazette*, Sept. 13, 1794, for an apprentice to learn cabinetmaking. Monument to Head in Spring Hill Cemetery, Harrodsburg, reads: "Preacher, editor, craftsman and patriot." He was an ordained minister and the one who married Thomas Lincoln and Nancy Hanks. Sandburg says, "There was a Reverend Jesse Head he [Thomas Lincoln] had heard preach over at Springfield in Washington County, and he had a particular liking for Jesse Head, who was a good chair-maker, a good cabinetmaker, and an active exhorter in the branch of the Methodist church. . . ." (Whitley)

HEALY, Recompense, *Newport, R. I.*
Working as joiner in 1775. (Richardson)

HEATH, Nathaniel, *Barrington, R. I.*
His account book covering 1769–98 at Rhode Island Historical Society, Providence. In 1769 made for Asa Bickniell a "Sea Chest" and a "Rocken Chear," also a "Desk of tow tear of Draws." In 1771 made a "4 foot tabel at 7ˢ per foot" and a "low Case of Drawers." Book shows he also made coffins, sold lumber, and did carpentry work, plowing, and so on.

HEFFERMAN, John, *Charleston, S. C.*
Born 1765. Listed in directory for 1806 as cabinetmaker. Became a citizen in 1814, when he gave his age as forty-nine and his home as Ireland. (Burton)

HENDERSON, Thomas, *Salem, Mass.*
Born Oct. 13, 1811. Known to have been member of the cabinetmaking firm of Hill, Henderson & Co. (*q.v.*) at 24 County St., 1837–42. Partner of William R. Allen (*q.v.*) in 1846.

HENDERSON, ALLEN & CO., *Salem, Mass.*
Thomas Henderson (*q.v.*) and William R. Allen (*q.v.*) at 38 Washington St. in 1846.

HENDLEY, John D., *Providence, R. I.*
Listed in directory in 1824 as cabinetmaker and undertaker over 6 North Water St. and in 1832 at 48 Benefit St.

HENDREE, George D., *Richmond, Va.*
Working 1792–1834. Prominent merchant and cabinetmaker. A mahogany cylinder desk made by him and now owned by a granddaughter was shown at the exhibition of Southern Furniture, 1640–1820, at the Virginia Museum of Fine Arts, Richmond, 1952. (*Antiques*, Jan. 1952)

HENDRICK, David, *Boston, Mass.*
Chairmaker in Cow Lane, 1796.

HENRY, Julian, *Charleston, S. C.*
Listed in directories during 1802–22 as cabinetmaker.

HENZEY, Joseph, *Philadelphia, Pa.*
A pair of fan-back Windsors signed by Joseph Henzey included in loan exhibition of Windsor chairs held in Philadelphia at Old Congress Hall, May 17, 1952, for a meeting of the Society of Descendants of the Signers of the Declaration of Independence. These were made circa 1776–96. Hornor says that both David Stackhouse and Isaac Covert were apprenticed to Henzey in 1772.

HEPBOURNE, Francis, *Annapolis, Md.*
Advertised as cabinetmaker in 1769.

HEWITT, John, *Savannah, Ga.*
Advertised as cabinetmaker in 1801.

HEWS, Alpheus, *New Haven, Conn.*

In the *New Haven Gazette and the Connecticut Magazine* of New Haven, Conn., Feb. 22, 1787, appeared the following advertisement: "Alpheus Hews, from New Jersey, begs leave to inform his friends and the public . . . that he carries on the business of Windsor Chair Making in Chapel Street in New Haven, where may be had any number of Windsor settees, and Garden Chairs made in the neatest manner and different fashions, also some very convenient for children."

HICHBORNE, Thomas, *Boston, Mass.*

Listed as joiner in 1688.

HICKS & LAW, *Baltimore, Md.*

Listed in directory for 1796 as cabinetmakers.

HIGGINS, Gaylor, *Suffield, Conn.*

"Made a chest of drawers." (Bissell)

HIGGINS, Sylvester, *East Haddam, Conn.*

Advertised in *Connecticut Gazette*, Jan. 7, 1807: "Sylvester Higgins Wishes to inform his friends and the publick, that he is carrying on the Cabinet and Chair making business in East Haddam, 1st Society, half a mile north of the meeting house, where he can furnish his customers with all kinds of furniture in his line of the first fashions from New York, at a very short notice."

HILL, Isaac Preston, *Manchester, Mass.*

Born Nov. 3, 1819. Cabinetmaker. (Belknap)

HILL, James, *Lexington, Ky.*

Working as cabinetmaker in 1818. (Whitley)

HILL, William, *Charlestown, Mass.*

Chairmaker. Died 1820 in Cambridge.

HILL, HENDERSON & CO., *Salem, Mass.*

Employed William R. Allen (*q.v.*) 1837–42. *See* entry for Thomas Henderson.

HILLIARD, Robert, *Boston, Mass.*

Listed as joiner in 1681.

HILTON, Aaron Swett, *Salisbury, Mass.*

Born Aug. 18, 1819. Cabinetmaker. (Belknap)

HISS & AUSTIN, *Baltimore, Md.*

Cabinetmakers on south side of Fayette St. between Howard and Park 1833. "[Keep] a complete assortment of furniture, and execute, according to order in the neatest manner." (Varley)

HITCHCOCK, Aaron (Captain), *Suffield, Conn.*

Born in Springfield, Mass.; died in Suffield, Conn. Married Experience Kent, daughter of John Kent. For half a century was a leading citizen in Suffield. The town meeting, May 17, 1740, "Also granted to Aaron Hitchcock Seventeen shillings and six pence in Town pay for sundreys—viz. his bottoming a chair for the schoolhouse and making a coffin for Goodman Segar [Joseph, the cabinetmaker]; and mending the Schoolhouse." Kept a tavern for a long time on the Ruggles Minister Lot, High St. (Sheldon)

HITCHCOCK, Lambert, *Hitchcocksville, Conn.*

Born in Cheshire, Conn., June 28, 1795, Lambert was the son of John Lee Hitchcock, a Revolutionary soldier who traced his ancestry back to Matthias Hitchcock who came to Boston from London in 1635. In 1818 Lambert settled in the little town of Barkhamsted in western Connecticut, where he established a cabinet and chair factory. In his little shop, Hitchcock at first made chair parts which he shipped to Charleston, S. C., and other points in the South. The chair-part business flourished and soon became the leading industry of Barkhamsted, account books showing that chairs were shipped as far west as Detroit and Chicago, as well as to the southern states. By 1825 Hitchcock gave up making parts and turned his attention to the construction of complete chairs. This new venture was most successful and soon he found it necessary to have more room. About 1826 he built a big new shop, three stories high of brick and large enough to care for the more than one hundred men, women, and children employed to fill the ever-increasing orders. With so many employees needing to live near their work, a group of houses sprang up around the factory, and the little settlement was called Hitchcocksville—today Riverton.

the front than at the back, with straight sides and a rolled or rounded edge in front. Chair backs are of several kinds; the "turtle-back"; the "pillow-top"; a "cut-out" back slat; a rounded top; a curved back with spindles; and a crest or "cut-in" oval back. The "cut-out" back slat is probably the most rare, and is sometimes in the form of cornucopias, eagles, or scrolls.

At first the chairs were grained to resemble rosewood, the red of the first coat of paint showing through the black.

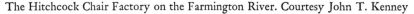

The Hitchcock Chair Factory on the Farmington River. Courtesy John T. Kenney

The Hitchcock chair was an early example of mass production, a chair selling at that time for about $1.50 retail. Although the Hitchcock chair is of several types, the characteristics are the same in all. The frames are generally of birch or maple. The backs have a curved top with a broad gently curved back slat, usually with a narrow crosspiece below. The uprights are continuations of the legs. The front legs and the stretcher between are nicely turned in spool, ring, or vase shapes. The seats are wider at

Later a lemon-yellow was sometimes used as the background color. Seats were first of rush, then cane or plank, all three styles made over a period of many years. Chair seats were marked on the back with the stencil "L. Hitchcock, Hitchcocksville, Connecticut, Warrented," usually all on one line. Hitchcock chose his wood with much care and allowed none to be used with knots or other imperfections. To find suitable wood for this purpose, he traveled far and wide, and "warrented" was his way of assuring his customers of the high quality of both wood and workmanship.

The stenciled designs used in decorating the chairs added much to their popularity. Very few were originally undecorated. The stencils were cut from strong but light-weight paper with a design of small checks, overlaid by blocks an inch square. This made it possible to keep the stenciling on a straight line. Popular among the stenciled designs were the basket of fruit containing pears and plums or a bunch of grapes with leaves and a rose; the horn of plenty, of which there

Hitchcock chair

are several varieties; a fountain with birds; and a conventionalized fruit and leaf pattern. Children applied the first coat of paint, the red undercoat. Then came a coat of silky but not glossy black, applied in such a way as to show faint hairlines of the red beneath. This was followed by the stenciling of the designs on the top, the back slat, the uprights of the back, and the rounded seat front. The stenciling was the women's work, the paints applied literally by their fingers. Their finger tips, first dipped in oil, then in the dry bronze or gold powder, were rubbed over the stencil, thus transferring the design to the chair. The color of the fruit, flowers, or birds was then painted in with a brush. Although the chief stencil design was on the wide back splat, decorative motifs were frequently used on the top rail and uprights of the back

and the front seat rail as well. The narrow marginal lines were usually in gilt, sometimes in yellow or off-white, and the turnings of legs and back were often touched with gilt.

Boston rockers in both the large and small sizes, as well as a child's Boston rocker with rolling seat and crest, were made. Cape Cod rockers, or "Mammy benches" as some call them, were made at the Hitchcock factory. Probably the rarest of all the many types of chairs made at Hitchcocksville is the high-back armchair with rockers. The very high back has the "pillow top," and the slat below is very narrow, as is a second slat at the bottom of the back. Four finely shaped arrow uprights connect these slats. Sturdy arms extend below the rush seat, and the rockers are short and stubby.

Everything went well at the Hitchcock factory and business was good until sometime in 1828; then on July 20, 1829 Lambert Hitchcock was forced into bankruptcy with liabilities of $21,525.31. The business was transferred to Rufus Holmes, Theron Rockwell, Jesse Ives, and William L. Holabird, who, as trustees, were to sell, manage, and dispose of the property in a manner most beneficial to Lambert's creditors, while he carried on as agent for the chair business. This arrangement must have worked out well for all, for in the *Hartford Courant* under date of Nov. 27, 1832 appeared the following:

Notice is hereby given that the chair business lately carried on by Lambert Hitchcock as agent is now resumed by him on his own account and responsibility, and that his trustees are no longer interested in or responsible for the same. The subscriber will continue to manufacture chairs, and now has on hand a large and elegant assortment of chairs, made after the latest fashions, and finished in the best manner.

LAMBERT HITCHCOCK
Hitchcocksville, November 17, 1832

In 1829, Arba Alford, Jr., who had been employed by Hitchcock from the very beginning of the business, was taken into partnership, and the name stenciled on the back of the chairs became "Hitchcock, Alford & Co. Warranted." While Hitchcock traveled through the South, the western states, and New England selling the products of his factory, Alford managed the shop. On Oct. 30, 1830 Hitchcock married Eunice Alford, a sister of his partner. The name of the firm remained "Hitchcock, Alford & Co." until 1843, when Hitchcock opened an independent factory in Unionville, where he manufactured chairs similar in every way to those made at Hitchcocksville. These were marked "Lambert Hitchcock, Unionville, Connecticut."

After Hitchcock moved to Unionville in 1843, Arba Alford took his brother Alfred into partnership and continued manufacturing chairs at the Hitchcocksville factory under the name of "Alford & Company." They also conducted a general store in one wing of the factory. In 1846 the chair business was discontinued. Naturally during all these years chairs similar in type were constructed at other factories in various parts of New England.

Holmes & Roberts (q.v.) made chairs at Colebrook during 1838–40 but sold out to Hitchcock in 1840.

In 1836, a year after the death of his first wife, Hitchcock married Mary Ann Preston at Cazenovia, N. Y., and they were the parents of three sons and a daughter. He died in 1852, and his will named his former partner, Arba Alford, Jr., executor of his estate.

(Mr. John T. Kenney, President of the Hitchcock Chair Company, Riverton, furnished the data relating to history of Hitchcock factory.)

HITCHINS, Samuel, *Boston, Mass.*
Cabinetmaker at 40 Middle St. in 1804.

HODGE, David, *Charleston, S. C.*
Listed in directory for 1809 as cabinetmaker at 62 Meeting St.

HODGINS, Martin, *Savannah, Ga.*
Advertised during 1779–1814 as cabinetmaker.

HODGKINS, John, *Ipswich, Mass.*
Baptized Aug. 16, 1713. Died 1797. Married Elizabeth Hovey, 1738. Known as "carpenter John." (Little)

HODGKINSON, John, *Baltimore, Md.*
Fancy chair manufacturer in all its varieties at 32 Hanover St., 1833. "Orders promptly executed." (Varley)

HODGSON & NICHOLSON, *Baltimore, Md.*
Advertised as cabinetmakers in 1790.

HOFFMAN, John, *New York City*
Will dated 1773 calls him a cabinetmaker.

HOLDEN, Asa, *New York City*
In 1812 advertised ball-and-spindle-back fancy chairs. Shop at 32 Broad St.

HOLDEN, Oliver, *Charlestown, Mass.*
Born 1765 in Pepperell; died 1844. Arrived in Charlestown, 1788. Cabinetmaker.

HOLDEN & JONES, *Boston, Mass.*
Chairmakers at Boston Neck in 1807.

HOLLAND, John, *Boston, Mass.*
Listed as cabinetmaker in 1796.

HOLMAN, Levi, *Salisbury, Vt.*
"Chairmaker in the village in 1814." (Weeks)

HOLMES, Isaac, *Lexington and Frankfort, Ky.*
In 1806 listed in Lexington, Ky., on Main St. In *Western World*, March 3, 1808, advertised he "has commenced business on High St." Windsor chair maker. (Offutt)

HOLMES, Nathan, *Boston, Mass.*
Born 1664. Listed as joiner in 1693

when he became a member of Ancient & Honorable Artisans Co.

HOLMES, Robert, *Lexington, Ky.*

In 1804 listed as "wheel and chair maker." Had a brush factory at corner of Cross & Short streets where he made chairs. In 1806 listed in directory as chairmaker. (Offutt)

HOLMES (Rufus) & ROBERTS (Samuel), *Robertsville, Conn., southeast section of Colebrook*

Partnership began 1838. Holmes apparently was not a chairmaker but financed the company. In 1840 sold plant to Lambert Hitchcock and Arba Alford for $2,000. Made wood-bottom chairs similar to those by Hitchcock. *See* entry for Roberts.

HOLT, Stephen, *Salem, Mass.*

Married Abigail Brown of Ipswich, 1803. Cabinetmaker on North St. Sold his tools June 25, 1805. (Belknap)

HOLTON, Thomas, *Charleston, S. C.*

In 1721 married Anne Mindemen but in 1731 they were separated. He died in 1732. On Aug. 5, 1732 an advertisement in the *South Carolina Gazette* read as follows: "At the House of the late T. Holton, Chairmaker on the Green, the same business is carried on where Chairs and Couches are made and mended, after the same manner, and at reasonable Rates." (Burton)

HOMER, Andrew, *Boston, Mass.*

A Pembroke breakfast table in Hepplewhite style, circa 1780, with Homer's label is at the Henry Ford Museum, Dearborn, Mich.

HOOCKEY, John, *Newport, R. I.*

John Banister's account book (at Newport Historical Society) under date of April 2, 1750 reads that John Hoockey was credited with "a black walnut desk and caseing rec'd in January last and shipped in ye Hannah £44; mending and caseing a desk 8/52; mending a chair 1/15."

HOOK (or HOOCK), William, *Salem, Mass.*

Born Feb. 19, 1777; died May 15, 1867 at Roxbury. Apprenticed to John Swett, joiner and cabinetmaker, Salisbury, Mass. Moved to Salem, 1796. Married Abigail Greenleaf in Salem, March 2, 1800. Worked for Edmund Johnson for two years; then for Jacob Sanderson. In 1800 established own business at Essex and Court streets, and was patronized by leading families of Salem. His furniture was so much in demand that orders were placed sometimes a year in advance. He was located in 1803 on Federal St.; in 1804 on Marlborough St.; in 1818 at 20 Essex St. Much of his work is in Sheraton style, richly veneered and inlaid. Characteristic are carved water leaves on capitals terminating corner posts. These are slightly serrated and have an undulating outline, and the concave face of each lobe

Detail showing carved water leaves, characteristic of work of William Hook

is marked by four or five shallow groovings. It is possible that Hook occasionally collaborated with Nehemiah Adams since features found on some pieces attributed to Adams are also seen on some furniture attributed to Hook—elongated bulb feet and long cylindrical necking. Several pieces of documented furniture have been located, most privately owned by descendants of those for whom they were made. At the Essex Institute, Salem, there is a chest of drawers and dressing mirror bequeathed to it by George R. Curwen, who stated that it had been made by Hook in 1818. This has a bow front with drawers veneered in crotch mahogany. Ball feet terminate the short turned legs. The knobs are of wood. Also at the Essex Institute is a bureau-desk attributed to Hook. This has a serpentine front, corner capitals with carved water leaves (identical with those on a sideboard attributed to him at the Boston Museum of Fine Arts), reeded corner columns, straight lion-paw feet. One of the most elaborate pieces, which tradition says was made by Hook in 1809 as a wedding present for his sister, is a sideboard at the Boston Museum of Fine Arts. This has a swell front, veneered and inlaid with a sunburst of contrasting bands. The corner posts and legs are reeded; the capitals carved with water leaves. (Belknap; F. Kimball, *Antiques*, April 1934)

HOOPER, Thomas, *Charlestown, Mass.*
Born 1779; died 1868. Joiner.

HOPE, Thomas, *Charleston, S. C.*
Born 1757 in England; died 1820. Listed in directory for 1790 as cabinetmaker living at 15 Friend St. Essentially an architect but built an outstanding cupboard in a Knoxville, Tenn., house. (Nutting, Vol. 3)

HOPKINS, Gerrard, *Baltimore, Md.*
Died 1796. Son of Samuel Hopkins of Philadelphia, a prominent Quaker. Served his apprenticeship with Robert Moore, according to Nutting. Arrived in Baltimore from Philadelphia in 1767. On April 9, 1767 he advertised in the *Maryland Gazette* as follows: "Gerrard Hopkins, son of Samuel, Cabinet and Chair-Maker from Philadelphia at the sign of the Tea Table and Chair in Gay Street Baltimore-Town Makes and sells the following goods in the best manner and in the newest Fashions in Mahogany, Walnut, Cherry-tree and Maple viz. Chests

of drawers of various sorts, Desks, Bookcases, Scrutoires, Cloth-Presses, Tables, of various sorts such as Bureaus, Card, Chamber, Parlour, and Tea Tables, Chairs of various sorts such as easy arm, Parlour, Chamber or Corner Chairs, Settees, Clock-cases, Couches, Candle stands, Decanter stands, Tea Kettle Stands, Dumb-Waiters, Tea-Boards, Bottle Boards, Bedsteads &c. &c. N.B. Any of the above Articles to be done with or without carved work."

About 1934 in the West River section of Anne Arundel County were found a number of pieces of furniture made between 1700 and 1776 with original bills relating them to Hopkins. These included nine ladder-back walnut chairs from an original set of twelve, a mahogany sideboard, fiddleback chairs in Queen Anne style, a mahogany drop-leaf table, and mahogany side chairs. On Jan. 19, 1773, Hopkins advertised in the *Maryland Journal*: "Gerrard Hopkins, son of Samuel, cabinet and chair maker hath for sale in Gay Street Baltimore Town, mahogany boards, planks, also logs. He still continues business in its various branches as usual."

In 1780 Hopkins made a mahogany ladder-back chair for Charles Carroll (illustrated in *American Collector*, June 1944). In 1787 he entered into a partnership with a cabinetmaker by the name of Haines and changed the name of his shop to "Sign of the Bureau and Coffin." This partnership ended in 1795 and Hopkins resumed business for himself. Apparently he did not use a label since none has been found.

(*American Collector*, June 1944; *Antiques*, Sept. 1934; Berkley; Downs, p. xix, Nutting)

HOPKINS, John G., *Providence, R. I.*
Listed in directories from 1824 to 1832 as cabinetmaker at 192–194 Benefit St.

HORNBY, Gaulter, *Baltimore, Md.*
Listed in directories during 1792–1810 as cabinetmaker.

HORNBY, William, *Baltimore, Md.*
    Listed in directories during 1796–1800 as cabinetmaker.

HORNBY & TURNER, *Baltimore, Md.*
    Listed in directories during 1788–92 as cabinetmakers.

HORTON, Samuel, *Boston, Mass.*
    Chairmaker at Boston Neck in 1807.

HOSMER, Joseph, *Concord, Mass.*
    James Hosmer, the first of that name to arrive in Concord, reached there in 1635. In an old deed he is called a carpenter and architect. Doubtless he learned his trade in England. He built a house and a sawmill near the village mill-dam, and on Oct. 13, 1638 married Sarah White, of London. Sarah was a sister of Mrs. Rowlandson, wife of the Rev. Joseph Rowlandson (the first minister of Lancaster, Mass., and the minister in Wethersfield, Conn., in 1677; he was the owner of the Sunflower chest now in the Lancaster Library, a key piece in dating Sunflower chests). The eldest son of James and Sarah White Hosmer was also named James. He was a carpenter or cabinetmaker and is said to have hidden his tools before going to fight under Captain Wadsworth at the battle of Sudbury. There he was killed and his tools were never found. He left two sons—James III and Thomas. James III sold his half of the property inherited from his father and moved to Farmington, Conn. Thomas married Hannah Hartwell of Lincoln. His second son was also called Thomas; received a farm and the sawmill when he was twenty-one from his father; and married Prudence Hosmer, his third cousin. The cabinetmaker Joseph, his eldest son, was born Dec. 27, 1735. When Joseph was twenty-one, his father divided the farm which he then owned between Joseph and his other son, Benjamin. Living near the Hosmers was Robert Rosier, a Frenchman, who had married Mary Shevally, a second cousin of Joseph. Rosier was an excellent cabinetmaker and

with him Joseph learned the trade of cabinetmaking. Rosier later moved to Albany, N. Y.

In 1758, at the age of twenty-three, Joseph built his own house. On Christmas Eve 1761 he married Lucy Barnes of Marlboro, and from then until the outbreak of the Revolution he worked steadily at cabinetmaking, employing several apprentices, who lived in his home. In addition to cabinetmaking, he managed a large farm and apparently raised cattle since he also owned pastures in Rutland, New Ipswich, Princeton, and Acton. On April 19, 1775 he acted as adjutant of the American Forces at the battle of Concord at the North Bridge. After the Revolution, he held many important positions in town, county, and state. He died in 1821.

Hosmer's furniture shows some likeness to that of Benjamin Frothingham. It is of excellent design and workmanship. At the Concord Antiquarian Society there are two fine pieces attributed to him, a cherry chest of drawers and a cherry desk. (PLATE XVIII, No. 2) These came directly to the Society from Joseph's great-grandson, the late Cyrus Hosmer. At the Winterthur Museum, Delaware, there is a cherry and maple block-front highboy, circa 1770, on high slender legs that seem almost too delicate to support the piece. This is attributed to Hosmer. The author is grateful to Mrs. Howard W. Kent of the Concord Antiquarian Society for her helpfulness in securing data regarding Hosmer and Rosier.

(*Centennial of the Social Circle in Concord*, 1782–1882; Downs, No. 189; G. L. Hosmer, *Hosmer Genealogy*, 1928; *Memorial of George Washington Hosmer*, 1882, privately printed; Shattuck)

HOW & ROULAIN, *Charleston, S. C.*
    On Nov. 13, 1762 advertised in the *South Carolina Gazette*: "How & Roulain, Joiners & Cabinet-Makers, next door to Miss Hester Simons in King-street, Gives notice, that they carry on the said business in all its branches."

HOWARD, Joseph, *Suffield, Conn.*
Born 1738; died 1810. Married Hannah Dewey. Account book in Kent Memorial Library, Suffield, beginning 1783, shows he made a quantity of furniture.

HOWARD, Thomas, *Pawtuxet and Providence, R. I.*
Advertised in *Providence Gazette* on June 9, 1804 and in *Rhode Island Gazette & General Advertiser* on Oct. 30, 1810 and constantly throughout that year: "Thomas Howard, jun. Cabinet Manufacturer. He continues to prosecute it at the Factory above mentioned, where he has now on hand for sale on such terms as he thinks will be considered reasonable, a great variety of cabinet-work . . . also At his Furniture Ware-House in Providence near Mr. Wilkinson's Book-Store, an extensive and valuable assortment of articles in the line of his profession, etc."

HOWD, Whitehead, *New Hartford, Conn.*
Advertised in the *Connecticut Courant*, Oct. 28, 1807: "Whitehead Howd, Has for sale at his Shop 20 rods north of Cowles tavern Most of the articles in the CABINET LINE of mahogany and Cherry-tree, viz. Secretarys, Desks, Swelled and plain Bureaus, dining and breakfast Tables, Sewing and Candle Stands, high post, field and common Bedsteads. Also a handsome assortment of Chairs."

HOWE, James B., *Roxbury, Mass.*
Cabinetmaker who married a daughter of Stephen Badlam circa 1800.

HOWE, John, *Boston, Mass.*
Cabinetmaker and turner on North St., 1796.

HOWE & ALEXANDER, *Boston, Mass.*
Cabinetmakers on Back St., 1793.

HOWELL, William, *Boston, Mass.*
In notice of death in 1717 listed as cabinetmaker.

HOYT, Thaddeus, *Ridgefield, Conn.*
Married Elizabeth A. Hawley, Nov. 2, 1844. *See* entry for Rufus H. Pickett.

HOYT, BABCOCK & APPLETON, *Dorchester Lower Mills, Mass.*
See entry for John Osborn.

HUBBARD, *Boston, Mass.*
Member of firm of Curtis & Hubbard advertising "Fancy & Bamboo chairs" in 1828.

HUBBARD, Miles, *Salem, Mass.*
Married Lucy Peabody, Oct. 27, 1771. Shop in Water St., where he made chairs, burned in 1774.

HUBBARD, Richard, *Boston, Mass.*
Working as chairmaker in 1733.

HUBBELL, John, *Alexandria, Va.*
Working circa 1798. "Combined cabinetmaking with tavern keeping." (Comstock)

HUBON, Henry, *Salem, Mass.*
Son of Stephen and Anna N. Rousseau Hubon, who went to Santo Domingo from Baltimore sometime before 1790. Henry born there May 1, 1790. His father sent him, when twelve years old, on a ship, commanded by a Captain Knight, to be educated in Massachusetts, entrusting the captain with money for this purpose. Knight apprenticed Henry to William Appleton of Salem but kept the money. Henry served his apprenticeship for nine years and became an excellent cabinetmaker. He married Nancy Bedford on Jan. 5, 1812, and in that same year left to fight in the War of 1812. He was captured and taken to England as prisoner. When the war was over he returned to Salem to find his wife dead and himself the father of a daughter Eliza Ann. In 1812 he formed a partnership with Jeremiah Stanniford, with a shop on Charter St., and they made a great deal of furniture for export. The partnership dissolved in 1823 and Stanniford moved to Old Paved St. In 1818 Henry married Frances Dwyer and they were the parents of a son, Henry G. Hubon. In 1842 Hubon was at 30 Neptune St.; in 1850, back at

Charter St. The son, trained as a cooper, joined his father about this time and they devoted their business to the making of coffins. In 1863 Hubon married a third wife, Mrs. Jane Goodridge. He died Sept. 20, 1864. (*American Collector*, Aug. 1939, Feb. 1945)

HUEY, J., *Washington County, Pa.*

A desk of walnut and poplar wood attributed to him has two inscriptions. On the bottom of a small drawer of the cabinet is one which reads, "James Boyar his Desk made June 1808 By me J. Huey Washington County & State of Pennsylvania. DESK for Mr. James Boyar." In another drawer is a second inscription which reads, "James Boyar's desk made of poplar and walnut. James Boyar of Peters Creek, Washington County. Robert Jones, George Rose, Simon Snyder, Governor Dutch." (*Antiques*, Dec. 1931)

HULTKIN, Magnus, *Salem, N. C.*

Working in 1806. Moravian cabinetmaker. (Fries, *Records of the Moravians in North Carolina*)

HUMESTON, Jay, *Charleston, S. C.*

Listed in 1802 directory as Windsor chair maker at 136 Meeting St. Probably the Humiston of Humiston & Stafford.

HUMISTON & STAFFORD, *Charlestown, S. C.*

Advertised in the *Charleston City Gazette and Advertiser*, Nov. 29, 1798: "Humiston & Stafford, Chair Makers. Warranted Windsor Chairs and Green Settees, Of the newest fashion, and of an excellent quality, superior to any ever imported into this city."

HUMPHREYS, A., *Warren, R. I.*

Advertised in the *Clarion of Bristol County, Advertiser*, Jan. 10, 1824: "Cabinet Furniture & Winsor Chairs. The Subscriber, respectfully informs the public that he continues to manufacture Cabinet Furniture of every description at his shop, opposite Capt. Nathan Child's Store, where they can be supplied on favorable terms, Also, Just received an assortment of Chairs of various kinds from 87 cents to $2.75. All orders attended to with punctuality and dispatch. A. Humphreys." The same advertisement continued for many issues.

HUNNEWELL, Richard, *Charlestown, Mass.*

Born 1713; died 1788. A joiner who lost house, shop, furniture, and many tools in fire of 1775.

HUNT, Abel, *Gilford, N. H.*

Arrived in Gilford in 1773. Carried on the carpenter's and cabinetmaker's business. Had the only turning lathe in Gilford and made chairs and other furniture.

HUNT, Benjamin, *Newport, R. I.*

Working as joiner in 1740. (Richardson) It is probable that he moved to Providence, because he signed Providence Cabinet Makers' Agreement (at Rhode Island Historical Society), March 24, 1757.

HUNT, Caleb, *Providence, R. I.*

Listed in directories from 1824 to 1837 as cabinetmaker at Middle and Union streets.

HUNT, Clifford, *Savannah, Ga.*

Advertised from 1785 to 1810 as a coach- and chairmaker.

HUNT, Francis, *Boston, Mass.*

Listed as joiner when he died in 1753. (Nutting, Vol. 3)

HUNT, Ward, *New York City*

Subscribed to *Life of Whitefield* in 1774 as cabinetmaker.

HUNTER, Ebenezer M., *Manchester, Mass.*

Born circa 1822 at Bowdoinham, Me. Married Freelove H. Decker of Wiscasset, Feb. 11, 1849 in Manchester. Cabinetmaker. (Belknap)

HUNTING, Asa, *Boston, Mass.*
Working as cabinet- and chairmaker in 1790.

HUNTINGTON, David, *Newport, R. I.*
Had shop on Elm St. Mason says he sold furniture in New York and West Indies.

HUNTINGTON, Joel and Charles, *Hartford, Conn.*
Advertised in the *American Mercury,* July 30, 1801, as cabinetmakers.

HURD, Jacob, *Charlestown, Mass.*
Born 1676; died 1749. Joiner.

HURDLE, Levi, *Alexandria, Va.*
Advertised in *Alexandria Gazette,* Jan. 1, 1835, announcing that he had taken his brother Thomas I. Hurdle into partnership and "will continue at the old stand, south-west corner of King and Columbus streets, to carry on their business as Chair Manufacturers & Ornamental Painters, and where they will make, and keep constantly for sale at fair prices, a general assortment of Grecian, Fancy, and Windsor Chairs. . . ."

HUSE, John, *Newburyport, Mass.*
Born 1783; died 1827. Cabinetmaker. Married Elizabeth G. Pearson, April 13, 1807. (Belknap)

HUSE, William, *Boston, Mass.*
Cabinetmaker in Boston in 1820 but in Newburyport in 1857. (Belknap)

HUSSEY, Elijah, *Andover, Mass.*
Born in Rochester, N. H. Married Rosanna Moore of Andover, Aug. 15, 1827. Working as cabinetmaker as late as 1848. (Belknap)

HUTCHINSON, John, *Charlestown, Mass.*
Listed in directory for 1803 as cabinetmaker.

HUTCHINSON, Thomas, *Charleston, S.C.*
Not known whether he was born in Charleston or not. Associated with Thomas Elfe (*q.v.*) for some years. Died during the British occupation in 1782. Left most of his property to his godson, Thomas Elfe, Jr. (*q.v.*). (Burton)

HUTCHINSON, Thomas, *Salem, Mass.*
Cabinetmaker. At 16 Walnut St. in 1837; 112 Essex St. in 1857; 205 Essex St. in 1864.

HYDE, Henry, *Boston, Mass.*
Chairmaker on Russell St., 1807.

HYDE, Nathaniel, *Boston, Mass.*
Cabinetmaker on Vine St., 1807.

HYNSON, Nathan, *Baltimore, Md.*
Listed in directories from 1800 to 1810 as cabinetmaker.

INGLIS, Thomas, *New York City*
Subscribed to *Life of Whitefield* in 1774 as cabinetmaker.

INGRAM, Alexander, *Baltimore, Md.*
Listed in directory for 1810 as cabinetmaker.

IVORY, Silas, *Charlestown, Mass.*
Listed as joiner when he married in 1734.

JACKSON, Amos D., *Providence, R. I.*
Listed in directory for 1824 as cabinetmaker on President St.

JACKSON, E., *Providence, R. I.*
Listed in directory for 1824 at Hydraulion St. and 77 North Main.

JACQUES, Richard, *New Brunswick, N. J.*
Made Windsor chairs about 1750. Was a "Spinning Wheel and Windsor Chairmaker." (*Antiques,* Sept. 1928)

JACQUES (or JAQUES), Stephen (Sergeant), *Boston and Newburyport, Mass.*
Working as a joiner in Boston in 1680, but town records of Newburyport show him there as early as 1684, when he married Deborah Plummer. On Dec. 21, 1698 "The towne voted that Serg. Stephen

Jacques should build a meeting house sixty feet in breadth and twenty feet in the stud, for five hundred and thirty pounds." In February 1699 the town voted to pay Serg. Jacques twenty pounds more and to have the meeting house twenty-four feet in the stud rather than twenty. Jacques kept a combination account book and diary, still extant, which ends in 1741. In the Newburyport Historical Society headquarters there is an oak table with heavy turned legs connected by stretchers, with top overhanging the frame on either side, attributed to Jacques.

JAMES, Edward, *Philadelphia, Pa., and New Jersey*

Died 1798. Used an engraved label, "Cabinet & Chair Maker." In 1783 paid an occupation tax of £100. Also worked at some time in New Jersey. (*Catalogue, State Museum*, Trenton, N. J., 1953; Hornor, *International Studio*, Feb. 1929)

JAMES, George W., *Providence, R. I.*

Listed in directories during 1836–37 as chairmaker on Green St.

JAMES, John, *Baltimore, Md.*

Listed in directory for 1796 as cabinetmaker.

JAMES, Samuel, *Baltimore, Md.*

Listed in directory for 1796 as cabinetmaker.

JANVIER, John, *Odessa, Del.*

Born 1777; died 1850. Son of John and Elizabeth Janvier. His father a joiner or cabinetmaker. John learned trade in father's shop. John's account book (in Delaware State Archives, Hall of Records, Dover, Del.) shows he was in business as early as January 1794, and that he did considerable work for Daniel Trotter. Married Ann Jane Wiley in 1807. Inventory of his estate in 1850 showed furniture in Chippendale, Hepplewhite, and Sheraton styles. Did not use a label, but a Sheraton sideboard has an inscription

in his handwriting: "John Janvier, Cantwell's Bridge, 1812." Cantwell's Bridge is the old name for Odessa. Several pieces of his furniture still owned by descendants.

JARVES, John Jackson, *Boston, Mass.*

Father of Deming Jarves of Sandwich-glass fame. Came to Boston from England in 1787, at which time he advertised that he was on Newbury St. He occupied several buildings there; later was at 6 Beech St. There is a copy of his first, very long advertisement at the Massachusetts Historical Society, in which he calls himself both cabinet- and chairmaker. When he died in 1823 he left his wife and children the large sum of $25,000 in addition to six buildings.

JASPER, William, *Charleston, S. C.*

Listed in directory for 1819 as cabinetmaker at 351 King St.

JELLIFF, John, *Newark, N. J.*

Born 1813 in Norwalk, Conn.; died 1893. Fourth of eight children. He and two brothers became cabinetmakers. Moved to Newark when seven years old and was apprenticed to James H. Crane during 1830–36. In April 1836 opened his own shop at 9 Court St., Newark. In 1836 married Mary Marsh of Elizabeth, N. J. In 1837–38 had partnership with Vantilburg at 333 Broad St.; apparently this dissolved by 1843 as directory for that year shows them at different addresses. Had prosperous career and retired in 1890. Much of his carefully made furniture is hand-carved, doubtless by himself. At the New Jersey Historical Society, Newark, there is a bed, dresser, and chair made by Jelliff about 1850. At the Newark Museum there are several pieces made by him.

JENKINS, Michael, *Baltimore, Md.*

Listed in directories during 1803–20 as cabinetmaker.

JENKINS, William, *Salem, Mass.*

Born circa 1760; died 1836. Had cabinetmaking shop on Washington St. in 1796. (Belknap)

JENKS, Edward B., *Providence, R. I.*
Listed in directory for 1828 as cabinetmaker at 68 Broad St.

JENNEY, Samuel, *Plymouth, Mass.*
Nutting says he was a cabinetmaker born circa 1633. Willison's *Saints and Strangers* shows that he moved to Dartmouth in 1652.

JEWETT, John, *Salem, Mass.*
Born 1795 at Ipswich; died 1874 in Salem. First worked in Beverly, where he was in 1817. By 1820 was in Salem with cabinetmaking shop at Liberty and Vine streets. In 1829 moved to shop of A. Hershey opposite Salem Hotel. In 1837 at 261 Essex St.

JOHNS, Isaac, *Baltimore, Md.*
Listed in directory for 1796 as cabinetmaker at 25 North Gay St.

JOHNSON, Edmund, *Salem, Mass.*
Son of Edward. On Nov. 10, 1793 married Betsy Smith. In 1796 had shop at River and Federal streets. Employed many carvers and apprentices. Produced furniture of a fine quality, particularly for export. Johnson evidently at times accompanied his cargo south because notice of his death in 1811 says he was "on his passage from the Southland."
Lockwood in his 1926 edition of *Colonial Furniture in America* illustrates (Fig. XLVI) a four-door secretary bearing the label of Edmund Johnson of Salem. This is apparently one of the earliest of the Salem secretaries. In the side sections there is a cupboard door below a shallow drawer. The upper doors are glazed with straight bars in the familiar thirteen-pane pattern. The cupboard doors have veneered ovals surrounded by a double line of inlay. On the posts, which have square tapered legs, there are inlaid pendants of bellflowers. *Antiques*, May 1933, illustrates a secretary similar to that described above. In

Antiques, June 1954, there is illustrated a tambour desk in Hepplewhite style containing a perspective glass behind the upper door. In the base there are tambour slides instead of drawers. Behind these are the candle and "prospect." A door in the back makes it possible to change the views to be shown without opening the tambour slides in front. This piece has Johnson's label pasted on the back. At the Henry Ford Museum, Dearborn, Mich., there is a Hepplewhite-style breakfront with Johnson's paper label.

JOHNSON, Edward, *Boston, Mass.*
Working as cabinetmaker in Boston in 1639. Apparently moved to Charlestown and then to Woburn, where he died in 1672.

JOHNSON, Edward, *Salem, Mass.*
Born 1722 in Lynn; died 1799 in Salem. Father of ten children, of whom Edmund was one. Employed by the Sandersons during 1793–95.

JOHNSON, Emery, *Providence, R. I.*
Listed in directory for 1828 as cabinetmaker at 133 High St.

JOHNSON, Jedediah, *Salem, Mass.*
Born circa 1759; died 1821. Brother of Edmund. Was an excellent chairmaker. Made chairs for Derby in 1798.

JOHNSON, John, *Annapolis, Md.*
Working as cabinetmaker in 1763.

JOHNSON, Jonathan, *Lynn, Mass.*
Born circa 1683; died 1741. Chairmaker. (Belknap)

JOHNSON, Micaiah, *Salem, Mass.*
Born circa 1767; died 1817 in Boston. Another brother of Edmund. Employed by Sandersons as chairmaker during 1793–95.

JOHNSON, Thomas, *Boston, Mass.*
Born in Charlestown in 1715. Married in 1739. Listed as cabinetmaker in 1761.

JOHNSON, Thomas, *Baltimore, Md.*
    Listed in directory for 1799 as cabinet-maker.

JOHNSON, William, *Lowell, Mass.*
    Working in 1833. *See* entry for Elwin C. Shaw.

JOHNSTON, Edward, *Charleston, S. C.*
    Advertised in *South Carolina Gazette,* April 23, 1796: "Johnson, Edward, Cab-inet-Maker, late from Philadelphia Begs leave to inform the public in general, that he has opened a Ware-Room in Meeting-street, nearly opposite the Scotch-Church, where he has for sale, A general Assort-ment of Modern and Elegant Cabinet work, Finished in a style of Elegance and Neatness that Surpasses anything of the kind, hitherto offered for Sale in this City. Amongst which are: Capital cylin-der fall desks and bookcases, side boards, ladies commodes, drawers of different patterns, card tables of various patterns, and figures, breakfast ditto, ditto; and a variety of Chairs of newest patterns, with sundry other articles in the above branch. Likewise, Two suits of Tables, superbly finished for a Drawing-Room, Beautiful Japanned Chairs, or painted for do. or bed chambers. And various kinds of Fire Skreens. N.B. E Johnson, having engaged workmen of the first abilities, intends carrying on the Cabinet-Making Business, in all its various branches at his Ware-room, where orders are received and exe-cuted with dispatch." Burton says he died four months later, at which time he was listed as Edward Johnston, cabinetmaker.

JONES, Abraham, *Charleston, S. C.*
    Died Jan. 13, 1857. Listed in directories during 1813–57 as cabinetmaker. Had shop on Beaufain St.

JONES, Hamilton, *Baltimore, Md.*
    Cabinetmaker at corner of Sharp St. and German Lane in 1833. (Varley)

JONES, Nathaniel, *Southington, Conn.*
    Died 1825. Advertised in *Connecticut Courant,* June 7, 1809: "Nathaniel Jones,

Cabinet & Chairmaker, Respectfully in-forms the public, that he carries on the CABINET and CHAIRMAKING business, in the various branches. Also that he has ob-tained a letter, patent from the President of the United States, for the exclusive right of making and vending eagle top HAIRCOMBS. This is therefore to caution all persons, not to intrude on the said patent, on penalty of the law, without purchasing the right of said Jones; will be sold on liberal terms." (*Southington Vital Statistics*)

JONES, Robert W., *Charleston, S. C.*
    Listed in 1807 directory as cabinet-maker.

JONES, Thomas, *Philadelphia, Pa.*
    Arrived in Philadelphia from London and served a four-year apprenticeship with Gostelowe from 1773. (Hornor)

JONES, William, *Salem, Mass.*
    Baptized in 1790 at Marblehead. In 1823 had cabinetmaking shop at 2 South St. Still there in 1837.

JONES, William, *Charleston, S. C.*
    Died 1792. Listed in 1790 directory as cabinetmaker at 51 Broad St. On April 9, 1791 advertised in *City Gazette or Daily Advertiser* that he intended to carry on the upholstering business as well as cab-inetmaking and that he needed one or two journeyman cabinetmakers. (Burton)

JONES, William F., *Salem, Mass.*
    Born Feb. 15, 1817. Doubtless son of William Jones of Salem; *see* above. Listed as sawyer in 1861 and as cabinetmaker in 1864.

JUDD, David, *Northampton, Mass.*
    Cabinet- and chairmaker about 1800. (Judd)

KECKLEY, John, *Charleston, S. C.*
    Listed in directories during 1809–22.

KEELER, George, *Ridgefield, Conn.*
    See entry for Rufus H. Pickett.

KELSA, James, *Boston, Mass.*
Cabinetmaker on Water St. in 1796.

KELSO, John, *New York City*
Made a freeman in 1774 as a Windsor chair maker. In same year advertised that he "served a regular apprenticeship in one of the first shops in that way in Philadelphia."

KENDALL, Gilman, *Dunstable, Mass.*
Born Sept. 22, 1827; died Nov. 11, 1847. Cabinetmaker. (Belknap)

KENN, Lenier, *Boston, Mass.*
Working in 1739. Nutting says he was a cabinetmaker, partner of Thomas Gibbons.

KENNEDY, George, *Northcutt's Mills, Townsend Creek, Ky.*
Advertised in 1815 that he had had previous experience as a cabinetmaker in Baltimore and New York.

KENNEDY, Samuel, *Baltimore, Md.*
Listed in directories for 1802 and 1803 as cabinetmaker.

KENNEDY, William, *Williamsburg, Va.*
Advertised as cabinetmaker in *Virginia Gazette,* 1769.

KENT, Ebenezer, *Charlestown, Mass.*
Listed as a cabinetmaker who suffered loss in fire of 1775.

KERWOOD, William, *Trenton, N. J.*
Born 1779 in Monmouthshire, Wales. Came to America and settled at Morrisville near Trenton in 1785. In 1794 was apprenticed to a cabinetmaker in Philadelphia. In 1803 moved to Trenton. In loan exhibition at the N. J. State Museum, Trenton, 1929, he was represented by a Sheraton-style mahogany table with reeded legs.

KESLER, Michael, *Philadelphia, Pa.*
Paid an occupation tax in 1783. Died in 1794. (Hornor)

KETTELL, Jonathan, *Newburyport, Mass.*
Born 1759 in Charlestown; died 1848. Cabinetmaker who moved to Newburyport after Charlestown fire in 1775.

KIMBALL, Abraham, *Salem, Mass.*
Chairmaker. Member of firm of Kimball & Sargent, on Essex St. in 1821; at 4 Holyoke Place in 1831. Disappears from directory in 1846.

KIMBALL, Elias, *Salem, Mass.*
Cabinetmaker at 199 Essex St. in 1837.

KIMBALL, James, Jr., *Salem, Mass.*
Born Oct. 14, 1808. Chairmaker at 127 Essex St. in 1837. Working until 1861.

KIMBALL, Jeremiah, *Ipswich, Mass.*
Cabinetmaker about 1790. (Waters)

KIMBALL, Joseph, *Canterbury, N. H.*
Advertised in 1812 for an apprentice.

KIMBALL, Samuel T., *Salem, Mass.*
Born Nov. 3, 1810. Cabinetmaker working for Hill, Henderson & Co. In 1846 with Henderson, Allen & Co. In 1850 member of Henderson & Kimball, 38 Washington St.

KIMBALL & SARGENT, *Salem, Mass.*
See entries for Abraham Kimball, Winthrop Sargent, John Whipple, and Alexander White.

KING, Ashbel (Captain), *Suffield, Conn.*
Born Jan. 26, 1747/8; died May 21, 1806. Son of Joseph and Hannah King. Married Jemima Smith, Dec. 19, 1782. Probably worked with his brother Eliphalet. Inventory of his estate lists "one half of a joiner's shop." His account books at Kent Memorial Library, Suffield, reveal he made some furniture but was more of a housewright than cabinetmaker. Doubtless learned his trade with Joseph Howard. (*Suffield Vital Statistics*)

KING, Isaac B., *Suffield, Conn.*
Born 1801; died 1870. Inventory of estate listed "one half of a joiner's shop."

KING, Jacob, *Baltimore, Md.*
    Listed in directory for 1799 as cabinet-maker.

KING, John, *Suffield, Conn.*
    Born 1777; died 1835. Chest of his joiner's tools at Suffield Historical Society. (Bissell)

KING, Nathaniel Phippen, *Danvers and Salem, Mass.*
    Baptized Aug. 28, 1796. Son of William. He attempted to carry on his father's trade in Salem. Advertised in *Salem Gazette*, Jan. 26, 1819, the removal of his shop to Essex St., "a few doors east of North Street where he intends manufacturing the Grecian and Gothic Cabinet Work, also Mahogany Chairs in the most fashionable and elegant style." Died Nov. 3, 1819. His mother was appointed administrator of the estate and his tools and shop were sold at auction. (Bentley)

KING, William, *Salem, Mass.*
    Ancestors came to Salem from England. William baptized Feb. 24, 1754. Married daughter of Deacon Nathaniel Phippen. On July 21, 1789 advertised in *Salem Mercury* cabinetwork in its various branches carried on at his shop. He was evidently irresponsible, for he soon left a letter saying he was going away and deserted his family. He stole a horse and buggy and was apprehended at New Haven, Conn. In 1793 he started off with his family but somewhere along the line left them stranded. The Rev. William Bentley notes under date of July 3, 1796: "News from Philadelphia that William King belonging to a good family in this Town after having dragged his family from Town to Town, left a note that he was going to drown himself and disappeared. It is supposed that he means to ramble unincumbered. The family are to return to Salem." Apparently William did go on alone, and in 1806 he was advertising in Hanover, N. H. Much data about the family appear in Bentley's diary.

KINGMAN, Seth, *Boston, Mass.*
    Cabinetmaker on Fish St. in 1789.

KINKAID, Alexander, *Charleston, S. C.*
    Listed in 1809 directory as cabinet-maker at 84 Tradd St.

KINSMAN, Nathaniel, Jr., *Gloucester, Mass.*
    Born Oct. 5, 1745; died before Sept. 4, 1797. Cabinetmaker. (Belknap)

KINSMAN, Obed Carter, *Manchester, Mass.*
    Baptized March 25, 1817. Cabinetmaker. (Belknap)

KINSMAN, William Henry, *Manchester, Mass.*
    Baptized circa 1824. Cabinetmaker. (Belknap)

KIRKPATRICK, James, *Baltimore, Md.*
    Listed in directories of 1807 and 1808 as cabinetmaker.

KIRKWOOD, James, *Charleston, S. C.*
    Born 1716; died 1781. Cabinetmaker living on Broad St. (Burton)

KITFIELD, Benjamin K., Jr., *Manchester, Mass.*
    Born Nov. 4, 1817. Cabinetmaker. (Belknap)

KITFIELD, Thomas Hooper, *Manchester, Mass.*
    Born March 19, 1818. Cabinetmaker. Brother of Benjamin.

KNEELAND, Samuel, *Hartford, Conn.*
    Born 1755; died 1828. In partnership with Lemuel Adams (q.v.). This association dissolved in 1795 and each established himself in his own shop. Not known where he learned his trade but Hartford had any number of cabinetmakers who could have taught him. From advertisements it seems probable that he was in business for himself from 1789 at least. In the *American Mercury*, April 13, 1789, he advertised "his shop near the bridge."

In the same paper, Aug. 10, 1789, he announced that he had "Removed from the bridge to his house near Mr. Blis's tan works, where he still continues to carry on the Cabinet and Chair making business in the various branches as usual." On March 28, 1791 he again advertised that he continued to carry on the cabinet- and chairmaking business at his house a few rods west of Mr. Jonathan Butler's Tan Works. On Feb. 6, 1792 he advertised for "one or two likely Boys that can be well recommended, as apprentices to the Cabinet-Making Business; such may find a place by applying to Samuel Kneeland, a few rods West of Mr. Jonathan Butlers Tan-Works, etc."

After the partnership with Adams was dissolved in 1795, Kneeland apparently moved to Farmington, not far from Hartford. On Feb. 5, 1798 he advertised in the *Connecticut Courant*: "Samuel Kneeland, Cabinet and Chair Maker, Farmington, Begs leave to acquaint his friends and the public, that he has lately removed from Hartford to the noted stand occupied by Mr. Thomas Bulkley, cabinet maker, deceased; where he intends to carry on the above business in all its branches, in the most modern fashions of cherry or mahogany. He likewise quicksilvers, frames and gilds Looking Glasses of every description. He wants a Journeyman that is a workman. Likewise a likely active Boy as apprentice to the above business; such may find good encouragement by applying as above." On the bill rendered by Jeremiah Halsey for furnishings supplied the Old State House in 1796 (photostatic copy at Connecticut State Library) Kneeland's name is listed for "Tables, &c 53."

KNEELAND & ADAMS, *Hartford, Conn.*

In partnership from 1792 to 1795, when each established himself independently. The first advertisement of Kneeland & Adams appeared in the *American Mercury*, Sept. 17, 1792. They again advertised in October and November 1793: "Kneeland & Adams Respectfully informs the Gentlemen and Ladies, that they can supply them with every kind of Cabinet work, on very short notice, as they have in constant employ the best workmen, from New York and Boston. They now have on hand, and ready for sale, an elegant assortment of Cabinet furniture, consisting of Parlour, chamber and Hall Chairs, Mahogany with swelled and concave seats, neatly covered with Satten— Hair seating—mahogany and cherrytree Desks and Book-Cases, ditto Commode and Plain Beuroes, Mahogany Sectretarys and Sideboards, Dining, Tea and Breakfast Tables, Mahogany Card and Pembroke Tables, square, round and oval inlaid and Plain, Pier, Writing and Kitchen Tables, High post, Field, Cross and Cord Bedsteads, Clocks and Time-Pieces, Clock Cases of various prices, Candle Stands, Tea-Trays and Sarvers, Kitchen Chairs, Elegant Looking Glasses, from one to thirty Dollars each, and a good assortment of China faced Clock Pins. All which they offer for sale on reasonable terms for Cash, Country produce and Lumber of every kind. Old Looking Glass Plates Quicksilvered, Framed, Gilt and Burnished as usual." The partnership apparently did no advertising in the Hartford papers in 1794 although they were advertising in the *New Hampshire Journal* during that year that they would "supply all sorts of fine furniture." On March 16, 1795 and again on March 23, the *American Mercury* contained the following: "The Co-Partnership of Kneeland & Adams is this day by mutual consent dissolved. Samuel Kneeland. Lemuel Adams. Hartford March 5, 1795."

At the Winterthur Museum, Delaware, there is a cherry serpentine-front chest of drawers (Downs, No. 173) made in 1793 with the engraved label of Kneeland & Adams in the top drawer.

KNIGHT, Enoch, *Newbury, Mass.*

Born Jan. 26, 1771; died Nov. 16, 1844. Cabinetmaker at 46 North St., 1837-42. (Belknap)

KNOLTON, David, *New York City*

Made a freeman in 1770; listed as cabinetmaker.

KNOWLTON, Abraham, *Salem, Mass.*

Probably born in Ipswich in 1756; died Dec. 5, 1797. Cabinetmaker who arrived in Salem with his brother Nathaniel (*q.v.*) in 1783. (Belknap; Bentley)

KNOWLTON, Ebenezer, *Boston, Mass.*

Born at Ipswich, and baptized Jan. 18, 1769. Grandson of Abraham Knowlton, a well-known carpenter who built the third building of the First Church in Ipswich in 1749; a church so fine architecturally that a replica of it was later built in Boston. Ebenezer evidently served his apprenticeship in Ipswich. In 1796, at the age of twenty-seven, he was established in a shop on Ann St., Boston. Later he was on Moore's Wharf. In 1805 his shop was on Fish St., his home on North Sq. Last mentioned in Cotton's City Directory in 1810, when his shop was still on Fish St., his home at 36 Prince St. The following notice appeared in the *Columbian Centenil* on Dec. 26, 1810: "In this town on Saturday night, Mr. Ebenezer Knowlton, Ae. 41, after a long and painful illness, which he bore with fortitude; funeral from his late dwelling house No. 36 Prince-street, this afternoon at one half past two o'clock, weather permitting; relations and friends are requested to attend without further notice." In the same paper, Jan. 26, 1811, appeared the following: "On Monday, next at 10 o'clk. At the Shop lately occupied by EBENEZER KNOWLTON, deceased. All the stock in Trade of said Knowlton consisting of finished and unfinished Mahogany and other Furniture; Chairs of all kinds; Mahogany and other Boards and Planks; Tools &c. ALSO AT 12 O'CLOCK—at the House lately occupied by said deceased in Prince-street—Several articles of useful and Handsome FURNITURE. J. Jutau, auct'r."

In 1933 a Sheraton-style mahogany secretary with tambour front was located.

On the bottom of the first long drawer a much worn label read: "Ebenezer Knowlton Makes and has for Sale at his Shop in Fore-Street, at the head of Moore's Wood-Wharf, Boston, Cabinet Furniture and Chairs of all kinds. On reasonable Terms for Cash." In discussing this piece Ormsbee said, "This piece . . . does show that Knowlton was a competent and capable workman who knew how to employ crotch veneering and inlay for the decorative effects so essential for a well executed piece in the Sheraton manner." (Ormsbee, *American Collector*, Dec. 1933)

KNOWLTON, Nathaniel, *Salem, Mass.*

Baptized Feb. 22, 1761. Bentley listed him as a cabinetmaker in 1785. He considered him and his brother Abraham clever workmen but unreliable.

KNOWLTON, Nathaniel, Sr., *Eliot, Me.*

Born 1786 in Eliot; died 1859. Learned his cabinetmaking trade in Eliot. In the later years of his life devoted much time to carriage-making. (*Biographical Review . . . Leading Citizens of York County, Maine*, Boston, 1896)

KNOWLTON, William, *Salem, Mass.*

Born March 15, 1805 in Brandon, Vt.; died before 1850. Working as turner in Salem from 1837 to 1846. In 1840 appears as cabinetmaker on the Charitable Mechanics list.

KNOWLTON, Willis Sargent, *Manchester and Salem, Mass.*

Born Oct. 5, 1808. Cabinetmaker in Manchester. In 1855 located in Salem at 12 March St.

KOONES, Charles, *Alexandria, Va.*

Advertised in *Alexandria Gazette*, Jan. 1, 1835, as a "cabinet, chair and sofa maker."

LACROIX, Francis Joseph, *Charleston, S. C.*

Born 1775. Listed in directory for 1806 as cabinetmaker at 53 Meeting St. Died

Aug. 17, 1806. His death notice gave his age as thirty-one and said he was a native of the province of Champagne, France. (Burton)

LAMBERT, Porter R., *Salem, Mass.*
Born Aug. 14, 1813. In 1842 and as late as 1855 located at 296 Essex St. Cabinetmaker. (Belknap)

LAMPRELL, Benjamin A., *Providence, R.I.*
In 1836 and 1837 listed as cabinetmaker at Fulton and Walnut streets.

LAMSON, Amos, *Salem, Mass.*
Born circa 1769; died May 20, 1821. Cabinetmaker with shop on Marlborough St. (Belknap)

LAMSON, Benjamin, *Boston, Mass.*
Listed as cabinetmaker in 1833.

LAMSON, Francis, *Charlestown, Mass.*
Designated as a joiner on list of those who lost tools in fire of 1775.

LAMSON, William, *Charlestown, Mass.*
Listed as chairmaker in 1789.

LANDER, William 2nd, *Salem, Mass.*
Chairmaker. Died April 22, 1778. (Belknap)

LANE, John, *Boston, Mass.*
Notice of death in 1737 lists him as chairmaker.

LANE, John, *Candia, N. H.*
Working 1796–1800. Built pews and steeple for church as well as furniture and spinning wheels. (*American Collector,* June 1937)

LANE, Nicholas, *Salem, Mass.*
Listed as cabinetmaker at 6 Charter St. in 1837.

LANGLEY, Nathan, *Newport, R. I.*
Working as joiner in 1750. (Richardson)

LANGWORTHY, James, *Newport, R. I.*
Working as joiner in 1732. (Richardson)

LANNING, John, *Salem, N. J.*
Working as cabinet- and chairmaker in 1778. (*Antiques,* Sept. 1952)

LANNUIER, Charles Honoré, *New York City*
Born 1779; died Oct. 16, 1819. Arrived from France with two brothers sometime in the 1790s. It is possible that for some years after his arrival he worked in Duncan Phyfe's shop. In 1805 listed in the New York Directory as "Henry Lannuier, cabinetmaker, 60 Broad St." Here he had a combination shop and warehouse; he and his family living upstairs. Apparently he was successful and employed another Frenchman, John Gruez, as his shop foreman. Lannuier worked in Sheraton and French Empire styles and at times his work so closely resembles that of Phyfe as to be confusing. He used two types of labels; the first a simple printed sticker, the second an elaborate engraved one, but both were in English and French. The engraved label is as follows:

> HRE. LANNUIER
> CABINET MAKER FROM PARIS
> KIPS IS WHARE HOUSE OF
> NEW FASHION FOURNITURE
> BROAD STREET, NO. 60
> NEW-YORK
>
> ───────────
>
> HRE. LANNUIER
> EBENISTE DE PARIS
> TIENT FABRIQUE &
> MAGASIN DE MEUBLES
> LES PLUS A LA MODE
> NEW-YORK

At times he used a steel die that stamped his name "H. Lannuier" into the wood in the usual French method of marking.

His successful career was a short one. In the *Spectator* of Oct. 18, 1819 appeared the following notice: "On Saturday evening after a lingering illness, Charles Honore Lannuier, Aged 40." He was buried in old St. Patrick's Cathedral, Mulberry St., Oct. 18, 1819. Gruez attempted unsuccessfully to carry on the business. A transcript of the minutes of the New York Common Council for

July 13, 1812 shows that Lannuier made mahogany chairs, etc. for the Common Council room at a cost of $409. There is a labeled card table at the Metropolitan Museum of Art, New York City, and other labeled pieces are at many museums, including that of the City of New York and the Winterthur Museum, Delaware. At the Albany (N. Y.) Institute of History and Art there is a sleigh-type mahogany bed with ormolu mounts. Both the head and foot boards bear the label of Lannuier. (PLATE XXXI) This bed was formerly in the Van Rensselaer Manor House, Albany. (*American Collector*, June 1935; *Antiques*, Jan. 1954)

LAPIERE, Gilbert Bernard James, *Charleston, S. C.*
  Born 1774. Listed in 1806 directory as cabinetmaker at 30 Union St. When taking out citizenship papers, Nov. 13, 1807, said he was thirty-three and a native of Metz, France. Died 1814. In his will, probated Oct. 28, 1814, left his tools to his copartner Thomas Lejeune. (Burton)

LARKIN, Edward, *Charlestown, Mass.*
  At the time of his death in 1677 listed as turner.

LARKIN, Edward, Jr., *Charlestown, Mass.*
  Born 1689; died 1751. Doubtless grandson of Edward. Chairmaker.

LARKIN, Elisha, *Boston, Mass.*
  Cabinetmaker on Back St. in 1796.

LARKIN, John, *Charlestown, Mass.*
  Possibly a brother of Edward. Turner. Married Nov. 9, 1664.

LARKIN, John, *Charlestown, Mass.*
  Born 1690; died 1720. Brother of Edward Jr. Chairmaker.

LARKIN, John, *Boston, Mass.*
  Born 1724; died 1798. Son of Edward Jr. Chairmaker in Black Horse Lane in 1798. Married Katharine Frothingham. Worked in Cambridge, from where he

enlisted in army. In Boston at time of death.

LARKIN, Samuel, *Charlestown, Mass.*
  Born 1701; died 1784. Chairmaker who claimed loss insurance from fire of 1775. Then moved to Southborough.

LARKIN, Thomas, *Charlestown, Mass.*
  Born 1730; died 1799. Chairmaker who went to Marlborough after fire of 1775.

LASKY, Benjamin, *Marblehead, Mass.*
  Born 1734/5; died 1778. Chairmaker. (Belknap)

LASKY, Thomas, *Marblehead, Mass.*
  Baptized 1696/7. Chairmaker. (Belknap)

LATHAM, Edward, *Baltimore, Md.*
  Listed as cabinetmaker in 1810.

LATTA, William, *Boston, Mass.*
  On arrival from Scotland in 1768 listed as joiner.

LAW, Anthony, *Baltimore, Md.*
  Listed in directories during 1799–1818 as cabinetmaker.

LAW & DENMEAD, *Baltimore, Md.*
  Listed in directories for 1804 and 1805 as cabinetmakers.

LAWRENCE, Daniel, *Providence, R. I.*
  Advertised in 1787: "Daniel Lawrence informs the respectable citizens that he carries on the chair-making Business in Westminster street where he makes and sells all kinds of Windsor Chairs, such as Round About Chairs, Dining Chairs, Garden-Chairs, also sofas, settees, etc. in the newest and best Fashions, neat, elegant and strong, beautifully painted, after the Philadelphia mode, warranted of good seasoned Materials, so firmly put to-gether as not to deceive the Purchasers by an untimely coming to pieces."

LAWRENCE, Edward, *Charlestown, Mass.*
  In partnership with Charles Forster

(at times spelled Foster) about 1800 under name of Forster & Lawrence and then with Abraham Crowninshield under name of Forster, Lawrence & Co.

LAWRENCE, John, *Charlestown, Mass.*
Listed as joiner in 1696.

LAWRENCE, Samuel, *New York City*
Advertised in newspaper in 1766 as chairmaker.

LAWSON, John, *Baltimore, Md.*
Listed in directory for 1808 as cabinetmaker.

LAWSON, Richard, *Baltimore, Md.*
Worked for thirteen years with Seddons of London. Bordley says in his unpublished manuscript at the Maryland Historical Society: "A designer as well as a cabinetmaker, who drew and sold shop designs. He was the only cabinetmaker to advertise for Mahogany Toys (inlay motives). For 13 years enjoyed the traditional training of an English cabinet maker in the shop of Seddons, the most fashionable cabinet maker of this time in London." Bordley believed that Jean Garnier was Lawson's decorator and that James Smith who advertised as a carver, gilder, glass painter, mirror maker, and oval-panel turner was his carver and gilder. In 1785 became a partner in firm of Bankson & Lawson (*q.v.*).

LAWTON, Robert, Jr., *Newport, R. I.*
Maker of a Hepplewhite-style table, privately owned, that bears the date "Newport 20th of 5th Mon. 1794." At that time Lawton was on Broad St. Carpenter shows a table (No. 58) belonging to him with Lawton's label; it shows the date July 4, 1798, at which time he was on Spring St. (Richardson)

LEACH, Daniel, Jr., *Manchester, Mass.*
Born March 10, 1822. Cabinetmaker.

LEACH, Lewis, *Dorchester Lower Mills, Mass.*
Born 1777; died 1841. Cabinetmaker.

At this time there were many cabinetmakers in Dorchester Lower Mills. *See* entry for Badlam, Sr.

LEARNED, Elijah, *Boston, Mass.*
Born 1765; died 1827. Cabinetmaker on Back St. in 1796.

LEATHERS, William, *Charlestown, Mass.*
Cabinetmaker who suffered loss in fire of 1775.

LEAVER, Gabriel, *Savannah, Ga.*
Working 1757-95. Owned a plantation house three miles west of Savannah and kept two apprentices. His obituary in the *Georgia Gazette*, Oct. 29, 1795. (Comstock)

LEAVITT, John, *Suffield, Conn.*
Born 1724; died 1798. Inventory lists a chest of joiner's tools, a cherry framed chair, and a compass chair. (Bissell)

LEAVITT, Thaddeus, *Suffield, Conn.*
Born 1750; died 1813. Bissell shows a commode (pl. 13) with Leavitt's name burned on it. Leavitt's account book, at the Kent Memorial Library, Suffield, indicates he made furniture.

LEE, Ariel P., *Manchester, Mass.*
Born circa 1821. Cabinetmaker. (Belknap)

LEE, Chapman, *Charlton, Mass.*
Born 1799; died 1849. Country craftsman who made several hundred pieces of furniture including chests, tables, beds, cradles, chairs, desks, stands, cupboards, and coffins. (*Antiques*, Aug. 1953)

LEE, Charles, *Manchester, Mass.*
Born circa 1817. Cabinetmaker. (Belknap)

LEE, Henry F., *Manchester, Mass.*
Born circa 1808. Cabinetmaker. (Belknap)

LEE, Robert, *Newport, R. I.*
In partnership with Adam S. Coe on Long Wharf, 1820. (*Records,* Newport Historical Society)

LEE, Samuel, *Baltimore, Md.*
Listed in directories during 1796–1800 as cabinetmaker.

LEE, Thomas, *Charleston, S. C.*
Born 1780. A native of Scotland. Probably trained there. In 1804 formed a partnership with John Gros (*q.v.*) which lasted until Lee's death on Feb. 10, 1814.

LEES, Samuel, *Philadelphia, Pa.*
Cabinetmaker. Died 1798. (Hornor)

LEGARE, Solomon, Jr., *Charleston, S. C.*
Born 1703; died November 1774. Son of silversmith Solomon Legare of Charleston. On Sept. 26, 1754 advertised in the *South Carolina Gazette:* "Any Person may be supplied with black chairs at 12 1 per dozen, white ditto a 9 1. low chairs at 15 s. a piece, and children's chairs at 12 s. 6 d. and 15 s. by applying to me at my plantation on *John's-island,* or Mr. *Thomas Legare* next door to the EXCHANGE COFFEE-HOUSE in Charles-Town. *Solomon Legare,* junior." In addition to chairmaking, he cultivated his plantation and later operated a tannery in Charleston. (Burton)

LEHMAN, Benjamin, *Philadelphia, Pa.*
Born 1760. Apprenticed to Jacob Knorr, carpenter, of Germantown. In addition to his carpenter business and furniture making, carried on a lumber business and livery stable. In 1786 compiled a book of prices in his own handwriting. This has been discovered. It consists of forty-three pages and has the title *Prices of Cabinet and Chair Work.* This was written ten years earlier than the *Book of Prices* published by the Federal Society of Philadelphia Cabinetmakers. It is not known whether he marked his pieces or not. (Gillingham, *Bulletin,* Historical Society of Pennsylvania, Oct. 1930; Hornor)

LEIGH, John E., *Trenton, N. J.*
A writing-arm chair (No. 39) in the loan exhibition at the N. J. State Museum, Trenton, in 1953, had beneath the seat the printed label "John E. Leigh, Cabinetmaker, 107 Factory Street, Trenton, N. J."

LEIGHTON (or LAIGHTON), Daniel, *Gloucester, Mass.*
Born 1764; died 1794. Cabinetmaker. (Belknap)

LEJEUNE, Thomas, *Charleston, S. C.*
Listed in directory for 1816. *See* entry for Lapiere.

LEMASTER, George, *Marblehead, Mass.*
Baptized July 7, 1793. Cabinetmaker.

LEMON, Charles, *Salem, Mass.*
Probably born in Boston. In partnership with his brother John on Court St., Salem, in 1796. (Perley, *Salem in* 1700)

LEMON, John, *Salem, Mass.*
Brother of Charles (*q.v.*) and senior partner.

LEMON, William, *Salem, Mass.*
A double chest of drawers, in the Karolik Collection, Boston Museum of Fine Arts, attributed to Lemon with carving by Samuel McIntire, is said to be the richest piece of eighteenth-century American furniture "architecturally." (PLATE XXII) On Oct. 22, 1796, McIntire billed Elizabeth, daughter of Elias Hasket Derby, for carving "a Case Drawers Made by Mr. Lemon." Lemon is believed to have moved from Salem to Boston and to have been residing there at the time of his death in 1827. (Hipkiss)

LESTER, William, *Boston, Mass.*
Listed in directory for 1800 as cabinetmaker.

LETCHWORTH, John, *Philadelphia, Pa.*
Born 1759. Hornor says that Letchworth made no less than eight distinct

types of Windsor chairs in addition to benches. A feature of his work was the use of mahogany for arms, which were left unpainted even on painted chairs. In 1791 made chairs for the "New City Hall" at Fifth and Chestnut streets. In 1796 made two sets of side chairs and armed "Oval Windsor Chairs" for William Meredith. One set was painted green, the other white. Hornor shows illustrations of several chairs made by Letchworth: a bamboo turned Windsor with mahogany arms (pl. 475); a marked, balloon-back Windsor with center splat similar to those found on English Windsors (pl. 476); and a marked ladderback, made about 1790, with legs of maple, seat of poplar, arms of mahogany, uprights of hickory, and the pierced slats of walnut (pl. 477). Letchworth retired from business about 1805. He was a member of and minister in the Society of Friends. Pictured in *Antiques*, January 1951, is a pair of Windsor loveseats with mahogany arms and Letchworth's mark.

LEVELY, William, *Baltimore, Md.*
Listed in directory for 1804 as cabinetmaker.

LEVERETT, William, *Boston, Mass.*
Listed in directory for 1804 as cabinetmaker who also maintained a warehouse.

LEWIS, George, *Boston, Mass.*
Listed in directory for 1807 as cabinetmaker on Spring Lane.

LEWIS, James, *Stratford, N. H.*
"Uncle Jimmy's [James known as such locally] pieces are usually cherry inlaid with delicate lines of a light wood." (Thompson)

LEWIS, William, *Charleston, S. C.*
Listed in directory for 1809 as cabinetmaker at 99 Queen St.

LIHAULT, Augustus, *Baltimore, Md.*
Listed in directory for 1803 as cabinetmaker.

LILLY, William, *Baltimore, Md.*
Listed in directory for 1799 as cabinetmaker.

LINCOLN, Amos, *Boston, Mass.*
Listed in directory for 1799 as cabinetmaker.

LINCOLN, Ebed, *Gloucester, Mass.*
Born 1748; died 1817. Cabinetmaker. (Belknap)

LINCOLN, Jedediah, *Boston, Mass.*
Listed in directory for 1799 as cabinetmaker.

LINCOLN, Thomas, *Hardin County, Ky.*
Born 1778; died 1851. Married Nancy Hanks, June 12, 1806. History lists Thomas as a migratory carpenter living in a log cabin when his son Abraham was born. Carl Sandburg, in *Abraham Lincoln, The Prairie Years*, calls him a "carpenter and cabinetmaker" and says, "His neighbors knew him as a good workman, a handy man with the ax, the saw, the drawknife, and the hammer." He also states that "Tom worked at the carpenter's trade, made cabinets, door-frames, window sash and coffins." At the J. B. Speed Art Museum, Louisville, Ky., there is a cupboard known as the "Lincoln corner cupboard." Although this is unsigned, it is attributed to Thomas.

LINDENBERGER, Charles, *Baltimore, Md.*
Listed in first Baltimore directory, 1796, as cabinetmaker.

LINDSAY, Joseph, *Marblehead, Mass.*
Died 1764. Cabinetmaker. (Belknap)

LINDSON, John, *Baltimore, Md.*
Advertised as cabinetmaker in 1785.

LINING, Thomas, *Charleston, S. C.*
First advertisement, May 2, 1748, in *South Carolina Gazette* states that he was "lately arrived from London." At that time on Broad St. In 1754 advertised again: "Thomas Lining, Cabinet and

Chair Maker from London, has removed into the House lately possessed by Mr. Macarton . . . opposite to Isaac Mazyck Esq.; in Broad-street." Lining died September 1763 and the inventory of his estate showed him to have been prosperous. Considerable cypress was listed in the inventory, showing that, like others in Charleston, he used this as secondary wood in the construction of his furniture. (Burton)

LINSEY, Daniel, *Boston, Mass.*
Arrived in Boston in 1637 with Samuel Dix, to whom he was apprenticed. (Nutting, Vol. 3)

LINSLEY, Harvey J., *Woodbury, Conn.*
Made furniture in the Sheraton style of cherry and mahogany. Mrs. William Minor of Woodbury owns a two-drawer stand of cherry with mahogany veneered front, a three-drawer bureau similar in some details to the stand, and an oval tip-top table made by Linsley. Standing today, practically on the dividing line between the towns of Woodbury and Southbury, is a house where lived the Trowbridge family. A large cherry tree was cut down on this property and the wood taken to Linsley's cabinet-shop, where it was made into the above furniture. Two matching stands were made to stand between the windows in the front rooms. When Mrs. Minor's family—the Grahams—bought the property from the Trowbridges, they were given the furniture. The second stand belongs to Mrs. Minor's sister.
When the First Congregational Church of Woodbury was built about 1818, Linsley brought from Central America the mahogany for the railing on the back of the pews. Linsley's tombstone in the Old Cemetery, Woodbury, gives the following dates: born August 24, 1797; died March 25, 1853.
The author is grateful for the data on Linsley furnished by Mrs. William Minor, Miss Clara Nichols, and Mrs. Julia P. Strong, all of Woodbury. (Cothren)

LISCOMB, Samuel, *Providence, R. I.*
Listed in directory for 1824 as cabinetmaker on President St.

LITTLE, John, *Amesbury, Mass.*
Died July 9, 1812. Married in 1798. Cabinetmaker. (Belknap)

LITTLE, John, *Salisbury and Manchester, Mass.*
Born circa 1814. Cabinetmaker. (Belknap)

LITTLE, William, *Sneedsborough, N. C.*
Born May 10, 1775 at Marlsgate, England; died 1848. Trained as cabinetmaker in shop of man named Graham. Arrived in Charleston in 1799 and worked for a short time with John Watson (*q.v.*). Burton tells of a letter arriving from his brother George in 1800 addressed to "Mr. William Little, Charleston, S. C. Cabinet Maker to the cair of John Watson Kingstrail, No. 12." In 1801 moved to Sneedsborough, N. C. In 1806 married Elizabeth Steels, daughter of a wealthy planter, and retired from cabinetmaking in 1817. Known locally for about twenty-five pieces of furniture still in the families of those for whom they were made. Worked in the Hepplewhite and Sheraton styles, some pieces showing features reminiscent of the Chippendale period. Later pieces showed a trend toward the Empire. Worked in walnut, cherry, and mahogany. (*Antiques*, June 1955; Burton)

LIVERMORE, Thomas, *Boston, Mass.*
Working as joiner in 1710.

LLOYD, William, *Springfield, Mass.*
Born 1779. Son of John and Marianna Wright Lloyd; grandson of Maj. John Lloyd. His father was a leather dresser with a house on Ferry Lane—now Cypress St. It is not known where William learned his trade. On July 6, 1802 his first advertisement appeared in the *Springfield Federal Spy:* "William Lloyde Informs the Public, that he carries on the CABINET BUSINESS, one door north of

Zebina and Thomas Stebbins Store, where may be had SIDEBOARDS, CLOCK CASES, DESKS, BOOK CASES, BUREAUS, AND CARD TABLES. All shall be had at shortest notice, cheap for Cash or Country produce." The location referred to was the corner of Main and Ferry streets. In 1808 advertised he had a good chairmaker. In the *Springfield Gazette and Republican*, Sept. 13, 1845, appeared the following: "Died In this town on the 10th Mr. William Lloyd, age 66."

At the Connecticut Valley Historical Museum, Springfield, there is a documented card table and bureau made by Lloyd. The bureau is in the Hepplewhite style. Illustrated on back cover of *Antiques*, June 1948, is a mahogany bow-front sideboard with Lloyd's label of Feb. 16, 1811. This is attached inside the right-hand compartment. This sideboard is a beautifully proportioned piece with inlay. (*American Collector*, May 1935)

LONG, Melchor, *Savannah, Ga.*
Died in 1774, at which time listed as cabinetmaker.

LONG, Samuel, *Newburyport, Mass.*
Born 1762; died 1794. Cabinetmaker.

LONGE, M. Antoine, *Louisville, Ky.*
Advertised in *Western Courier*, Dec. 21, 1815: "He will also execute all kinds of cabinetmaker's work."

LOOKEY, Christian, *Baltimore, Md.*
Listed in directory for 1810 as cabinetmaker.

LORD, Daniel, *Ipswich, Mass.*
Cabinetmaker on High St. about 1790. (Waters)

LORD, David Wells, *Ipswich, Mass.*
Born Sept. 13, 1812. Cabinetmaker. (Belknap)

LORD, Jeremiah R., *Manchester, Mass.*
Born circa 1823 in Ipswich. Worked in Manchester as cabinetmaker.

LORD, Joseph, *Ipswich, Mass.*
Cabinetmaker about 1790. (Waters)

LORD, Josiah 3rd, *Ipswich, Mass.*
Born Jan. 8, 1821. Cabinetmaker.

LORD, Moses, *Ipswich, Mass.*
Cabinetmaker about 1790. (Waters)

LORD, Moses, Jr., *Ipswich, Mass.*
Chairmaker, probably working with his father.

LORD, Moses Goodhue, *Ipswich, Mass.*
Born July 2, 1820. Cabinetmaker.

LORD, Nathaniel, *Ipswich, Mass.*
Cabinetmaker on High St. about 1790. (Waters)

LORD, Samuel, *Charlestown, Mass.*
Cabinetmaker who moved to Cambridge after the fire of 1775.

LOUD, Solomon, *Boston, Mass.*
Partner of Nathaniel Bryant (*q.v.*) in firm of Loud & Bryant on Court St., 1813.

LOUD & BRYANT, *Boston, Mass.*
See entries for Solomon Loud and Nathaniel Bryant.

LOUGEE, Joseph L., *Salem, Mass.*
Cabinetmaker. Member of firm of Haskell & Lougee at 296 Essex St. in 1859.

LOVE, William, *Newport, R. I.*
John Banister's receipt book, at Newport Historical Society, records in 1750 that "Wm. Love is paid in full for a round about chair."

LOWREY, John, *Savannah, Ga.*
Died 1796. Cabinetmaker on Barnard St. Left a fairly large estate which included fourteen chairs. (Theus, *Antiques*, Feb. 1954)

LUKENS, Thomas, *Pittsburgh, Pa.*
Advertised in *Pittsburgh Gazette*, Nov. 28, 1795: "The subscriber begs leave to

inform his friends and the public in general that he has commenced the Cabinet-Makers Business in all its branches, at the house lately occupied by Mr. Samuel Mahon, etc." For over a year kept an advertisement in the paper for an apprentice.

LUMMUS, David, *Ipswich, Mass.*
Cabinetmaker about 1790. (Waters)

LUNT, Abraham, *Newburyport, Mass.*
Born 1683. Cabinetmaker.

LUNT, Joshua, *Newburyport, Mass.*
Cabinetmaker working in 1736–72 with his brother (?) Abraham. Account book at Essex Institute, Salem.

LUPTON, William, *Charleston, S. C.*
Arrived in Charleston from London and advertised in the *South Carolina Gazette*, Sept. 19, 1743. At that time on Broad St. In this advertisement said that he would make "all sorts of Cabinets and Chairs in the best and neatest Manner and at the lowest Prices." Married Alice North, March 3, 1744. Again advertised Dec. 10, 1750. In August 1751 his house was sold at auction to pay debts. Doubtless left Charleston at that time. (Burton)

LUTHER, John, *Providence, R. I.*
Listed in directory for 1824 as cabinetmaker working over 6 N. Water St., living at 137 Broad St.

LUTHER, Joseph, *Providence, R. I.*
Listed in 1824 directory as cabinetmaker working over 6 N. Water St., living at 60 Weybos St. Doubtless working in shop with John.

LUTHER, Nathan P., *Providence, R. I.*
Listed in directories for 1836 and 1837 as chairmaker on Green and Elm streets.

LUTHER, Thomas S., *Providence, R. I.*
Listed in directories during 1824–28 as cabinetmaker at 192 Benefit St.

LUTHER, William T., *Salem, Mass.*
Shipped mahogany furniture to Brazil on *Welcome Return* in 1803. Invoice marked "Will Luther." A William T. Luther is listed as chairmaker at Buffum's Corner in 1803, moving to "over Mr. Ferguson's store" in 1805. Doubtless the same man.

LUYTEN, William, *Charleston, S. C.*
Died Oct. 24, 1800 in Camden, S. C. Did work for Thomas Elfe. Married Mary Ann Collins, May 29, 1764. When she died in 1770 she was buried in St. Michael's Cemetery and her husband made a cypress bedstead for her tombstone. This may be seen today. In 1784 apparently gave up cabinetmaking.

LYDON, Samuel, *Newport, R. I.*
Working as joiner in 1741. (Richardson)

LYELL (or LYLE), Fenwick, *Middletown, N. J.*
Working in the late 1700s. Account book at Monmouth Historical Society, Freehold, N. J.

LYNDON, Caleb, *Newport, R. I.*
Mentioned in Elnathan Hammond's account book in 1772 as mending a case of drawers and making a mahogany table for Hammond's daughter Elizabeth. Job Townsend's account book, at Newport Historical Society, shows Lyndon billed for work, Feb. 9, 1803.

LYNHAM, George, *Boston, Mass.*
Listed as cabinetmaker with a shop called "Chest of Drawers" in 1719.

MACHE, Nicholas, *Baltimore, Md.*
Listed in directory for 1804 as cabinetmaker.

MACKMILLION, Alexander, *Salem, Mass.*
Chairmaker and turner living in 1720. (Perley, *History of Salem*)

MACKMILLION, Jonathan, *Salem, Mass.*
Born Aug. 23, 1708; died before De-

cember 1739. Chairmaker. Married Rachel Procter, July 20, 1732. (Perley, *History of Salem*)

MAGRATH (or McGRATH), Richard, *Charleston, S. C.*
Advertised in *South Carolina Gazette*, Aug. 8, 1771, that he was lately from London and was moving his shop "up the Path, a little way without the Town Gate; where the Cabinet-maker's and Upholsterers Business will be carried on in a more extensive Manner." At that time he was on King St. In 1772 he advertised that he was carrying on his business in King St. and could supply "Double chest of Drawers, with neat and light Pediment Heads, which take off and put on occasionally; Ditto with a desk Drawer; Dining-Tables; commode Card Tables; Sophas, with Commode fronts divided with three sweeps, which give them a noble look; caned Chairs of the newest fashion, splat Backs, with hollow slats and commode fronts of the same Pattern as those imported by Peter Manigault, Esq. &c." Again advertised in 1773. (Burton)

MAIN, James, *Baltimore, Md.*
Working 1813-22. Listed in directory for 1813, in which year he married Mary Ann Smith on March 18. Again in directory in 1822 as cabinetmaker at 63 Broad St.

MALLARD, Prudent, *New Orleans, La.*
Son of Sir Peter Nicholas Mallard of Scotland and Lady Michael Louise Oger of France. He was born in Sèvres in 1809 and is thought to have received his training as a cabinetmaker in France. He arrived in New York in 1829 and is believed to have worked with Duncan Phyfe. In 1838 he opened a shop on Royal St. in New Orleans. In 1841 he moved to more spacious quarters at 305 Royal St. His business was most successful and in 1860 he purchased the adjoining building. At this time he had a business partner by the name of John M.

Robinson. He made frequent trips to Europe for new ideas. His furniture was an adaptation of the Louis XV style, and in the days when he was the fashionable cabinetmaker of New Orleans his furniture brought higher prices than that of any of his contemporaries in the South. It is known that he received as much as $3,000. for a bedroom set. He did not use a label but many pieces attributed to him by tradition are still in existence. Today Mallard's work does not bring the prices of works by many other cabinetmakers of that time who did not have his prestige. Several pieces attributed to him are illustrated in *Antiques*, September 1943. (*American Collector*, May 1936; *Antiques*, Aug. 1944)

MANDERFIELD, John, *Philadelphia, Pa.*
Died 1793, a victim of the yellow fever epidemic. Hornor says Governor John Penn was one of his clients.

MANNING, Caleb, *Salem, Mass.*
Died circa June 15, 1810. Cabinet- and chairmaker. Was on Daniel St. in 1803, but before that had been on Federal St. in partnership with Samuel Harris. In 1805 was on Fish St. near Gray's Wharf, where he did cabinetwork as well as made Windsor chairs. In 1806 on Derby St. (Belknap)

MANNING, Charles H., *Salem, Mass.*
Born June 19, 1813 (?). Cabinetmaker at 6 North St. in 1842. In 1850 partner in the firm of Manning & Sargent. (Belknap)

MANNING, Daniel A., *Salem, Mass.*
Born January 1825; died before 1864. Cabinetmaker. (Belknap)

MANNING, Thomas, *Charlestown, Mass.*
Cabinetmaker. Moved to Salem after fire of 1775.

MANSFIELD, Benjamin Bream, *Salem, Mass.*
Cabinetmaker. Given one-fourth inter-

est in his father's long house in 1791. In 1792 deeded his share to his brother. (*Essex Registry of Deeds*)

MARCH, Jones, *Lexington, Ky.*

Announced in the *Lexington Observer and Kentucky Reporter*, Aug. 21, 1833, that "Jones March formerly of Gaunt & March makes Fancy and Windsor chairs." (Offutt)

MARCOTTE, Leon, *New York City*

Arrived from France in 1854. Brought with him much French furniture and soon became a fashionable New York cabinetmaker. His wife was the daughter of Ringuet Le Prince, a celebrated Parisian cabinetmaker. In 1860 advertised in the *New York Evening Post*: "Very rich suites of Blackwood and Gilt, covered in Moire Antique, do. In Tapestry; elegant Rosewood Parlor-Suites, covered in rich Satin; Black and Gilt Centre Tables with very rich Gilt Bronzes; etc." Elaborate pieces with rich marquetry were made in his shop. He used butterfly motifs in shaded wood, and mother-of-pearl for stars. At the Theodore Roosevelt Birthplace, 28 East Twentieth St., New York City, there is a satinwood bedroom set, in a master bedroom, that is attributed to him. (*Antiques*, Sept. 1943)

MARLEN, William, *Charleston, S. C.*

Listed in directories in 1803, 1807, and 1809 as cabinetmaker.

MARLIN, James, Sr., *Baltimore, Md.*

Advertised as cabinetmaker in 1791.

MARQUAM, Edward, *Baltimore, Md.*

Listed in directories during 1800–1803 as cabinetmaker.

MARSH, Charles, *New York City*

A Windsor armchair and side chair with bamboo turnings bearing the label "Charles Marsh, Windsor Chair Maker of Number 75 John St., New York," are illustrated in *Antiques*, May 1930.

MARSH, Samuel, *Newport, R. I.*

Working in 1860 as chairmaker on the south side of Bannister's Wharf and Thames St., "upstairs." (Richardson)

MARSHALL, John, *Suffield, Conn.*

Died 1755. Inventory of his estate listed a shop and turning tools.

MARSHALL, John, *Charleston, S. C.*

Died June 1820. Listed in directory of 1790 as cabinetmaker at 219 Meeting St. Evidently prosperous since he was the owner of two plantations. Apparently gave up cabinetmaking in 1800 and left Charleston. (Burton)

MARSHALL, Nathaniel, *Portsmouth, N. H.*

A trained cabinetmaker who in 1792 was overseer of the poorhouse. Under his supervision the inmates constructed furniture. In that year advertised in the *New Hampshire Spy* that chairs, bureaus, Pembroke tables, a desk, and a cedar bureau were available at the poorhouse.

MARTIN, George Whitefield, *Salem, Mass.*

Born 1771; died 1810. Cabinetmaker whose shop and tools were sold at auction June 19, 1810, apparently to settle his estate.

MARTIN, James, *Baltimore, Md.*

Listed in directories during 1799–1816 as cabinetmaker.

MARTIN, Thomas, *Salem, Mass.*

In 1816 working as cabinetmaker in shop on Water St. opposite Captain Peabody's wharf.

MARTIN, William, *Baltimore, Md.*

Listed in directories for 1807 and 1808 as cabinetmaker.

MASON, David, *New York City*

Signed as cabinetmaker when witness to a will in 1772.

MASON, Ralph, *Boston, Mass.*
Working in 1670 as a joiner. Possibly a son of Roger.

MASON, Roger, *Boston, Mass.*
Working in 1635 as a cabinetmaker.

MASON, Samuel, *Boston, Mass.*
Working as a joiner with his father Ralph in 1670.

MATHIOT, August, *Baltimore, Md.*
Fancy chair maker at 18 North Gay St. in 1833. (Varley)

MATTOCKS, John, *Litchfield, Conn.*
Windsor chair maker. Shop a mile west of center. Advertised in 1797 that he would take in exchange for his work "Bass wood Plank proper for chair seats." (White)

MATTOCKS, Samuel, *Boston, Mass.*
Listed in 1728 and 1729 as chairmaker at "Sign of the Cross."

MAY, John, *Charleston, S. C.*
Born 1792; died 1859. Appears to have formed a partnership with one Munro in 1819, when they are listed at 29 Queen St. In 1822 May was listed as cabinetmaker at 61 Queen St., where he continued for over thirty years. In the last years of his life apparently gave up furniture making and devoted his time to making coffins. (Burton)

McCABE, Thomas, *Baltimore, Md.*
Listed in directory for 1796 as cabinetmaker.

McCLELLAN, James, *Charleston, S. C.*
Advertised in *South Carolina Gazette*, Jan. 27, 1732: "James McClellan, Cabinet-Maker, from London, living next door to Mr. Joseph Massey, in Church-Street, Makes and sells all sorts of Cabinet Ware; viz. Cabinets, Desks & Book-Cases, Buroes, Tables of all sorts, Chairs, Tea-boxes, and new fashioned Chests &c." Burton thinks it possible he may have been working in Charleston earlier than this since the *Gazette* was first issued in 1732. Advertised March 30, 1738 that he was leaving the province. (Burton)

McCOMB, Joseph, *Salem, Mass.*
Cabinetmaker. Had shop at Liberty and Charter streets which was taken over by Thomas Needham, Jr., Oct. 11, 1811.

McCORMICK, George, *Chillicothe, Ohio*
Working 1806–16. In Chillicothe at Adena, one of the historic houses owned by the Ohio Historical Society; there is a mahogany card table in the Hepplewhite style made by McCormick about 1809. This table is documented by estimates and bills submitted by Mc-Cormick to Thomas Worthington. Worthington had brought McCormick from the East to construct his mansion, Adena. McCormick worked on Adena during 1806 and 1807 and subsequently made a number of pieces of furniture for Worthington. Mrs. Elizabeth W. Costello, West Liberty, Ohio, a great-granddaughter of Thomas Worthington, owns a Hepplewhite-style mahogany sideboard made by McCormick about 1809. This is also documented by estimates and bills. When the first state house was built in Columbus, McCormick did the woodwork. (Data kindly furnished by John S. Still, Curator of Historical Collections, Ohio Historical Society, Columbus, Ohio.)

McCORMICK, James, *Baltimore, Md.*
Advertised in 1786 as cabinetmaker.

McCORMICK, James, *Alexandria, Va.*
In 1786 advertised "long experience in some of the first shops in England and Ireland." This could be the same man listed above, who perhaps was working in both towns; however, the name was not uncommon at that time.

McDONALD, William, *Boston, Mass.*
Listed as cabinetmaker and carver on North St. in 1796.

McDOUGLASS, Hugh, *Newark, N. J.*

A letter written to his relatives in 1805 reads: "The last time I wrote you I lived in Newark, New Jersey and was in the cabinetmaking business. Six years ago I retired from business and purchased a farm on which I live, raising my own Bread, much more independent of man, but apparently much more dependent on God." Letter written from Morris County, N. J. (*Antiques*, Sept. 1953)

McDOWELL, James, *Duck Creek Cross Road, Del. (later called Smyrna)*

Died 1838. Sideboard and a signed chest of drawers in exhibition at the Wilmington Society of Fine Arts, 1950. The chest of drawers is of mahogany with swell front, an unusual valanced skirt, tapered bracket feet, and canted corners inlaid to simulate reeded columns. The name is written in ink beneath one of the drawers. The sideboard was made in 1816 and has the signature of William McDowell, a son. James established his business in 1785. Bought a lot in 1786 on what is now Commerce St., and he and his son James established a cabinetmaking business. This was later carried on by James's sons and grandson. (*Antiques*, Aug. 1950; Hornor, *Antiquarian*, Nov. 1930)

McELWEE, C. B., *Lexington, Ky.*

In the *Kentucky Gazette* for Jan. 15, 1819 announces his removal to a new address. In this advertisement calls himself a cabinetmaker. (Offutt)

McGEE, Samuel, *New York City*

Made a freeman in 1757, at which time listed as cabinetmaker.

McILVANE, Archibald, *Lexington, Ky.*

Listed in County Court Orders for January 1804 as cabinetmaker. (Offutt)

McINTIRE, Samuel, *Salem, Mass.*

The name Samuel McIntire, particularly in New England, stands not only for beautiful pieces of carved furniture in the Hepplewhite and Sheraton manner but for eminence in architecture and building. He was not only one of America's finest carvers of mantels, doorways, and interior trim but also the designer of some of the most beautiful buildings of the Federal Period in New England.

Samuel McIntire was born in Salem in 1757, the son of Joseph and Sarah (Ruck) McIntire, and was baptized Jan. 16, 1757 in the First Church. We know little of his early life except that he came from a family of carpenters and wood carvers. It is probable that during his youth he carved figureheads and other parts of ships being constructed in the Salem shipyards. He was undoubtedly a real student since the inventory of his estate in the Probate Court for the County of Essex at Salem shows that he possessed innumerable books. Listed in the inventory were Rees' Encyclopedia and volumes on architecture by Palladio, Ware, Langley, and Paine. There were a "Dictionary of Arts and Sciences," a "Book of Sculptures," a two-volume set of "French Architecture," and a number of books on history, travel, and music.

On Aug. 31, 1778 McIntire married Elizabeth Field. Their son Samuel Field McIntire was born in 1780. Quite suddenly in 1782, McIntire came into prominence as the architect and builder of the lovely Peirce-Nichols House in Salem. Part of this building was not completed until 1801; and in this the details are in his charming Adam-influenced style; the earlier part in the Georgian manner.

McIntire's home was at 29 Summer St. In the rear of it he opened a large woodworking shop, employing several of his brothers—without intent, doubtlessly, following in the footsteps of his English master, Robert Adam, and his Adelphi in London. It is probable that McIntire drew the designs for his houses and that his brothers did the actual building. He himself, however, did the carving of the beautiful doorways, the exquisite mantels, and the interior trim. In the years between the building of his first house in 1782 and his last in 1810, McIntire confined his work almost entirely to Salem. During that time this seaport was at the peak of its prosperity, and McIntire, the outstanding builder in the town, was employed by the wealthy merchants and shipowners to construct their mansions. In 1800 he was commissioned by Elias Hasket Derby to design and build Oak Hill at Peabody for his daughter Elizabeth, wife of Capt. Nathaniel West. He worked on it continually during 1800 and 1801. McIntire died in 1811, but even after his death, his son was adding to or repairing this mansion. Although the house is still standing, three of the rooms—the parlor, parlor chamber, and dining room—have been removed and reconstructed at the Museum of Fine Arts, Boston. They are furnished with objects of the period, many of them originally at Oak Hill, and some of these pieces are attributed to McIntire.

By the time of his death, McIntire had designed and built some twenty mansions, many along Chestnut St., and fortunately not one was destroyed in the disastrous fire of 1914. Today, Chestnut St. is one of the most beautiful streets in America, lined as it is with these lovely houses. The Gardner-Pingree House, built in 1810 and now owned by the Essex Institute, was his last and most beautiful.

McIntire was a simple man, never attaining a position of social equality with those for whom he built such beautiful homes; a man with a love of his work, of sculpture, of music. However, he was evidently not without desire for recognition, for in 1793 he entered the competition for the Capitol building at Washington. His plan was not chosen, but neither were those of Benjamin Henry Latrobe and Charles Bulfinch, professional architects who had such an effect upon the architecture of America—Latrobe in Greek Revival, Bulfinch with his Adam-inspired influence upon New England.

McIntire, like his mentor Robert Adam, not only designed beautiful houses, but also decorated the interiors, and designed appropriate furniture for them. At one time it was the fashion to attribute everything that came out of Salem to him. Again, some attempted to prove he was no cabinetmaker, and even questioned his ability as a carver. The facts indicate that McIntire designed furniture which was doubtlessly constructed in his own workshop, that he carved furniture, and that he and his son were the outstanding carvers of Salem, often employed to carve the pieces made by other cabinetmakers. The Rev. William Bentley, pastor of the East Church in Salem, was a meticulous diarist. His diary, published in several volumes and covering the years 1783–1819, contains the most intimate details of Salem life. He records the story of his employment of McIntire to carve a bust of John Winthrop. Evidently he was not too pleased with the results, but that was in 1798. By 1802 it would appear that McIntire had progressed a great deal (although the Winthrop bust is considered today a competent piece of carving), since under date of Oct. 8, 1802, Bentley records: "As a Carver we place Mr. Macintire with Skillings of Boston. In some works he has succeeded well. He cuts smoother than Skillings but he has not his genius. In architecture he excells any person in our country & in his executions as a Carpenter, or Cabinet maker. His Brother executes the work at Allen's farm." The bust is now owned by the American Antiquarian Society at Worcester.

When Samuel McIntire died, Feb. 6, 1811, it is apparent that his contemporaries realized their loss. At this time Bentley wrote: "This day Salem was deprived of one of the most ingenious men it had in it. Samuel McIntire, aet. 54, in Summer street. He was descended of a family of Carpenters who had no claims on public favour & was educated at a branch of that business. By attention he soon gained a superiority to all of his occupation & the present Court House, the North & South Meeting houses, &

indeed all the improvements of Salem for nearly thirty years past have been done under his eye. In Sculpture he had no rival in New England & I possess some specimens which I should not scruple to compare with any I ever saw. To the best of my abilities I encouraged him in this branch. In Music he had a good taste & tho' not presuming to be an Original composer, he was among out best Judges & most able performers. All the Instruments we use he could understand & was the best person to be employed in correcting any defects, or repairing them. He had a fine person, a majestic appearance, calm countenance, great self command & amiable temper. He was welcome but never intruded. He had complained of some obstruction in the chest, but when he died it was unexpectedly. The late increase of workmen in wood has been from the demand for exportation & this had added nothing to the character & reputation of the workmen so that upon the death of Mr. McIntire no man is left to be consulted upon a new plan of execution beyond his bare practice."

McIntire is buried in the Charter Street Burying Ground, Salem, and his slate tombstone bears this inscription:

In Memory of
Mr. Samuel McIntire
who died February 6, 1811
Aet. 54

He was distinguished for Genius in Architecture Sculpture and Musick; Modest and sweet Manners rendered him pleasing: Industry and Integrity respectable: He professed the Religion of Jesus in his entrance on manly life; and proved its excellence by virtuous Principles and unblemished Conduct.

The furniture designed, constructed, and carved by Samuel McIntire covers a wide field. He seems, however, to have been fond of sofas and chairs—or else there was a particular demand for them—because they are in greater numbers than other pieces. Hipkiss in speaking of the

furniture to be seen in the three McIntire rooms at the Boston Museum of Fine Arts says, "Among them are examples of American chairs and cabinetmaking of the first order, examples that place the designer-craftsmen of Salem among the best of Philadelphia, Boston and Newport." Many of the individual pieces in these rooms are described as "designed and carved by Samuel McIntire" or "at-

Sheaf of wheat carving
design by Samuel McIntire

Carving design of alternating fluting and rosette by Samuel McIntire

tributed to Samuel McIntire." At the Essex Institute, Salem, is a signed McIntire sketch showing a chair back identical with one attributed to him. Also at the Institute is a carved and painted pear about which Mr. Bentley wrote, Sept. 25, 1802: "Saw an imitation of a wonderful pear which grew in Ipswich. It was carved by Macintire and painted by Corné and was said to be an exact imitation. It might easily be mistaken excepting its size might make suspicion."

Motifs used on furniture attributed to McIntire are closely related to those known to have been carved by him in the houses he built and decorated. These include a basket of fruit and flowers, a basket of fruit with festoons of flowers or drapery, a distinctive eagle in relief, wheat in a stack, a pendant of husks, a cluster or spray of grapes, a cornucopia spilling out its contents, an Adam-type urn with festoons of flowers, a spray of laurel. The alternating blocks of fluting and rosettes are constantly seen both in room decoration and on furniture. While much of the furniture attributed to Mc-Intire is of mahogany, many pieces are of a combination of woods, particularly mahogany, bird's-eye maple, and satinwood. He also used inlay to secure a rich effect, and at times gilding.

Sofas made by McIntire are of two general types—Hepplewhite with a curved back, Sheraton with a square back. Since Sheraton's book did not reach the American market until 1791, any sofa of the second type was naturally constructed after that date. The Hepplewhite type is represented in the Karolik Collection at the Boston Museum of Fine Arts. (PLATE XXIII, No. 1) This has the curving top rail carved with the characteristic band of fluting and rosettes, surmounted by carved cornucopias with fruit and ribbons. The rolled upholstered arms are faced in mahogany carved with leafage and rosettes. There are four square tapered legs in front with carved grape design on each. In the same collection is a sofa of the second type made about 1800. The

Basket of fruit carving design by
Samuel McIntire

top has a band of fluting and rosettes, surmounted by three panels—one oblong, flanked on either side by one of the console type—each of which is carved with a fruit basket and leafage against a punch-marked field. The four front legs are turned and reed-molded. A third sofa is similar to the second one described above except that the four front legs are square tapered with grape-design carving. In the Karolik Collection at the Boston Museum of Fine Arts is a pair of card tables, design and carving attributed to

McIntire. (PLATE XXIII, No. 2) These are Hepplewhite in style, were made 1790–1800, and reveal some of McIntire's finest carving. The top edge shows the alternate fluting and rosettes. On the face of the square tapered legs is the carved grape pendant that appears on several of the sofa and chair legs. The four spade feet are cased in ebony. On the apron above each leg is an oval beaded rosette, and each apron panel has an applied carved motif. That in the center is crossed cornucopias, while each side panel shows

Center panel of Sheraton-style sofa back showing characteristic McIntire carving designs—alternate fluting and rosette, eagle, and a punch-marked field

a basket of fruit. Rays of richly grained veneers on the top leaf fan out from a semi-elliptical panel with a shell pattern of inlaid boxwood, colored or charred by the hot-sand method.

Chairs attributed to McIntire follow the same trends as do the sofas—Hepplewhite with shield back, Sheraton with square back. There are many at the Boston Museum of Fine Arts, the Essex Institute at Salem, the Philadelphia Museum of Art, and the Metropolitan Museum of Art, New York City. The Hepplewhite shield-back chair generally had an elongated vase-shaped medial splat flanked by curved and shaped bars. Sometimes the flanking bars have oval medallions; at other times, instead of the central vase-shaped splat, there are three bars, all with the oval medallions. Occasionally drapery swags extend across the chair back from the central splat to the others. The front legs are square tapered with spade feet, the face carved with pendant flowers, husks, or grape design. The Sheraton-type chair with square back may have the top panel carved with one of several McIntire designs. An interesting eagle with outstretched wings—

somewhat different from the usual Mc-
Intire eagle but evidently designed to fill
the panel—appears on several chairs of
a set at the Essex Institute.

At the Boston Museum of Fine Arts
there is a pair of superb upholstered armchairs with typical McIntire carving on
the exposed wood surfaces. They were
made about 1790. At the Metropolitan
Museum of Art, New York City, there
is an armchair carved in 1801 for
Jerathmeel Peirce.

One of the most beautiful pieces of
furniture to come from Salem is a double
chest of drawers in the Karolik Collection
at the Boston Museum of Fine Arts.
(PLATE XXII) This was constructed by
William Lemon and carved by McIntire.
Hipkiss calls it "the masterpiece of
Salem." He also says that its only rival
is the double chest of drawers in the
Garvan Collection at Yale University Art
Gallery, which is less rich in carving (see
PLATE XXI, also the entry for Stephen
Badlam). The Lemon piece is said to have
been made as a wedding gift from Derby
to his daughter. The front and sides are
of crotch-mahogany veneer on pine. The
drawers are edged with bead molding of
ebony and satinwood. The band dividing
the two parts of the piece is wider than
usual to accommodate a row of alternate
flutings and rosettes, and narrower bands
are carried along the bottom and the
top of the case. The center panel in the
frieze has an urn of fruit. The side panels
have small seated figures in relief with
baskets on their heads. Cornucopias are
in the lower corners, and a small basket
flanked by leafage is on the skirting.
Beautifully carved urns form the end
finials, while a gilded figure of Justice or
Peace is at the center. At the Essex Institute, Salem, there are quantities of papers
and records from the Derby estate.
There one may see the bill for carving
this chest of drawers:

Madam Elizabeth Derby
to Samuel McIntire Dr.
To Carving Base
Mouldings & Brackets

for a Case Drawers
Made by Mr. Lemon
at 39   1:19:0
To Carving Freeze
Roses &c for the top
at 24   1: 4:0
                               _____
                               £3: 3:0

Salem 22d Octo 1796
Received payment
Saml McIntire.

At the William Rockhill Nelson Gallery of Art, Kansas City, Mo., there are
three pieces of furniture attributed to
McIntire: a card table purchased in
Marblehead; a two-drawer work table; a
bed that, although attributed to Mc-
Intire, might have been made by Nathaniel Appleton (see 1928 edition of
Nutting, Vol. 1, pl. 1513-15).

At the Henry Ford Museum, Dearborn, Mich., there is a Hepplewhite-style
card table attributed to McIntire.

Anyone studying the work of Samuel
McIntire should visit the three McIntire
rooms at the Museum of Fine Arts, Boston. These demonstrate his genius as an
architect. Much of the furniture in them
came from Salem, was made for the first
owner of Oak Hill, Elizabeth Derby
West, and includes many pieces by Mc-
Intire. A study of these and of the large
number of pieces by McIntire in the
Karolik Collection will give a comprehensive understanding of his role as cabinetmaker and carver.

The author is grateful to the many
people who helped with this interpretation, among them: Mrs. Yves Henry
Buhler, Assistant Curator, Dept. of
Decorative Arts, Museum of Fine Arts,
Boston; Russell Kettell, of Concord,
Mass.; the late Fiske Kimball, former Director of the Philadelphia Museum of
Art; Mrs. Amelia R. MacSwiggan, formerly of the Essex Institute, Salem; and
staff members of the Essex Institute.

(*Antiques*, Feb. 1929, Nov. and Dec.
1930, Jan., March, Nov., and Dec. 1931,
Jan. and Feb. 1932, Dec. 1933, Oct. 1934
[A series of articles relating to McIntire
written by two authors having different

PLATE XVII, NO. 1
Mahogany block-front chest-on-chest marked "N B 1774." Attributed to Nathan Bowen, Marblehead, Mass. Detroit Institute of Arts.

PLATE XVII, NO. 2
Mahogany block-front secretary attributed to Benjamin Frothingham, Charlestown, Mass. William Rockhill Nelson Gallery of Art, Kansas City, Mo.

PLATE XVIII, NO. 1
Cherry block-front desk, Connecticut, inscribed, "This desk was maid in the year 1769 buy Benj^m Burnam that sarvfed his time in Felledlfey." The Metropolitan Museum of Art, New York City.

PLATE XVIII, NO. 2
Cherry serpentine-front desk attributed to Joseph Hosmer, Concord, Mass. Concord Antiquarian Society.

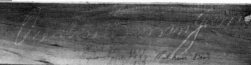

PLATE XIX, NO. 1

Cherry chest-on-chest made by Reuben Beman, Kent, Conn. Inscribed with his name and the date 1801. Henry Francis Du Pont Winterthur Museum, Winterthur, Del.

PLATE XIX, NO. 2

Mahogany Chippendale-type highboy attributed to Elijah Booth, Southbury, Conn. Society for the Preservation of New England Antiquities, Boston.

PLATE XX, NO. 1
Mahogany block-front desk with label of
Ursual Daniel, Halifax, N. C. Virginia
Museum of Fine Arts, Richmond.

PLATE XX, NO. 2
Unusual desk made by John Skillin, Boston, Mass., for Governor Hancock and
known as the Hancock Desk. American
Antiquarian Society, Worcester, Mass.

PLATE XX, NO. 3
Walnut tea table, Chippendale type, 1750–
60. Formerly attributed to the Philadel-
phia school. Now evidence attributes it to
John Bachman, Lancaster, Pa. M. and M.
Karolik Collection, Museum of Fine Arts,
Boston.

PLATE XXI

Mahogany chest-on-chest made in 1791 by Stephen Badlam of Dorchester Lower Mills, Mass., with carved figures by the Skillins of Boston. Mabel Brady Garvan Collection, Yale University Art Gallery, New Haven, Conn.

Inscription on mahogany chest-on-chest by Stephen Badlam.

PLATE XXII
Mahogany chest-on-chest attributed to William Lemon of Salem, Mass. Design and carving attributed to Samuel McIntire of Salem, 1796. Known as "the masterpiece of Salem."
M. and M. Karolik Collection, Museum of Fine Arts, Boston.

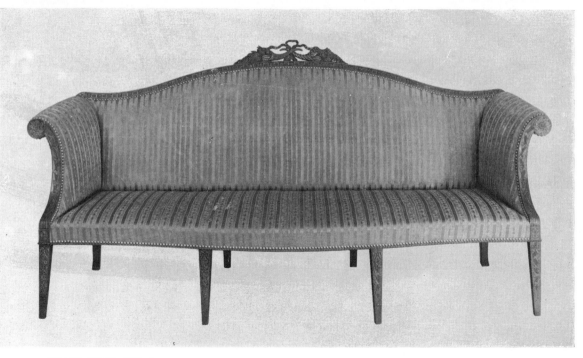

PLATE XXIII, NO. 1
Hepplewhite sofa with carving attributed to Samuel McIntire, Salem, circa 1795. M. and M. Karolik Collection, Museum of Fine Arts, Boston.

PLATE XXIII, NO. 2
One of a pair of mahogany Hepplewhite-style card tables. Design and carving attributed to Samuel McIntire, Salem, 1790–1800. M. and M. Karolik Collection, Museum of Fine Arts, Boston.

PLATE XXIV, NO. 1

Tambour sideboard attributed to John Seymour, Boston, Mass., circa 1800. Front of mahogany, rosewood, and satinwood. Three tambour doors enclosing compartments painted in blue. M. and M. Karolik Collection, Museum of Fine Arts, Boston.

PLATE XXIV, NO. 2

Mahogany tambour desk attributed to John Seymour & Son, circa 1800. Tambour shutters of alternating strips of mahogany and curly satinwood enclosing spaces under semi-elliptical arches. M. and M. Karolik Collection, Museum of Fine Arts, Boston.

PLATE XXV, NO. 1
Mahogany Pembroke table with inlay, Hepplewhite style, with label of Holmes Weaver, Newport, R. I., 1790–1800. M. and M. Karolik Collection, Museum of Fine Arts, Boston.

PLATE XXV, NO. 2
Hepplewhite-style card table, circa 1790, with label of Stephen and Thomas Goddard, Newport, R. I. The Metropolitan Museum of Art, New York City.

PLATE XXVI, NO. 1
Mahogany side chair, Philadelphia, 1770–80. Made by James Gilling-ham. The Metropolitan Museum of Art, New York City.

PLATE XXVI, NO. 2
Mahogany Hepplewhite shield-back side chair, circa 1795. Possibly made by Elbert Anderson. The Metro-politan Museum of Art, New York City.

Mahogany sideboard with satinwood inlay, Hepplewhite style. Attributed to Matthew Egerton, Sr., New Brunswick, N. J., circa 1785. M. and M. Karolik Collection, Museum of Fine Arts, Boston.

Mahogany sideboard with inlay, Sheraton style, made by John Shaw, Annapolis, Md., 1770–80. Baltimore Museum of Art.

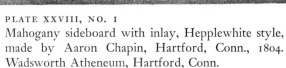

Bill of sale for Aaron
Chapin sideboard by which
attribution was made.

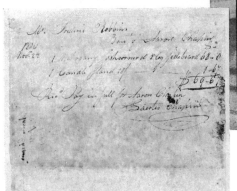

PLATE XXVIII, NO. 1
Mahogany sideboard with inlay, Hepplewhite style,
made by Aaron Chapin, Hartford, Conn., 1804.
Wadsworth Atheneum, Hartford, Conn.

PLATE XXVIII, NO. 2
Mahogany secretary, Hepplewhite style, attributed to
Henry Connelly, Philadel-
phia, circa 1805, and mahogany side chair, late eighteenth
century, attributed to Ephraim Haines. Now at Adena,
Chillicothe, Ohio, owned by
the Ohio Historical Society.

PLATE XXIX, NO. 1
Mahogany library table attributed to Duncan Phyfe, New York City. The Metropolitan Museum of Art, New York City.

PLATE XXIX, NO. 2
Mahogany worktable-desk, 1823, with label of Michael Allison, 46–48 Vesey St., New York City. The Metropolitan Museum of Art, New York City.

PLATE XXX
One of a pair of carved and gilded rosewood sofas by John Henry Belter, New York City, circa 1850. Virginia Museum of Fine Arts, Richmond.

PLATE XXXI
Mahogany sleigh bed with ormolu mounts and labels of Charles Honoré Lannuier, New York City. Albany Institute of History and Art.

Mahogany cabinet probably made by John Goddard II, Newport, R. I., toward the end
of his life. Newport Historical Society.

points of view. In part illuminating, in part confusing; entire series should be read to prevent misunderstanding. One wonders at negative side of the discussion since Bentley's facts have never been questioned and his statements regarding McIntire are definite.]; Bentley; Cousins and Riley; Hipkiss, *Three McIntire Rooms*, Museum of Fine Arts, Boston, 1931)

McINTIRE, Samuel Field, *Salem, Mass.*

Born 1780; died 1819. Son of Samuel. Worked closely with his father, and upon his death advertised in the *Salem Gazette*, on April 30 and May 3, 1811: "The subscriber carries on Carving as usual at the Shop of the deceased in Summer Street where he will be glad to receive orders in that line. He returns thanks for past favors." On April 18, 1815 he advertised: "Samuel F. McIntire, carver, Cheap Side, Summer Street, Ship Heads, Festoons for Sterns, Tablets and Blockings for Chimney Pieces, Brackets, Draperies—Eagles from 5 inches to 2 feet 6. A variety of Figures, Butter and Cake Stamps, Furniture Carving and Bellows tops." The only known, documented work by Samuel Field McIntire is described in the bill at the Boston Museum of Fine Arts for work done at Oak Hill in 1813–14 to supplement or repair the work done there by his father. It is agreed that he lacked the genius of his father although he did competent work. It is probable, however, that some pieces attributed to the father were actually executed by the son.

McINTOSH (or M'INTOSH), John, *Charleston, S. C.*

Born in Edinburgh, Scotland, in 1771. It is believed he arrived in Charleston some years before 1813, when he became an American citizen. The Charleston directory of 1806 lists M'Intosh (*sic*) and Foulds as cabinetmakers at 133 Meeting St. Burton believes this M'Intosh was probably John McIntosh. It is thought that he served his apprenticeship in Scot-

land. He died in 1822. Inventory of his estate listed bedstead posts, unfinished furniture, and a lot of mahogany and pine boards. (Burton)

M'INTOSH & FOULDS, *Charleston, S. C.*

Listed together in directory for 1806 at 133 Meeting St. Burton says they were still working together in 1808, when it was recorded that they made a pair of sofas for which they were paid $65. In 1813 the two men are listed in the directory at separate addresses.

McKELLER, John, *Boston, Mass.*

Arrived from Greenwich, England, in 1766, at which time listed as joiner.

McKIM, Robert, *Richmond, Va.*

Listed as chairmaker in directory of 1819. A Windsor loop-back side chair has his label "Robert McKim, Windsor Chair Maker, Post office Richmond." (Comstock)

McMILLAN, James, *Boston, Mass.*

Notice of his death in 1769 listed him as cabinetmaker.

McMORRAN, John, *Windsor and Suffield, Conn.*

Born 1727 in Windsor; died 1812 in Suffield. Lived in Windsor until 1757, when he moved to Suffield. His account books at the Kent Memorial Library, Suffield, reveal that he made a great deal of furniture—chests of drawers, stands, tables, chairs, chests, bedsteads—during the years he lived in Windsor. It seems apparent that he gave up cabinetmaking in 1757, when he moved to Suffield. (Bissell)

MEAD, John, *Salem, Mass.*

Born 1787; died 1824. Cabinetmaker. (Belknap)

MEANO, Peter A., *Savannah, Ga.*

Advertised 1787–1817 as cabinetmaker.

MEARS, Warren, *Essex, Mass.*

Baptized July 20, 1828; died Oct. 3, 1845. Listed as cabinetmaker.

MEDCAFF, William, *Frankfort, Ky.*
In the *Guardian of Freedom*, March 16, 1804, "informs citizens of Frankfort he has commenced the cabinet business on his own account."

MEEKS, John and Joseph, *New York City*
Working first half of nineteenth century. Competitors of John Henry Belter. Their rosewood furniture, however, lacks the charm of Belter's. It is severely rectilinear, with turned decoration and without any of the evidences of Belter's skill.

MEEKS, Joseph, *Savannah, Ga.*
Advertised in 1798 as cabinetmaker.

MEGOWAN, James, *Lexington, Ky.*
Working in 1818 as cabinetmaker. (Whitley)

MERRIKEN, James, *Baltimore, Md.*
Listed as cabinet- and chairmaker in directories as early as 1810. Varley says he was still there in 1833.

MERRILL, Moses, *Newburyport, Mass.*
Born 1798 at Newbury. Working during 1849–60 as cabinetmaker. (Belknap)

MESSINGER, Henry II, *Boston, Mass.*
Died 1681. Inventory of his estate lists him as chairmaker and joiner and showed tools, chest of drawers, and other furniture.

METCALF, Joseph, *Medway, Mass.*
Born 1765; died 1849. Younger brother of Luther. Learned his trade with brother. In 1789 went by oxcart to Hallowell, Me., and thence to Winthrop. Set up first cabinetmaking shop in Winthrop. Had many apprentices, among them Samuel Benjamin (*q.v.*). (Stackpole)

METCALF, Luther, *Medway, Mass.*
Born 1756; died 1838. Apprenticed to Elisha Richardson of West Wrentham in 1770–78. Apprenticeship, as so often was the case, was interrupted by necessary army service, after which he was always known as Major. In 1778 opened his own shop in the village and employed some workmen. On April 14, 1801 advertised in the *Columbian Mercury*: "Wanted to Hire—A journey man Windsor Chair Maker—also wanted one or two active Boys not exceeding 16 years of Age as apprentices to the Cabinet and Chairmaking Business. Inquire of Luther Metcalf." In 1816 helped make the chairs and communion table for the new meetinghouse. Furniture by Metcalf still in existence in vicinity of Medway. (Jameson)

METHENEY, John, *Lexington, Ky.*
Working in 1818 as cabinetmaker. (Whitley)

MEW, Edmond, *Annapolis, Md.*
Advertised in 1770 as cabinetmaker.

MICKLE, Samuel, *Haddonfield, N. J.*
Apprenticed to Jonathan Shoemaker of Philadelphia. Afterwards stayed with Shoemaker for a short period and then returned to Haddonfield in 1776. In 1779 gave up cabinetmaking and moved to Woodbury, N. J. (Downs, No. 121)

MILES & LYONS, *Greenfield, Mass.*
Isaac Miles and Joel L. Lyons established a partnership in the cabinetmaking business in 1837, on Main St., Greenfield. They were considered to be good workmen, employing several journeymen and training apprentices. They maintained a warehouse and produced a wide variety of furniture—secretaries, bureaus, tables, chairs, four-post beds, organ cases, store fittings, etc. They also made coffins. The partnership continued for thirty-two years. After 1869 Lyons carried on alone until he became deaf and infirm. He died in 1893 at the age of eighty. (Data supplied by Mrs. Burton N. Gates, Worcester, Mass.)

MILLARD, James, *Providence, R. I.*
Listed in directories for 1836 and 1837 as cabinetmaker working on Williams St., living at 196 South Main St.

MILLARD, William, *Providence, R. I.*
Listed in directory for 1832 as cabinet-maker at 196 South Main St., in those during 1836–37 at 115½ South Main St.

MILLER, James, *Charlestown, Mass.*
Designated as cabinetmaker on list of those who suffered loss in fire of 1775. Later moved to Needham.

MILLER, John, *Charlestown, Mass.*
Born 1713; died 1763. Listed as joiner.

MILLER, John, *Baltimore, Md.*
Listed in directories during 1796–99 as cabinetmaker.

MILLER, Peter, *Savannah, Ga.*
Born 1765; died 1810. Inventory of his estate in 1810 showed "a walnut table, red bay [Persea borbonia] bedstead," several mahogany pieces and chairs.

MILLER, Stephen, *Bridgeton, N. J.*
Working 1788–1822. At loan exhibition at State Museum, Trenton, N. J., 1953, was a receipt for a coffin made by "STEPHEN MILLER, Cabinetmaker." Receipt dated "January 24, 1790."

MILLER, William, *Charlestown, Mass.*
On list of those who suffered in fire of 1775. Working for Benjamin Frothing-ham in 1789. Moved to Waterville, Me., in 1794.

MILLERD & TILLEY, *Providence, R. I.*
Listed in directory for 1832 as cabinet-makers on William St.

MILLETT, Benjamin R., *Salem, Mass.*
See entry for Seth S. Currier.

MILLS, William, *New York City*
During 1793–98 partner of Deming in Mills & Deming (*q.v.*). After partnership was dissolved apparently worked alone for five or six years.

MILLS & DEMING, *New York City*
First mentioned in New York City Directory of 1793 at 140 Queen St., which became Pearl St. in 1794. Their label, however, reads "Mills & Deming, No. 374 Queen Street, two doors above the Friends Meeting, New York. Makes and sells, all kinds of Cabinet Furniture and Chairs after the most modern fashions, etc." Directory still lists them as late as 1798, after which there is no further mention of them. They do not seem to have advertised during these years. It is believed that Simeon Deming of the firm was born in Wethersfield, Conn., in 1769 and that he married Eliza-beth Deming there in 1797. According to Deming Genealogy, they moved to East Bloomfield, N. Y., in 1813, and Simeon died there in 1855. In the Geneal-ogy, he is called a skillful cabinetmaker. This company seems to have specialized in sideboards and secretaries in the Hep-plewhite style. Among their finest work is a Hepplewhite sideboard made about 1795 for Governor Oliver Wolcott of Connecticut, 1796–97. This is an elabo-rate piece, with matched mahogany veneers and inlaid satinwood urns, drapery swags, and garlands. There is a fine picture of this in color on the cover of *Antiques*, December 1928. In the same magazine for January 1947, it is again pictured, this time offered for sale. See also *American Collector*, June 1935.

MINARD, Stephen, *New York City*
French émigré cabinetmaker working in New York City. Contemporary of Duncan Phyfe and Charles Honoré Lan-nuier.

MINOT, Martin, *Boston, Mass.*
Cabinet- and chairmaker in Rawson's Lane, 1789.

MINSKY, Samuel, *Baltimore, Md.*
Listed in directory for 1810 as cabinet-maker.

MIRICK, Benjamin, *Charlestown, Mass.*
Designated as cabinetmaker on list of those who suffered loss in fire of 1775.

MIRICK, Edward, *Charlestown, Mass.*
Born 1704; died 1765. Obituary in 1765 called him a cabinetmaker. Probably father of Benjamin.

MONAT, John, *New York City*
Made a freeman in 1765 and listed as cabinetmaker.

MONCRIEF, Richard, *Charleston, S. C.*
Died 1789. Cabinetmaker and house builder. Advertised in *South Carolina Gazette*, March 27, 1749: "This is to give Notice . . . that the subscriber is now at leisure, and will be obliged to any person that will employ him to do all the carpenter's and joiner's work in any one building. At whose shop in Queen-street all sorts of cabinetwork is neatly made, and all kinds of lumber sold." Will probated Sept. 18, 1789. (Burton)

MONTAGU, Richard, *Savannah, Ga.*
Advertised occasionally from 1794 to 1819 as joiner.

MOODY, Benjamin, *Newburyport, Mass.*
Died 1781. Joiner. All Newburyport cabinetmakers by the name of Moody evidently members of the same family.

MOODY, Enoch, Jr., *Newburyport, Mass.*
Born 1754; died 1804. Cabinetmaker.

MOODY, Ezra, *Newburyport, Mass.*
Died 1793. Chairmaker.

MOODY, James, *Newport, R. I.*
Working as joiner in 1739. (Richardson)

MOODY, John, *Newburyport, Mass.*
Born 1759; died 1793. Chairmaker.

MOODY, Matthew, Jr., *Williamsburg, Va.*
Advertised in *Virginia Gazette* in 1766 as cabinetmaker.

MOODY, Oliver, *Newburyport, Mass.*
Died 1775. Prominent in the town and at his death left a mansion on King St.

MOODY, Oliver, Jr., *Newburyport, Mass.*
Died 1776. Chairmaker. Carried on the family business but did not do so well as his father and when he died left but a small estate.

MOODY, Oliver III, *Newburyport, Mass.*
Died 1786. Son of Oliver Jr. Carried on the business of chairmaker but at his death his estate was even smaller than his father's.

MOORE, Philip, *Charleston, S. C.*
Married Besheba Hariet Hanlins, April 16, 1797. In 1800 leased land on the east side of Meeting St., on the corner of Rope Lane, for five years from John McIver. In directories until 1809 as cabinetmaker at 28 Meeting St. In 1806 advertised a "Mahogany Double Desk." Apparently gave up cabinetmaking in 1816 to become a lumber sawyer. (Burton)

MOORE, Robert, *Savannah, Ga.*
Advertised in 1734 as cabinetmaker.

MOORE, Robert, *Philadelphia, Pa.; Baltimore, Md.*
It is believed he had Thomas and William Moore working with him in Baltimore in 1774. Advertised in Maryland paper, Nov. 3, 1778 (Downs, No. 53). Gerrard Hopkins advertised that he had worked with him in Philadelphia. *See* entry for William Wayne. (*Baltimore Furniture;* Nutting)

MOORE, William, Jr., *Barkhamsted, Conn.*
Chairmaker working in Barkhamsted about 1790. Forced out of business in 1829. His inventory at that time showed a hundred chairs on their way to Philadelphia; and others in Massachusetts, New York, and elsewhere. Stamped his name on the back of the seat.

MOREHOUSE, Levi, *New Milford, Conn.*
"Mr. Levi Morehouse occupies a water privilege about a mile above the paper mill, with a saw and turning mill and a

cabinet shop where he conducts the cabinet and undertaking business." (Orcutt, *History of . . . New Milford, Connecticut, 1703-1882*)

MORGAN, Benjamin, Jr., *Manchester, Mass.*
Born Aug. 30, 1805. Cabinetmaker. (Belknap)

MORGAN, Douglas, *Georgetown, Conn.*
Working about 1830. *See* entry for Rufus H. Pickett.

MORGAN, John, *Manchester, Mass.*
Born June 7, 1813. Cabinetmaker. (Belknap)

MORGAN, Joseph Marsters, *Manchester, Mass.*
Born Oct. 19, 1817. Cabinetmaker. (Belknap)

MORISON, Simon, *Charleston, S. C.*
Born 1796. Arrived in Charleston from Scotland in 1817. Died Sept. 23, 1839. His obituary in the *Courier*, Oct. 5, 1839, stated: "In his vocation as a Cabinet Maker he was indefatigable; by his industry he had secured a competency for life, and about three years since, retired from the business." (Burton)

MORRELL, W., *Savannah, Ga.*
Advertised in 1824 as a cabinetmaker.

MORRISON, James, *Pittsburgh, Pa.*
Advertised in *Pittsburgh Gazette*, March 25, 1803, for an apprentice who had run away.

MORRISON, Spindelow, *Newburyport, Mass.*
Died 1768, at which time listed as joiner.

MORTON, John, *Baltimore, Md.*
Listed in directories during 1807-10 as cabinetmaker.

MOSES, Artemas, *Salisbury, Vt.*
Working as carpenter and joiner in the middle of the village in 1815. (Weeks)

MOULTON, Jonathan, *Boston, Mass.*
Born 1726; died 1787. Listed in directories as cabinetmaker.

MUCKENFUSS, Michael, *Charleston S. C.*
Born 1774; died 1808. Doubtless born in Charleston of German ancestry. May have learned his trade with Charles Desel (*q.v.*), who, it is believed, married his sister. In 1798 bought large amounts of real estate. In his will left his son James Custer Muckenfuss the contents of his shop, which included considerable furniture lumber. (Burton)

MULL, James, *Boston, Mass.*
Arrived from Scotland in 1766, when listed as joiner.

MUNROE, George, *Providence, R. I.*
Listed in directories for 1836 and 1837 as cabinetmaker on Friendship St.

MUNROE, Nehemiah, *Roxbury, Mass.*
Cabinetmaker working with the Roxbury group in 1800.

MUNSON, Ephraim, *Bethlehem, Conn.*
Born October 1762; died Nov. 27, 1834. Sixth child of Obadiah Munson (1731-1805) and Rachel Tyler Munson. Before moving to Bethlehem had lived in Woodbury. His cabinet shop in Bethlehem was at the Capt. Hawley place about three quarters of a mile southeast of the village. He was burned out and then moved to Nonnewog, about three and a half miles southeast of the center of town. "As a cabinetmaker, he was considered a first rate workman." In his inventory there are listed a "compass saw," two "match planes," a long plane, a fluting plane, and two handmade and rather crude chisels. (Myron A. Munson, *Munson Family*, 1896, Vol. 1)

MURPHY, James, *Boston, Mass.*
Arrived from Newfoundland in 1739, when listed as a joiner.

MURRAY, John, *Charlestown, Mass.*
Born 1783; died 1861. Chairmaker. At time of death was in Andover.

MURRAY, John, *Manchester, Mass.*
Born Oct. 20, 1804. Cabinetmaker. (Belknap)

NASER, Frederick, *Charleston, S. C.*
Born 1786; died 1860. Listed in directory for 1809 as cabinetmaker at 58 Meeting St. Brother-in-law of Michael Muckenfuss (*q.v.*).

NEAL, James, *Easton, Md.*
From 1802 to 1807 John Needles (*q.v.*) worked in Neal's shop as an apprentice.

NEEDHAM, Daniel, *Salem, Mass.*
Married in 1728/29. Working as cabinetmaker in Salem in 1732. Father of Thomas, and first of a family of well-known cabinetmakers.

NEEDHAM, J., *Salem, Mass.*
Born 1755; died 1787. Son of Thomas and grandson of Daniel. Cabinetmaker, doubtlessly working with his father.

NEEDHAM, Jasper, *Danvers, Mass.*
Born circa 1707; died April 3, 1794. Son of Anthony Needham, Jr., who died in winter of 1757–58 and left Jasper the old Needham house on north side of Lowell St. in Peabody. Jasper listed as joiner. When he died he left the house to his son Stephen. (Perley, *History of Salem*, Vol. 3)

NEEDHAM, Thomas, *Salem, Mass.*
Born circa 1729; died 1787. Married Mary Twist in 1751; Seeth Phippeny in 1754; and Lydia Lefavour after 1779. Listed as joiner and cabinetmaker.

NEEDHAM, Thomas, Jr., *Salem, Mass.*
Baptized Aug. 3, 1755; died after 1820.

Married Mary Bell in 1799 and Abigail Peirce in 1808. Took Joseph McComb's cabinetmaking shop on Charter St., Oct. 11, 1811. In business as late as 1821. With John Osgood, a merchant, and Jabez Baldwin, a jeweler, was an appraiser of the estate of Mrs. Nathaniel West, daughter of Elias Hasket Derby, for whom Samuel McIntire built at Peabody. Mrs. West died March 9, 1814. At the Winterthur Museum, Delaware, there is a carved mahogany daybed made about 1820 and signed by Thomas Needham. *Antiques,* October 1953, illustrates a Hepplewhite-style mahogany table with oval satinwood inlays and Needham's label. (Kettell; Perley, *History of Salem*, Vol. 2)

NEEDLES, John, *Baltimore, Md.*
Born 1786; died 1878. Apprenticed to James Neal of Easton during 1802–7. Moved to Baltimore in 1808 and opened a shop at 10 Hanover St. In directories from 1812 to 1820 at 54 Hanover St. On May 28, 1811 married Eliza Matthews. Retired from business in 1853. Worked largely in mahogany in Sheraton style, although some pieces in the Empire style are of curly maple. Occasionally used walnut and rosewood. Some twenty labeled or documented pieces have been located. His daughter wrote *Memoirs of Eliza Needles*, which is in the possession of the family, as are other records. (*Antiques*, May 1940 and April 1954)

NEILD, Elias, *Birmingham, Pa.*
Described as cabinetmaker in deed dated 1785. (Stockwell, *American Collector*, April 1939)

NELSON, Stephen R., *Hartford, Conn.*
In the *American Mercury*, Aug. 8, 1826, appeared the following: "B. Hudson & Co., Auctioneers, advertise sale of stock by the order of Assignees of Stephen R. Nelson, Cabinetmaker."

NELSON, William, *Boston, Mass.*
Advertised in 1754 as cabinetmaker at the North End.

NELSON & GATES, *Burlington, Vt.*
Listed as makers of and dealers in chairs in 1840.

NEVILLE, Henry, *Charleston, S. C.*
Born 1796; died 1857. Son of Joshua. In 1819 listed at 134 East Bay. In 1820 joined his father and they moved to 282 King St. Burton believes he gave up cabinetmaking at time of his father's death in 1840.

NEVILLE, James, *Charleston, S. C.*
Listed in 1801 directory as cabinetmaker on Broad St.

NEVILLE, Joshua, *Charleston, S. C.*
Born 1768; died 1840. From Ireland. Became citizen in 1814. In directory of 1801 as cabinetmaker living at 11 Clifford Alley. In 1802 at 43 Tradd St. In 1820 his son Henry joined him in business and they moved to 282 King St. In the year he died he was at 98 Church St. (Burton)

NEWELL, Jonathan, *Boston, Mass.*
Listed as cabinetmaker when he arrived from Ireland in 1765.

NEWMAN, Benjamin, *probably Massachusetts*
Mrs. Burton N. Gates of Worcester, Mass., has a set of late side chairs, having a broad straight band at top, three arrow spindles, and Newman's mark. These were purchased in 1918 near Amherst, Mass.

NEWMAN, Elisha, *Ipswich, Mass.*
Cabinetmaker about 1790. (Waters)

NEWMAN, Mark, *Gloucester, Mass.*
Born Nov. 4, 1822. Cabinetmaker. (Belknap)

NEWMAN, Mark, Jr., *Andover, Mass.*
Born July 13, 1804. Cabinetmaker.

NEWTON, Ebenezer, *Oxford, Mass.*
Born 1772; died 1829. Chairmaker. (Data supplied by Mrs. Burton N. Gates of Worcester, Mass.)

NEWTON, Thomas, *Charleston, S. C.*
Advertised in *South Carolina Gazette*, June 4, 1744, that he was a carpenter, joiner, cabinetmaker, and frame maker from London and was located at "Mr. Graham's Wig maker in Broad St."

NICHOLS, Isaac, *New York City*
On subscription list for *Life of Whitefield*, 1774, as cabinetmaker.

NICHOLS, John, *Boston, Mass.*
Born 1654; died 1715. Listed as joiner in death notice in 1715.

NICHOLS, Joseph, *Savannah, Ga.*
Advertised in 1800 as a Windsor chair maker.

NICHOLS, Meric, *Providence, R. I.*
Listed in directories during 1832–37 as cabinetmaker at 148 and 186 High St.

NICHOLS, Walter, *Newport, R. I.*
Listed on Marlborough St., "West of house." "The White Horse was a noted inn on the corner of Marlborough and Farewell Streets kept by Jonathan Nichols in 1739. It was in his coffee shop that the project of building the Long Wharf begun that year was discussed and there the proprietors of the wharf, after their frequent meetings, had a good time at the table of Nichols. In 1782 Walter Nichols succeeded his father in the management of the house and his descendents still reside there. Walter Nichols, a cabinetmaker, had his shop in the small building to the west of the house and a part of the same premises." (Mason)

NICHOLS, William, *Boston, Mass.*
Born 1692. Listed as joiner.

NICKERSON, George, *Boston, Mass.*
Listed as joiner in 1690.

NOBLE, Mathew, *Chatham, Conn.* (*now East Hampton*)
Advertised in the *Connecticut Courant*, March 27, 1797: "Chairs of all kinds

(except cabinet) made and sold by the subscriber, and new seats furnished to old chairs offered. He has few sets common ones on hand, and wants to purchase WHITE WOOD or Bass Plank, 18 inches wide and 2 inches thick."

NOBLETT, Dell, *Wilmington, Del.*

Listed in directory for 1814 as cabinetmaker on Shipley St. between Broad and Kent.

NORMAN, Moses, *Newport, R. I.*

Cahoon's ledger, at Newport Historical Society, records that he paid Norman for a maple desk on Nov. 29, 1755.

NORRIS, Edward, *Salem, Mass.*

Baptized Aug. 18, 1657; died December 1700. Married Mary Symonds (daughter of James Symonds, the cabinetmaker), Dec. 3, 1686. Joiner. (Perley, *History of Salem*, Vol. 2)

NORRIS, Edward, Jr., *Salem, Mass.*

Baptized July 6, 1690; died July 19, 1759. Married Remember White, Dec. 30, 1715. Chairmaker and turner. (Perley, *History of Salem*, Vol. 2)

NORRIS, James C., *Charleston, S. C.*

Working as cabinetmaker on King St. from about 1819 to 1822. Burton believes he gave up cabinetmaking in 1822 and that he died about 1853.

NORTON, George (Captain), *Suffield, Conn.*

Born 1641 in Salem, Mass.; died 1696. Son of George Norton, who came from London in April 1629. Arrived in Suffield in 1674. Made a freeman in 1681. Married Sarah —— before coming to Suffield; married Mercy Gillette, June 20, 1683. Inventory of his estate in 1696 showed joiner's tools. (Bissell; Perley, *History of Salem; Suffield Vital Statistics*)

NORTON, Jacob, *Hartford, Conn.*

Advertised in the *American Mercury*, Nov. 8, 1790, as maker of Windsor chairs.

"Informs the public he continues to make all kinds of Windsor chairs, a few rods west of the Great Bridge, Hartford: where those who will please to favor him with their custom, may be supplied at the shortest notice, and on the most reasonable terms. Pay made easy."

NORTON, William, *New York City*

Advertised in papers in 1740 as cabinetmaker.

NOYES, Edwin, *Newburyport, Mass.*

Born circa 1824. Known as cabinetmaker.

NOYES, Francis, *Newport, R. I.*

Working in 1727 as a joiner. (Richardson)

NOYES, Isaac, *Newburyport, Mass.*

Born 1737; died 1800. Listed as joiner.

NOYES, Samuel S., *East Sudbury, Mass.*

Label on bow-front chest of drawers made about 1810 reads: "House Furniture of the most fashionable kind made, sold and exchanged by Samuel S. Noyes, cabinet maker, East Sudbury, near the Causeway." (*Antiques*, Oct. 1944)

NUTT, John, *Charleston, S. C.*

Advertised in *South Carolina Gazette*, Aug. 2, 1770: "To Be Sold for Ready Money, At the Very Lowest Prices, by John Nutt, Cabinet-Maker, Facing the Cross-Keys in King-Street, a Parcel of Well Manufactured Mahogany Furniture, consisting of Chairs of different patterns, Dining Tables of different sizes, Tea-Tables, Half Chest of Drawers, etc." Burton believes he left the province after the sale.

NUTTING, Joseph G., *Salem, Mass.*

Cabinetmaker listed at 11 North St. in 1842 and at a new address in each successive directory until 1864. Evidently had shop in building where he lived.

OGDEN, Benanial, *West Chester, Pa.*

On West Chester tax list of 1796 as

owner of an unfinished stone house and a shop. When this stone house was purchased at a later date a small Chippendale mirror with signature of Thomas Beale was found in it. No known piece of furniture by Ogden in existence. Had an apprentice named Beale. (Stockwell, *American Collector*, April 1939)

OGDEN, Benjamin, *Elizabethtown, Ky.*
Working circa 1800. "Methodist minister who was a chair-maker and worker in wood." (Sandburg, *Abraham Lincoln, The Prairie Years*)

OGDEN, Thomas, *West Chester, Pa.*
Son of Benanial. Advertised in *The Village Record* before 1810. Working after 1840. Made clock cases for Joseph Cave of West Chester. (Stockwell, *American Collector*, April 1939)

OLDHAM, John and Jacob, *Baltimore, Md.*
Listed in directories as cabinetmakers, 1796–1820.

OLDHAM, Thomas, *Baltimore, Md.*
Listed in directory for 1804 as cabinetmaker.

OLMSTEAD, *Hartford, Conn.*
See entry for Daniel Dewey.

O'NEAL, Hugh, *Philadelphia, Pa.*
Turner and chairmaker. Hornor quotes a bill of 1736 for turning and framing several dozen slat chairs.

ORDWAY, Henry, *Newburyport, Mass.*
Listed in directory for 1848 as cabinetmaker.

ORMESTON, John, *Williamsburg, Va.*
Advertised as cabinetmaker in *Virginia Gazette* in 1763.

ORMSBY, Orrin, *Windham, Conn.*
Born Aug. 14, 1766. Son of John and Deborah Ormsby. His twin brother Oliver died in infancy. Around 1785

working as a Windsor chair maker and joiner. (Bayles)

ORNE, *Salem, Mass.*
Partner in the firm of Seccomb & Orne on Boston St., Salem, 1821. (Belknap)

ORR, John, *Boston, Mass.*
In 1796 listed as cabinetmaker at 12 State St.

OSBORN, John, *Dorchester Lower Mills, Mass.*
An apprentice in firm of Hoyt, Babcock & Appleton, 1822.

OSBURN, Walter, *Annapolis, Md.*
Advertised as cabinetmaker in 1771.

OTIS, Isaac, *Boston, Mass.*
Listed as cabinetmaker in 1818.

OTIS, John, *Boston, Mass.*
Working as cabinetmaker before 1780.

OTTIGNON, William A., *Salem, Mass.*
Born Feb. 27, 1823. Married Dorcas J. Hodgdon, Oct. 7, 1847. At 6 Summer St. in 1846.

OVERSTREET, Thomas, *Louisville, Ky.*
Advertised in *Western Courier*, Jan. 24, 1814: "Three or four journeymen will find constant employment. One or two apprentices will be taken."

PABST, Daniel, *Philadelphia, Pa.*
Active during middle of the nineteenth century. Worked largely in walnut. Furniture by him at the Philadelphia Museum of Art.

PACKARD, Fearnot, *Newport, R. I.*
Working as joiner in 1733. (Richardson)

PACKROW, John, *Charleston, S. C.*
Born in Charleston. Family name originally Pasquereau. Advertised in *South Carolina Gazette*, Aug. 21, 1762, "that he still continues to carry on his business of

CABINET and CHAIR-MAKING &c. at his shop in Charles-Town, and will be obliged to those who will favour him with their custom, and he engages to have their work done well, and with the greatest dispatch, having very good workmen." In 1761 his mother gave him a lot at 115 Tradd St. One month later he mortgaged the property to John Rutledge, and in 1765 the property was taken over for the mortgage. In 1763 moved to Jacksonboro, S. C., but in a year was back in Charleston. Advertised in the *South Carolina Gazette*, Nov. 12, 1764, that he was resuming his business in Charleston. No advertising after 1767. (Burton)

PADDOCK, Zac, *Middletown, Conn.*
Joiner on Main St. between Parsonage St. and Episcopal Church about 1770–75. (Barber)

PADELFORD, John, *Taunton, Mass.*
Hepplewhite-style secretary, shown in *Antiques*, November 1940, has the following inscription of owner and maker: "Robert Deans Property, made by John Padelford, 1806."

PAGE, Benjamin *Boston, Mass.*
Listed in directory for 1789 as cabinetmaker on Fish St.

PAGE, John, *Newburyport, Mass.*
Born Feb. 3, 1810. Cabinetmaker at Market Landing in 1849 and as late as 1860.

PAGE, Thomas, *Savannah, Ga.*
Working as cabinetmaker during 1783–1828. (*Antiques*, Feb. 1954)

PAINE, Stephen, *Charlestown, Mass.*
Arrived in Charlestown as a child in 1738. Apprenticed to a chairmaker by the name of James Perry. Finished his apprenticeship with a chairmaker in Cambridge. Worked in Charlestown as chairmaker in 1743–52, then moved to Medford.

PAINTER, Samuel, *Wilmington, Del.*
Listed as chairmaker at 148 Market St. in Porter's Register, 1814.

PALMER, Richard, *Philadelphia, Pa.*
Hornor says he paid an occupational tax as cabinetmaker in 1783 of £60 and in 1786 of £200.

PALMER, William, *New York City*
Located at 2 Nassau St. In 1802 advertised "black and gold fancy chairs with cane and rush seats."

PARISH, Benjamin, *Lexington, Ky.*
Listed in directory for 1806 as cabinetmaker on Main St.

PARKER, Alba D., *Providence, R. I.*
Listed in directories during 1824–28 as cabinetmaker at 115½ and 82 South Main St.

PARKER, G., *Newburyport, Mass.*
Had cabinetmaker's shop with Southey Parker on Middle St. in 1809.

PARKER, Medad, *Salisbury, Conn.*
Died 1781. Wife's name was Tryphena. A son Ralph was born on Sept. 17, 1772 and a daughter Tryphena on Sept. 14, 1774. Inventory of his estate listed: "Joiners Shop, Cherry stuff in shop, three Joiners Benches, Turning Wheel and Lathe, 4 Jointers," many planes of various kinds, augers, gouges, paring chisels, broad and narrow chisels.

PARKER, Samuel, *Marblehead, Mass.*
Died 1771. Cabinetmaker. (Belknap)

PARKER, Silas, *Newburyport, Mass.*
Born circa 1748; died Dec. 7, 1832. Cabinetmaker. (Belknap)

PARKER, Southey, *Newburyport, Mass.*
Had cabinetmaker's shop with G. Parker on Middle St. in 1809.

PARKER, Thomas M., *Providence, R. I.*
Listed in directory for 1832 at 125 Broad St. and at Green St. Made chairs

similar to Hitchcock's. His label as quoted by Nutting reads: "Manufactured by Thomas M. Parker, Green Street, Providence, R. I."

PARKER, William, *Newburyport, Mass.*
Born 1748; died 1842. Cabinetmaker.

PARKIN, Richard, *Philadelphia, Pa.*
A pair of footstools in Empire style made about 1840 has his label. (*Antiquarian*, March 1931)

PARKMAN, William, *Boston, Mass.*
Born 1685; died 1776. Working as cabinetmaker in 1723.

PARR, John, *Baltimore, Md.*
Listed in directories during 1803–10 as cabinetmaker.

PARSONS, Edmund, *Boston, Mass.*
Listed in directory for 1825 as cabinetmaker.

PARSONS, John, *New York City*
Made a freeman in 1754, when listed as joiner. Advertised in 1754 that he did "all sorts of cabinet work." His will, dated 1756, was probated 1761.

PARSONS, John Fitch, *Suffield, Conn.*
Born April 12, 1775. Son of Ebenezer and Anne (Fitch) Parsons, who were married Sept. 16, 1772. Mother came from Hatfield, Mass. John married Clarissa Hovey, Nov. 11, 1804. Had shop on west side of Crooked Lane (now Mapleton Ave.). His account books are at the Kent Memorial Library in Suffield. These made it possible to identify some of the furniture made by him since he used no label. Worked almost entirely in pine and cherry. Sold his home in 1835 and apparently moved away. At a loan exhibition featuring work of craftsmen in and near Springfield, Mass., at the Springfield Museum of Art in the summer of 1936, a Hepplewhite sideboard of mahogany with whalebone inlay, a semicircular end table from a three-part dining table of cherry, and a cherry stand by Parsons were shown. The account books showed the sideboard and table had been made for Ebenezer King. The sideboard was made about 1807. (*American Collector*, June 1936; *Antiques*, November 1938, illustration of sideboard; Bissell, illustration of sideboard)

PARSONS, Theodosius, *Windham, Conn.*
Advertised in *Connecticut Gazette*, New London, Oct. 18, 1792: "WANTED IMMEDIATELY A JOURNEYMAN that is a good workman at the Windsor Chair and Cabinet business—to such an one good wages in cash will be given by applying to THEODOSIUS PARSONS. WINDHAM (Scotland Parish)."

PARSONS, William, *Boston, Mass.*
Born 1615; died 1702. Notice of death listed him as joiner.

PATTEFACE, William, *Baltimore, Md.*
Listed in directory for 1799 as cabinetmaker.

PATTEN, Matthew, *Bedford, N. H.*
Working 1754–67. Kept a diary in which he listed his furniture and customers. (*American Collector*, June 1937)

PATTERSON, Moles, *Baltimore, Md.*
Listed in directory for 1799 as cabinetmaker.

PATTERSON, William, *Baltimore, Md.*
Listed in directories during 1796–1818 as cabinetmaker.

PEABODY, Benjamin, *Newport, R. I.*
Mason says, "Benj. Peabody carried on a large trade in furniture with Surinam. He was an ingenious mechanic and was known as one of the best gun stock makers in the colonies." According to Richardson, Peabody was working as a joiner in 1750. The following appears in

the Aaron Lopez memorandum book (at Newport Historical Society) under date of 1761:

Peabodie, Benjamin   at the Point
Cr. by 4 Maple Desks £75   300
      by Caseing 1 Ditto   7
                                  ___
                                  307

PEABODY, John C., *Bradford and Manchester, Mass.*

Born June 12, 1825. Cabinetmaker in Manchester, 1848. (Belknap)

PEARCE, Abraham, *Charleston, S. C.*

In Charleston as early as 1766, when he was granted land by the Provincial Council. In 1768 advertised in the *South Carolina Gazette* as a cabinetmaker and carver and that he was opening a shop on Broad St. two doors from the Beef Market. That was his last advertisement. Elfe's account book shows that Pearce carved chair splats for him. Directory of 1782 lists him as an undertaker at 32 Broad St. Pearce apparently left Charleston with the British when they evacuated the town in December 1782. (Burton)

PEARCE, Ashael L., *Providence, R. I.*

Listed in directories for 1836 and 1837 as cabinetmaker at 34 Williams St.

PEARCY, Jonathan, *New York City*

Subscribed to *Life of Whitefield* in 1774 as cabinetmaker. Referred to in advertisements of Marinus Willett (*q.v.*) in 1773 and 1774 as Peasey. His name spelled in other ways also.

PEARSON, Jeremiah, *Newburyport, Mass.*
Born 1699; died 1768. Cabinetmaker.

PEASE, John, Jr., *Enfield, Conn.*

Born in Salem, Mass., May 30, 1654; died 1734. "Joiner and carpenter." He married Margaret Adams of Ipswich, Jan. 30, 1676/7 and was already the father of two children when the Pease family and neighbors left Salem for Springfield,

Mass., in 1681. Some records seem to indicate that he and his brother Jonathan had made an earlier trip in 1679 to Enfield to search out a home for the family, for in 1685 they were given extra allotments of land by the town because they had been among the "first cummers," and Enfield was settled in 1679. Family records indicate that John Pease, Sr., (1630–89) served an apprenticeship under John Symonds (*q.v.*) of Salem, the earliest of many Symonds' listed as chairmakers, cabinetmakers, and turners. In his will John Symonds assigned his apprentice (John Pease) to his son James "during the term of time in the indenture, pay £40 in four years, £10 per annum."

To John Pease, Jr., is attributed the Hadley chest at the Museum of Fine Arts, Boston. This was made for his daughter, Mary Pease, born in Enfield, May 24, 1688. She married Thomas Abbe in 1714, and died in 1746. This is one of three Hadley chests with the full name of the owner inscribed on the top rail. Some have thought John Pease, Jr., may also have made the "Thankfull Taylor Chest," but tradition in the Taylor family attributes it to Thankful's father, John Taylor (*q.v.*).

John Pease, Jr.'s eldest son John married Elizabeth Spencer, a member of the Hartford family of turners and joiners closely associated by friendship and marriage with Nicholas Disbrowe (*q.v.*). Eliphalet Chapin (*q.v.*) was a great-grandson of John Pease, Sr., a great-nephew of John Pease, Jr., and a second cousin of Elizabeth Spencer Pease; thus he was connected by birth with several in the cabinetmaking craft.

To understand the background of John Pease, Jr., "joiner and carpenter," one must go back a bit in his family history since in published data of his ancestry there are many conflicting facts. Robert and Margaret Pease of Great Baddow, Essex County, England, came to America in 1634 accompanied by their eldest son Robert (born 1607) and John, a brother of the senior Robert. This John has been confused with the many other Johns in the Pease family and has been assumed by some to be the ancestor of the John Pease, "joiner and carpenter," with whom this entry is concerned.

Robert, the father, died in Salem in 1644. His son Robert had a son named John, apparently born in England circa 1630. It is probable that John was left an orphan at an early age and that he became the responsibility of his grandmother Margaret Pease, since in her will she gave him to a Thomas Watson "as his own child." John married Mary Goodell. He was made a freeman in Salem, April 29, 1668. In the fall of 1681 he and his family, the families of his two eldest sons, John and Jonathan, and the families of several neighbors left Salem for Freshwater Brook, near Springfield, Mass., later called Enfield. He became known as the "father of Enfield." Salem Records show that he was back in Salem in 1682 to sell his house, land, and other property. In the deed he described himself as "late of Salem, now of Enfield." He died suddenly on July 8, 1689. By that time his son John Jr., "joiner and carpenter," was firmly established in Enfield, where he became one of its outstanding citizens. (Allen; Luther; Perley, *History of Salem*, Vol. 1; Rev. David Pease, *The Pease Record*, privately printed, 1869)

PECK, Benjamin, *Hamilton, Mass.*
Born circa 1749; died 1838. Cabinetmaker. (Belknap)

PECK, James, *Savannah, Ga.*
Born 1783; died 1812. Coach- and chairmaker. (Comstock)

PECKHAM, Isaac, *Providence, R. I.*
Listed in directory for 1828 as cabinetmaker at Westminster St.

PECKHAM, Reuben, *Newport, R. I.*
Working as joiner in 1732. (Richardson)

PEELE, Benjamin, *Danvers, Mass.*
Born 1740; died 1811. Cabinetmaker. (Belknap)

PENNINGTON, John, *Annapolis, Md.*
Advertised as cabinetmaker in 1750.

PERKINS, Elijah, *Salem, Mass.*
Born circa 1757; died Jan. 25, 1841. Served in the Revolution, for which he received a pension. In 1837 was working as cabinetmaker at 5 Ash St.

PERKINS, Thomas, *Salem, Mass.*
Advertised March 1831 that he was selling out. In 1826 listed on Essex St., four doors west of North St., as maker of fancy chairs.

PERRING, Charles, *Boston, Mass.*
Arrived from London in 1768, at which time listed as joiner.

PERRY, James, *Charlestown, Mass.*
Listed as chairmaker in 1736.

PETERSEN, Carsten, *Salem, N. C.*
Working circa 1800. Born near Flensburg, Denmark, in 1776. Arrived in Salem soon after 1800 with his wife and two sons, William and Edward, who learned their trade with him. Is known as the maker of several curly maple secretaries. (Fries, *Records of the Moravians in North Carolina*)

PEW, George, *Gloucester, Mass.*
Married Mary Ann Babbage, Nov. 5, 1829. Listed as chairmaker at 37 Mill St. in 1837 and as cabinetmaker at 272 Essex St. in 1842. Still living at 26 Lafayette St. after 1850 but no shop is listed separately.

PFENINGER, Martin, Sr., *Charleston, S. C.*
Mentioned in Elfe's account book in May 1772, when he paid him £40 for work. Advertised in *South Carolina Gazette*, April 12, 1773, when he was located in New Church St. Evidently successful

in business. Advertised in the same paper, Oct. 28, 1777: "Martin Pfeninger is sorry for want of material to oblige him to leave off his business of Cabinet-making &c." Died Sept. 20, 1782. (Burton)

PHELPS, Timothy, *Hartford, Conn.*
Born May 24, 1702; died Sept. 9, 1756. Son of Timothy and Sarah Pratt Phelps. His father died when he was twelve and shortly thereafter he was apprenticed—perhaps to one of the Spencers. None of his work has been identified. In 1730 he was associated with Obadiah Spencer, Jr. (*q.v.*) in settling an estate. In 1737 he co-operated with Jarrard Spencer, Jr. (*q.v.*) in work on the new meeting house for the First Church of Hartford.

PHELPS, Timothy, Jr., *Hartford, Conn.*
Baptized Aug. 8, 1725; died 1784. Married Abigail Edwards in 1751. His home and shop were on the east side of Main St., about 200 yards north of the courthouse. Barber says that in 1775 he was on Main St., between Dr. John Endicott and Richard Shepherd, tailor. For over thirty years he carried on an extensive business and tradition says he was the "leading cabinetmaker of his day," but none of his work has been identified. It may well be that some of the pieces attributed to Chapin were made by him. He fought at the Battle of Ticonderoga and after the battle was given the task of making coffins. Inventory of his estate on file at the Connecticut State Library, Hartford, shows a great many cabinetmaker's tools. Also listed: "Unfinished Desk; 3 Chairs unfinished; 1 Unfinished Desk & Book Case; Refuze Board and Stuff in Chamber Entry, Mahogany Plank; Old Brass Escutcheons." The unfinished desk and bookcase was appraised at £5.8.0, which was a comparatively high value.

PHILLIPS, Henry Lee, *Manchester, Mass.*
Born Sept. 4, 1823 at Lynn. Married Mary Frances Dennis of Gloucester, Nov. 7, 1847. Cabinetmaker. (Belknap)

PHILLIPS, John, *Charlestown, Mass.*
Born 1694; died 1755. Listed as joiner.

PHILLIPS, John M., *Charleston, S. C.*
Died 1825. Advertised in *City Gazette and Daily Advertiser*, May 23, 1796, as cabinetmaker on Beaufain St. In 1809 and 1813 listed in directories as cabinetmaker.

PHILLIPS, William, *Newport, R. I.*
Listed as joiner in 1729. (Richardson)

PHIPPEN, Ebenezer, *Salem, Mass.*
Born circa 1750; died March 29, 1792. Married Elizabeth Simmes, Oct. 27, 1772. The Rev. Bentley listed him as cabinetmaker in 1785. On April 1, 1792 Bentley recorded: "Mr. Ebenezer Phippen died after long confinement. Since the war he paid little attention to business tho a carpenter."

PHIPPEN, Samuel, *Salem, Mass.*
Born 1744/5; died Feb. 22, 1798. Married Mary Swain, Oct. 27, 1782. Lived near Union Wharf. Perley calls him a cabinetmaker. Evidently retired from cabinetmaking in 1793, when he sold a house in Danvers. (Perley, *History of Salem*, Vol. 2)

PHIPPEN, Stephen, *Salem, Mass.*
Died circa 1774. Cabinetmaker.

PHIPPS, Solomon, *Charlestown, Mass.*
Born 1700. Listed as joiner.

PHYFE, Duncan, *New York City*
In 1783 or 1784, a couple by the name of Fife and their several children, including a son named Duncan, set sail from Scotland for the New World. Two of the children died on the voyage. Upon arrival in America, the family settled in Albany, where the father opened a cabinetmaking shop. There Duncan, a lad of sixteen, worked under his father's supervision. Duncan was born in 1768 at Loch Fannich, thirty miles from Inverness, Scotland, and no doubt he had already

served an apprenticeship in his native country. Soon he was established in New York City. In William Duncan's New York Directory and Register for 1792, he is listed as Duncan Fife, joiner, at 2 Broad St. In 1794 he has moved to 3 Broad St., is listed as a cabinetmaker, and has changed his name from Fife to Phyfe. Phyfe seems not to have been happy in this location and after several changes settled at 35 Partition St., near the "Common." Before very long his shop was producing fine furniture. Records show that in a few years he was receiving orders from fashionable people not only in New York City but in Philadelphia and other parts of the country as well. Lachlan Phyfe is listed in the Baltimore Directory at 27 Gay St., 1807-9, and may well have been an agent for his relative Duncan, who, it is believed, had other agents in the South as well. Sales were good and more room became necessary to care for the expanding business. In 1807 Phyfe acquired the adjoining building at 34 Partition St. and this became the workshop. In 1811 he purchased No. 33 Partition St. The house at No. 35 continued to be his home until 1815, when he bought one directly across the street from No. 34 for that purpose. In 1816-17, Partition St. was renamed Fulton and the houses renumbered. From that time on the buildings owned by Phyfe were Nos. 168, 170, and 172 on one side of the street, and his home was No. 169, on the opposite side. A contemporary view in water color of this group of buildings may be seen at the Metropolitan Museum of Art, New York City. The building which was originally his home, and at the time of the painting the warehouse, is a three-story brick structure with marble trimming, well-designed door with semicircular fanlight, wrought-iron stoop railing, and slate roof. The middle building, which served as the showroom, is two stories in height, charming in design, with show windows on the first floor and a bank of three large windows on the second. The third

building, the workshop, has large windows on all three floors. The pediment displays a huge eagle with spread wings filling the entire space.

Until 1837 Duncan Phyfe carried on the business under his own name but in that year it became Duncan Phyfe & Sons. In 1840 it was changed to Duncan Phyfe & Son and remained thus until his retirement. By 1847 Phyfe had accumulated a large fortune and decided to discontinue the business. He sold the stock on hand at auction, retired, and lived in the house at 169 Fulton St. until his death in 1854.

When Phyfe began his career as an independent cabinetmaker in New York City, many published books of designs were available from which he could choose those appealing to his own tastes and to those of his wealthy clients. He seems to have selected largely from those of Sheraton. Later he came under the influence of the more classic Directoire style and then of the more architectural French Empire, of which he became the leading representative in America. As the years advanced he was increasingly obliged to make furniture in the styles demanded by his clients, and by the time he retired in 1847 the products of his shop were massive, heavy, and of the type known as American Empire.

In the beginning of his career Phyfe worked in the reddish mahogany which he imported from Cuba and Santo Domingo. It is said he often paid as high as one thousand dollars for a single log and supervised the cutting of the veneers which he used at times so effectively. He depended upon the choice mahogany for rich effects, seldom using contrasting wood as did many other cabinetmakers of the day, his only exceptions the bandings of matched veneers used to emphasize small panels. After 1830 much of his furniture was made of rosewood. Until his latest period he not only chose his wood with care, but also selected designs with consideration for proportion and line, and the result is clearly shown in examples of his best work. After 1830 the worsening fashions of the day were too strong even for him to combat and he was obliged to make furniture in the styles demanded by his clients. He himself belittled much of this later work, calling it "butcher furniture." In the decoration of his furniture he used turning, veneering, reeding, and carving.

Duncan Phyfe is the only cabinetmaker in America whose name is associated with a type of furniture which includes chairs, window benches, footstools, sofas, tables, sewing tables, sideboards, etc. And yet little of this socalled Phyfe furniture, even that made during his lifetime, was made by his own hands. It is safe to say that in his earliest days in New York City a great deal of the work was done by him personally, and it is the furniture of those years that is of the finest quality in design and workmanship. Doubtless, the great quantity made in his shop during its fifty-five years of existence, by more than one hundred journeymen, cabinetmakers, apprentices, turners, upholsterers, and carvers, was made under his supervision and from his selected designs and materials. Again, other pieces attributed to him and to his workshop were made in the workshops of other, contemporary cabinetmakers. Some pieces long attributed to him are now known to have been made by others. A gaming table at the Museum of the City of New York was attributed to Phyfe until Lannuier's name was accidentally discovered on the edge of a drawer.

Clients paid well for the furniture that came from the Phyfe workshop, bills dated 1816 showing that a "piere" table cost $265 and a sofa $122, extremely high prices for those days. All agree, however, that Phyfe's work deteriorated as the years of the nineteenth century advanced and that much that came from his workshop in the last years of its existence has little to recommend it to the connoisseur.

Phyfe used at least two different labels, the earlier one reading "D. Phyfe's Cabinet Warehouse, No. 35 Partition-street, New York," and the later one having the address 170 Fulton St. The amount of work produced in his shop during its fifty-five years must have been enormous and yet but a comparatively small number of labeled pieces are known today. Many articles can be attributed to his shop by documentary evidence and others by comparison with labeled pieces.

The lyre, which had been used for a long time in Europe as a decorative motif, was a favorite of Phyfe for chair backs,

Detail of carved sofa back by Duncan Phyfe, showing use of lyre motif

sofa and bench arms, and table bases, with strings of brass or whalebone and with a key of ebony running through the top. Among his favorite motifs for carving, and the carving on all Phyfe furniture is clearly defined and expertly executed, were acanthus leaves, somewhat flatter in style than usual with other carvers of the day, plumes, cornucopias, drapery swags, crossed branches of laurel, leaf and dart, wheat ears, thunderbolts, trumpets, and rosettes. At times the rosettes will be found on corner blocks on tables, on lyres, and at the intersection of the diagonal or curved bars in chair backs.

Reeding is found on almost every piece of Phyfe furniture, and quite individual with him is the contraction of reeding from top to bottom of a tapered surface such as a leg. His turnings are delicate and of the finest quality. Typical of his furniture are bulbous turnings which terminate the delicately straight reeded legs on chairs, sofas, and tables. Some of his early work shows small paw feet on the front legs of chairs, benches, and tables, so finely carved that each separate hair is plainly suggested by the use of small irregular grooves. Phyfe was fond of brass for trimming feet and for furniture mounts. Table skirtings often show a

Duncan Phyfe armchair showing Sheraton influence

narrow border of veneer, the grain of which is at right angles to that of the rest of the wood. At times corner blocks are veneered. His gaming and card tables usually have a drawer, as do his Pembroke tables. Carefully selected white wood rather than pine is used for drawer linings and the dovetailing is small and delicate.

The Phyfe-type chairs are quite dis-

Duncan Phyfe chair showing Sheraton influence

tinctive. The Sheraton-influenced chair was followed by one in which the Directoire trend is apparent. In this the lyre, so much a favorite of Phyfe, makes its appearance. In the lyre-back chair, the back posts are not continuations of the back legs as in the earlier chair but are separate pieces of wood, the break appearing at the juncture of the back and seat, and they appear to form a continuous curve with the seat. Reeding extends from the top of the face of the back posts down through the juncture, along the upper side of the side seat rails, and over the edge to the top of the front legs, which have a slightly concave curve. At times the top crosspiece is carved, at times veneered.

Duncan Phyfe lyre-back chair

The third division of the Phyfe chairs shows the influence of the French Empire styles. Here the front legs are double reversed curves, crossed in the center, either reeded or plain, and ending in brass lion's feet. The back legs remain square as in the earlier chairs, with a stretcher extending from the crossing of the front curves back to join a stretcher between the two rear legs. This chair is also found with curved legs at the sides, joined by a turned stretcher. The backs of these Empire-influenced chairs have either curved or diagonal cross bars and carved decoration similar to that of the other types. Naturally, each of the three general types shows variations, but a Duncan Phyfe chair is easily recognized. Mahogany was the wood of choice for the chairs, the seats either upholstered, of the slip type, held in place by screws, or caned, with a squab cushion for comfort.

Duncan Phyfe chair showing Directoire influence

Duncan Phyfe chair showing French Empire influence

Closely related to the chairs in design and decorative treatment are the window benches, in which the arms are similar in every way to the chair backs, although reduced somewhat in size.

Phyfe often made sofas to match his chairs, and the designs follow the same general trend from Sheraton to Directoire to Empire. The most usual sofa is that with a straight wooden top rail, usually decorated; curved wooden arms resting on small balusters; front and side rails of wood, either straight or partly curved; and six or eight legs—four in front, two and sometimes four in back. The top rail usually has three rectangular panels, generally carved with one of Phyfe's favorite motifs. The front edge of the arms forms a continuous curve with the back, is generally reeded, and ends in a slight scroll which bends back under and rests upon a delicately turned baluster. As in the chairs, the seat frame is reeded. Legs are short, reeded, and terminate in a small turning. This early sofa has an upholstered back, seat, and arms, or is caned. Variations have the upholstery carried down over the front seat rail. Few sofas have been found corresponding to the second type of chair, that showing the Directoire influence and making use of the lyre. The few that were made in this style usually have a double lyre for the arms, the back and seat upholstered, and the side and front seat rail a continuous reeded curve. The legs are of the scroll type and are also reeded. In the third type, that showing the Empire trend, the legs are crossed reverse curves with a brass lion's head at their crossing and brass lion's feet at their base. This type is either upholstered or caned. When caning is used, loose cushions are fastened over the back panels and seat.

To many the pedestal-base table is synonymous with the name Phyfe but this style was popular with all cabinetmakers in the first quarter of the nineteenth century, although Phyfe as an outstanding cabinetmaker with a fashionable clientele had many constructed by the workmen under his supervision. Some of his finest tables are in the Sheraton-influenced style with four delicately reeded legs. In this style he made card and gaming tables, Pembroke and dining tables, serving and sewing tables. Since he used the curved line in preference to a straight one whenever possible, his table tops generally show a subtle curving, at times being shaped in a clover-leaf pattern. The pedestal table is of two types: (1) that in which the pedestal is composed of a column, either plain or turned in an urn shape, supported by three or four curving widespread legs, and (2) that in which a platform rests upon the curving legs, and upon this platform a section which upholds the table top. This second type may be further divided into two groups: (1) that in which the top is supported by four posts which rest upon the platform, and (2) that in which crossed lyres support the table top. Whatever the type, there are three or four curving widespread legs, with, as a rule, Phyfe's favorite acanthus-leaf carving and reeding of the top surfaces. Feet are generally lion's paws. The tops are of great variety: oval, round, or oblong, and in many sizes, from two- and three-part dining tables to Pembroke, "piere," sewing, gaming, and card. These tops are usually curved or of the clover-leaf pattern with a border of veneer, the edges at times reeded, the skirtings veneered. In the dropleaf tables, there are corner blocks with a delicately turned pendant.

Phyfe also constructed many sofa, library, and dressing tables which have their tops supported at the ends either by a lyre or by coupled colonettes. The curving legs spread out from the base block of either the colonettes or lyre supports and are connected near the top by a delicately turned stretcher. About 1790 the sewing tables, often called Martha Washington, were introduced, and many of these were constructed in the Phyfe workshop either in the Sheraton style with delicately reeded legs or with the pedestal base. Although chairs, sofas, window benches, and tables were made in the Phyfe workshop in large numbers and are most characteristic of his work, he also made sideboards, piano cases, beds, and other furniture.

Examples of Phyfe's work may be seen in many museums, among them, the Metropolitan Museum of Art, New York City (PLATE XXIX, No. 1), the New-York Historical Society, the Museum of the City of New York, the Brooklyn Museum, the Boston Museum of Fine Arts, the William Rockhill Nelson Gallery of Art, Kansas City, Mo. An outstanding collection of Phyfe's works at the Henry Ford Museum, Dearborn, Mich., includes among other things a piano.

At the Ohio Historical Society at Columbus there is a bill for an interesting item made by Phyfe in 1827. At that time Thomas Worthington, who had been Ohio's governor, a United States Senator, and the holder of many other important positions, died in New York City and his body was shipped home to Chillicothe, Ohio, in a Phyfe-made coffin. The author is indebted to John S. Still, Curator of Historical Collections at the Ohio State Museum, for this fact.

(*American Collector*, May 1929, Jan. and June 1935, March 1942; *Antiquarian*, March 1930; *Antiques*, Nov. 1922, Dec. 1929, April 1934; Cornelius, the most comprehensive study of Phyfe)

PICKERING, George, *Philadelphia, Pa.*
Died 1784. In 1783 paid an occupational tax of £60. In 1784 advertised as cabinet- and chairmaker and stated that he had on hand "17 walnut chair feet, 9 mahogany and walnut Bannisters." Hornor says that "George Pickering made a set of six slat back Mahogany chairs before 1784."

PICKERING, Theophilus (Reverend), *Ipswich, Mass.*
Born Sept. 28, 1700 in Salem; died Oct. 19, 1747. A skillful cabinetmaker, as shown by a set of chairs in William and Mary style as well as other pieces of furniture still in the possession of the Pickering family.

PICKETT, Rufus H., *Ridgefield, Conn.*
Working circa 1820. Samuel Hawley and Rufus H. Pickett had a cabinet shop which stood on the site of the south end of the old Bailey Inn (no longer standing) and extended beyond the fence to the grounds of Joshua I. King. Pickett

lived in a house opposite the shop. This partnership continued for some years but was then dissolved and Pickett continued alone. He employed many apprentices and was always called "Boss" Pickett. John Bouton, who later had a shop in Norwalk, learned his trade with Pickett and was very skillful at mahogany veneering. Pickett used to take Bouton with him on trips through the woods around Ridgefield to help select trees to be cut down for making furniture. Rockwell, in his *History of Ridgefield, Connecticut,* says, "Many fine examples of furniture to be seen in Ridgefield and adjacent towns were made by 'Boss' Pickett and his men. Mr. Pickett did all the turning and carving and was especially fine and expert as a mahogany carver. High four-post beds, stands, ornamental chairs, center tables and card tables with claw feet, every kind of furniture was made in Ridgefield. Much of their product was sent to the southern states, especially counting house desks—as they were called—of mahogany and cherry." Among those whom Rockwell says learned their trade with Pickett were William Stone, Charles A. Smith, George Keeler, Douglas Morgan (who came over from Georgetown), Nelson B. Sherwood, Thaddeus Hoyt, and Pickett's two sons Starr and Edwin. Starr was killed in the Civil War. Just below Cooper Station, in that part of Ridgefield known as Florida, the remains of an old dam indicate the location of "Boss" Pickett's mill where he sawed out lumber to use in his cabinet shop.

PIERCE, Azel, *Lebanon, Conn.*
Advertised in the *New London Gazette* as cabinetmaker on March 17, 1813.

PIERCE, Joseph, *Manchester, Mass.*
Cabinetmaker. Married Martha S. Burnham, April 13, 1840, in Essex.

PIERCE, Thomas, *Charlestown, Mass.*
Joiner who claimed loss of tools in fire of 1775.

PIGNOT, William, *Boston, Mass.*
Listed as cabinetmaker in 1805.

PIMM, John, *Boston, Mass.*
Working 1736–53. Purchased house and land on north side of Fleet St., Aug. 10, 1736. In the *Boston Weekly News Letter* for June 23-30, 1737 he advertised this land and added, "Inquire of Mr. John Pimm cabinet-maker near Scarlet's Wharfe, and know further." It is believed that he was the maker of a highboy which bears the name Pim on each drawer and that he sent it to a japanner to be lacquered—probably Thomas Johnson, the leading japanner of Boston, who advertised in 1732 "At the Golden Lyon in Ann Street." This highboy is now at the Winterthur Museum, Delaware. A similar one with matching lowboy is at the Metropolitan Museum of Art, New York City. (*Antiques,* May 1929)

PITMAN, John, *Salem, Mass.*
Died 1800. Cabinetmaker. (Belknap)

PITMAN, John, Jr., *Newport, R. I.*
Chairmaker. Working in 1752. (Richardson)

PITMAN, Mark, *Salem, Mass.*
Baptized June 20, 1779. In *Antiques,* May 1933, there is illustrated and described a small mahogany secretary which was purchased from Pitman by the present owner's direct ancestor and which has never been out of the family. This has a hinged leaf that rests on slides to form the writing surface. It bears Pitman's label, which reads:

CABINET WORK,
of all kinds,
MADE AND WARRANTED
by
MARK PITMAN
ESSEX STREET,
Nearly opposite Cambridge Street,
SALEM

Mahogany secretary with label of
Mark Pitman

At the Essex Institute, Salem, there is a
Pitman label identical with the one in
the secretary.

PITMAN, Mark, Jr., *Salem, Mass.*
Baptized Aug. 21, 1814; died circa 1859.
Learned his trade with his father and
carried on business at 324 Essex St. until
1855.

PITON, Thomas, *Baltimore, Md.*
Advertised as cabinetmaker in 1783.

PITTEE, David C., *Manchester, Mass.*
Born circa 1818. Married Mrs. Sarah J.
Webber, daughter of James Ridley, Nov.
23, 1848 in Beverly. Cabinetmaker.
(Belknap)

PLUMB, Ebenezer, Jr., *Litchfield, Conn.*
Working in 1797. *See* entry for Oliver
Clark.

PLYMPTON, Calvin, *Medway, Mass.*
Working 1775–1816. Apprenticed to
Luther Metcalf (*q.v.*).

POALK, George, *New York City*
Signed as chairmaker when witness to
a will dated 1772.

POE, Thomas, *Baltimore, Md.*
Listed in directories during 1803–18 as
cabinetmaker.

POIGNAND, David, *Boston, Mass.*
Arrived in Boston from St. Heliers,
Isle of Jersey. At the City Art Museum,
St. Louis, Mo., there are three pieces of
furniture made by Poignand—a secretary,
chest of drawers, and folding card table.
The secretary was made in 1788 and was
willed to the second son, David R. Poignand, of Lancaster, Mass. It is believed
he took this and the other pieces with
him when he went to Kentucky, where
he was married in 1814. From him they
descended by inheritance to the Plant
family and were given to the museum
by a member of that family. The lock
plate of the secretary is marked "D P
1788."

POINTER & CHILDRES, *Richmond, Va.*
Makers of a labeled Windsor chair.
Pointer is in the Richmond census of
1782.

POOR, John, *Newburyport, Mass.*
Baptized May 31, 1812. Advertised as
cabinetmaker. Worked as late as 1860.
Married Nancy Titcomb of Cumberland, Me., Aug. 20, 1843. (Belknap)

POOR, Samuel, *Newburyport, Mass.*
Died Nov. 29, 1727. Chairmaker. Married Rachel Baily, Feb. 16, 1679, in Newbury. (Belknap)

PORTER, Benjamin R., *Charleston, S. C.*
Died 1825. From 1797 to 1822 worked
as cabinetmaker. In 1797 entered into a
partnership for a short time with Jacob
Labach. Their one advertisement appeared in the *South Carolina Gazette*,
June 20, 1797: "Cabinet Makers. The subscribers beg leave to inform their friends
and the public, that they have commenced

the Cabinet-making Business, No. 187 Meeting Street." (Burton)

PORTER, John, *Hartford, Conn.*

Advertised in the *Connecticut Courant*, Sept 27, 1802: "Manufactures all kinds of CABINET WORK, in the best manner, of the latest and most approved pattern and at the shortest notice. An assortment of the most fashionable and common articles, constantly for sale at his cabinet shop Hartford, State St. 30 rods East of the State House. N.B. Journeymen at the above business wanted, please to inquire of said Porter."

PORTER, William, *Charlestown, Mass.*

Cabinetmaker. Married Sally Fosdick, 1806.

POTTER, Daniel, *Ipswich, Mass.*

Located on Windmill Hill. Described as "a cunning maker of chairs circa 1790." On March 3, 1818 adjudged *"non compos mentis."* (Waters)

POTTER, Joseph, *Marblehead, Mass.*

Died July 14, 1768. Cabinetmaker and carver. (Belknap)

POTTER, Phillips, *Providence, R. I.*

At the Rhode Island Historical Society there is an agreement signed by several Providence cabinetmakers on March 24, 1757. It concludes with a list of prices for various items of furniture such as "Mahogany high Cases of draws at £100:00:0," Walnut do with tear of Draws £75:00:0," "Black Walnut high Case of Draw at £85." The agreement was signed by Grindall Rawson, Benjamin Hunt, John Power, Phillips Potter, and Joseph Sweeting.

This agreement is on one side of what was evidently a paper used by Potter the year before which is entitled "Rule and Price of Joyners Work, Phillips Potter His Book 1756." Potter's prices in 1756 were considerably lower than those in the agreement.

POUILHAN, C., *Baltimore, Md.*

Listed in directories for 1807 and 1808 as cabinetmaker.

POWELL, Joseph, *New York City*

Records of colonial treasurer in 1768 showed he was ordered to pay "Joseph Powell £11:43:3 for making two Book Cases and a large Table for the use of the General Assembly."

POWER, John, *Providence, R. I.*

Cabinetmaker working in 1757. Signed agreement of Providence cabinetmakers, March 24, 1757. *See* entry for Phillips Potter.

POWERS, Stephen, *Lexington, Ky.*

Working in 1818 as cabinetmaker. (Whitley)

PRATT, Joel, Jr., *Sterling, Mass.*

A painted armchair, made circa 1830–40, with paper label of "Joel Pratt, Jun.," is at the Henry Ford Museum, Dearborn, Mich.

PRATT, Joseph, *Newport, R. I.*

Listed in William Langley's account book (at Newport Historical Society) as a chairmaker in 1790.

PRATT, Phineas, *Weymouth, Plymouth, and Charlestown, Mass.*

Born 1593, probably in London. Arrived in America early in 1622 and settled at Wessagusset (Weymouth). Fled to Plymouth in 1623. Purchased land there in 1626. Married Mary Priest in 1630 and they had nine children. Moved to Charlestown in 1650 and died there in 1680. It is possible that while in Plymouth he worked with John Alden and Kenelm Winslow, makers of much of the oaken furniture produced in that locality.

In 1931 the R E B Chest (Luther's No. 15) was discovered near Boston. This chest by its structure and history seems to be somewhat older than the one by Disbrowe (*q.v.*). It has four panels with grooved stiles and dentiled posts and lower rail. The tulip and leaf decoration, the leaves with rounded stems as on the Hadley chests of the Hartford group, and the initials common to the Hadley chests are present. Structurally this four-panel chest is closer to the earlier Jacobean models than are the other Hadleys, and it is the only one with four panels. A possible date of 1650 is assigned to it, some thirty years earlier than the date of the Mary Allyn chest by Disbrowe. It is deemed possible that this chest was constructed by Pratt, who was one of the earliest cabinetmakers in America. (Luther; Willison)

PRATT & WALKER, *Boston, Mass.*
Listed in 1816 as cabinetmakers on Washington St.

PRENTICE, Oliver, *Hartford, Conn.*
See entry for Tibbils & Prentice.

PRICE, Ephraim S., *Salem, Mass.*
Died August 1839. Married Mary B. Doyle, June 10, 1828. Member of firm of Price & Averill. Took John Jewett's shop on Vine St., July 3, 1829. At Charter St. in 1837. (Belknap)

PRICE, Joseph, *Manchester, Mass.*
Born at Tamworth, N. H. Married Abigail S. Abbott, June 14, 1841 at Manchester, and Mrs. Nancy Rust of Lynn, Dec. 21, 1844. Cabinetmaker. (Belknap)

PRICE, R., *Baltimore, Md.*
Listed in directory for 1804 as cabinetmaker.

PRICE, Warwick, *Baltimore, Md.*
Working 1790–1810. Listed in directories during 1800–10 as cabinetmaker at 45 Bridge St. A shield-back chair attributed to him and made 1790–1800 is at the Baltimore Museum of Art. (Bordley)

PRICE, William, *Boston, Mass.*
Born 1684 in England; died 1771. In 1726 advertised chests of drawers, corner cupboards, tables, and Japan work. In 1733 advertised at "King's Head & Looking Glass."

PRICE & AVERILL, *Salem, Mass.*
See entries for Ephraim S. Price and James K. Averill.

PRICE & PARR, *Baltimore, Md.*
Listed in directory for 1804 as cabinetmakers.

PRIESTLEY, Edward, *Baltimore, Md.*
Listed in directories during 1810–20 as cabinetmaker.

PRIESTLEY & MINSKY, *Baltimore, Md.*
Listed as cabinetmakers in 1807.

PRINCE, Samuel, *New York City*
Advertised from 1772 until the time of his apparent retirement in 1776. Located on Cart & Horse St. His advertisement in 1772 reads: "All sorts of CABINET-WORK in the neatest manner, and on the lowest terms. Orders for the WEST-INDIES, and elsewhere, completed on the shortest notice." Died in 1778 in New Jersey and his will showed a considerable estate. At the Winterthur Museum, Delaware, there is a mahogany desk and bookcase (Downs, No. 224) believed to have been made by Prince since it is similar to one made between 1770 and 1775 with his label. The piece at the Winterthur Museum has a pitch pediment, fluted, chamfered corners, and knuckled feet, and is decorated with Chinese frets. *Antiques*, July 1946, illustrates a "Beau Brummel"—a combination desk, dressing table, and chest of drawers—in the Chippendale style with Prince's label. He used a finely engraved trade card which reads: "Joyner at the Chest of Draws in Cart & Horse Street New York Makes and Sells all Sorts of Joyners Work on the Lowest Terms."

PROUD, Daniel and Samuel, *Providence, R. I.*
Listed in directory for 1824 as chairmakers at 105 Broad St. and residents at

23 Chestnut St. Swan, in *Antiques*, April 1946, lists Daniel as a joiner and cabinetmaker in Newport in 1780. It might well be that Daniel was Samuel's father and that in his late years he came to Providence to work and live with his son.

PULCIFER, Francis, *Salem, Mass.*
Born 1771; died June 24, 1823. Partner of Samuel Frothingham (*q.v.*) on Church St. until they removed to Court St. in 1795, when partnership dissolved. Pulcifer continued in the cabinetmaking business by himself. In 1803 shipped furniture on *Welcome Return* to Brazil.

PULCIFER, James, *Salem, Mass.*
Cabinet- and chairmaker on Court and Water streets in December 1795.

PULCIFER & FROTHINGHAM, *Salem, Mass.*
See entries for Francis Pulcifer and Samuel Frothingham.

PULSIFER, Israel Eliot, *Beverly, Mass.*
Baptized June 26, 1774. Died Dec. 21, 1809. Cabinetmaker. (Belknap)

PURCELL, Henry, *Baltimore, Md.*
Listed in directories for 1799 and 1800 as cabinetmaker.

PURSE, W. W., *Charleston, S. C.*
Born 1797; died 1858. Listed in directory from 1822 to 1831. Burton says that Purse has the distinction of being one of the few cabinetmakers of Charleston to whom a definite piece of furniture can be attributed. He made a bookcase of mahogany for James Jervey in 1822 and it and the receipted bill are in the possession of a descendant.

PUTNAM, Joseph, *Lexington, Ky.*
Advertised in *Kentucky Gazette* of Lexington, March 15, 1795, that he was "doing cabinet work." Trained many apprentices. (Offutt)

PUTNAM, Nathaniel, *Danvers, Mass.*
Died Nov. 15, 1800. Cabinetmaker

whose estate was sold at time of his death to pay debts.

QUACKINBUSH, Laurence, *Charleston, S. C.*
Married Mary Pringle, Sept. 3, 1801. Listed in directory for 1806 at 3 Cock Lane. His daughter Ann baptized in 1808. No further record and Burton believes he moved to some other locality.

QUERVELLE, Anthony, *Philadelphia, Pa.*
Listed in Philadelphia directories during 1835–49. Mentioned in Watson's *Annals of Philadelphia*, 1846, as among the wealthy men of the community and worth upwards of $75,000. Watson says he was a native of France and an extensive manufacturer of furniture who "made his money by steady industry and strict economy." In *American Collector*, November 1943, Downs shows a secretary made circa 1835 with Quervelle's label, which reads, "Cabinet and Sofa Manufactory, South Second Street a few doors below Dock, Philadelphia."

QUIMBY, John, *Springfield, N. H.*
In 1813 advertised: "Wanted Immediately a journeyman to the Cabinet Business. One who is master of making Tables, Bureaus, Sideboards, Clock Cases, and will receive large wages for six months or more by applying to John Quimby." (*American Collector*, June 1937)

QUIMBY, Moses, *Newburyport, Mass.*
Listed as cabinetmaker in 1849 and 1850.

RALPH, John, *Charleston, S. C.*
Died 1801. Worked for Elfe during winter of 1773–74. Elfe paid him £35 each month. After that probably worked as independent cabinetmaker until 1793, when he formed a partnership with Nicholas Silberg. This lasted for about three years, after which Ralph resumed work by himself. (Burton)

RALPH & SILBERG, *Charleston, S. C.*

Partnership of John Ralph and Nicholas Silberg formed October 1793. Advertised in the *City Gazette & Daily Advertiser*, Oct. 1, 1793, that they were "Cabinet Makers, Chair Makers, and Undertakers at 52 Church St." In the same paper, April 1, 1796, appeared the notice of their dissolution. (Burton)

RAND, Ebenezer, *Charlestown, Mass.*

Born 1688; died 1743. Notice of death listed him as joiner.

RAND, Jacob, *Charlestown, Mass.*

Born 1778; died 1840. Cabinetmaker who was an apprentice of Jacob Forster in 1797. After finishing his apprenticeship went to Hardwick.

RAND, Thomas, *Charlestown, Mass.*

Died 1786. Notice of death called him a joiner.

RANDALL, Charles E., *Providence, R. I.*

Listed in directories for 1836 and 1837 as cabinetmaker working on Cranston St., residing at 151 High St.

RANDLE, William, *Boston, Mass.*

Advertised in 1715 when he was located on Queen St. that he made chests of drawers, desks, bookcases, etc.

RANDOLPH, Benjamin, *Philadelphia, Pa.*

Born in Monmouth County, N. J.; date of birth unknown. Woodhouse says he was the son of Isaac Fitz-Randolph of Monmouth County, N. J., a descendant of Edward Fitz-Randolph of Nottingham, England, who arrived in Scituate, Mass., in 1634 and moved to New Jersey about 1670. (In 1637 Edward married Elizabeth Blossom, whose family arrived in Salem, May 15, 1629, on the *Mayflower*, but not the original Pilgrim ship.)

On Feb. 17, 1762, Benjamin Randolph married Anna Bromwich, only daughter of William Bromwich, a staymaker on Sassafras St., Philadelphia. At that time he was already established in business, his

shop the "Golden Eagle" located on Chestnut St. between Third and Fourth. In 1770 he was using a very elaborate advertising card engraved by J. Smither and adapted from plates in Chippendale's

Elaborately carved chair back of Philadelphia Chippendale side chair, circa 1770-80

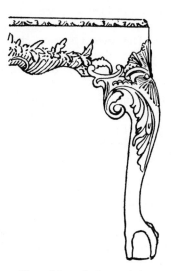

Carved leg of above chair

Director, and his label read "All Sorts of Cabinet and Chair Work Made and Sold by Benj. Randolph, at the Sign of the Golden Eagle in Chestnut Street, Philadelphia." His receipt book for the years 1763-77 is now in the collection of the

Winterthur Museum, Delaware. In 1792 he retired from business and returned to his home at Speedwell Mills, on Wading River, near Burlington, N. J. By this time his first wife had died, and he married Mary Wilkinson, widow of William Fenimore.

Furniture made by Randolph reveals him to have been one of the greatest cabinetmakers and carvers of America. His famous six "sample" chairs (attributed to him by family history since they descended in the family of his stepson Nathaniel Fenimore) are superb examples of cabinetmaking and carving. Three are here illustrated. The Chippendale wing chair now at the Philadelphia Museum of Art is massive in proportion, richly carved on arms, legs, and apron, and the legs terminate in heavily furred paw feet. (PLATE X, No. 2) It is thought that the mask in the center of the apron front may be a portrait of Benjamin Franklin. In 1929 this chair was sold at the Reifsnyder auction in New York City for $33,000, the highest price ever paid at that time for an American-made armchair. The second sample chair that is illustrated is also at the Philadelphia Museum of Art; it is one of the most beautiful of Randolph's side chairs, elaborate with incomparably rich carving. (PLATE XI, No. 1) Also illustrated is a much simpler chair, with Randolph's label, from the Karolik Collection at the Boston Museum of Fine Arts. (PLATE XI, No. 2) This shows some similarity to chairs made by James Gillingham (q.v.). It will be noticed that even in the most elaborate side chair the back legs are somewhat crude and without ornamentation. This was intentional, as such chairs when not in use were meant to stand against the wall, and when in use at the table would be seen only by the servants.

It is a matter of record that Jefferson commissioned work by Randolph and to him is attributed the table upon which the Declaration of Independence was drafted. In 1930 when an exhibition was being arranged at the New Jersey State

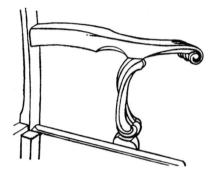

Detail of arm supports of Philadelphia Chippendable-style armchair

Museum at Trenton to celebrate the city's 250th anniversary, six walnut chairs bearing Randolph's label were shown. At the Metropolitan Museum of Art, New York City, there is a table made about 1770 that is attributed to Randolph, and there are chairs attributed to him in the Garvan Collection at Yale University, in the northeast bedchamber of the Palace at Williamsburg, Va., at Kenmore, Alexandria, Va., and at the Wintherthur Museum.

(Cescinsky, *Antiques*, Nov. 1925; Downs; Hipkiss; Hornor; Miller; Nutting; Ormsbee; Willison; Woodhouse, *Antiques*, May 1927)

RANGER, Edmund, *Boston, Mass.*
Listed as cabinetmaker on Purchase St. in 1789.

RANK, Johannes, *Jonestown, Pa.*
As in the case of the Seltzers (q.v.), it is believed the Ranks came to Pennsylvania from the Palatinate and at about the same time. Johannes was born April 15, 1763 and died May 4, 1828. It is thought he learned the art of decorating chests from Christian Selzer. Chests with his signature are dated 1795 and 1796 and show him to have been a competent painter who followed Selzer's lead closely. Painting, however, did not seem to have the attraction for him that it did for his gifted teacher, and he became better known as the keeper of the White Horse Tavern on the town square of

Jonestown, the same square where his brick mansion, now a store, still stands.

RANK, John Peter, Sr., *Jonestown, Pa.*

Born Nov. 3, 1765; died June 26, 1851. Thought to have been a brother of Johannes. A chest believed to have been made about 1790, which is similar to the work of Christian Selzer, has on the right-hand vase "Peter Rank His Hand." The work on this chest, however, does not equal that of Christian Selzer. John Peter used a cinnamon-brown for his leaves instead of the rich brown used by Christian. In signing his name he never used "John."

RANK, Peter, *Jonestown, Pa.*

It was believed by Esther Stevens Frazer that Peter was a grandson of Johannes Rank. In the Rank Mansion at Jonestown in 1933 there was a chest in the attic marked "Januar der 23, 1800." The work on this is similar to that of John Peter Rank, Sr., but is less competent. It shows many dots on the flowers and leaves as well as on the border. A second chest with this feature is dated "Peter. 1807." For details concerning these chests *see* entries for Christian Selzer and John Seltzer. For data on the Rank and Seltzer chests the author is greatly indebted to Ray Boeshore, Borough Secretary of Jonestown, Pa., Miss Evelyn Isele, of Jonestown, Pa., and Raymond E. Krape, of Mechanicsburg, Pa. (*Antiques*, Feb. and April 1927)

RANKIN, Samuel, *Lexington, Ky.*

Working in 1818 as cabinetmaker. (Whitley)

RAWSON, Grindall, *Providence, R. I.*

Born 1719; died 1803. Fourth son of Wilson Rawson of Mendon, Mass. Settled in Providence in 1741. Carried on his trade of cabinetmaking on Long Wharf. Married four times. At the Rhode Island Historical Society there is a mahogany chair from a set made at the Rawson Shop in 1801 for Jacob Whitman as a wedding present for his granddaughter. Although Grindall was in his eighties at this time, it is probable that he was still the head of the shop; however, the chairs were undoubtedly made by his son Joseph. Grindall was the first of three generations of Rawsons in the cabinetmaking business in Providence from 1741 to 1809. He was one of the signers of the Providence cabinetmakers agreement, March 24, 1757.

RAWSON, Joseph, *Providence, R. I.*

Died July 19, 1835. Learned his trade in his father's shop. Became a lieutenant in the Revolution. In 1791 a member of the firm of Wallen & Rawson, manufacturers of fifes, on Westminster St., "next door east of Theodore Foster, Esq." Listed in directory for 1824 as Joseph Rawson & Sons, 102 Westminster St., and Sugar Lane. In 1828 Joseph and Joseph Jr. are listed at 68 Broad St.; during 1832–37 George B., Samuel, and Joseph Jr. are listed at same address. (*Mechanics Festival and Historical Sketches*)

RAYMOND, Benjamin, *Beverly, Mass.*

Born April 26, 1768. Married Mary Procter of Marblehead, April 29, 1799, and Betsy Raymond, March 5, 1809. Cabinetmaker.

RAYMOND, William, *Beverly, Mass.*

Cabinetmaker. Married Dec. 4, 1785.

RAYNER, James, *Charlestown, Mass.*

Suffered loss in fire of 1775, after which moved to Newburyport.

RAYNSFORD, Solomon, *Boston, Mass.*

Listed as joiner in 1696.

READ, John, *Baltimore, Md.*

Listed in directories during 1808–10 as cabinetmaker.

READMOND, Jeremiah, *Savannah, Ga.*

Advertised from 1802 to 1820 as cabinetworker.

REDIN, Henry, *Boston, Mass.*
Listed as chairmaker in 1714.

REDMOND, Andrew, *Charleston, S. C.*
Died 1791. Advertised Jan. 13, 1784 in *South Carolina Gazette and General Advertiser* that he "still carries on, at No. 27 Meeting-street near the New Church or corner of St. Michaels Alley, Turnery in all its branches. All kinds of House, Cabinet and Ship-Joiner's Work; Jobbing, ditto, etc. Likewise Philadelphia Windsor Chairs, either armed or unarmed, as neat as any imported, and much better stuff; etc." In 1774 did some work for Elfe. Will probated Feb. 1, 1791. (Burton)

REED, Daniel T., *Newburyport, Mass.*
Moved to Newburyport from Nashua, N. H. Listed in directory for 1848 as cabinetmaker. Also made reed organs. Working as late as 1860. (Belknap)

REES, Edward, *Philadelphia, Pa.*
Died 1793. Cabinet- and chairmaker on South Third St. Inventory of his stock showed: "1 Lot Mahogany Chair feet; Mahogany Front Rails and Slats, 1 Lot Chair Stuff; 7 Doz. Mahogany Back feet; 4 doz. do do; 3 Doz. walnut do; 15 Mahogany Banisters." (Hornor)

REID, William, *Lexington, Ky.*
Working 1793–1806. When taking out citizenship papers in 1798 stated he came from Scotland. In *Kentucky Gazette* in 1793 advertised that he was making chairs "next door to Lawyer Hughes and opposite J. Postlewaite's." Listed in directory of 1806 as chairmaker on Mulberry St.

RENSHAW, Thomas, *Baltimore, Md.*
Listed in Baltimore Directory in 1814 and 1815. At the Baltimore Museum of Art there is a painted settee in Sheraton style made by Renshaw. It is decorated with landscapes which at one time were erroneously described as Baltimore scenes. The inscription reads: "Thos. Renshaw, No. 32 S. Gay St., Balti. (the maker)— John Barnhart Ornamenter." (Bordley)

RESIDE, William, *Charleston, S. C.*
In *City Gazette and Daily Advertiser,* April 9, 1799, advertised that his shop was at 131 Meeting St. Listed in 1809 directory on Church St.

RETTINGER, A., *Louisville, Ky.*
Advertised in the *Western Courier,* Dec. 31, 1813: "A. Rettinger Informs his friends and the public that he now has on hand a large supply of stuff for Cabinet Work, etc."

REYNEL, John and Jacob & Co., *Uniontown, Pa.*
Advertised in the *Genius of Liberty,* Jan. 13, 1816, that they "Wish to inform their friends and the public in general that they carry on the Cabinet Making Business in all its branches in Uniontown at the East end of Main street opposite the Widow Gilman."

REYNOLDS, Jonathan, *Newport, R. I.*
Working as chairmaker in 1764. (Richardson)

RHEA, Robert, *near Freehold, N. J.*
Working circa 1695. In exhibition of the early arts of New Jersey held at the New Jersey State Museum in 1953 there was shown a wainscot chair made by Rhea on his plantation near Freehold in 1695. This chair has a rectangular back framing a center panel carved with a thistle, rows of ornamental gouge work, and the inscription "16 R 95/R. I."
The initials are those of Robert Rhea and his wife Jennett (Hamtom) Rhea. Rhea is known as a Scotch house carpenter, and the crest rail on the chair is treated in an architectural manner unlike that found on other wainscot chairs of American origin.

RHOADES, Nathaniel A., *Dedham, Mass.*
Born circa 1810 in Sharon, Mass. Moved to Dedham at some unknown date. Married Sarah Wilson of Dedham, Sept. 14, 1849. Cabinetmaker.

RICHARD & DIKE, *Montague, Mass.*
Listed as makers of stenciled furniture circa 1850.

RICHARDS, Edward, *Boston, Mass.*
Listed as cabinet- and chairmaker on Devonshire St. in 1796.

RICHARDS, John, *Manchester, Mass.*
Born March 24, 1806; died Dec. 23, 1834. Married Hannah Hilton, Nov. 10, 1830. Cabinetmaker. (Belknap)

RICHARDSON, Christopher Columbus, *Beverly, Mass.*
Cabinetmaker. Died before Feb. 21, 1826. (Belknap)

RICHARDSON, Ebenezer, *Newport, R. I.*
Working as joiner circa 1733. (Richardson)

RICHARDSON, Elisha, *Franklin, Mass.*
Working 1743–98, at which time Franklin was known as West Wrentham. He was a maker of Windsor chairs. These were sturdy, with well-molded saddle seats and generous turnings. Mrs. Burton N. Gates of Worcester possesses one with his name marked on it. He also made a banister-back chair, a slat-back rocker, and a roundabout chair which are in existence and bear his name. Luther Metcalf (*q.v.*) was an apprentice in his shop from 1770 to 1778. (Jameson)

RICHARDSON, Stephen W., *Salem, Mass.*
Cabinetmaker at 199 Essex St., 1837–50.

RICHMONDE, *Philadelphia, Pa.*
Working in 1763. It is believed he made Windsor chairs in Independence Hall. His shop was on Arch St. (*Bulletin, Pennsylvania Museum of Art,* Dec. 1925)

RICKER, Henry, *New York City*
Subscribed to *Life of Whitefield* in 1774 as cabinetmaker.

RIDER, Elijah, *Providence, R. I.*
Listed in 1824 directory as chairmaker at 181 South Main St.

RIDGEWAY, Ebenezer, *Boston, Mass.*
Listed as cabinet- and chairmaker on Fish St. in 1789.

RIDGWAY, Samuel, *Boston, Mass.*
Notice of death in 1773 listed him as chairmaker. A second Samuel Ridgway was listed on Ann St. in 1786 as chairmaker—perhaps a son.

RILEY, John, *Charleston, S. C.*
Born 1751; died 1804. Burton believes he served as apprentice in some shop in Charleston. After Revolution moved to Jacksonborough, about twenty-five miles from Charleston. Listed as cabinetmaker when administering an estate in 1804.

RILEY, Samuel, *Wilmington, Del.*
Listed in Porter's Register about 1814 as chairmaker at 27 East Front St.

RINDGE, John, *Ipswich, Mass.*
Baptized Oct. 7, 1759. Died Oct. 18, 1801. Cabinetmaker on High St. Married Sarah Baker, May 14, 1786.

RITTER, Charles, *Lexington, Ky.*
Working in 1818 as cabinetmaker. (Whitley)

RIVINGTON, James, *New York City*
Advertised between 1760 and 1770. Shop on Hanover Square.

ROBBINS, John, *Charlestown, Mass.*
Married in 1798, when he was listed as cabinetmaker.

ROBERTS, Aaron, *New Britain, Conn.*
Born April 20, 1758; died 1831. Son of Dr. Aaron and Hepzibah Shepherd Roberts of Middletown. He married Ruth Hart, eldest daughter of Thomas Hart, Feb. 17, 1785, and Mary Wadsworth, May 20, 1829. Concerning him Camp wrote: "While young he learned the trade of joiner and cabinetmaker at Rocky Hill. He bought of a fellow apprentice, Daniel Ames, a house which had been built by the latter on the west side of South Main St. He also became owner of the Bassett Farm and for many

years worked the farm with hired help in connection with his trade." Mr. Houghton Bulkley of Hartford, Conn., who owns several pieces attributed to Roberts, has been delving into his background for years. He has had writing on the back of one piece identified as that of Roberts, which makes attribution certain. Several pieces were in the Three

Chest-on-chest of the type attributed to Aaron Roberts. Shape of pediment, cornice with notching, shell carving, finials, and feet are characteristic of work attributed to this man. Circa 1785

Centuries of Connecticut Furniture exhibition at the Wadsworth Atheneum, Hartford, in 1935. Number 90 was a cherry chest-on-chest with scroll top, cornice with notching, carved rosettes, and handsomely carved base for urn-shaped finials. There was raised carving on the square drawer, quarter columns, and curved bracket feet. This piece was dated

1780–90. Numbers 145, 220, 223, and 235 were similar to the above. Number 147 was a cherry highboy with scroll top, carved rosettes, urn finials, carved upper and lower square drawers, quarter columns, cabriole legs with some carving on the knees, and claw-and-ball feet. This was indicated as characteristic of Roberts' work circa 1780. Number 151 was a mahogany highboy with scroll top, carved rosettes, urn finials at ends, center piece carved in a mushroom shape, columns full twisted, underpart of skirt carved, cabriole legs, claw-and-ball feet, made 1770–80. Two chest-on-chests in Chippendale style, made circa 1785 and attributed to Roberts, are at the Henry Ford Museum, Dearborn, Mich. A cherry chest-on-chest attributed to Roberts is on loan at the Wadsworth Atheneum, Hartford.

Furniture attributed to Roberts shows him to have been a competent cabinetmaker. He worked largely in cherry although some pieces were made of mahogany. He created some pieces in the block-front style and several show characteristic rope-twist columns, sometimes in the upper section of a chest-on-chest, at times in both upper and lower sections. He also used a dentil cornice, carving on the center and sometimes lower square drawer showing interlaced stems instead of the usual fan or shell, and an individual portion of an applied shell at the base of the center finial. From time to time pieces attributed to him are advertised for sale. *Antiques*, May 1946, shows a cherry chest-on-chest with blocked front, carved shells, rope-carved columns, bonnet top with carved cornices and finials. There are distinctive notches or dentils below scrolls of the pediment. This chest-on-chest shows features common to those pieces attributed to Roberts.

ROBERTS, S., *Pemberton, N. J.*

Shown at loan exhibition at the State Museum, Trenton, N. J., 1953, was a fancy armchair (No. 42). Beneath the seat was the maker's brand mark "S. ROBERTS NEW MILLS."

ROBERTS, Samuel, *Robertsville, Conn.* (*southeast section of Colebrook*)

Working 1805–40. Samuel's father, John E. Roberts, operated a chair shop on the site of an old iron forge built in 1770 by Richard Smith, who also had an iron furnace in Salisbury. Smith returned to England at the beginning of the Revolution and Jacob Ogden took over the forge. Later the forge was taken over by Joseph and Elisha Buell, and in the latter part of the eighteenth century the place came into the possession of Samuel's father and Samuel inherited it from him. At first the chairs, similar to those made by Lambert Hitchcock, were turned by hand but eventually were milled. There were apparently several varieties, all with wooden seats, the earliest without stenciling. In November 1838 Roberts formed a partnership with Rufus Holmes of Colebrook under the firm name of Holmes & Roberts (*q.v.*) and the firm made stenciled chairs. In 1839 they began to mark them with the firm name. In November 1840 they sold the plant to Hitchcock (*q.v.*) and Alford.

ROBILLIARD, Samuel, *Savannah, Ga.*

Advertised from 1766 until 1806 as turner.

ROBINSON, John M., *New Orleans, La.*

In partnership with Prudent Mallard (*q.v.*) in a flourishing business at 305 Royal St. from 1860.

ROBINSON, Richard, *Boston, Mass.*

"Made a square table in 1747 for ye Speaker 7:0:0." (*Province Records*)

ROBINSON, William, *Newport, R. I.*

Working as joiner in 1734. (Richardson)

ROBINSON & GWYNN, *Wilmington, Del.*

"Chair manufacturers" circa 1814 at 15 Market St. (*Porter's Register*)

ROCKWELL, Thomas H., *Ridgefield, Conn.*

Married Deborah Townsend, July 20, 1795. In 1799 bought a shop at upper end of Main St., having learned his trade with Elisha Hawley. On December 30, 1799 advertised in the *Republican Journal* of Danbury as cabinetmaker. (Rockwell)

ROCKWELL, Warren, *Salisbury, Vt.*

Working as chairmaker in the village in 1816. (Weeks)

RODGERS, Fitz William, *Andover, Mass.*

Cabinetmaker working in 1847. (Belknap)

ROGERS, Ebenezer, *Newburyport, Mass.*

Listed in directory for 1848 as cabinetmaker. In 1849 at corner of Olive and Merrimac streets. Working as late as 1860, but no shop address given after 1854.

ROLFE, Ebenezer, *Newburyport, Mass.*

Born Feb. 24, 1818. Listed in directory of 1848 as cabinetmaker. Working as late as 1860.

ROMAN, Alexius, *Baltimore, Md.*

Listed in directory for 1809 as cabinetmaker.

ROSETT & MULFORD, *Elizabethtown, N. J.*

Makers of inlaid case furniture in Hepplewhite style. (*Catalogue, State Museum*, Trenton, N. J., 1953)

ROSI, John E., *Philadelphia, Pa.*

Large Empire sideboard owned privately in Texas bears notation "Made January 29, 1828 in Philadelphia by John E. Rosi." Illustrated in *Antiques*, January 1930.

ROSIER, Robert, *Concord, Mass.*

Robert Rosier, a Frenchman, married a relative of Joseph Hosmer (*q.v.*) and lived in Concord near the bridge. He was an excellent cabinetmaker and Hosmer learned his trade with him. Later the Rosiers moved to Albany. The author is grateful to Mrs. Howard W. Kent of the Concord Antiquarian Society for her helpfulness in securing data regarding Rosier and Hosmer. (*Centennial of the Social Circle in Concord*, 1782-1882)

ROSS, Horace, *Manchester, Mass.*
Born April 13, 1818. Cabinetmaker at Manchester, then moved to 25 Forrester St., Salem, in 1846.

ROSS, John G., *Boston, Mass.*
Listed in directory for 1832 as cabinetmaker.

ROSS, Lorenzo D., *Newburyport, Mass.*
Born April 14, 1810. Married Joanna Janvrin, March 17, 1833. Working as cabinetmaker as late as 1850.

ROSS, W. B., *Baltimore, Md.*
Cabinet- and chairmaker at 8 Hanover St. in 1833. (Varley)

ROU, George D., *Charleston, S. C.*
Listed in directory for 1819 as cabinetmaker on Warren St.

ROU, M., Jr., *Charleston, S. C.*
Listed in directory for 1802 as cabinetmaker at 22 George St., in that for 1806 as M. Rou without the "Jr."

ROULAIN, Abraham, *Charleston, S. C.*
Born Aug. 6, 1738; died 1787. Son of Abraham Roulain and Mary Ann Guerin Roulain, French Huguenots. Not known in whose shop he was apprenticed. On Dec. 6, 1768 advertised in the *South Carolina Gazette*: "ABRAHAM ROULAIN Acquaints the Public, in General, and his friends and former customers that he hath removed into Tradd Street, next Door to George Saxby, Esq., where he carries on the Joiners and Cabinet Business; he will be much obliged to those Ladies and Gentlemen who please to favour him with their custom. —— Mrs.

Roulain carries on the Mantua-Makers Business at the same place." (Burton)

ROUSBY, John, *New York City*
Signed as cabinetmaker when witness to a will in 1766.

ROW, George Daniel, *Charleston, S. C.*
Listed in directory for 1801 as cabinetmaker at 11 Federal St.

ROWE, Abram, *Manchester, Mass.*
Born in Gloucester. Baptized Aug. 3, 1807. Married Olive Maria Goldsmith, December 1832, in Manchester, where he was working as cabinetmaker.

ROWE, George W., *Portsmouth, N. H.*
A single labeled example by him is known. This is a Hepplewhite secretary made circa 1780. (*American Collector*, May 1937)

RUGGLES, Levi, *Boston, Mass.*
Listed in directory for 1810 as cabinetmaker.

RUSH, William, *Philadelphia, Pa.*
Born 1756; died 1833. The chief carver in Philadelphia. Evidently employed to carve furniture in addition to figureheads for merchantmen and frigates and cigarstore Indians. Hornor believed he studied with Edward Cutbush. Rush was a founder of the Pennsylvania Academy of Fine Arts.

RUSS, Nathan K., *Lowell, Mass.*
Listed as cabinetmaker in 1835.

RUSSELL, Porter, *Newburyport, Mass.*
Married Elizabeth Oaks, Nov. 20, 1808, and Mrs. Ann Pearson, Aug. 24, 1817. Advertised as cabinetmaker in 1833. Listed in directories from 1848 to 1857 at Brown's Wharf and Merrimac St.

RUST, Henry, *Boston, Beverly, and Salem, Mass.*
Born 1737 at Ipswich. Cabinetmaker who was in Boston in 1773, in Beverly in

1782, and then in Salem. On Jan. 22, 1771 received part of house of Samuel Ruck (Rust?). (Perley, *Salem in* 1700)

RUTTER, John, *Baltimore, Md.*
Advertised in the *Maryland Gazette*, April 10, 1786, as maker of Pembroke tables. (Miller)

RYCHMAN, John, *New Brunswick, N. J.*
Advertised in 1793 that he was a cabinet- and chairmaker who had "lately removed from New York."

SACKETT, Isaac, *Providence, R. I.*
Listed as cabinetmaker in directory in 1824 at foot of Union St., in 1828 at 105 Westminster St., during 1832–37 on Walker St.

SAFFORD, Ebenezer, *Newburyport, Mass.*
Born March 4, 1822 in Newbury. Listed in directory for 1849 as cabinetmaker at 10 Middle St. Married Emily Ann Wormstead, Sept. 12, 1847.

SAFFORD, Nathaniel, *Salem, Mass.*
Employed by the Sandersons (*q.v.*) as a turner in 1800.

SAFFORD, Samuel Henry, *Newburyport, Mass.*
Born Dec. 3, 1819. Listed in directory for 1849 as cabinetmaker at 10 Middle St., doubtless in association with Ebenezer, who was probably a brother. Married Lucretia B. Story, Nov. 28, 1844.

SAGE, Lewis S., *Northampton, Mass.*
"Cabinetmaker north of meeting house." On March 17, 1793 advertised in *Hampshire Gazette*: "Desks, cases of Drawers, tables, bureaus, frame chairs, Windsor chairs, plain do, & other articles." (Judd)

SALISBURY, Benjamin, *Boston, Mass.*
Listed as cabinetmaker in 1751 on a wharf on Bangs Alley.

SAMPSON, William, *New Orleans, La.*
Advertised in old sugar and rice journals, "William Sampson, New Orleans, Established 1830. Plantation Furniture, Mahogany or Rosewood, a Specialty." (*American Collector*, May 1936)

SANBORN, Reuben, *Boston, Mass.*
Listed in directory for 1789 as chairmaker on Doane St.

SANDERSON, Elijah, *Salem, Mass.*
Born 1752 in Watertown; died 1825. In 1781 married Mary Mulliken of Lexington, sister of Samuel Mulliken, clockmaker. After death of his brother Jacob (*q.v.*), who had been his partner, Elijah formed a partnership with Benjamin Swan, Joel Tay, and Captain John Waters, owner of the schooner *Molly*, and continued to make furniture for export. During the years he and his brother worked together (about 1790 to 1810) they were among the outstanding furniture-makers of Salem, employing many workmen and apprentices. It is a matter of record that Samuel McIntire carved some furniture for them. The Sanderson Papers at the Essex Institute, Salem, show shipments of furniture to Alexandria, Baltimore, Charleston, Savannah, New Orleans, the East and West Indies, and South America. Elijah thought his work superior to that of his partners or workmen, branded his initials on those pieces made by him, and gave instructions to the ships' captains to sell his furniture separately. He was shipping furniture to Brazil as early as 1803 on the *Welcome Return*.

When he died the following appeared in the *Salem Gazette* of Feb. 18, 1825: "Died in this town Deacon Elijah Sanderson, Aged 73, a worthy and honest man and a useful member of society. He was at the Battle of Lexington. On the evening of the 18th of April, 1775, he saw a party of nine British officers pass up through Lexington where he then resided. It being unusual to observe British officers pass into the country at evening his attention was attracted. In the evening he and one or two of his neighbors followed to ascertain what were their intentions; when they had followed as far as Lincoln, the officers who had so posted themselves as to command the road, made prisoners of Mr. Sanderson and his companions and led them aside into the fields and detained them there until about 3 o'clock in the morning, when the officers in the road made prisoner of Colonel Paul Revere who had escaped from Boston after the British troops had embarked and was rushing into the country to sound the alarm. Colonel Revere informed them that their movements were detected and the country alarmed, notwithstanding their precautions. They then ordered their prisoners to mount and returned toward Lexington. When they arrived near the Meeting House they heard the alarm Bell ringing; the British officers then ordered their prisoners to dismount, cut their saddle girths and bridles to prevent them reaching their countrymen. The British officers then started off at full speed and soon met the British troops marching on to Concord. When they came up to the Meeting House at Lexington they rushed on Huzzaing and fired. The militia soon dispersed."

(Belknap; Downs, No. 168; *Sanderson Papers*, Essex Institute, Salem, Mass.)

SANDERSON, Jacob, *Salem, Mass.*

Born circa 1758 in Watertown; died 1810. The Sanderson shop was on Federal St.; the "Sanderson Cabinet Wares," as it was called, employed many journeymen and apprentices. In June 1791 Elias Hasket Derby purchased furniture from the Sandersons at a cost of £177—a considerable sum—much of which was shipped to Calcutta, where it was sold at auction. In 1799 the Sandersons had Josiah Austin as a partner and the company began shipment of their furniture on their own account. At the Pingree House, Salem, there is a Sheraton-style mahogany tester bed with reeded posts

and carved sheaves of wheat made by Jacob Sanderson in 1807 for Aaron Waitt. (Belknap; Downs; *Sanderson Papers*, Essex Institute, Salem, Mass.)

SANDERSON, John, *Salem, Mass.*

Born 1794. Married Abigail Haskell, Dec. 7, 1824. Had cabinetmaking shop at 51 Federal St., 1837-53. Died circa 1857, after which his wife carried on the business until 1861.

SANFORD, John, *Boston, Mass.*

Listed as carver on Cornhill in 1789.

SANFORD, Samuel, *Newport, R. I.*

His will (at the Newport Historical Society), probated Jan. 6, 1806, designated him as cabinetmaker.

SANFORD, Zachariah, *Saybrook, Conn.*

Will probated Dec. 29, 1732. Inventory listed: "11 rope hooks, 3 spindles, 2 hooks, 2 burning irons, branding iron, 3 swigle knifes, 5 Turning Chisells and a gouge, Joyners plow, 4 small plains, 2 hand plains, 2 cove plains, long plain, two squares, chair bit, 3 small bitts, 3 chisels, 2 gouges." (*Probate Court Records*, Guilford, Conn.)

SANFORD & NELSON, *Hartford, Conn.*

Advertised in *American Mercury*, April 6, 1824: "SANFORD & NELSON Cabinetmakers offer for sale at their Cabinet Warehouse, a few rods South of Bennett's City Hotel, Main Street, an extensive assortment of new and fashionable Furniture CONSISTING of the FOLLOWING ARTICLES: Sideboards, Lockers, Sofas, Pillar & Claw Tables, Card Tables, Cherry breakfast and dining tables, Workstands, Secretaries, Bedsteads, Music Stools, etc. of various descriptions, which will be sold as low as can be purchased at any warehouse in the State. Those who wish to purchase would do well to call and look for themselves. Lumber of all kinds taken in exchange."

SANGER, Stephen S., *Alexandria, Va.*

Advertised in *Alexandria Gazette*, Jan. 9, 1834 "that he still continues to manufacture and has now on hand Beds, Mattresses & Chairs and Cabinet Furniture at his Upholstering & Cabinet Ware Room. Repairs in either line done neat, cheap & expeditiously."

SARGENT, Jabez, *Charlestown, Mass.*

Born at Malden. Married in 1716, at which time he is called a cabinetmaker.

SARGENT, Solomon 3rd, *Gloucester, Mass.*

Cabinetmaker. Married Charlotte W. Plummer, Nov. 19, 1843. (Belknap)

SARGENT, Winthrop, *Salem, Mass.*

Member of cabinetmaking firm of Kimball & Sargent on Essex St. opposite Union St. from April 25, 1821 to 1829; at 4 Holyoke Place from February 1831. Firm listed in directory for 1837 but Sargent's name is not. Still living, however, since he was a member of Charitable Mechanics Association in 1840.

SASS, Edward George, *Charleston, S. C.*

Born 1788. Son of Jacob, with whom he doubtless served his apprenticeship. Associated with father in 1811 when they advertised as Jacob Sass & Son. In 1813 directory they are both listed at 38 Queen St. In directory for 1822 Edward is listed at Northern Warehouse, 77 Queen St. Immediately after father's death in 1836 advertised in *Courier* that he intended to carry on the business. Died Jan. 20, 1849. Left his tools and workbenches to his son George Washington Sass. (Burton)

SASS, Jacob, *Charleston, S. C.*

Born 1750. Arrived from Germany in 1773 and in 1776 married Dorothea Vielham, daughter of a German planter. For almost fifty years worked as a cabinetmaker in Charleston. Held many positions of honor and trust in American Army during Revolution. Became a member of the German Friendly Society in 1777 and its president in 1789. His portrait hangs in the Hall of the Society. Acquired a great deal of property in and around Charleston. His wife died March 31, 1812 and he died in February 1836. They are buried in St. John's Lutheran Churchyard. A mahogany desk-bookcase in the Miles Brewton House has this inscription in ink on the side of an interior drawer: "Made by Jacob Sass, October, 1794." Other pieces of furniture have been attributed to him but this is the only labeled piece to come to light. (Burton)

SAUNDERS, David Elwell, *Salem, Mass.*

Cabinetmaker. At 261 Essex St. during 1837–46. Married Henrietta A. Felt, Feb. 11, 1838.

SAUNDERS, John, *Bradford, Mass.*

Died before April 1819. Cabinetmaker. (Belknap)

SAUNDERS, Moses, *Bradford, Mass.*

Born circa 1765; died 1819. Cabinetmaker. (Belknap)

SAUNDERS, Philip H., *Salem, Mass.*

Born June 23, 1800. Cabinetmaker. Had shop on Danvers Place near Aborn St. His stock and tools were sold there April 10, 1823, when he either had died or was discontinuing business.

SAVERY, William, *Philadelphia, Pa.*

Born 1721; died 1788. Comparatively unknown until some years ago when his label was discovered on the underside of a carved lowboy at the Van Cortlandt Manor, New York City. This reads: "All Sorts of Chairs and Joiners Work Made and Sold by William Savery at the Sign of the Chair a little below the Market in Second Street, Philadelphia." Immediately many pieces of Philadelphia-made furniture, now known to have been made by other Philadelphia cabinetmakers, were attributed to Savery.

Savery was a Quaker and catered to the Quaker trade in a little shop the size of its lot, 12′ 6″ wide. Inventory of his estate showed no carving tools, so it is probable that he constructed the furniture but had others do the carving, a custom among many cabinetmakers. He advertised frequently in the *Pennsylvania Journal* and the *Pennsylvania Packet* during the years 1750–72. The discovery of the lowboy with his label made it possible to identify pieces in various collections as having been made by him. Some twenty with his label have come to light. Although he is no longer considered the outstanding cabinetmaker of his day, he is judged to be one of the fine craftsmen "whose gamut of work," according to Downs, "ranged from maple rush-bottom chairs to carved mahogany high chests of quiet elegance." The earliest pieces made by him are in the Queen Anne style; the later pieces in Chippendale. At the Winterthur Museum, Delaware, there is a plain walnut armchair in Chippendale style, made 1755–60, bearing his label. At the Detroit Institute of Arts there are two side chairs and an armchair attributed to him, made about 1750. These were in the Reifsnyder sale in 1929. At the Philadelphia Museum of Art there are several pieces attributed to him. At the Henry Ford Museum, Dearborn, Mich., there is a Chippendale-style armchair with Savery's initials and the date 1758. Hornor illustrates a Chippendale chest-on-chest made about 1770 and attributed to Savery (fig. 146). A walnut chest made about 1760 and having Savery's label pasted within a secret drawer of the till is illustrated in *Antiques*, February 1929. (*Antiquarian*, July 1930; Cescinsky; Downs; Hornor; Nutting)

SAYWELL, David, *Boston, Mass.*
Notice of death in 1673 listed him as joiner.

SCHOLZE (or SCHOLZEN), P. W., *Baltimore, Md.*
Working circa 1790. In the Schuyler Mansion at Albany, N. Y., there is a Hepplewhite-style mahogany chest of drawers made about 1790 with the inscription

"P. W. Scholze [rubbed, could be Scholzen] Cabinetmaker, 7 East Lexington St., Baltimore." A search of the Baltimore directories for 1796 and 1799–1802 did not reveal any such name. The piece was illustrated in *Antiques*, April 1954.

SCOTT, Charles, *Providence, R. I.*
Directory of 1828 lists his cabinet warehouse at 115 South Main St. at corner of Benefit and Transit streets. It is possible that he and Adrian Webb (*q.v.*) were the partners who used the label "Webb & Scott, Cabinet & Chair Makers, Benefit-Street, Providence, Rhode Island" found in a cherry secretary-bookcase, with ogee feet, arched top, and inlay, mentioned by Nutting.

SCOTT, Edward, *Boston, Mass.*
Listed as Windsor chair maker in 1801.

SCOTT, John, *Newport, R. I.*
Working as "Joyner" in 1696. (Richardson)

SCOTT, Mathew, *Baltimore, Md.*
Listed as cabinetmaker in 1807 and 1808.

SCOTT, Peter, *Williamsburg, Va.*
Advertised in *Virginia Gazette* in 1755 as cabinetmaker.

SCOTTOW, John, *Boston, Mass.*
Notice of his death in 1678 listed him as joiner.

SCOTTOW, Joshua, *Boston, Mass.*
Arrived in Boston in 1639, when listed as joiner.

SCOTTOW, Thomas, *Boston, Mass.*
Working as joiner in Boston as early as 1638.

SCUDDER, John (Captain), *Westfield, N. J.*
Working during the late 1700s. Used a label. Maker of inlaid furniture. (*Catalogue*, State Museum, Trenton, N. J., 1953)

SEAVER, William, *Boston, Mass.*

Chairmaker "At the Sign of the Chair," Vose's Wharf, 1796. Just discovered is a Windsor cradle with a label which indicates that William Seaver and James Frost (*q.v.*) were in partnership circa 1798. Label reads: "Warranted / Windsor Chairs / and Settees / in the newest stile, and of a superior quality / Made and sold by Seaver and Frost / Sign of the Windsor chair / No. 57 . . . Street, Boston. / They offer to return money should quality not answer the expectation of purchaser." Illustration of hooded cradle with bamboo notched spindles shown by Ginsburg & Levy, *Antiques*, January 1957.

SECCOMB, *Salem, Mass.*

Partner in the firm of Seccomb & Orne on Boston St., Salem, 1821. (Belknap)

SEGAR, Joseph, *Suffield, Conn.*

Died 1740. In Land Records at Northampton, Mass., listed as "Chairmaker." At town meeting, May 19, 1740, Aaron Hitchcock was granted town pay for making a coffin for Segar. (Judd)

SEIDENBERG, Henry, *Newburyport, Mass.*

Married Nancy Woodbury, Dec. 11, 1832. Listed as cabinetmaker in 1849, and also as a dealer in furniture on Market Square from 1849 to 1854.

SEIGNOURET, Francois, *New Orleans, La.*

Born 1768. Arrived in New Orleans from his birthplace, Bordeaux, France, about 1800. Established his furniture business at 520 Royal St. and by 1832 was the most fashionable cabinetmaker in New Orleans. The wealthy planters engaged him to furnish their houses, and he sold his products as far away as Mobile and Charleston. He made massive furniture to fit the high ceilings and large rooms of the southern homes, a typical Seignouret armoire being between eight and ten feet in height. Although he used mahogany, he seems to have preferred rosewood. His carving was done directly on the piece of furniture rather than being applied. Tradition says that every piece of furniture made by him has the letter S somewhere about the carving. Since he used the S curve in his carving design, particularly at the corners of panels, this may have given rise to the legend. His tables, chests, and so on usually have marble tops. He made a particular type of chair—an adaptation of a popular First Empire design—that is known even today as the "Seignouret chair." This has a rounded top rail which extends forward and downward to form low arms which curve to the front legs. In his earliest chairs of this type the front legs were a part of the arms; in his later chairs they were made separately and then joined to the frame. The chair back has one splat in the center. The front legs are modified cabriole and the back legs curve slightly backward. Seignouret did not use a label and furniture is attributed to him only by style and tradition. Some pieces attributed to him are illustrated in *Antiques*, September 1943. He returned to France in 1853. His business was carried on a few years longer under his name but unsuccessfully. (*American Collector*, May 1936; *Antiques*, Aug. 1944)

SELDON, Isaac, *Hadley, Mass.*

Married Esther Ingram, Oct. 14, 1725. Esther's mother was one of the Smiths of Hadley. In 1762 Isaac was recorded as being "noncomposmentis" and an inventory of his estate listed a chest. When he died in 1764 a second inventory listed "a Chest 2/8, a Chest in ye Chamber 2/8, a Chest in ye garret 2/8." Seldon was a carpenter and Luther believed that he may have made the E I Chest (Luther's No. 42).

SELLARS, William, *Baltimore, Md.*

Listed as cabinetmaker during 1796–1810.

SELTZER, John (Johannes), *Jonestown, Pa.*

Born Aug. 9, 1774; died Feb. 1, 1845.

Eldest son of Christian Selzer (*q.v.*). He is buried near his father in Trinity Lutheran Cemetery, Jonestown. When John's brother, Christian Jr., died in 1814, John was an administrator of his estate and was listed as "house carpenter of Bethel township." It is deemed probable that he made the chests which the Seltzers and Ranks painted. The Seltzer house was directly across the street from the brick mansion of the Ranks, on land where today's bank is located. It may well be that Christian Selzer constructed the earliest chests which he painted since there is a difference in the base molding of those made before and after 1790. After 1790 there is no difference whatever in the construction of the many chests painted by the Seltzers and the Ranks. A few chests with John Seltzer's signature have a drawer at the bottom. Eighteen hundred is the earliest date yet found on a chest with his signature. His method of decoration follows closely that of his father, and his mottling and graining are similar. Instead of the rich brown used by his father for leaves, however, John used green, and he introduced a lovebird into his design. After 1810 his chests show a decline in both workmanship and decorative design.

SELZER, Christian, *Jonestown, Pa.*

Doubtless the Seltzer family (like the Ranks [*q.v.*]) came to Pennsylvania early in the eighteenth century from the Palatinate. The name is found with several spellings. In the Census of 1790 two Christian Sulsers and one John Selser are found. Christian spelled his last name without the "t," as shown on his tombstone in Trinity Lutheran Cemetery at Jonestown. On the tombstone of his son John (Johannes), in the same cemetery, however, the name is spelled Seltzer, and from that time onward his descendants used that spelling.

Christian was born Feb. 16, 1749 and died Feb. 3, 1831. His will, probated Feb. 10, 1831, divided his estate among his ten children. The inventory showed an estate valued at $30,000, which was con-

siderable at that time. His wife, Elizabeth, had died in 1824.

Painted dower chests bearing Christian Selzer's signature reveal him to have been a creative artist. These chests vary slightly in size and in the spacing of the panels, and no two are painted with exactly the same design. Chests bearing his signature carry dates from 1771 to 1796. Those dated before 1790 show broad panels, large and flamboyant flowers, and somewhat thick vases with simple S-curve handles. His signature is in German script with the name "Christian" on one line, the letters of which could not be confined within the vase-form on which they are scratched. On later chests "Christian" is on two lines, "Selzer" on one, and the date on another. This inscription was lightly scratched with some sharp instrument and apparently was done while the paint was still wet. In the same manner, the chest design was embellished with zigzags, rosettes, and borders for the vases.

As Christian's skill and experience developed, he produced a design more delicate and refined. Chest panels became taller with a corresponding increase in the height of the vase painted on them. The vases themselves are more competently designed and have well defined handles.

By 1795 Christian was evidently instructing his son and various members of the Rank family in the methods of decorating the dower chests. None, however, succeeded in equaling his work in this field. Raymond E. Krape of Mechanicsburg, Pa., has made a most thorough study of these chests and was of assistance to Esther Stevens Fraser, who wrote detailed articles on the chests in 1927. He has kindly furnished the author with a summary of his findings. The chests are made of whip-sawed white wood (up-and-down sawmill lumber). They are generally forty-eight inches in length. This means that on a three-panel chest there are three-inch spaces at either end and between each panel, and three twelve-inch panels into which the design is fitted. The chests generally have a German rat-trap type lock, the top part riveted through the lid. This lock has a large key with escutcheon. Around the escutcheon, a unique circular design resembling graining was achieved by rolling the wet paint with a corncob. The strap hinges are usually hand-wrought, ornate, and often of a tulip design. Inside the chest are sometimes one, sometimes two trinket drawers. The lid of such drawers was doweled to the side of the chest so that it could not be removed without destroying the chest. The front, back, and ends of the chests are neatly dovetailed. The chest interior is never finished. In some there is a small secret drawer that is opened by pressure at a certain spot. Mr. Krape has found this drawer in chests made by both the Ranks and Seltzers. The last descendant of Christian Selzer to bear the family name died Dec. 25, 1955 in Harrisburg, Pa., and now none of the two families of Seltzers and Ranks remain.

A chest signed and dated 1785 by Christian Selzer is at the Metropolitan Museum of Art, New York City. (PLATE VII, No. 1) A chest dated 1796 is at the Philadelphia Museum of Art.

(*Antiques*, Aug. 1925, Feb., April, and June 1927)

SEYMOUR, John, *Boston, Mass.*

About 1794 John Seymour arrived in Boston with his wife Jane and their son Thomas. They came from Portland, Me., but since there is no record of their being in Portland and since Portland was an active seaport it is likely they came from England on a boat that landed at Portland and went directly from there to Boston. When Jane died in 1815 notice of her death in the *Columbian Centinel* said that she "was the wife of John Seymour, formerly of Axminster, England." This would mean that John had received his cabinetmaking training there. In the directory for 1796 John Seymour, cabinetmaker, is listed on Creek Square; this was the location of his shop until it was closed

in 1808. The first mention of him in a newspaper was in *Russell's Gazette*, June 28, 1798, when Dr. J. Flagg, in announcing an auction at his house, listed much furniture "of the workmanship of Mr. Seymour."

Seymour is considered the greatest designer and craftsman of Boston after the Revolution. He had his son Thomas (*q.v.*) associated with him from at least 1800, but it is probable that he himself designed and largely constructed most of the furniture that is attributed to him or that has the label "John Seymour & Son." Characteristic of his work and considered as significant as his label is a curious robin's-egg blue paint used on compartment interiors. Other characteristic features include inlaid pilaster forms, sliding tambour shutters, inlaid festoons on reeded tambour slides, a lunette or half-ring pattern inlay on top edges and skirts, and a variety of secondary woods in a single piece. All his furniture shows delicate proportions and fine workmanship.

As early as 1804 his son Thomas was advertising his Boston Furniture Warehouse and in 1805 is listed separately in the directory as "Thomas Seymour, Furniture Warehouse, Common St." In 1808 the cabinetmaking factory of John Seymour & Son closed. The John Seymours lived on Portland St., and when Jane died in 1815 Thomas and his wife moved from their home on Milk St. to the Portland St. house.

There are a great many pieces of furniture attributed to Seymour in the Karolik Collection at the Boston Museum of Fine Arts. Among them are a tambour sideboard (PLATE XXIV, No. 1) and a tambour desk (PLATE XXIV, No. 2). In 1929 a mahogany and satinwood Hepplewhite secretary made about 1790–1800 and bearing the label of John Seymour & Son was sold at auction for $30,000. This had inlaid festoons on the reeded shutters—details rarely found—and the four ring handles had circular plaques of Battersea enamel. At the Boston Museum of Fine

Arts and at the Winterthur Museum, Delaware, one may see similar pieces.

One of the most beautiful pieces at the Boston Museum of Fine Arts is a commode of mahogany, satinwood, bird's-eye maple, and rosewood, made 1790–1800. This semicircular chest of drawers was sold to Elizabeth Derby of Salem by Thomas Seymour, in 1809. Doubtless, however, it was made by his father. On its top, radiants of alternating woods converge toward the back in a small semicircular area painted with seashells in a manner most skillful and unusual. It is believed the painting was done by John R. Penniman, who is listed in the Boston Directory as a painter at 57 Warren St. This richly beautiful piece of furniture has lion's-head brasses similar to those used in Boston and Salem by other cabinetmakers and brass feet identical with those used by Duncan Phyfe. Other pieces attributed to Seymour at the same museum are: a mahogany and satinwood tambour basin stand, made 1790–1800; a mahogany and satinwood marble-top bedside stand, 1800–1810; a mahogany and bird's-eye maple sideboard in Sheraton style, 1800–1801; a wine cooler of mahogany and satinwood hooped with brass, circa 1795; a lady's work table of mahogany and curly maple in Sheraton style, 1800; a pair of armchairs with upholstered backs and sides and with arm rests carved with leaf patterns, the ends supported by turned and carved posts; and a pair of chairs of mahogany with satinwood veneers in Sheraton style, circa 1800. In the Haverhill Room of the American Wing, at the Metropolitan Museum of Art, New York City, there is a mahogany bed with richly carved posts at the foot attributed to Seymour.

(*Antiques*, April 1947, April 1948; Hipkiss)

SEYMOUR, Thomas, *Boston, Mass.*

Son of John (*q.v.*). Arrived in Boston about 1794. By 1800 apparently associated with his father in the cabinetmaking business on Creek Square. On Dec. 4, 1804, advertised in the *New England Palladium*:

BOSTON FURNITURE WAREHOUSE

The Subscriber respectfully informs the Public that he has taken and fitted up in a most commodious manner those extensive premises at the bottom of the Mall (lately occupied as the Washington Museum) for the purpose of a Commission Furniture Warehouse where he now offers for sale a handsome assortment of Cabinet Furniture, Chairs, Looking Glasses; and from the daily addition to his Stocks and to the prices of the Furniture he flatters himself that persons purchasing any of the above articles will find it to their advantage to call as above.

THOMAS SEYMOUR

N.B. As it is his intention to keep constantly on hand a general assortment of every article necessary to furnish the house completely, those who may have second hand furniture to dispose of will have an opportunity of obtaining its full value by depositing the same at the said warehouse where the Cabinet business is carried on in all its branches and any article made on the shortest notice.

In 1805 Seymour enlarged the warehouse and added upholstering to his services. About 1807 Thomas entered into a partnership with James Cogswell (*q.v.*), a cabinetmaker on the same street. This partnership did not last long, because on May 30, 1812 Thomas advertised: "On Tuesday next the Ware Room of the Boston Cabinet Manufactory Congress Street will be opened when will be for sale Useful, and Ornamental Cabinet Furniture all made by or under the direction of Thomas Seymour. Ladies and Gentlemen particularly the former customers of Thomas Seymour are respectfully invited."

When Stephen Badlam died in 1815 the accounting of the Badlam estate at the Norfolk County Probate Office showed that Thomas Seymour owed him $1,369.15, undoubtedly for furniture Badlam had sent to the warehouse to be sold on commission. Thomas continued his shop on Congress St. until 1821 and then moved to 837 Washington St. He was listed there until 1842.

(*Antiques*, Oct. 1937, April 1947, April 1948, May 1954; Hipkiss)

SHAW, Alexander, *Philadelphia, Pa.*

Listed as cabinet- and chairmaker. Married Elizabeth, daughter of Stephen Phipps, Oct. 15, 1801, when he was at 99 South Front St. Later he was at North Front St., but in 1807 moved back to South Front. Hornor shows a swell-front mahogany bureau and a bureau with squared corners and round tapering feet made by Shaw in the *Antiquarian*, March 1931.

SHAW, Daniel, *New York City*

Listed as joiner when made a freeman in 1754. Advertised in newspapers in 1761 as cabinetmaker.

SHAW, Elwin C., *Lowell, Mass.*

Cabinetmaker working for William Johnson in 1833.

SHAW, F., *Massachusetts (?)*

Name branded with a die in Roman letters on a Chippendale desk made about 1755–85, probably in Massachusetts; see *Antiques*, May 1940. Same name branded with a die in italics on a mahogany tea-table; see *Antiques*, April 1938.

SHAW, George, *Philadelphia, Pa.*

Born 1750; died 1792. Name appears in MacPherson's Directory, 1785, as cabinet-maker on Market St. between Third and Fourth. In 1791 working at 127 Chestnut St., residing at 240 Sassafras St.

SHAW, John, *Annapolis, Md.*

It would appear that John Shaw was an English-trained cabinetmaker. He first appears on the Annapolis scene in May 1773, when he and his partner, Archibald Chisholm, advertised in the *Maryland Gazette* that they had imported for their own use and for sale "a neat and general assortment of Joiners and Cabinetmakers

tools." In 1775 they advertised in the same paper, "Cabinet & Chairmakers in Church St., Annapolis. . . . A quantity of mahogany, in logs, plank and boards and a variety of looking-glasses in mahogany frames. They likewise do various kinds of turner's work." In November 1776 the following appeared in the *Gazette*: "The partnership of Shaw & Chisholm, cabinet-makers in Annapolis, being now dissolved, those persons who are indebted to them in company are requested to settle the same, as soon as possible, with JOHN SHAW at the house lately occupied by the company or with ARCHIBALD CHISHOLM, at the house lately possessed by Mr. Charles Peale in Church-street, where each party intends carrying on their business of cabinet and chair making as formerly." During part of 1776 there must have been a third partner since some advertisements carry the firm name of "Middleton, Shaw & Chisholm." It is apparent, however, that any and all partnerships, so far as Shaw was concerned, ended with the November 1776 advertisement and that he continued in business by himself at the old shop.

Bordley says that over a period of time Shaw used three different labels, but the best-known one is elaborate, octagonal in shape, with "John Shaw, Cabinetmaker, Annapolis" in the center, surrounded by a wreath, and with a small oval in the top center enclosing thirteen stars. When the new State House at Annapolis was being built Shaw was selected to make the furniture for the House of Delegates. At the Maryland Historical Society, Baltimore, there is a mahogany chair with modified shield back, and line inlay around rail and saddle seat, that is similar in design to those in a set made for the Senate Chamber at Annapolis, for which John Shaw's bill is preserved in the Hall of Records, Annapolis. Also preserved is another bill of Shaw's, which reads: "2 Tables for the Bar of the House of Delegates/ 2 pine Tables for the Committee rooms at the Stadt house/6 Spitting Boxes for the Senate/a Coffin for an Old Soldier." At the Maryland Historical Society there is a mahogany armchair with a heart-shaped back having lines of inlay around the frame and an inlaid oval shell medallion at the top. There is also a line of inlay on the legs. This chair was used by the governor of Maryland before 1836 and is a mate to the president's chair now in the Senate Chamber at Annapolis. Both are attributed to Shaw. A serving table made about 1789 and attributed to Shaw was at one time the property of Charles Carroll but is now in St. John's College Museum, Annapolis.

At the Baltimore Museum of Art there are several pieces either with Shaw's label or attributed to him. Carrying his label is a shield-back chair with so-called "double eagle" carving on top of splat; and a mahogany sideboard (PLATE XXVII, No. 2), made 1770–80, Sheraton style, with serpentine front, the body decorated with three large ovals outlined with wide crossbanding. The crossbanding of the center oval is zebra wood. There are fan inlays on the spandrels, line inlay in the form of rectangles with cut corners on the stiles, and line inlay with scalloped top on the legs. As often seen on such pieces attributed to Shaw each pair of forelegs is close together and the intervening central section of unusual length. There are ovoid spade feet with line inlay around the spades. In the American Wing of the Metropolitan Museum of Art, New York City, there is an inlaid mahogany side chair in Hepplewhite style, made about 1803, attributed to Shaw.

Bordley, in speaking of Shaw, says that at times he used the blocked feet so typical of English workmen whereas other cabinetmakers of the period used instead a band of leg inlay. He also says, "Shaw expressed an individual peculiarity in inlays around oval panels. He never mastered the art of keeping blocks in their proper positions in a circle. On every piece of his I have seen where such inlays were used the same fault occurs." Shaw was the only southern cabinetmaker, as far as Bordley knew, who used chestnut for the lining of drawers.

(*American Collector*, May and June 1944; *Antiques*, Sept. 1930, July 1942; *Baltimore Furniture*; Bordley; *International Studio*, March 1931; Miller)

SHELDON, Jonathan, *Newport, R. I.*
Listed as joiner in 1787. (Richardson)

SHEPARD, Edward, *Wethersfield, Conn.*
Advertised in *Connecticut Courant*, Nov. 1, 1814, as cabinetmaker.

SHEPARD, Lemuel, *Charlestown, Mass.*
Married Henrietta Vose in 1788. Listed as cabinetmaker when he died in 1825.

SHEPARD, Lemuel B., *Providence, R. I.*
Listed from 1832 to 1837 as cabinetmaker at 99 Westminster St. Apparently a member of Shepard & Cook in 1832. Listed separately in 1836 and 1837.

SHEPARD & COOK, *Providence, R. I.*
Listed in directory for 1832 as cabinetmakers at 99 Westminster St. Company not listed in 1836 and 1837, but each partner is—Lemuel B. Shepard and Ebenezer C. Cook.

SHERBURN, Thomas, *Boston, Mass.*
In 1765 advertised as cabinetmaker on Back St. who made "desks and bookcases, cases of drawers, bureaus, tables of many kinds and screens." Working at same address until death in 1806.

SHERIDAN, John J., *Charleston, S. C.*
Began working circa 1825. On April 26, 1825 advertised in the *Courier* that he had "GRECIAN SOFAS, Easy Chairs, etc." for sale. Advertised at intervals during the next few years, always stressing the desirability of Charleston-made furniture. Still living in 1855. (Burton)

SHERIDAN, John J., *Louisville, Ky.*
Working 1838–50. Made furniture in various styles, including Sheraton. (Offutt)

SHERWOOD, Nelson B., *Ridgefield, Conn.*
Working circa 1830. *See* entry for Rufus H. Pickett.

SHERWOOD, Thomas, *Baltimore, Md.*
Listed during 1802–4 as cabinetmaker.

SHEWARD, John and Perry, *Wilmington, Del.*
Cabinetmakers, each of whom was a brother-in-law of George Whitlock. Listed at 207 Market St. in directory for 1814.

SHILLING, Tobias, *Baltimore, Md.*
Listed in directory for 1799 as cabinet-maker.

SHIPMAN, William, *Middletown, Conn.*
Working as Windsor chair maker circa 1785.

SHOEMAKER, Isaac, *Philadelphia, Pa.*
Born in Germany. Listed as turner in 1669. (Hornor)

SHOEMAKER, Jacob, Sr., *Philadelphia, Pa.*
Records show he did work for James Logan during 1714–16. (Hornor)

SHOEMAKER, Jacob, Jr., *Philadelphia, Pa.*
Signed the Non-Importation Agreement of 1765 as a turner. Member of Library Company in 1743. (Hornor)

SHOEMAKER, Jonathan, *Philadelphia, Pa.*
Believed to have been the grandson of Richard Gove, cabinetmaker and carver of Penn's time. Working from about 1757 until his death during the yellow fever epidemic of 1793. To him are attributed a chest-on-chest and a low bureau (Hornor, pls. 102 and 103). Both have bracket feet. He is also credited with having made an armchair (Hornor, pl. 159) which has a beautifully strap-scrolled back with exquisite carving. He made a folding card table (Hornor, pl. 157) with gadroon molding and acanthus carving.

SHOEMAKER, Peter, *Philadelphia, Pa.*
Arrived in Philadelphia in 1685. Settled in Germantown section. Listed as turner. (Hornor)

SHORT, John, *Newburyport, Mass.*
Working as early as 1736.

SHORT, Joseph, *Newburyport, Mass.*
Born June 30, 1771; died Nov. 10, 1819. One of a family of several generations of cabinetmakers by the name of Short but the only one to label his furniture. His label reads: "Warranted Cabinet Work of all Kinds, Made and Sold by Joseph Short,

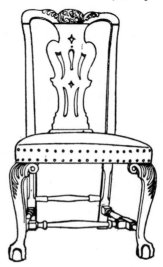

Side chair of the type attributed to
Joseph Short

At his Shop Merrimack Street, between Market-Square and Brown's Wharf, Newburyport. All orders for Work will be gratefully received and punctually executed." Another label added, "He also makes Martha Washington chairs." His labels have been discovered on a mahogany swell-front bureau with inlay and crossbanding, finished with beading around edge, and on a mahogany tripod table with snake feet. Illustrated in *Antiques*, October 1953, is the framework of a Martha Washington chair attributed to Short. This shows his method of construction. His claw-and-ball foot has been likened to that of Frothingham.

SHORT, Sewell, *Newburyport, Mass.*

Born 1735; died 1773. At the time of his death his shop and warehouse were valued at £105 and his stock at £96:17:0. Included in the stock of unfinished furniture were a desk and bookcase, four mahogany table frames, a mahogany desk, and a cedar desk and bookcase. This last item would indicate that some of his pieces were for export since a great deal of furniture made in New England for export was of cedar. Indeed, one will find little or no cedar furniture in New England today although quantities were made there.

SHORT, Stephen, *Newburyport, Mass.*

Born April 9, 1807. Cabinetmaker. Still working in 1860.

SHOVE, Theophilus, *Boston, Mass.*

Opened a joiner's shop in 1739.

SHREEVE, Thomas, *New York City*

Advertised in the *New York Gazette or the Weekly Post Boy,* June 17, 1754: "A Board Yard kept by Thomas Shreeve, House Carpenter & joiner from Burlington, West New Jersey, living opposite William Walton's Esq.: in Queen Street."

SHURTLEFF, Ezekiel L., *Chelmsford, Mass.*

Born circa 1824 in Westford. Married Mercy H. Hildreth, Dec. 26, 1848. Listed as cabinetmaker.

SIGWALD, Thomas, *Charleston, S. C.*

Listed in directories from 1806 to 1816 as cabinetmaker on southwest corner of King and Queen streets. Burton thinks it quite possible he was apprenticed to and worked for Jacob Sass.

SIKES, Victory, *Suffield, Conn.*

Born 1649; died 1708. Son of Richard Sikes of Springfield, Mass. Carpenter by trade. Moved to Suffield in 1682, where he became a successful citizen. Married Elizabeth Granger, July 16, 1684. In August 1699 sold his house lot of twenty-one acres with a "Mansion" thereon to Joseph

Sheldon for £55. In 1699 engaged by town to finish work on house of minister, Mr. Benj. Ruggles. It is believed he also did cabinetmaking. (Bissell; Sheldon)

SILBERG, Nicholas, *Charleston, S. C.*

Died December 1801. Came from Sweden. In 1793 formed partnership with John Ralph (*q.v.*). Partnership lasted about three years. In 1796 Silberg was established as cabinetmaker and undertaker at 132 Queen St.

SILL, Thomas, *Middletown, Conn.*

Advertised in the *Middlesex Gazette,* May 17, 1799: "Barnes, Nath. & Thos. Sill Have Commenced a Copartnership together in carrying on the business of Cabinet Making In all the Several Branches thereof, at their shop in Middletown (lately occupied by Mr. Duc) a little North of the Church:—Those Ladies and Gentlemen who will please to favor them with their custom, may depend on having their work done in the neatest and best manner, with dispatch, on as reasonable terms as can possibly be afforded."

SILLOWAY, Joseph, *Newburyport, Mass.*

Listed in directory for 1848 as cabinetmaker. Still active in 1860.

SILSBEE, Nathaniel, Jr., *Salem, Mass.*

Baptized Feb. 3, 1805. Married Mary Anne C. Devereaux, Nov. 9, 1829. Listed in directory for 1849 as cabinetmaker.

SIMMONS, Andrew, *Baltimore, Md.*

Listed in directory for 1810 as cabinetmaker on East St. near Bridge St.

SIMMS, Isaac P., *probably Massachusetts*

A fine loop-back Windsor side chair in collection of Mrs. Burton N. Gates of Worcester has Simms' name branded on it.

Brand mark of Isaac P. Simms

SIMPKINS, John, *Boston, Mass.*
Listed as cabinetmaker in 1789.

SIMPSON, John, *Charlestown, Mass.*
One of the early settlers of 1661. Cabinetmaker.

SIMPSON, Joseph, *Boston, Mass.*
Listed in directory for 1789 as cabinetmaker on Exchange St.

SINCLAIR, William, *Flowertown, Pa.*
Philadelphia directories list a cabinetmaker by this name from 1819 to 1837 at Hinckel's Court, then at 9 Rachel St., and then at Paschall's Alley. Label in a mahogany-veneer secretary with inlay, made about 1803, gives address as Flowertown. (*Antiques*, Oct. 1929)

SINGLETON, William, *Baltimore, Md.*
Listed in directories during 1796–1802 as cabinetmaker.

SINGLETON & McFADDEN, *Baltimore, Md.*
Advertised as cabinetmakers during 1790–95.

SKILLIN (or SKILLINGS) FAMILY, *Boston, Mass.*
The Skillins were primarily carvers. They are included herein since they worked in close association with various cabinetmakers of their day. Moreover, at least one of them—John—was himself a cabinetmaker. The entries below are concerned with six members of this family. Simeon Skillin (1716–78) was the eldest of the group. He had four sons who were carvers: Samuel (1742–1816); James; John (1746–1800); and Simeon Jr. (1757–1806). Simeon III (1766–1830) was the son of Samuel.
(*Antiques*, Dec. 1931, April 1933, July 1934, Oct. 1935, March 1936, June 1938, April 1948; Bentley; *Davis Papers*, Massachusetts Historical Society, Boston; *Derby Papers*, Essex Institute, Salem; Downs; Hornor; *Index of American Design;* Nutting)

SKILLIN, James, *Boston, Mass.*
Son of Simeon and Ruth Skillin. Apparently went to Philadelphia with Samuel and worked there as a carver.

SKILLIN, John, *Boston, Mass.*
Born 1746; died 1800. Son of Simeon and Ruth Skillin. John and Simeon Jr. worked closely together for some twenty years, and all bills were rendered under their joint names. As early as 1786 they were advertising Windsor chairs for sale at "Mess'rs Skillins' Carver's Shop near Governor Hancock's Wharf," but whether they were also making the chairs is not known. John did make furniture at some time during his life. At the American Antiquarian Society, Worcester, Mass., is an unusual desk made by him for Governor John Hancock. (PLATE XX, No. 2)

John's third wife was Mary Fowle, a member of the family of carvers by that name who were closely associated in business with the Skillins. A chest of drawers made 1760–75 with claw-and-ball feet, one of the pieces he made for this wife at the time of their marriage, is owned in Portsmouth, N. H. In 1778 John carved the figurehead for the *Confederacy*, built at Norwich, Conn.

He and Simeon Jr. did much work for Elias Hasket Derby. Among the Derby Papers, 1780–95, at the Essex Institute, Salem, are innumerable bills for such work. One dated May 10, 1791 is for two figureheads, the cost amounting to £31: 15:0 with ten per cent deducted for prompt pay. Another bill, dated Oct. 3, 1791, itemizes carving a "Grand Turk Head 11 feet long" at a cost of £16, and "Carv'd work done for a chest of drawers" at a cost of £6:15:0. Under date of Sept. 25, 1793 is the following interesting bill:

Elias Haskett Derby Esq. To John and Simeon Skillin, Dr.

To a figure of a Hermit for a Garden	7:10:0
To a Figure of a Shepherdess	6: 0:0
To a Figure of Plenty	7:10:0

To a Figure of a Gardener   7:10:0
To Priming the above   0:15:0
                                   ───────
                                   29: 5:0

Received payment in full of
    Benj. Pickman Junr
        John & Simeon Skillin

In 1795 Bulfinch chose the Skillins to carve the eighteen Corinthian columns for the new State House at a cost of £360. When John died in 1800, six years before his brother Simeon, the Rev. William Bentley wrote in his Diary, "John Skillings, an eminent Carver in Boston, died suddenly January 28, age 54. This man has long been known in this branch particularly by our seamen, in all our Seaport Towns."

SKILLIN, Samuel, *Boston, Mass.*

Son of Simeon and Ruth Skillin. Hornor says that Samuel was a carver of great ability "engaged at one time in embellishing the ships owned by Joseph Carson and the vessels for the Pennsylvania Navy during the Revolution." He adds that Samuel, who was born in Boston, July 5, 1742, came from a family of woodcarvers, that as a young man he had come to Philadelphia, and that after the Revolution he went to New York to ply his trade. It is apparent that he did not stay in New York, because his name appears on the Boston tax list of 1780 and in the directories from 1796 until his death in 1816. Hornor further says that Samuel carved the bust of Benjamin Franklin now at the Franklin Institute and that he executed the figurehead for the frigate *Constitution.*

SKILLIN, Simeon, Sr., *Boston, Mass.*

Born 1716; died 1778. In 1738 married Ruth Phillips in New North Church, Boston. They were the parents of ten children, of whom at least four were carvers—Samuel, James, John, and Simeon Jr. In 1741 Simeon bought a house and land on Salutation Alley and a few years later property on Charter St. It is known that he carved the figurehead

Minerva for the brig *Hazard* in 1777 for Caleb Davis. Among the Davis Papers at the Massachusetts Historical Society there is a bill dated Oct. 10, 1777 for the piece. The bill is receipted by Simeon Skillin, Jr., but it and the work itself gives evidence that the carving was done by the father. At the Beverly Historical Society there is a mahogany Chippendale secretary known as the Captain Moses Brown secretary. This was made about 1775. In the center of the broken pediment is a bust of Milton, 6½ inches tall, carved from a single block of mahogany. The head wears a chaplet of laurel leaves to signify Milton's literary fame. This bust has been attributed to Simeon. Also attributed to him, because all are apparently by the same person, are the three figures on the chest-on-chest made by Stephen Badlam in 1791 and now in the Garvan Collection at Yale University (PLATE XXI), and two carved mahogany figures on a secretary in the Bolles Collection at the Metropolitan Museum of Art, New York City. However, since Simeon died in 1778, it is obvious that he did not make those on the Badlam piece and it may well be that John was the carver of all. Naturally there would be a resemblance between the work of the various Skillins but John seems to have been the foremost when it came to carving.

SKILLIN, Simeon, Jr., *Boston, Mass.*

Born 1757; died 1806. Son of Simeon and Ruth Skillin. When but twenty years old, he receipted a bill for work done by his father for Caleb Davis and had doubtless by this time been working in the Skillin shop for some years. The Rev. Edward G. Porter in his *Rambles in Old Boston,* 1884, says that when John died Simeon continued the art and "not only did he carve figureheads for ships but innumerable chairs, sideboards, desks, and other pieces of furniture."

How much of the carving was done by John and how much by Simeon is impossible to tell. Probably they worked together on many pieces, and doubtless their work was much alike. All figures attributed to them have common characteristics, as if done by one person; always present are the sloping shoulders, slender proportions, spiral-shaped drapery over the breasts, a somewhat heavy neck, and a distinctive head shape.

SKILLIN, Simeon III, *Boston, Mass.*
Born in Philadelphia, June 9, 1766; died in Boston, Jan. 31, 1830. Son of Samuel. Hornor credits him with being a carver.

SKILLMAN, Robert, *Baltimore, Md.*
Listed in directory for 1810 as cabinetmaker.

SKINNER, Augustus, *Providence, R. I.*
Listed in directory for 1824 as cabinetmaker working at Union St., residing at 4 Weybosset St.

SLEEPER, Henry, *Newburyport, Mass.*
Cabinetmaker. Married Sarah Morse, March 29, 1749. Died circa 1782.

SLICER, William, *Annapolis, Md.*
Advertised in the *Maryland Gazette*, 1769: "Cabinet and Chair Maker at Mr. James Cannan's a little below the Market-House, in Annapolis Takes this Method to inform the Public, that he makes and sells the following Articles, all constructed in the most neat and fashionable manner, viz. Desks, Book-Cases, Escritoires, Bureaus, Card, Chamber, Parlour and Tea-Tables; Easy Arm, Parlour and Chamber Chairs; Corner Settees, Clock-Cases, Couches, Dumb-Waiters, Tea Boards, Bottle Boards. . . ."

SMALL, Isaac, *Newport, R. I.*
Listed in 1803 as Windsor chair maker on Marlborough St. near Friends Meeting House. (Richardson)

SMITH, Adams, *Beverly, Mass.*
Born circa 1760; died 1789. Cabinetmaker in partnership with Moses Adams. Married Mrs. Anna Wallis, Nov. 9, 1783. (Belknap)

SMITH, Alanson, *Providence, R. I.*
Listed in directory for 1824 as cabinetmaker on Stewart St.

SMITH, Amos F., *Salem, Mass.*
Cabinetmaker. Married Martha H. Dwinnell, Oct. 10, 1829. Died Sept. 12, 1833 in Portsmouth, N. H.

SMITH, Caleb, Jr., *Salem, Mass.*
Born Jan. 1, 1785. Married Jenny Miles, Dec. 25, 1803. Listed in directory until 1855 as cabinetmaker but no shop address is given.

SMITH, Charles A., *Ridgefield, Conn.*
See entry for Rufus H. Pickett.

SMITH, David, *Ipswich, Mass.*
Cabinetmaker working circa 1790. (Waters)

SMITH, Ebenezer, *Beverly, Mass.*
A mahogany tilt-top candle stand is in existence with bill attached "To Ebenezer Smith, Dr. July 20, 1805."

SMITH, Eliakim, *Hadley, Mass.*
Born 1735. Served in volunteer group in the Revolution and died in 1775 in camp at Watertown, N. Y. Among the Judd Papers at the Forbes Library, Northampton, Mass., are his account books for the years 1757–80. The prices are in "Old Tenor." Of interest are the following four entries:

1757 Case of Dras for Rebecca 40/
1761 19 days work & a part at 25/
1763 John Eastman—case of draws 26/0/0
1764 A Desk upon French feet 13/0/0

In 1758 he made for James Meacham a pewter cupboard and other work at "56/" and a square table for "75/." He did not sign or label his work. Sideboards attributed to him are of cherry. It has been thought he might be the maker of several highboys similar to those made in Connecticut with a vine type of carving on the pilasters. His work must have been of

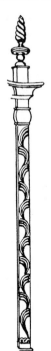

Vine-carved detail found on pilasters of a small number of highboys found in Connecticut River Valley, circa 1760-80

high quality, otherwise he could not have charged John Eastman £26 for a case of drawers in 1763.

SMITH, Elihu B., *Lyme, Conn.*
Advertised as cabinetmaker in *New London Gazette*, June 17, 1813.

SMITH, Ellingwood, *Manchester, Mass.*
Born March 20, 1805 in Beverly. Cabinetmaker. Married Sally Lee, May 12/14, 1830.

SMITH, Elliott, *Salem, Mass.*
Born 1796; died July 21, 1841. Married Nancy C. Loves, April 23, 1821. He and John Jewett leased part of the mills built in 1663 on South River from William Mucklefield, tobacconist and snuff-maker, to use as a cabinetmaking shop. Smith was hurt by the machinery and died.

SMITH, George, *Baltimore, Md.*
Listed in directories during 1799-1818 as cabinetmaker.

SMITH, George Elias, *Charleston, S. C.*
Listed in directories during 1806-16, first as a cabinetmaker then as a carpenter at 115 Meeting St.

SMITH, Ira, *Salisbury, Vt.*
Listed as joiner working in the northwestern part of the town in 1791. (Weeks)

SMITH, Jeremiah Francis, *Marblehead, Mass.*
Baptized Sept. 24, 1809. Listed in 1847 directory as cabinetmaker.

SMITH, John, *Boston, Mass.*
Advertised in 1804 as cabinetmaker on Back St. in former shop of Smith & Hutchins.

SMITH, John, *Lexington, Va.*
Made a chest of drawers about 1817 for Robert McCluer, a surgeon in the War of 1812. This is still in the possession of a descendant. (Comstock)

SMITH, John Bodwell, *Salem, Mass.*
Baptized Aug. 2, 1820; died Sept. 20, 1847. Cabinetmaker at 6 North St. in 1846.

SMITH, Joseph, *Newport, R. I.*
Listed as joiner in 1733. (Richardson)

SMITH, Joseph A., *Salem, Mass.*
Listed as cabinetmaker at 199 Essex St. in 1842. After that listed until 1861 with no shop address.

SMITH, Purchase, *Ipswich, Mass.*
Born Aug. 17, 1774; died June 10, 1828. Listed as cabinetmaker.

SMITH, Richard, *Charleston, S. C.*
Began work as a cabinetmaker in 1809 and worked steadily until his death in 1857. (Burton)

SMITH, Roswell, *Charlestown, Mass.*
Served his apprenticeship with Jacob Forster (*q.v.*).

SMITH, Samuel, *Manchester, Mass.*
Listed as cabinetmaker in 1825.

SMITH, William, *Boston, Mass.*
On tax list of 1687 as joiner.

SNODEN, David, *Boston, Mass.*
Notice of his death in 1747 listed him as chairmaker.

SNOWDEN, Jedidiah, *Philadelphia, Pa.*
Died 1797. Advertised in 1773 as a "Cabinet and Windsor Chair-maker." Was a member of the Library Company of Philadelphia in 1748 and 1749. In 1786 paid an occupational tax of £100. (Hornor; Nutting, Vol. 3)

SNUDGRASS, William, *Baltimore, Md.*
Listed as cabinetmaker from 1800 to 1803.

SOMMERVILLE, James, *Baltimore, Md.*
Advertised as cabinetmaker in 1784.

SOULE, Nathaniel, *Providence, R. I.*
Listed in directory for 1828 as cabinetmaker at 68 Broad St.

SPALDING, Hiram, *Providence, R. I.*
Listed in directories for 1836 and 1837 as cabinetmaker working at 101 Westminster St., residing at 67 Broad St.

SPANGLER, John, *Lexington, Ky.*
Advertised in *Kentucky Gazette*, Lexington, Aug. 11, 1794, "making cabinets and furniture." Again advertised Sept. 13, 1794.

SPEAR, John, *Newport, R. I.*
Listed as chairmaker in 1775. (Richardson)

SPEAR, Joseph, *Alexandria, Va.*
Advertised in *Alexandria Herald*, June 21, 1815: "Joseph Spear Respectfully informs his Friends and the Public that he continues to carry on the CABINET BUSINESS in all its various branches, on Royal Street near the Market, and has on hand some well made FURNITURE."

SPENCER, Abiel, *Newport, R. I.*
Mason says Spencer trained under John Goddard, and states: "He had a shop on the Point Bridge. One might have passed the shop a hundred times and not have noticed it, so little was there about the place to attract attention. Probably no man ever lived a more methodical life than Dr. Spencer, for so he was called; certainly no one could have been less disturbed by what was going on in the world around him for he had a little world of his own, of which he was the center. In 1810 he bought the place and with the exception of about ten years when he had charge of a woolen mill in Portsmouth, he passed his whole life under his own roof dying in 1878 at an advanced age. For 68 years he had kept this little shop and so averse was he to leaving it that he rarely went as far as Thames Street. Seems to have sold almost anything in his shop."

SPENCER, Daniel, *Newport, R. I.*
Mentioned in Dr. William Hunter's account book (Newport Historical Society) as a joiner in 1775 and 1776.

SPENCER, Jarrard, *Hartford, Conn.*
Born circa 1650; died 1712. Son of Thomas (*q.v.*). About 1681 took over his father's shop. In 1681 made for John Tolcott "2 great chayrs, 2 high chairs, 4 womens chairs" for £1:04:0. These were part of the dowry of his daughter, who was married a few months later. When Spencer died he left his son Jarrard Jr. his tools, "a pres cubard and a small chest." (For all Spencers of Hartford, see *Antiques*, May 1933; *Collections of the Connecticut Historical Society*, Hartford, Vol. 14; Luther; Nutting, Vol. 3)

SPENCER, Jarrard, Jr., *Hartford, Conn.*
Born 1684; died 1754. Carried on his trade of turner and joiner in the shop of his father. He was Jarrard's only son and inherited his father's equipment, which was valued at fifty shillings. In 1737 he and Timothy Phelps co-operated in work

for the new meetinghouse for the First Church of Hartford, making many of the balusters in the steeple. Moved to New Hartford, where he died. Several of his descendants followed his trade as turners.

SPENCER, Obadiah, Jr., *Hartford, Conn.*
Born 1666; died 1741. Grandson of Thomas Spencer. Married daughter of Nicholas Disbrowe. Evidence shows that the Spencers were turners and chairmakers. In 1730 Obadiah was associated with Timothy Phelps in settling an estate, and it is possible Phelps worked in one of the Spencers' shops. He had a son who also was trained and at his death he left him his "joiners tools of all sorts."

SPENCER, Thomas, *Hartford, Conn.*
Died 1687. An Englishman who came with Thomas Hooker's group in 1639. A close friend of Nicholas Disbrowe (*q.v.*), whose home lot was not more than a hundred yards from that of Spencer. Owned and operated a woodworking shop which he gave to his son Jarrard some years before his death. For five generations the Spencers carried on the trade of joiners and turners.

SPENCER, William, *Suffield, Mass.*
Listed in Land Records of 1724 as chairmaker. It may well be that this Spencer was a member of the cabinetmaking family of Hartford. There was close relationship between the people of Hartford and Suffield, and the year of his death, 1745, would place him as a contemporary of Obadiah Spencer, Jr., and Jarrard Spencer, Jr.

SPENSER, Daniel, *Lexington, Ky.*
Advertised in the *Kentucky Gazette*, May 24, 1793, that he had "opened a cabinet and chairmaking business at Mr. Hustons on Mulberry Street, south of Main street." In June 1793 advertised that he made "reed-bottom chairs."

SPIERS, James, *Williamsburg, Va.*
Advertised as cabinetmaker in the *Virginia Gazette* from 1745 to 1751.

SPILLER, Moses, *Salem, Mass.*
Died 1817. Listed as cabinetmaker.

SPOONER, Sherlock, *Boston, Mass.*
Listed as cabinetmaker at Washington and Warren streets in 1830.

SPOONER, Thomas, *Newport, R. I.*
Chairmaker. (Richardson)

SPOONER & FITCH, *Athol, Mass.*
Antiques, October 1952, illustrates a cherry chest of drawers in Hepplewhite style with firm name branded on back. This piece with its fine inlays and ivory fittings shows these men to have been expert craftsmen but little is known about them.

SPRAGUE, Ebed, *Boston, Mass.*
Listed as chairmaker on Liberty Square in 1796.

SPROSEN, I., *Connecticut*
In the *American Collector*, October 1935, is shown a set of braced bow-back chairs made about 1770 of hickory and maple and having Sprosen's mark.

STACKHOUSE, David, *Philadelphia, Pa.*
Apprenticed to Joseph Henzey (*q.v.*) in 1772.

STACKHOUSE, Stacy, *Hartford, Conn.*
Advertised in the *Connecticut Courant*, Jan. 30, 1786: "Stacy Stackhouse From New York . . . has established his business in this city; where he makes and sells all sorts of Windsor Chairs in the neatest manner. . . ." On Oct. 8, 1792 again advertised in the *American Mercury;* "Stacy Stackhouse Informs the public that he continues to make WINDSOR CHAIRS in the best manner, at his house, a little north of the State House in Hartford. —— Those Ladies and Gentlemen who will please to favor him with their custom, may depend on having their work done in the genteelest manner, and on as reasonable terms for pay in hand, as in New York. Wanted by said Stack-

house, one or two likely lads 14 or 15 years old, as apprentices to the above business." In 1796 apparently no longer in business. *See* entry for John Wadsworth.

STAFFORD, Samuel, *Boston, Mass.*
Listed as cabinetmaker on Kilby St. in 1789.

STAFFORD, Theodore, *Charleston, S. C.*
Partner of Jay Humiston (Humeston?). In 1798 they advertised as Windsor chair makers. In 1801 directory Stafford is listed as working alone at 98 Tradd St. Not listed after 1802. (Burton)

STALL, *Newport, R. I.*
Listed as chairmaker in 1795 but no first name given. (Richardson)

STANDLEY, Paul, *Manchester, Mass.*
Baptized 1792. Listed as cabinetmaker when married on June 28, 1845.

STANNIFORD, Jeremiah, *Salem, Mass.*
Partner of Henry Hubon (*q.v.*) on Charter St. from 1812 to 1823. In 1823 Stanniford moved to Old Paved St. while Hubon continued in shop on Charter St. Married Sarah Clifton, March 11, 1827. It is recorded that a Jeremiah Stanniford died in Lynn, Sept. 30, 1832.

STANWOOD, Ebenezer, Jr., *Ipswich, Mass.*
Baptized 1747. Cabinetmaker working as late as 1786. Married Anne Badger, Sept. 12, 1782.

STANWOOD, Samuel, *Salem, Mass.*
Listed as cabinetmaker at 3 North St. in 1837 and at 21 North St. in 1846.

STAPLEFORD, Thomas, *Boston, Mass.*
On tax lists of 1684 as chair- and cabinetmaker.

STAPLES, John, *Baltimore, Md.*
Listed in directory for 1810 as cabinetmaker.

STARKEY, William, *Lowell, Mass.*
Listed in directory for 1837 as cabinetmaker.

STARR, Jonathan, *New London, Conn.*
Advertised in *New London Gazette*, Dec. 17, 1773, for a journeyman cabinetmaker.

STARR, L. S., *Baltimore, Md.*
Listed in directories for 1807 and 1808 as cabinetmaker.

STEPHENS, David, *Boston, Mass.*
On tax lists of 1688 as joiner.

STEVENS, John, *Boston, Mass.*
Married in Andover in 1731. Notice of death in 1745 listed him as joiner.

STEVENS, John, *Charlestown, Mass.*
Listed in directory for 1815 as cabinetmaker. Moved to Walpole.

STEVENSON, J., *Baltimore, Md.*
Listed in directories during 1806–10 as cabinetmaker.

STEVENSON, Thomas, *Dover, Del.*
Born 1787; died 1865. A bureau by him was exhibited at Wilmington Society of Fine Arts, 1950. (*Antiques*, Aug. 1950)

STEWART, Samuel, *Savannah, Ga.*
Advertised during 1789–1820 as a turner.

STICKNEY, Jacob, *Newburyport, Mass.*
Listed in directories during 1848–52 as cabinetmaker.

STICKNEY, Samuel, *Beverly, Mass.*
Baptized 1795. Listed as cabinetmaker in 1817.

STITCHER & CLEMMENS, *Baltimore, Md.*
Listed in directory for 1804 as cabinetmakers on South St. At the Baltimore Museum of Art there is a mahogany secretary made 1795–1810 with the follow-

ing label on the bottom of one of the drawers: "Stitcher & Clemmens, Cabinet and Chair Makers Corner of South and Water-Streets, Baltimore. Orders from the city or country attended to with punctuality. They have St. Domingo Mahogany of the best quality for sale." Below the cornice of the secretary there is a frieze of intertwined semicircles simulating fretwork. There are mullioned glass doors. In the lower section there are four large ovals outlined in satinwood and set into mitred panels. (*Baltimore Furniture;* Miller)

STOCKS, Thomas, *Charleston, S. C.*
    Died 1760. Formed partnership with Stephen Townsend (*q.v.*), which was ended by Stocks' death. (Burton)

STONE, Ebenezer, *Boston, Mass.*
    Born 1763. Advertised as Windsor chair maker and cabinetmaker in *Massachusetts Gazette* in 1787.

STONE, Gillman, *Providence, R. I.*
    Listed in directory for 1828 as cabinetmaker at 121 North Main St.

STONE, Isaac, *Salem, Mass.*
    Married Sarah Marshall, March 10, 1805. In 1809 was chairmaker on Essex St.

STONE, Samuel, *Boston, Mass.*
    Born 1760. Brother of Ebenezer. Advertised in *Massachusetts Gazette* in 1794 as cabinetmaker.

STONE, Thomas, *Providence, R. I.*
    Listed in directories during 1824–32 as cabinetmaker at 128½ North Main St.

STONE, William, *Ridgefield, Conn.*
    Working circa 1830. *See* entry for Rufus H. Pickett.

STONE & ALEXANDER, *Boston, Mass.*
    Among the few Boston cabinetmakers who labeled their work. At the Henry Ford Museum, Dearborn, Mich., there is a pair of Hepplewhite style side chairs

with their label, dated 1792. Directory lists the partnership on Prince and Back streets in 1796. Later each had a separate listing. There were three Alexanders—Giles, William (*q.v.*), and James.

STOREY, William, *Boston, Mass.*
    Arrived in Boston in 1637 with Samuel Dix, whom he served as apprentice. (Nutting, Vol. 3)

STOVER & TAYLOR, *New York City*
    A Sheraton-style sofa made about 1795, at the Metropolitan Museum of Art, New York City, shows a typical detail used by these partners—a carved daisy. In

Carved daisy, a typical detail of work of Stover & Taylor, circa 1795

Antiques, November 1923, there is illustrated one of a set of Sheraton chairs. When these were being upholstered bits of an old label were found. Pieced together they formed the label of Stover & Taylor. At the top of these square-backed chairs is a rectangular blocking with the typical daisy.

STOW, George, *Savannah, Ga.*
    Advertised during 1800–1827 as cabinetmaker.

STRACHAN, James, *New York City*
    In 1768 after his partner David Davidson had died, Strachan advertised as carver and cabinetmaker, saying that he hoped to carry on the business and that he was ready to undertake "house carvings of every kind, gilding and all sorts of cabinet work." Died in 1769.

STRANGE, Owen, *Savannah, Ga.*
    Working 1776–1814. Advertised as cabinetmaker.

STRATFORD, Samuel, *Boston, Mass.*
    Listed in directory for 1784 as cabinetmaker.

STRINGER, F., *Baltimore, Md.*
Listed as cabinetmaker in 1804.

SUTTON, Bartholomew, *Boston, Mass.*
Working in 1664 as joiner.

SWAGGER, Elisha, *West Chester, Pa.*
Advertised in *The Village Record* prior to 1810. (Stockwell, *American Collector*, April 1939)

SWALLOWE, Benjamin, *Newport, R. I.*
Listed as chairmaker in 1709. Made chairs for Jedediah Newland. (Richardson)

SWAN, Benjamin, *Salem, Mass.*
Born 1786; died 1842 in Worcester. Moved to Salem from Charlestown, Mass. Listed in 1837 at 30 Court St., in 1842 at 16 Church St. After Jacob Sanderson's death in 1810 was in partnership with Elijah (*q.v.*), who died in 1825.

SWAN, Joshua, *Charlestown, Mass.*
Born 1743. Listed as chairmaker. Also was in West Cambridge and Waltham.

SWAN, Timothy, *Charlestown, Mass.*
Listed as joiner when he married in 1715.

SWANEY, William, *Charlestown, Mass.*
In 1801 advertised in the *Salem Register* for journeyman cabinetmaker.

SWANEY, William, *Charleston, S. C.*
Listed in directories for 1806 and 1807 as cabinetmaker.

SWEAT, Nathaniel, *Marblehead, Mass.*
Died April 6, 1810. Married in 1794. In directory as cabinetmaker.

SWEENEY, Paul, *Baltimore, Md.*
Listed in directories during 1802–20 as cabinetmaker.

SWEENEY, Richard, *Boston, Mass.*
Listed in directory for 1796 as chairmaker.

SWEETING, Joseph, *Providence, R. I.*
Signed Providence Cabinetmakers Agreement, March 24, 1757. This is on file at the Rhode Island Historical Society, Providence.

SWETT, John, *Salisbury, Mass.*
Working 1794–95 as cabinetmaker and joiner. (Belknap)

SWETT, Jonathan, *Newport, R. I.*
Made cedar desk for John Cahoon in 1758 for £25 and a walnut and cedar chest for £53. (*Cahoon's Ledger*, Newport Historical Society)

SYMMES, Andrew, *Boston, Mass.*
Born 1704. Son of the Rev. Thomas Symmes. Joiner.

SYMONDS, Benjamin, *Salem, Mass.*
Born May 14, 1719; still living in 1783. Chairmaker. Married Hannah Bolton, Dec. 14, 1738. (Perley, *History of Salem*)

SYMONDS, Benjamin, *Salem, Mass.*
Chairmaker and turner. Married Margaret Skerry, Feb. 6, 1744/5. Died between 1764 and 1780. (Perley, *History of Salem*)

SYMONDS, James, *Salem, Mass.*
Born 1633; died 1714. Joiner. Married Elizabeth Browning, Nov. 20, 1661. The James Symonds lot on Main St. was granted to him by the selectmen April 5, 1672 and he owned it until his death in 1714. At that time it was valued at £30. John Pease served out his apprenticeship with him. (Perley, *History of Salem*, Vol. 1, and *Salem in* 1700)

SYMONDS, John, *Salem, Mass.*
Born July 8, 1666; died winter of 1728–29. Joiner. Married Sarah Roberts in 1689 and Sarah Foster in 1710. (Perley, *History of Salem*, Vol. 1)

SYMONDS, John, *Salem, Mass.*
Father of James. No data found regarding him other than his will, which

shows that John Pease, Sr., of Enfield, Conn., was apprenticed to him and at his death to his son James. (Rev. David Pease, *The Pease Record*, 1869)

SYMONDS, Jonathan E., *Salem, Mass.*
Baptized circa 1818. Died April 11, 1845. Cabinetmaker at 93 North St. in 1842.

SYMONDS, Joseph, *Salem, Mass.*
Born Aug. 12, 1721; died Aug. 7, 1769. Joiner and cabinetmaker. Married Mary Very, Nov. 15, 1743. (Perley, *History of Salem*, Vol. 1)

SYMONDS, Thomas, *Salem, Mass.*
Born April 1, 1677; died May 1, 1758. Joiner. (Perley, *History of Salem*, Vol. 1)

TAPPAN, Henry Story, *Manchester, Mass.*
Born Feb. 18, 1816. Married Elizabeth Eldridge, Dec. 17, 1846. Cabinetmaker.

TAPPAN, Samuel Forster, *Manchester, Mass.*
Born July 18, 1795. Married Nancy Smith of Beverly, Dec. 25, 1827. Cabinetmaker.

TAYER (or TAYRE), Benjamin, *Newport, R. I.*
During 1754-55 made many desks for John Cahoon (*q.v.*). Also worked for Aaron Lopez, whose account book (Newport Historical Society) contains the following item for the year 1773: "Cr Benjamin Tayer / 1 cabin table for Ship Benjamin £35:10."

TAYLOR, Galen, *Providence, R. I.*
Listed in directory for 1824 as cabinetmaker at 115½ South Main St.

TAYLOR, George, *Manchester, Mass.*
Cabinetmaker. Married Aurelia Burgess, June 8, 1843.

TAYLOR, James, *Newport, R. I.*
Listed as cabinetmaker on June 6, 1791 (Bond and Indenture Box, Vault A, New-

port Historical Society) and in 1796 (Richardson). His will, dated 1826, at Newport City Hall Probate Court, bequeathed "one large mahogany desk, 1 work bench, ½ tools to son, William; ½ to son Stephen."

TAYLOR, John, *Hadley, Mass.*
Doubtless the son of Stephen Taylor, who was one of the twenty-five persons who manifested their intention before March 25, 1661 to establish themselves on the west side of the river in that part of Hadley known as Hatfield. In 1662 John Taylor applied for land. In 1666 he married Mary Selden. In 1680 their daughter Thankful was born. It is family tradition that John was a cripple. Thankful became the second wife of Nathaniel Warner of Suffield on May 10, 1710. To John Taylor is attributed the "Thankfull Taylor" Hadley chest (Luther's No. 99). This is one of three chests with the owner's name inscribed in full on the top rail. This is in capital script and reads "Thankfull Taylor February the 18 1701." These chests were hope chests in most cases, thus this one was probably made as a gift for Thankful's twenty-first birthday. It has the usual tulip and leaf design continuous on rails and posts, indicating that the carving was done after the front was assembled. The posts of the chest are of oak, the end panels of pine, the rails and drawers of sycamore. A feature of the decoration distinguishing it from that on other chests of this type is the geometric design at each of the upper corners. In 1895 the chest was located in Suffield, where it had been ever since Thankful took it to her new home in 1710. *See* entry for John Pease. (Judd; Luther)

TAYLOR, John, *Boston, Mass.*
On tax list of 1674 as joiner.

TAYLOR, John B., *Alexandria, Va.*
Advertised in Alexandria in 1804. His label appears in a fruitwood chest of drawers. (Comstock)

TAYLOR, John B., *Baltimore, Md.*
Listed in directories during 1810–12 as cabinetmaker.

TAYLOR, John Matthias, *Manchester, Mass.*
Cabinetmaker who was born in England. Married Ann H. Lee, July 4, 1841.

TAYLOR, Robert, *Philadelphia, Pa.*
Working about 1799. Maker of labeled Windsors. Illustrated in Hornor is a chair by Taylor (pl. 502) and the label (pl. 501).

TAYLOR & KING, *Philadelphia, Pa.*
Makers of "fancy and Windsor chairs." Successors to John B. Ackley (*q.v.*). See Hornor, plates 499 and 500.

TEEL, William, *Haverhill, Mass.*
Cabinetmaker. Married Sarah Ann Choate, Dec. 31, 1827. Drowned Sept. 17, 1828.

TEST, John B., *Salem, Mass.*
Cabinetmaker in Palfray's Court in 1846; at 80 Derby St. in 1859.

THALWIG, Jacob, *Mount Vernon, Va.*
In 1806 when Bushrod Washington was living at Mount Vernon, the following entry was made in the manager's diary: "Today Jacob Thalwig, a Cabinet-Maker who has lived with Mr. Washington for near 3 years left this [place]." (*Antiques*, Jan. 1952)

THAXTER & ROUSE, *Boston, Mass.*
Their label appears in a Sheraton cherry and curly maple tambour desk made about 1780 when they were located on Ann St. Illustrated in *Antiques*, June 1955.

THAYER, Ziphion, *Boston, Mass.*
Listed as cabinetmaker in 1789.

THIESS, W., *Savannah, Ga.*
Advertised from 1797 to 1817 as chairmaker. (*Antiques*, Feb. 1954)

THOMAS, Lambert, *Baltimore, Md.*
Working as early as 1810. Had shop for cabinet- and chair-making at 128 High St. in 1833. (Varley)

THOMAS, Mahlon, *Mount Holly, N. J.*
His name appears on bottom of a chest of drawers made about 1797. (*Antiques*, Sept. 1952)

THOMAS, Spencer, *Roxbury, Mass.*
Cabinetmaker with the Roxbury group about 1800.

THOMPSON, Benjamin, Jr., *Manchester, Mass.*
Born Dec. 14, 1799. Cabinetmaker. Married Lydia Lee on Oct. 23, 1823 and Lydia Maria Littlefield on Nov. 13, 1849.

THOMPSON, Samuel, *Charlestown, Mass.*
Born 1779; died 1815. Listed as turner.

THOMPSON, William, *Baltimore, Md.*
Listed in directory for 1803 as cabinetmaker.

THOMSON, Edmund, *Salem, Mass.*
Listed in directory for 1803 as cabinetmaker on Federal St.

THOMSON, Samuel, *Baltimore, Md.*
Cabinet- and chairmaker at 21 Harrison St., opposite the bazaar, in 1833. (Varley)

THORN, William, *Pittsburgh, Pa.*
See entry for Giffin & Thorn.

THURSTON, Enoch, *Newburyport, Mass.*
Died 1805. Notice of death listed him as joiner.

THURSTON, Henry W., *Salem, Mass.*
Born Dec. 8, 1818. Cabinetmaker. Married Margaret E. McKenzie, April 5, 1849. Located at 14 Lynde St. during 1842–50; at 6 Howard St. during 1850–64. In 1864 was in business as furniture dealer with Thomas Henderson at 38 Washington St.

THURSTON, John, *Newport, R. I.*
Working in 1761 as joiner. (Richardson)

THWING, Benjamin, *Boston, Mass.*
Listed as joiner in 1670.

TIBBILS & PRENTICE, *Hartford, Conn.*
In the *American Mercury*, Nov. 11, 1828, B. Hudson & Co., auctioneers, advertised sale of stock of William Tibbils and Oliver Prentice, cabinetmakers.

TILESTONE, Thomas, *Boston, Mass.*
Listed as cabinetmaker on Purchase St. in 1789.

TILLEY, William, *Providence, R. I.*
Listed in directory for 1832 as cabinetmaker at William St. Probably a member of firm of Millerd & Tilley at same address.

TILLSON, William, *New York City*
Made freeman in 1761, at which time listed as chairmaker.

TILYOU, Peter, *New York City*
Advertised in 1770 as chairmaker.

TILYOU, William, *New York City*
Advertised in 1775 as chairmaker and turner. Doubtless relative of Peter.

TIMPSON, Thomas, *New York City*
Working 1801-5. A few marked examples of his work have been found, branded on the back "T. Timpson, N-York." Worked largely in the Chippendale style. (*American Collector*, June 1935)

TITCOMB, Edward, *Newburyport, Mass.*
Working 1690-1710. Four pieces made by him are known—one painted, one of oak, one of maple, and one bearing his name. All have the rather clumsy Flemish scroll leg. Illustrated in *Furniture of Our Forefathers* by Esther Singleton. (Nutting, Vol. 3)

TITCOMB, Isaac Cummings, *Newburyport, Mass.*
Born Sept. 8, 1813. Cabinetmaker. Married Sarah B. Stone, June 28, 1840.

TITCOMB, Jonathan, *Newburyport, Mass.*
Born 1727. Listed as cabinetmaker.

TITCOMB, Parker, *Newburyport, Mass.*
Died 1772. Notice of death listed him as cabinetmaker.

TITUS, Samuel, *Providence, R. I.*
Directory of 1828 lists him as cabinetmaker at rear of 32 Pawtuxet St.; that of 1832 at Stewart St.

TODD, William, *Boston, Mass.*
Cabinetmaker. Member of firm of Todd & Adams, Cambridge St., 1796.

TONKIN, W., *Alexandria, Va.*
Advertised in *Alexandria Gazette*, Jan. 11, 1794: "W. Tonkin, Joiner, Cabinet Maker and Glazier Begs leave to inform the public of his being commenced business in the back part of the house lately occupied by Mr. Sweeney, etc."

TOPPAN, Abner, *Newburyport, Mass.*
The Toppan family are descendants of the Abraham Toppan who settled in Newbury, Mass., in 1637. The following record of him appears in Coffin's *Sketch of the History of Newbury, Newburyport and West Newbury from 1635 to 1845*: "Abraham Toppan, being licensed by John Endicott esqr. to live in this jurisdiction was received into the towne of Newberry as an inhabitant thereof and hath heere promised under his hand to be subject to any lawful order, that shall be made by the towne." Abner was a son of Edward Toppan, the eleventh of twelve children. He was born April 7, 1764; died Dec. 31, 1836. He made a desk for William Little in 1795. This is of solid mahogany and has a reverse-serpentine front and claw-and-ball feet. The interior of the desk shows sunbursts

of inlaid satinwood. In the Newburyport Library there are several pieces of furniture that, according to records, were made for the Bannister family. These include a mahogany chest-on-chest, a mahogany secretary, and a block-front mahogany desk. The chest-on-chest and the secretary have identical scroll tops with carved rosettes and flame finials. There are fluted pilasters on the upper sections, and scrolled ogee-bracket feet. In both pieces the lower section has a reverse-serpentine front. The block-front mahogany desk shows rather sharp blocking and there is a mediocre pendant shell in the center of the base. The Toppan family house is still standing on High St.

TOWN, James D., *Lowell, Mass.*
Listed as cabinetmaker in 1834.

TOWNSEND FAMILY, *Newport, R. I.*
For a discussion of the work of this family, *see* the entries for the Goddards, the Newport cabinetmakers with whom the Townsends were closely associated not only by trade but also by marriage.

FIRST GENERATION

Solomon Townsend was the ancestor of the thirteen cabinetmaking Townsends listed below by generation. Each one of them is entered separately thereafter.

SECOND GENERATION

Job (1699–1765) and Christopher (1701–73): sons of Solomon.

THIRD GENERATION

Job Edward, Jr. (1726–1818); Edmund (1736–1811); Robert M. (died 1805); James (died 1827); Thomas (1742–1822): sons of Job.
John (1732–1809) and Jonathan (1745–72): sons of Christopher.

FOURTH GENERATION

Job E. (1758–78); Thomas (born 1785); James: sons of Edmund and grandsons of Job.
John F. (living in 1829): son of John and grandson of Christopher.

(References for all Townsend data include: Account books, Friends birth records, letters, photostatic copies of newspapers, Probate Court records and wills, at Newport Historical Society; Carpenter; Mason; Swan, *Antiques*, April and May 1946)

TOWNSEND, Christopher, *Newport, R. I.*
Born 1701; died 1773. Son of Solomon Townsend. On Dec. 26, 1723 he married Patience Easton. They were the parents of several children, of whom John and Jonathan are known to have been cabinetmakers. Christopher and his brother Job had their shops in the northwestern section of Newport, on land known as Easton's Point, which was the Quaker settlement, each working at the cabinetmaker's trade and producing good furniture in the Queen Anne tradition.

At the Newport Historical Society may be seen Abraham Redwood's Letter Book, 1723–40, and in it is the following letter from Christopher, under date of Feb. 4, 1738 (copy on file at Rhode Island Historical Society, Providence):

Cousin Abraham Redwood: According to thy Request In thine I indevoured to finish a Desk and Book Case Agreeable to thy directions to send thee by Brother Pope but could not quite finish it timely to send by him and understanding it was not for thee but a friend of thine, I concluded it would be Equal to thee, If I send it by another opertunity. And having an opertunity to send it by Brother Solomon, I shipped it by him and ordered him to Deliver it to thee or thy order, thou paying him one Moydore freight, the Desk and Book case amounts to Sixty Pounds, this currency; includeing the two Ruf cases which is equal to fourteen heavy Pistole at £4:5:8 or forty-four ounces and half of Silver which I desire thou would pay or cause to be paid to Brother Solomon. I may let thee know that I sold such a Desk and Book Case without any Ruf cases, for £58 in hand this winter. Brother Job, also sold one to our Collector for £59. I mention this, that thou may know that I have not imposed on thee. I now let thee know that our Relations are generally well and thy Wife and Children in Perticular. David Cheasbrows wife lies now dead and is to be buryed tomorrow. I have nothing more Particuler only that I hope to see thee here this summer and should be glad to hear that thou Prosper in the best of things, not only of this world, but of that which is to come. I now conclude with hearty Love to thee; and Brother Pope likewise, and Remaine thy affectionate Friend.

CHRISTOPHER TOWNSEND

Newport, Rhoad Island
   the 4:2m 1738

P.S. I did thy message to thy good friend Doctor Rodman. My wife desires yt her love may be remembered to thee.

This indicates that Christopher and Job were making desk-bookcases as early as 1738, which is contrary to what is usually assigned as the earliest working date of these men. Usually the year 1742 has been given—owing to oversight; this should have been 1746—a date based on the following entry on page 24 of Isaac Stelle's account book, at the Newport Historical Society:

Christopher Townsend's account
June 1744
  to 333 feet of Mahogany Plank
    at 22 and other things   30:10:16
Contra
July 1742 By one Coffin for my
           child
June 18   By one Walnut Coffin
         for my child   £3
Sept. 1746 By one Desk and Book
         Case   65
         By Mending a Desk   1:12
                          69:12
1747   By cash paid me   £50
        By 2 Desks

When Christopher died in 1773 he left to each of his three living children—Mary Wanton, daughter-in-law of Governor Gideon Wanton, John, and Christopher Jr.—one-third interest in "all my new desks and other joiner's ware that is

for sale, except one large mahogany Desk which my son Jonathan made." (Jonathan had died the year before in Long Island.) This desk he left to Christopher Jr. He left John, his other cabinet-making son, his tools, mahogany, and other "Shop Joinery Stock," as well as all the brasses, hinges, etc. "that shall remain after the said new Desks shall be finished."

No pieces of furniture are definitely attributed to Christopher, as is not the case with Job. However, his work probably would be much like that made by Job at any given time. Doubtless they both made many desk-bookcases since Christopher's letter to Redwood, the entries in Isaac Stelle's account book, and the furniture listed in Christopher's will indicate this.

TOWNSEND, Edmund, *Newport, R. I.*
   Born 1736; died 1811. Son of Job Townsend and brother of Job Edward Jr., James, Robert M., and Thomas. In Job Edward Jr.'s ledger there appears this entry: "Nicholas Anderrese, Dr. to Job & Edmund Townsend To a Large Mahogany Desk, Feb. 28, 1767." For this desk Anderrese was charged the very large sum of £330. An interesting item in the Aaron Lopez account book (at the Newport Historical Society), under date of Oct. 2, 1771, reads: "Memorandum that I have this day engaged a Cedar Bookcase from Edmund Townsend for which I am to allow him £340 and he is to deliver it compleated and cased in 12 days from the above date. Payable in goods." To this Lopez had added the remark "accomplished."

In the Karolik Collection at the Boston Museum of Fine Arts there is a mahogany block-front kneehole bureau made 1765–75; the original handwritten label on the upper side of a drawer bottom reads: "Made by Edmund Townsend In Newport, Rhode Island." This piece has the blocked drawer fronts cut from the solid mahogany, with the superbly carved convex shells applied. Chestnut is used as the secondary wood, the drawer sides being made of white wood. (PLATE XVI, No. 1)

TOWNSEND, James, *Newport, R. I.*

Died 1827. Son of Job. The inventory of his estate, dated October 1827, shows as many as thirty planes and a large number of chisels. Because of the similarity of the carving on most pieces of furniture made by the members of the Goddard-Townsend group, it has been suggested that one member did all the carving. The shells, it is true, show much variation: in the number of lobes, in curve and depth, in the treatment of the petals, and in the centers and outer edges. And yet these differences would not rule out their having been carved by one person. If one did serve as the carver, that man was doubtless James.

TOWNSEND, James, *Newport, R. I.*

Son of Edmund. As yet nothing is known about him as a workman.

TOWNSEND, Job, *Newport, R. I.*

Born 1699; died 1765. Job and his brother Christopher were the elders of the Townsend-Goddard group of cabinetmakers. Job and his wife, Rebecca, had many children, of whom five sons were cabinetmakers—Job Edward Jr., Edmund, Thomas, James, and Robert M. One daughter, Hannah, became the wife of John Goddard, his apprentice. According to Downing, in 1725 Job "took up Quaker lands on Easton's Point. His lot, numbered 86 of the First Division, lies along Third Street on the northwest corner of Bridge, and his house, now badly run down, still stands, its block modillion cornice mute evidence of the care with which it was built." Thus Job and Christopher were in the same area on Easton's Point, Christopher's house still standing at 74 Bridge St. Christopher's letter to Abraham Redwood dated 1738 seems to indicate that both brothers were well established in business for themselves by

that date. In miscellaneous account books at the Newport Historical Society, it would appear that they worked together on occasion, one entry mentioning "goods apprized by Job & Christopher Townsend June 26, 1741." In addition to his trade, Job was town treasurer for many years; when he died a notice in the *Newport Mercury*, Jan. 21, 1765, announced that "Job Townsend Town Treasurer Died last Saturday." A fragment of his will, filed at Newport, and dated "[—?] 3, 1764," lists him as "Townsend, Job Newport Shop Joiner."

At the Rhode Island School of Design, Providence, there is a desk-bookcase bearing his label, made shortly after 1730. This is of mahogany and has a flat top, bracket feet, arched paneled doors, and blocking and simple shell carving in the interior. It is the only labeled Job Townsend piece to date. At the Newport Historical Society is a high chest of drawers attributed to Job Townsend by family tradition. This is of mahogany without blocking and has one carved shell on the apron. (PLATE XIV, No. 1) It was presented to the Society by Miss Ellen Townsend, a granddaughter of John, and great-granddaughter of Christopher, Job's brother. Miss Townsend also presented the Society with a tray or silver table, made 1725–50, in Queen Anne style with slipper foot on cabriole leg. (PLATE XIV, No. 2). This was probably made by Job Townsend. At the Henry Ford Museum, Dearborn, Mich., is a Queen Anne style dressing table, 1740–60, attributed to Job Townsend.

TOWNSEND, Job Edward, Jr., *Newport, R. I.*

Born 1726; died 1818. Son of Job Townsend. His account books at the Newport Historical Society reveal that he and Edmund worked together in 1767, when they made a large mahogany desk for which they received 330 pounds. Under date of April 13, 1803 he charged Edmund "To Work on a Coffin for Mr. Coit." Other items in 1803 were:

May 9 Wm. Potter To a Cherry
   Stand   0/13/0
  14 John Taylor To a Low post
   Bedstedd   12/ 4/0

On May 19, 1808 he made a cherry desk for Gideon Dennis at "14/." Earlier entries show that he worked for the fashionable of Newport: for example, in 1762 he made a mahogany table for Joseph Wanton for £65 and in 1766 six chairs for Stephen Ayrault for £180. He died Oct. 18, 1818. Notice of his death was in the *Newport Mercury*, Oct. 24, 1818, and in the *Rhode Island Republic*, Oct. 21, 1818.

TOWNSEND, Job E., *Newport, R. I.*

Born 1758; died 1778. Son of Edmund. Nothing is known of the work of this Townsend who died when but twenty years old, but doubtless he worked with his father since boys began their apprenticeship at a young age. In Job Edward Jr.'s ledger is the terse entry "Job Townsend Died November the 5, 1778 at 10 Clock in the morning."

TOWNSEND, John, *Newport, R. I.*

Born 1732; died 1809. Time has awarded fame to John Townsend equal to that formerly accorded only to John Goddard. Some even believe that Townsend's work surpasses in beauty of design and workmanship that of his cousin by marriage, John Goddard. Some nine or ten pieces of furniture found bearing John Townsend's label are so outstanding in quality as to bolster this opinion and new evidence is constantly being uncovered.

The Friends Records at the Newport Historical Society state that "John Townsend, son of Christopher & Patience Easton his wife, was born in Newport ye 17th Day of 12th month in the year 1732-3." John doubtless served his apprenticeship in his father's cabinetmaking shop, beginning at a tender age, and he probably worked there with his father until his death in 1773. The following entries in the Aaron Lopez account book

(at the Newport Historical Society) indicate that John was selling furniture on his own account even before the death of his father:

1764
  Cr. John Townsend
    by 1 maple chair per bill   40
    by 8 mahogany chairs @ 40 320
    by 1 large tea board   14/10

1769
  Cr. John Townsend
    by 12 mahogany chairs and
       2 mahogany tables per bill
       of 3rd inst.   608/12

John was nine years younger than John Goddard, who was also apprenticed to the older Townsends, but it is reasonable to assume that by the time Goddard established his own place of business, John Townsend himself was already a well-trained cabinetmaker and that the two worked closely together, exchanging ideas and combining their knowledge and skill toward perfecting the beautiful block-front, shell-carved furniture which contributed so much to their fame.

On Sept. 6, 1764 John married Philadelphia Feke, daughter of Robert Feke the painter. It would appear that they had five children: Mary, who was born 1769, married Thomas Brinley on Feb. 27, 1823, and died Sept. 2, 1856; Sarah, who apparently died between 1801 and 1809; John F., who married Ann Easton on Feb. 6, 1804 and was still living in 1829; Solomon, who was living at the time of his father's death in 1809; and Charles F., who was also living at the time of his father's death. All five children are mentioned in the will of their uncle (Charles Feke), which is dated July 14, 1801, but John's will, dated 1809, makes no mention of Sarah, who apparently was no longer living. John's will, on file at the Newport City Hall Probate Clerk's office, in part makes the following provisions:

To my daughter Mary
  one of my best bedsteads with claw
    feet, which I made for my daughter
  Eight mahogany chairs with claw feet

black walnut chairs with hair bottoms

my easy chair

2 mahogany oval pembroke tables

1 square mahogany 4 ft. table with fluted legs

all mahogany 3 ft. square table with fluted legs

one square mahogany pembroke table with stretchers

one mahogany tea table.

To my son Solomon a mahogany clock which I made for him

To son Charles my mahogany desk which I made and now use and the mahogany desk which was his Sister Sarah's.

To three sons joiners tools and benches
9 feet mahogany
4 mahogany chairs not put together
4 feet mahogany bedposts
497 ft. mahogany
4 cherry bed posts
50 feet cherry tree.

As a Quaker John Townsend suffered during the days of the Revolution from the suspicion directed toward all of his religious group, whose belief forbade them to bear arms. In October 1777 he and some fifty others were captured by the British in Newport and taken aboard the prison ship *Lord Sandwich*. Some weeks later Governor Cooke of Rhode Island requested General Pigot to exchange these men for prisoners the Colonials were holding, and in the course of a few weeks the exchange was made. It is not known where John went upon his release but it is believed to have been Middletown, Conn. A block-front chest-on-chest was shown by Lockwood, in the third edition of his *Colonial Furniture in America*, which had the label "John Townsend, Middletown, Connecticut." This piece was not shown in subsequent editions of his book and much inquiry has failed to locate it today. If there was such a piece made by John Townsend then it would indicate that he was in Middletown between October 1777, when he is known to have been in Newport, and July 1780, when he wrote to Daniel

Cooke at Yale University from Norwich. The letter, now at the Rhode Island Historical Society, reads:

Dear Coonel

Had I but one Epistle to write by present conveyance, I should be less brief.

I should trouble you with the tedious detail of those friendly sentiments, I find revolving in my heart when I think of Coonelle. Sentiments founded on the solid basis of real esteem, sentiments bounded only by the Limits of the most extensive friendship.

This is perhaps the Last Letter I may have an opportunity to write. If it is believe it an earnest of sincere regard—please to comvince me that it is well received and answer this at Least, not according to its brevity or demerits but according to the charitable Candour which ought to be the principal Ingredient of every Literary mind.

Shall expect to see you at Norwich on your return from Yalensia, then to hear from your own mouth the numerous plaudits which grac'd the Characters of each commencing graduate.

Make such provision in your journey that you may spend some days in Norwich. Then in the recapitulation of those friendly scenes which formerly characterised our Intimacy, we shall take uncommon satisfaction.

Am in a prodigious hurry, pardon my inaccuracies and believe me your Friend and Humble

Servant

J. Townsend

Mr. Daniel Cooke
July 12, 1780

John was back in Newport on Jan. 17, 1782, when he appeared before a notary to collect money due him on work constructed in 1774 for Governor Wanton of Rhode Island, the father-in-law of John's sister Mary.

At the Metropolitan Museum of Art, New York City, there is a chest of drawers of the finest workmanship with block-front and carved shells. It has the written label inside the top drawer "Made by John Townsend, Rhode Island, 1765." (PLATE XVI, No. 2) At that time he was but thirty-three years of age. Also at the

Metropolitan is a mahogany breakfast table having square legs with stopped fluting and fret triangles in the corners where the legs join the table frame. This also bears John Townsend's label and the date 1766. Another labeled piece by John Townsend at the Metropolitan Museum is a clock case with the date 1769. In the Karolik Collection, Boston Museum of Fine Arts, there is a mahogany Pembroke table, made about 1790, with unusual pierced stretchers crossed diagonally, stopped fluting on square legs, and pierced brackets. The end aprons have borders of incised diaper pattern. The narrow drop-leaves are supported on hinged wooden wings. There is a drawer with sides of poplar and a bottom of chestnut. This is almost identical to a table at the Winterthur Museum, Delaware, which has John Townsend's label. At the William Rockhill Nelson Gallery of Art, Kansas City, Mo., there is a pair of card tables, one with John Townsend's label, dated 1794. This pair of card tables originally belonged to a set of four made for Colonel John Cooke. The tables are Hepplewhite in style, of mahogany inlaid with shaded holly, and were purchased at the Flayderman sale, 1930.

Antiques, February 1953, illustrates one of a set of six mahogany side chairs in Chippendale style attributed to John Townsend and made 1760–89. The set was made for Joseph Wanton, who was elected Governor of Rhode Island in 1769.

TOWNSEND, John F., *Newport, R. I.*
Living in 1829. Son of John. Married Ann Easton, Feb. 6, 1804. At the Newport Historical Society there is a cherry desk thought to have been made by John F. Townsend, although it has none of the fine carving found on pieces by his father.

TOWNSEND, Jonathan, *Newport, R. I.*
Born 1745; died 1772. Son of Christopher and brother of John. Christopher's will, 1773, mentions a "large mahogany

Desk which my son Jonathan made." Jonathan had died in Long Island the previous year.

TOWNSEND, Robert M., *Newport, R. I.*
Died 1805. Son of Job. There seems to be little data regarding Robert other than the following two items found by the author. The Probate Court Records at City Hall, Newport, have a reference for Nov. 4, 1805 to "Elizabeth Townsend, widow" and an inventory of Robert's shop and mahogany. The *Newport Mercury*, Nov. 16, 1805, contains the announcement that Job E. Townsend "has taken the shop of his late deceased brother in Pelham St. No. 3 where he carries on the cabinetmaking business in all its branches. Has now on hand a quantity of mahogany furniture which he will dispose of as cheap as can be purchased in Newport."

TOWNSEND, Thomas, *Newport, R. I.*
Born 1742; died 1822. Son of Job. In 1757, during the French and Indian War, he was captured by the French. He returned home and was working as a carpenter during the Revolution, but in 1775 was captured by the British. Upon his release he was not permitted to live in Newport but forced to reside in Mendon, Mass., until 1780. Thomas is mentioned in the ledger of his brother Job Edward Jr., who did work for several of his relatives. It is evident that Thomas gave up his carpenter's work before he died since he was called an innkeeper when his will was probated.

TOWNSEND, Thomas, *Newport, R. I.*
Born 1785. Son of Edmund. In the *Newport Mercury* for April 6, 1811 and in the *Rhode Island Republic* for April 3, 1811 there is notice of Thomas' marriage to Hannah B. Cornell on March 31, 1811.

TOWNSEND, M. B., *Baltimore, Md.*
Chair manufacturer and owner of cabinet furniture store at 36 Baltimore St. in 1833. (Varley)

TOWNSEND, Samuel, *Charlestown, Mass.*
Designated as turner on list of those who lost equipment in fire of 1775.

TOWNSEND, Stephen, *Charleston, S. C.*
On April 7, 1760 advertised that the partnership between Thomas Stocks and himself had been ended by Stocks' death. On Feb. 12, 1763 again advertised that he and William Axson had opened a shop on Tradd St. This partnership was ended in 1768 and Townsend opened a shop on Meeting St. Sold business to John Fisher (*q.v.*) on June 1, 1771. Believed to have given up cabinetmaking to devote himself to care of plantation. Died June 20, 1799. No evidence that Stephen had any connection with the Townsends of Rhode Island. (Burton)

TOWNSEND & AXSON, *Charleston, S. C.*
Partnership formed in 1763 by Stephen Townsend and William Axson. Had shop at corner of Tradd and Church streets, which was destroyed by fire in 1765. Partnership ended 1768, and each began working independently. (Burton)

TRACY, Ebenezer (Colonel), *Lisbon, Conn.*
Born April 20, 1744; died Nov. 10, 1803. Son of Andrew and Ruth (Smith) Tracy, who were married March 30, 1743. A study of the inventory of Ebenezer's estate indicates that he had a large cabinetmaking business and did not make just the Windsor chairs for which he is best known today. It suggests a close relationship between his family and that of Benjamin Burnham (Burnam). It raises the question as to whether he made the desk known as the General Ebenezer Huntington desk, formerly at the Metropolitan Museum of Art, for both Tracy and the General were Revolutionary officers, Huntington's mother-in-law was a Tracy, and both were living in Norwich. But these matters cannot be settled at this time. The inventory, dated April 21, 1803, shows an enormous amount of lumber, tools, and unfinished work. It listed:

"148 feet mahogany, 2148 feet cherry board, 491 do birch and beech, 111 mangrove do, 516 feet pine do, 1503 do white wood, 579 do maple, 707 do chestnut, 571 oak joists."

Among his tools were "52 moulding tools, 27 Joiners plains, 76 Chysils, Gouges &c. 14 fine and coarse hand saws, 50 Iron squair, 50 hold fast, Bench dog, Glue kettle, 2 Lead pots, Varnish pot, 12 lbs. glue, Stone yellow, 62 & 43 papers lamp black, etc." Among the finished and unfinished furniture were "2 low bureaus, 1 long table 7', 2 Pembroke do, 3 Candlestands, 50 clock cases, high post bed, 2 do, 2 Common beds, Chest Drawer, 103 Chairs of different sorts."

Other equipment included in part "Copal varnish, Marble paint vat & grinder, 6 lbs. emery, 12 gross screws, 4 drawer locks, 3 setts bureau trimmings, 35 escutchions, 50 sundry paints, copel and other varnish, Sideboard unfinished, Table, 6400 chair rounds & legs, 277 chair bottoms." In addition there was considerable furniture among the household listings.

Included in the inventory was an account of Uriah Rogers for various items, and credited against the amount due him, under date of Aug. 31, 1802, were the following charges for work done in Tracy's shop:

by 2 Shop Chairs at 4/3	0-17-0
by 3 Green Painted Chairs at 7/6	1- 2-6
by Painting 2 chairs at 2/	4-0

The entire inventory indicates that Tracy was a busy, prosperous cabinet-

Brand mark of Ebenezer Tracy

maker. As was not the case of so many workmen of his time, including his neighbor Benjamin Burnham, Tracy's estate did not have to be sold to pay his debts.

In addition to being a cabinetmaker he was a builder. Bishop in his *Historical Sketch of Lisbon* says that Tracy built the Second Church in Lisbon about 1773 while the Rev. Joel Benedick was pastor. He was also deacon in the church from 1795 until his death. Today we know only the Windsor chairs made by Tracy because he branded them "EB: TRACY." These are exceptionally well made, generally with chestnut seats, oak bows, and maple legs, with oak for the stretchers and hickory for the spindles. Mrs. Burton N. Gates of Worcester, Mass., who furnished the author with a rubbing, owns a horn-back side chair with Tracy's brand mark. In the Henry Ford Museum, Dearborn, Mich., is a Windsor braced bow-back armchair with Tracy's brand mark. (Bishop; *Inventory Probate Records*, Connecticut State Library, Hartford; *Vital Statistics, Norwich*)

TRACY, Elisha, *Scotland, Conn.*

Born Feb. 23, 1743/4; died 1809. Son of Eliphalet Tracy and his wife Sarah (Manning) Tracy. Listed as chairmaker. No inventory of estate found. Doubtless made by him is a Windsor chair with the brand mark "E. Tracy," owned by Mrs. Burton N. Gates of Worcester, Mass.

TREFETHERN, William, *Rye, N. H.*

Working about 1740 in the Queen Anne tradition. (*American Collector*, June 1937)

TREMAIN, John, *New York City and Charleston, S. C.*

Advertised in New York in 1751 as cabinetmaker. In 1755 a John Tremain appeared in Charleston, S. C., and advertised in the *South Carolina Gazette* on July 17: "John Tremain takes this opportunity to inform the public that he has set up his business of cabinet & coffin making in Elliott street; where those that please to employ him may be assured of having their work done in the neatest and cheapest manner. . . . Said Tremain is inclinable to take an apprentice for 5, 6,

or 7 years, if the boy be of sober family and well recommended." Burton finds no further evidence of this man's stay in Charleston. Is it possible that the New York and Charleston advertisements were by the same man?

TREVETT, Eleazar, *Newport, R. I.*

The Aaron Lopez account book (Newport Historical Society) records the following for 1766:

> Cr. Eleazer Trevett
> 2 Maple Desks per bill   £180
> 1 Mahogany Desk
> 2 Maple desks.

In 1802 Richardson says he was on Washington St. on the Point, just north of the Ship Yard. A copy of his will at the Newport Historical Society shows the date Jan. 25, 1804.

TROTTER, Daniel, *Philadelphia, Pa.*

Died 1800. Had shop in Elfreth's Alley. Worked with his son-in-law Ephraim Haines (*q.v.*). (Downs speaks of Benjamin Trotter as Haines' father-in-law. There was in Philadelphia a Benjamin Trotter working as chairmaker but it was Daniel Trotter's daughter who married Haines.) Together they made the so-called "pretzel-back" chair, a ladder-back with undulating cross slats, each with a small open design in center resembling a pretzel. Two similar chairs at the Metropolitan Museum of Art, New York City. (PLATE XII, No. 2) Trotter made chairs of this type for Stephen Girard. Hornor says he also made four bedsteads for Girard between 1786 and 1796; these were of mahogany with Marlborough bases. Hornor also says that Trotter used light-colored woods extensively to inlay mahogany in what in 1795 he called "stringing & shades."

TROWBRIDGE, Stephen, *New Haven, Conn.*

A news item in the *Connecticut Gazette*, New London, Jan. 14, 1791, reads: "Last Saturday afternoon a large building owned and occupied by Mr. Stephen Trowbridge, Cabinetmaker in this city [New Haven] was consumed by fire, together with a large quantity of finished and unfinished work, stock, tools, etc."

TRUELOCK, John, *Baltimore, Md.*

Listed in directory for 1799 as cabinetmaker.

TRUMBLE, Francis, *Philadelphia, Pa.*

Born circa 1716; died October 1798. Shipped furniture to Barbados as early as 1741. Hornor says that in 1754 he offered a large variety of articles for sale of "Mohogany, Walnut, Cherry-Tree, Mapple." He is mentioned in Benjamin Randolph's receipt book for the years 1763–77. In 1775 his shop was on "Front-street near Pine-street." In 1778 Trumble was paid for two tables and twelve chairs according to the cash book of the Pennsylvania Assembly. He branded his Windsor chairs with "FT." On May 17, 1952 a Windsor stamped with this mark was shown at the loan exhibition of Windsor chairs at Old Congress Hall, Philadelphia. This had been purchased when the original furnishings of Independence Hall were sold at auction in 1814. In 1802 they had been sent to Harrisburg for use by the Pennsylvania Assembly. In the first Philadelphia directory, 1785, Trumble is listed as a Windsor chair maker. In 1786, according to Hornor, he owned a dwelling house taxable at £900, and several wooden houses in Shippen St. taxable at £350. In 1796 a short-term partnership with Joseph Burden was dissolved. In March 1798 Trumble gave up chairmaking. (*Antiques*, June 1936; Hornor)

TRYON, Isaac *Glastonbury, Conn.*

Born 1741; died 1823. As yet it has been impossible to secure much definite data on Isaac Tryon. Glastonbury had innumerable Tryons, and it may well be he was a son of the Joseph Tryon who in 1723 had fifty acres of land there. In the Revolution Isaac served for three years. On Dec. 25, 1771 he married Elizabeth Kimberly, daughter of John and Mary (Hubbard) Kimberly; they had eight children, and the second son was named Isaac. It has been suggested that Isaac learned his trade with Eliphalet Chapin, but this seems improbable since they were the same age. Some features of Isaac's work are not unlike various ones seen in Chapin's furniture but this is not greatly significant since they worked in the same period. Tryon is the maker of an unusual cherry highboy with the following inscription marked in chalk in eighteenth-century script in one of the large drawers, "Glastonbury october 26th 1772 this Case of Draws made By me Isaac Tryon." This has a carved double sunflower on the center of the top middle drawer. It is illustrated in *Antiques*, August 1931. Illustrated in the same magazine, February 1955, is a cherry case of drawers inlaid with maple and mahogany and attributed to Tryon. Several pieces have been found and attributed to him by comparison with the marked piece. (Nutting, Vol. 3)

TUCK, Samuel J., *Boston, Mass.*

Listed as Windsor chair maker on Batterymarch St. in 1795.

TUCKER, Elisha, *Boston, Mass.*

Listed as cabinetmaker at 40 Middle St. in 1810.

TUCKER, Isaac, *Hartford, Conn.*

Listed as cabinetmaker at time he bought land from William Adams (*q.v.*) in 1739. (Love)

TUFFT, Thomas, *Philadelphia, Pa.*

It is not known where Tufft was born, but it is believed the time was about 1740. Neither is it known where he learned his trade. He married Martha Gamble of Nottingham, Burlington County, N. J., a sister of Patrick Gamble of that town. It is thought he was not in business for himself before 1768 but that he was well established by 1772 when he took an apprentice by the name of Edward Lewis. In 1773 he took over the shop formerly occupied by James Gillingham "Four Doors from the Corner of Walnut Street in Second Street, Philadelphia." He was listed in 1785 in the first Philadelphia directory. In 1779 he bought a house in Elfreth's Alley but in a year rented it to David Evans, another cabinetmaker, and moved to a dwelling in Norris Alley. In 1793 his wife was administering his considerable estate, although one writer says that contemporary records indicate he gave up business in October 1787 and died in Earl Township near Lancaster, Pa., in May 1788.

Downs says, "His carved high chests and matching dressing tables set a standard of exquisite detail." Downs believed, however, that Tufft hired professional carvers to do his carving as was the custom of many cabinetmakers. A pair of mahogany side chairs is at the Winterthur Museum, Delaware. These have engraved paper labels on the inside back rail which read, "Made and Sold by

Carved shell detail, mahogany lowboy, Chippendale style, Philadelphia, circa 1750–80

Thomas Tufft Cabinet and Chair Maker Four Doors from the Corner of Walnut Street in Second Street, Philadelphia." Hornor (pl. 231) shows a mahogany Chippendale sofa completed in 1783 and attributed to Tufft. A mate of this sofa is in the Winterthur Museum (Downs, No. 273). At the Philadelphia Museum of Art, there is a labeled lowboy. (PLATE XII, No. 1) The carved design on the knees is suggestive of the carving of James Gillingham. Chairs by Tufft also have certain features suggestive of those of Gillingham.

(*Antiques*, Oct. 1927, Oct. 1948; Downs; Hornor)

TUFTS, Uriah, *Lowell, Mass.*
Listed as cabinetmaker in 1834; still working in 1837. (Belknap)

TURNER, George, *Tyngsboro, Mass.*
Born circa 1823 in West Bridgewater. Married Almira Peirce Kendall, Oct. 26, 1848. Listed as cabinetmaker.

TURNER, J. B., *Lyme, Conn.*
Advertised in the *New London Gazette*, May 27 and July 15, 1829, as maker of "Fancy Chairs."

TURNER, Matthew, *Boston, Mass.*
On tax list of 1688 as joiner.

TUTTLE, Charles, *Boston, Mass.*
Listed in directory for 1806 as cabinetmaker on Common St.

TUTTLE, George, *Salem, Mass.*
Born circa 1803; died Aug. 1, 1832. Chairmaker.

TUTTLE, James Chapman, *Salem, Mass.*
Born circa 1772; died Aug. 14, 1849. Advertised in *Salem Gazette*, Aug. 19, 1796: "James C. Tuttle, Cabinet and Chair Maker Informs his customers and the public that whereas they have called on him . . . at his shop at the head of Federal Street on the corner adjoining Boston Road. . . ." Advertised again when he was located between Essex and Federal streets. Mrs. Burton N. Gates of Worcester, Mass., has a Windsor side chair with Tuttle's brand mark.

Brand mark of James Chapman Tuttle

TWEED, Richard, *New York City*
Born 1790. Served his apprenticeship with Thomas Ash, an outstanding Wind-

sor chair maker. Had shop at 24 Cherry St. and resided at 1 Cherry St. (T. Ormsbee, *Newtown Bee*, Conn., May 16, 1947)

TWEED, William Marcy (Boss), *New York City*

Born 1823; died 1878. Came from a family of furniture-makers. Although better known as Boss Tweed of New York City politics, he operated a chair factory until 1858. Learned his trade in his father's shop, where he began work when only eleven years old. By the time he was twenty-one he had his own shop at 357 Pearl St. Advertised "fine gilt and variegated colored chairs . . . also wood, cane, rush, willow and straw seat chairs." Few, if any, of his chairs were marked. (Ormsbee)

TYLER, Sylvester, *Hartford, Conn.*

Advertised in the *American Mercury*, Oct. 31, 1796, as cabinet- and chairmaker.

UNDERWOOD, John, *Charlestown, Mass.*

Working as cabinetmaker in Charlestown and Boston before 1788. (*Antiques*, Oct. 1944)

UNION CHAIR CO., *Winsted, Conn.*

Colebrook records for Jan. 7, 1847 show that Samuel Roberts conveyed a chairmill to "Moses 2nd, Paul N. & Caleb S. Camp of Winsted." From 1850 to 1865 these men, under the firm name of Union Chair Co., made many chairs similar to those by Hitchcock, some of them stenciled, marked with the firm name. They also made Boston rockers. In 1882 the company was sold to A. L. Rapp & Sons, New York. *See* entry for Holmes & Roberts.

UPTON, Henry, *Lowell, Mass.*

Born May 2, 1823 in Tewksbury. Married Frances Skelton, Oct. 6, 1849. Cabinetmaker. (Belknap)

VAIL, Joseph, *New York City*

First directory of New York City, printed in 1786, does not list Vail. Listed in 1790 as cabinetmaker at 153 Queen St.;

from 1791 to 1797 at Bowery Lane; in 1798 at Grand St. In 1799 and 1800 listed as Joseph Veal (*sic*), chairmaker, on Grand St. In 1802 and 1803 his name is again spelled correctly in directory. In 1804 moved to 54 John St., where he remained until 1806. His label is found in a mahogany slant-top desk—shown in *Antiques*, February 1944—the label giving 32 Beekman St. as his address. He was probably at this address before the first directory listing.

VALLEY, John, *Tolland, Conn.*

Advertised in the *American Mercury*, Hartford, Sept. 22, 1808: "WANTED IMMEDIATELY a Journeyman Cabinet-Maker to whom good wages will be given. Enquire of JOHN VALLEY, Tolland."

VAN GELDER, Garrett, *New York City*

Listed as chairmaker when made a freeman in 1765. His name appears in records of Common Council as early as 1738.

VAN MOLL, Augustin C., *Newburyport, Mass.*

Born in Lisle, France. On Jan. 25, 1840 married Honora Maria Broderickx (*sic*). Cabinetmaker from 1851 to 1860. (Belknap)

VANNEVAR, George, *Boston, Mass.*

Advertised in 1823 as cabinetmaker. Illustrated in *Antiques*, October 1929, is a mahogany sideboard of Sheraton style, found in Charlestown. In the center drawer is the penciled inscription "George Vannevar The Maker."

VENARD, Edward B. S., *Manchester, Mass.*

Cabinetmaker. Married Louisa A. Lee, Oct. 24, 1841.

VERY, Nathaniel, *Salem, Mass.*

Born April 23, 1809; died Jan. 25, 1897. Married Elizabeth Coombs, Sept. 11, 1836. Second wife was Eliza Ann Kimball. Working as cabinetmaker from 1833 to a few years before death. (Perley, *History of Salem*, Vol. 3)

VILES, William, *Boston, Mass.*
Working as cabinet- and chairmaker for John Doggett in Roxbury, 1806.

VINCENT, William, *Boston, Mass.*
Arrived from England in 1715, when listed as joiner.

VINSON, Samuel, *Newport, R. I.*
The Aaron Lopez account book, under 1763, records: "Cr. Samuel Venzant [Vinson?] by 1 maple desk £90."

VINYARD, John, *Charleston, S. C.*
Listed in directory for 1801 as cabinet-maker at 181 Meeting St. Burton says records indicate that Vinyard moved to Orangeburg, S. C., where a man by that name was married in 1806.

VOGLER, Christoph, *Salem, N. C.*
Came from Friedland in 1774. Working as late as 1794 as cabinetmaker and gunsmith. (Fries, *Records of the Moravians in North Carolina*)

VOGLER, John, *Salem, N. C.*
Born 1783; died 1881. Came to Salem in 1794 as an apprentice to his uncle Christoph. In the Wachovia Museum in Salem there is a "Vogler Room," where some of John's spoons and cabinetwork and a showcase with his tools are on exhibition. Evidently he was equally proficient as silversmith and cabinetmaker. His work has been identified and many pieces made by him are in the possession of his descendants. (Fries, *Records of the Moravians in North Carolina*)

VOSE, Daniel, *Milton, Mass.*
Born 1741; died 1807. Belonged to the same family as Ebenezer and had a business similar to his.

VOSE, Ebenezer, *Dorchester Lower Mills, Mass.*
Born 1766; died 1813. With other members of his family had a thriving cabinet-making shop with many apprentices at the time Stephen Badlam was working.

VOSE, Isaac, *Boston, Mass.*
Listed in directory for 1789 as cabinet-maker on Orange St. In 1819 the firm was Isaac Vose & Son.

VOSE, N., *Dorchester Lower Mills, Mass.*
Working as chairmaker in Ebenezer's firm.

VOSE, William, *Boston, Mass.*
Born 1778; died 1851. Advertised in 1803 as cabinetmaker.

VOSE & COATS, *Boston, Mass.*
In 1806 Joshua F. Coats (*q.v.*) was a member of this firm. Vose was undoubtedly one of the large family of cabinet-makers by that name in Dorchester Lower Mills. Firm apparently dissolved before 1817, when Coats opened his own shop on Roxbury St., Boston.

VOSE & TODD, *Boston, Mass.*
Listed in directory for 1796 as cabinet-makers on Cambridge St.

WADE, Francis Hodgkins, *Ipswich, Mass.*
Born Jan. 12, 1819. Married Eliza Ann Grant, May 20, 1845, in Salem. Working as cabinetmaker in Ipswich as late as 1846.

WADSWORTH, John, *Hartford, Conn.*
Advertised in the *American Mercury,* June 10, 1793: "John Wadsworth Takes this Method to inform his friends, and the Public in general, that he makes and sells, all kinds of Windsor Chairs at his shop about sixty rods north of the Court House, opposite to Mr. Daniel Jone's Store. Those who will be obliging as to favor him with their custom, may depend on having their work done in the neatest manner and on reasonable terms." Advertised in the same paper, Jan. 4, 1796: "WINDSOR CHAIRS. John Wadsworth Informs the Public that he has taken the Shop lately occupied by Stacy Stackhouse where he carries on the Windsor Chair-Making business:—Those who will please to employ him, may depend on having their work done in the best man-

ner, on reasonable terms and at the time agreed on:—Wanted by said Wadsworth as Apprentices to the above business, one or two likely Boys, 13 or 14 years old— Also to purchase, a quantity of square edged Whitewood Plank, from 18 to 20 inches wide."

On the bill rendered by Jeremiah Halsey for furnishings for the old State House at Hartford (photostatic copy at Connecticut State Library) John Wadsworth was listed in connection with "Settees & Chairs 70:13."

WADSWORTH, William, *Dorchester Lower Mills, Mass.*

Born 1768. Cabinetmaker. Married Mary Ruggles Vose of the cabinetmaking family.

WAINER, Thomas, Jr., *New York City*

Listed as chairmaker when made a freeman in 1750.

WAINRIGHT, James, *Baltimore, Md.*

Listed in directories from 1804 to 1808 as cabinetmaker.

WAITE, John, *Charlestown, Mass.*

Born 1651; died 1704. Notice of death listed him as joiner.

WALKER, Alexander, *Fredericksburg, Va.*

Advertised in *Virginia Herald* in 1799 as cabinetmaker.

WALKER, Moses, Jr., *Haverhill, Mass.*

Baptized Jan. 12, 1817. Married Abby D. Harris of Hudson, N. H., on April 3, 1841 and Betsy Clements George on March 19, 1844. Cabinetmaker.

WALKER, Robert, *Charleston, S. C.*

Born 1772; died July 30, 1833. A native of Scotland. In 1801 directory listed as cabinetmaker at 57 Broad St. Advertised in the *Times*, May 21, 1806, for two journeymen cabinetmakers. Between 1806 and 1810 bought considerable property. In 1810 moved shop from 39 Church St. to 19 Elliott St. In 1813 moved shop

to 53 Church St. Listed in directories until 1819. He is the only Charleston cabinetmaker whose label has survived. It is found on two pieces of furniture: a satinwood secretary-bookcase and a very fine clothespress acquired by the Charleston Museum in 1955. (Burton)

WALKER, William, *Charleston, S. C.*

In 1801 and for several years afterwards listed in directories on Hasell St. By 1806 located at 12 Archdale St. Died circa 1811. (Burton)

WALLACE, Robert, *New York City*

Advertised in the *New York Gazette* in 1753 "all Sorts of Cabinets, Scrutores, Desks and Book Cases, Drawers, Tables, either square, round, oval, or quadrile, and Chairs of any Fashion." Had shop on Beaver and New streets.

WALLACE, Thomas, *Charleston, S. C.*

Born 1758 in Ayreshire, Scotland; died Nov. 22, 1816. Married Agnes Rogers of Paisley, Scotland. In 1790 formed a co-partnership with Charles Watts (*q.v.*). Two years later Wallace opened his own shop. Advertised in the *City Gazette and Daily Advertiser*, March 31, 1792, as a cabinetmaker and undertaker. In 1796 again advertised that he was moving his shop from Meeting St. to Church St. between Broad and Queen and that "He has also on hand a quantity of ready made Furniture, among which are, a few dozen of fashionable Mahogany Chairs, which he will dispose of on lower terms than any in this city of the same quality." Burton says that Wallace doubtless prospered since he purchased several pieces of property in Charleston. Inventory of his estate lists one secretary and bookcase, one set of mahogany chairs, and two mahogany bedsteads. Thomas Elfe, Jr., was one of the appraisers. (Burton)

WALLACE & WATTS, *Charleston, S. C.*

Advertised in the *City Gazette and Daily Advertiser*, March 5, 1790, that they were cabinet- and pianoforte-makers from London. In 1791 Watts moved to the corner of Broad St. and Market Square. (Burton)

WALLIS, David, *Salem, Mass.*
Working as cabinetmaker for Nathaniel Appleton at 80 Derby St. in 1837.

WALLIS, Joseph, *Salem, Mass.*
Cabinetmaker at 281 Essex St. in 1837; at 29 Lafayette St. in 1842; at 205 Essex St. with furniture store in 1847; and later at 213 Essex St.

WALTON, Samuel, *Philadelphia, Pa.*
Mentioned in Benjamin Randolph's receipt book, 1763–77. In 1785 made "eight Chairs & a Sophy" at a cost of £36 for the Rev. Dr. Robert Blackwell of 224 Pine St. In 1783 paid tax as joiner of £55, and in 1786 £850 on a dwelling. (Hornor)

WAMMETT, Walden, *Newport, R. I.*
Working as joiner in 1825. (Richardson)

WARD, Ebenezer, *Salem, Mass.*
Baptized April 9, 1710; died March 3, 1791. Son of Miles Ward. Received lot and house from his father on March 7, 1755. Married Rachel Pickman, Oct. 23, 1735. His cabinet-shop and estate were in the hands of Benjamin Ward, Jr., for settlement in May 1791. (Perley, *Salem in 1700*)

WARD, John, *Salem, Mass.*
Born Jan. 10, 1738; died Dec. 1, 1789. Joiner and cabinetmaker. Married Sept. 14, 1758.

WARD, Miles, *Salem, Mass.*
Born March 11, 1673; died Aug. 29, 1764. Married Sarah Massey on Sept. 16, 1697 and Sarah Ropes in 1737. Joiner and chairmaker. The Miles Ward lot and house on lane leading to South River (see map facing p. 223 of Perley's *Salem in 1700*) belonged to Joshua Ward as early as 1669. He died in 1680, leaving this lot

and house, valued at £100, to his son Miles. On March 7, 1755 Miles conveyed it to his son Ebenezer.

WARD, Miles, *Salem, Mass.*
Born April 18, 1704; died June 17, 1792. Joiner. Married Elizabeth Webb on Jan. 3, 1727/8 and Hannah Derby Hathorne on Oct. 10, 1737. (Perley, *History of Salem*)

WARD, Moses, *Boston, Mass.*
Chairmaker in firm of Campbell & Ward in 1791. On Leveretts Lane in 1796. *See* entry for James Campbell.

WARDELL, Jonathan, *Boston, Mass.*
On tax list of 1690 as cabinetmaker.

WARDELL, William T., *Providence, R. I.*
Listed in directories during 1832–37 as cabinetmaker working at 148 High St., residing at 161 High St.

WARE, John, *Boston, Mass.*
Listed in directory for 1810 as cabinetmaker.

WARE, Maskell, *Roadtown, N. J.*
Born 1776; died 1855. The first of a family of chairmakers. Learned his trade

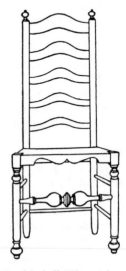

Chair by Maskell Ware, circa 1800

with John Lanning of Salem with whom he lived as a boy. Had seven sons, five of whom became chairmakers. Chairs made by Maskell had broad lines but were well proportioned. Frames usually were of curly or plain swamp maple; occasionally walnut was used for rockers. Chair posts were turned, slats were hewn by hand; and nails were not used. There were large ball turnings on front rung. Various types of finials were used. Seats were of rush; this was either "straight," each strand overlapping another, or it was "checkered," four strands overlapping the next four to form checkered diagonals across the seat, in a manner not unlike that used by the Shakers. (Nutting, Vol. 3)

WARE, John S. and William, *Bridgeton, N. J.*

Two of Maskell's sons. Advertised in 1826 as cabinet- and chairmakers. In exhibition at State Museum, Trenton, N. J., 1953 (see *Catalogue*), there was a child's chair with slat back and rush seat, made about 1850, that was attributed to some member of the Ware family. Also shown was a miniature chair with ladder back and rush bottom, made about 1816.

WARE, Samuel C., *Providence, R. I.*

Listed in directory for 1832 as cabinetmaker at 101–5 Westminster St.

WARFIELD, William, *Baltimore, Md.*

Listed in directory for 1799 as cabinetmaker.

WARHAM, Charles, *Charleston, S. C.*

Born 1701; died July 20, 1799. Arrived in Charleston from London by way of Boston in 1733. Doubtless trained in London. Worked as cabinetmaker in Charleston for some forty years. On Nov. 2, 1734 advertised in *South Carolina Gazette* that he was late from "Boston N. England" and that he "maketh all sorts of Tables, Chests, Chest-of-drawers, Desks, Bookcases &c. As also Coffins of the newest fashion, never as yet made in Charleston.

Whoever has a mind to treat with him for any of the above-mentioned may inquire at his shop in Trade-Street, next door to Mr. Joseph Moody's." (Tradd St. was often called Trade St. in early advertisements.) In 1735 he advertised, "I intend likewise to prepare all things necessary for and take care at Funerals in the same Manner as Mr. Walton, deceased did." Apparently he prospered, because he purchased much property. (Burton)

WARNER, Elijah, *Lexington, Ky.*

Directory of 1818 lists him as "Cabinet and wooden clock maker." (Whitley)

WARNER, Nathaniel, *Boston, Mass.*

Listed in directory for 1796 as cabinetmaker.

WARNER, William, *New York City*

Made a freeman in 1765. Listed as turner.

WARREN, Thomas, *Boston, Mass.*

On tax list of 1690 as joiner.

WATERHOUSE, Timothy, *Newport, R.I.*

Working as chairmaker in 1762. (Richardson)

WATERS, Daniel, *Charlestown, Mass.*

Designated as cabinetmaker on list of those who lost equipment in fire of 1775.

WATERS, Ebenezer, *Boston, Mass.*

Listed in directory for 1789 as chairmaker on Orange St.

WATERS, Edward, *Boston, Mass.*

Listed as cabinetmaker in 1789.

WATERS, William, *Baltimore, Md.*

Advertised in 1791 as cabinetmaker.

WATKINS, James, *Philadelphia, Pa.*

Cabinetmaker. Died 1794. (Hornor)

WATROUS, Seymour, *Hartford, Conn.*

Advertised in *Hartford Courant,* March

2, 1824: "Seymour Watrous, Informs the Chairmaker public that he has lately commenced the Cabinet and Chair Making business in Central Row, No. 6, at the sign of the Hartford Cabinet and Chair Warehouse. . . . Wanted immediately One Journeyman Chair Maker and two young lads from the country, fifteen or sixteen years of age as apprentices to the Chair Making business." Made chairs similar to those of Hitchcock. Married Mary Ann Barnard, Dec. 24, 1827.

WATROUS & DICKERSON, *Hartford, Conn.*
Cabinetmakers. Advertised in the *American Mercury* in 1830.

WATSON, John, *Charleston, S. C.*
Born 1751 in Mussilborough, Scotland. Listed in the directory for 1790 as cabinetmaker at 21 Tradd St. On July 9, 1796 advertised in *City Gazette and Daily Advertiser* that he was moving to 21 King St. At that time he was making a great variety of furniture. In February 1797 again advertised that he had secured workmen from "Auld Reekie [Edinburgh], London and Paris." On Jan. 1, 1798 formed a partnership with his "step-son" (son-in-law) John A. Woodill under the firm name of Watson & Woodill at 21 King St. Woodill died in 1805. Directories list Watson until 1812, the year of his death. (Burton)

WATSON, John, *New York City*
Made a freeman in 1770. Listed as cabinetmaker. According to its records the Common Council in 1770 "Ordered the Mayor issue his warrant to the Treasurer of this City to pay John Watson on order the Sum of £85 for making two large mahogany arm'd chairs for the use of the Common Council."

WATSON, John Horace, *Manchester, Mass.*
Born circa 1821 in Boston. Married Emily Pillsbury at Lynn, March 9, 1845. Listed as cabinetmaker in 1845.

WATSON, William, *Charleston, S. C.*
One of Charleston's earliest furniture makers. Married Mary Kemp, Sept. 26, 1723. Apparently successful in his work because he bought considerable property as early as 1729. On Aug. 14, 1736, a few days after his death, Mrs. Watson advertised in the *South Carolina Gazette*: "Notice is hereby given, That the Business lately carried on by Wm: Watson deceased will be continued by his widow, who has a considerable stock of fresh goods of all sorts necessary for Funerals, and Workmen fully capable of making Coffins and Cabinet ware, she has also ready made to be sold cheap, Tables, Chests-of-drawers, &c." (Burton)

WATTS, Charles, *Charleston, S. C.*
Died 1811. In 1790 formed a partnership with Thomas Wallace (*q.v.*). By 1791 Watts was established by himself at the corner of Broad St. and Market Square. His shop destroyed by fire and in 1795 he moved to Church St. In 1796 his shop again was destroyed by fire. He re-established his business on lower Church St. On July 19, 1796 he advertised that he was residing at John Milligan's, 6 Bedon's Alley, where he had a variety of furniture for sale. In 1797 he advertised in the *Diary* in New York City: "Wanted from 8 to 15 Journeymen Cabinet and Chair-Makers to go to Charleston, South Carolina where they will receive generous encouragement for further particulars, apply to Captain Joseph Baker, on Board the Sloop Romeo, laying at the Coffee House Slip.

"I hereby oblige myself to pay to any good workman, who is capable of doing the general run of Cabinet-work seventy-five percent advance on the New London book of Cabinet prices, published in 1793. I will also advance the passage money for whoever chuses to come in the above line; and find work for any, or all, of the above number, for 6, 9, or 12 months; board, or find them it at 3-½ dollars per week. The money for the work shall be paid weekly, or when the job is finished.

Charles Watts, Cabinet-Maker, Charleston."

Apparently he was very successful in his business ventures since he bought considerable property in Charleston. His name appears for the last time in the 1803 directory. His will was probated Nov. 30, 1811. (Burton)

WAYNE, Jacob, *Philadelphia, Pa.*

Son of William Wayne and Sarah Gillingham, oldest daughter of John Gillingham. In 1790 made two mahogany bureaus and six mahogany "slatt back Chairs" for Capt. Thomas Mason (Hornor, pls. 100 and 101). In 1783 paid occupation tax as cabinet- and chairmaker.

WAYNE, William, *Philadelphia, Pa.*

Married Sarah, oldest daughter of John Gillingham (*q.v.*). Father of Jacob. Partner of Robert Moore. In the *Pennsylvania Gazette*, Feb. 16, 1769, the following appeared:

> The partnership of Wayne and Moore, cabinetmakers, being expired, those who are indebted to said partnership are requested to make speedy payment and those who have any accounts against the partnership, to bring them in for payment to
>
> Robert Moore or
> William Wayne
>
> N.B. Robert Moore acquaints his Friends and the Public, that he now carries on the Cabinetmaking and Chair-Making Business in the Best Manner, and genteelest Taste, at his Work-Shop next but one to the Corner of Key's Alley, in Front St., above Race Street in the Shop which, during the partnership of him and Wayne, they used as a store and workshop.

Wayne continued in business and doubtless soon had his son working with him, first as an apprentice, and then as a partner. In 1770 Wayne made considerable furniture for Samuel Wallis, who married Lydia Hollingswood in 1769. Hornor (pl. 121) shows the so-called William Wayne highboy, one of the Wallis pieces. Wayne paid occupation

Detail of pediment of mahogany highboy, Chippendale style, Philadelphia, 1765–80

tax of £100 in 1783 and of £150 in 1786. In 1785 he and Jacob are both listed in the Philadelphia Directory but William's name does not appear in 1794.

The highboy made for Wallis shows that Wayne worked in the traditional Philadelphia practice. The piece is of very fine-grained mahogany. The cabriole legs are comparatively short with claw-and-ball feet, which makes the top section seem taller than usual. The central decoration of the scrolled pediment is an elaborately carved basket of leaves and flowers. The front legs are carved with a leafage design.

(*Antiques*, Sept. 1927; Hornor)

WEATHERS, James, *near Clintonville, Ky.*

Working 1802–62. Corner cupboards, tables, and sugar chests made by him are owned by collateral descendants. (Whitley)

WEATHERSTRAND, William, *Baltimore, Md.*

Listed in directories during 1796–1810 as cabinetmaker.

WEAVER, Holmes, *Newport, R. I.*

Born July 24, 1769 in Middletown, R. I.; died February 1848 in Newport. Holmes was the seventh child of Thomas and Alice Weaver of Portsmouth (*Weaver Genealogy* by Lucius E. Weaver,

1928). It is not known in whose shop he served his apprenticeship. On June 15, 1799 he advertised in the *Newport Mercury*: "Holmes Weaver, Chair and Cabinet-Maker, Has Taken a Shop in Meeting Street, North of the Mercury Printing Office." Sometime between 1806 and 1815 he moved to the north side of Broadway. There are several of his labeled pieces in existence. In the Karolik Collection at the Boston Museum of Fine Arts there is a Hepplewhite-style mahogany Pembroke table with the original label in the drawer. (PLATE XXV, No. 1) Inlays of satinwood and rosewood are on the legs, the satinwood embellished with engraved designs. Hipkiss says this table is "the finest known in this treatment." A second Hepplewhite-style Pembroke table, circa 1790, attributed to Weaver, is at the Henry Ford Museum, Dearborn, Mich. There are two clock cases with Weaver's label at the Rhode Island Historical Society, Providence. In *Antiques*, February 1924, there is shown a labeled chest of drawers. At the Newport Historical Society the die used by Weaver for his labels is displayed. This shows a serpentine-front sideboard above the following inscription:

HOLMES WEAVER
CABINET AND CHAIR-MAKER
MEETING STREET
NEWPORT

WEAVER, Isaac, *near West Chester, Pa.*
    Son of Joshua Weaver, silversmith. On tax list of 1807. Stockwell says that the first county newspaper, *The Village Record*, was founded in 1809, and that it contained the following advertisement in 1810: "Isaac Weaver, Cabinetmaker, takes the liberty of informing his friends and the public generally, that he continues to make all kinds of cabinet-ware in the best and most fashionable style either plain or inlaid, next door to his father's in the borough of West Chester, Chester County, where all orders directed to him will be attended to with punctuality and on the most reasonable terms. He also makes coffins and attends funerals on the shortest reasonable notice." (*American Collector*, April 1939)

WEAVER, William, *Coventry, Vt.*
    Born May 23, 1736 at East Greenwich, R. I. Family moved to Coventry about 1747. In 1773 moved to Bennington, Vt. While in Coventry "he led an active life being a house-carpenter, a cooper, and a shop-joiner." (L. E. Weaver, *Weaver Genealogy*, 1928)

WEBB, Adrian, *Providence, R. I.*
    Listed in directory in 1824 as cabinetmaker on North Main St.; in 1828 at 80 Benefit St.; in 1832 at 105 North Main St. It is possible that he and Charles Scott (*q.v.*) were the partners who used the label "Webb & Scott, Cabinet & Chair Makers, Benefit-Street, Providence, Rhode Island" found in a cherry secretary-bookcase, with ogee feet, arched top, and inlay, mentioned by Nutting.

WEBB, John Charles, *Manchester, Mass.*
    Born Jan. 31, 1815. Married Lucy Ann Procter, March 31, 1840. Listed as cabinetmaker in 1840.

WEBB, Thomas, *Boston, Mass.*
    Died 1728. Notice of death listed him as joiner.

WEBB, William 3rd, *Salem, Mass.*
    Baptized Nov. 11, 1805. Died Nov. 15, 1849. Married Margaret Perkins, March 2, 1833. Listed as cabinetmaker at 108 Essex St. from 1837 until death.

WEBB & SCOTT, *Providence, R. I.*
    A card table in Hepplewhite style, made circa 1790–1800 and attributed to Webb & Scott, is in the Henry Ford Museum, Dearborn, Mich. *See* entries for Adrian Webb and Charles Scott.

WEBBER, Charles E., *Saugus, Mass.*
    Born circa 1829 in Boothbay, Me.; died Dec. 22, 1847 in Saugus. Listed as cabinet-

maker at time of death. Buried in Charlestown, Mass.

WEBSTER, Francis, *Boston, Mass.*
Listed as cabinetmaker in 1793.

WEBSTER, John, *Salisbury, Mass.*
Born April 10, 1750; died Nov. 13, 1807. Listed as cabinetmaker. (Belknap)

WEDDESTRAND, Thomas, *Baltimore, Md.*
Listed as cabinetmaker during 1802–10.

WEEDEN, George, *Newport, R. I.*
The Aaron Lopez ledger (at Newport Historical Society) records the following for 1768:

Cr. George Weeden, Joyner by a /
    cabin table for ship Cleopatra   £32

Lopez recorded the following under date of 1772:

Cr. George Weeden, Joyner
    By a cabin table for Brigt. Brittania   £25
    By do for Brig. Neptune   £28

WEEDEN, Sam C., *Newport, R. I.*
Joiner in 1767. (Richardson)

WEEKS, Thomas, *Salem, Mass.*
Turner. Came from Charlestown to Salem, April 15, 1639. On Nov. 16, 1639 granted twenty acres at the Village. (Perley, *History of Salem*, Vol. 2)

WEIBLE, Daniel, *Strode's Station, near Winchester, Ky.*
Advertised in *Kentucky Gazette*, Lexington, Jan. 23, 1790: "Daniel Weible the Cabinet-maker resides at Strode's Station," adding that he was prepared to execute the wishes of his customers promptly. (Offutt)

WELCH, Benjamin, *Lowell, Mass.*
Listed as cabinetmaker during 1835–37.

WELCH, George, *Charleston, S. C.*
Married Mrs. Christiana Smith, Oct. 10,

1804. Listed in directory in 1806 at 21 Pinckney St., in 1819 on Charlotte St. (Burton)

WELCH, Thomas, *Charlestown, Mass.*
Born 1695; died 1755. Listed as joiner.

WELD, Edward, *Boston, Mass.*
Notice of death in 1751 listed him as cabinetmaker.

WELLS, John I., *Hartford, Conn.*
Advertised in *Connecticut Courant*, Feb. 19, 1798: "JOHN I. WELLS Wants an apprentice to the Cabinet Making business. He has as usual, Cabinet Furniture for sale, likewise, Windsor, Chamber, and Kitchen Chairs of various kinds. He wishes also to sell a new Brass Clock, payment can be made easy. He wants to purchase scantling suitable for Bedsteads, and Cherry-tree Boards; a little south of the Bridge." On May 31, 1809 he again advertised for seasoned plank and for "Long horse and Cattles HAIR." On April 12, 1812 he advertised in the *Connecticut Courant*: "JOHN I. WELLS Continues the CABINET & CHAIR making business at his shop south of the bridge Hartford. He has on hand for sale a variety of furniture, to which he is adding by the assistance of good workmen. The notice of such as may want any article in his line of business, is solicited, and would be gratefully received." In 1807 he had formed a partnership with Erastus Flint under the name of Wells & Flint.

WELLS & FLINT, *Hartford, Conn.*
On Oct. 28, 1807 the following advertisement appeared in the *Connecticut Courant*: "JOHN I. WELLS, ERASTUS FLINT. The subscribers inform their friends and the public, that they have formed a connection in business under the name of WELLS AND FLINT. Their business in future will be continued at their former stands in Main Street, where Cabinet Furniture in all its variety, Sofas, Tables, Chairs, Bedsteads, etc., etc. may be seen

and purchased on the most reasonable terms."

On Sept. 2, 1807 they had advertised in the same paper: "WELLS & FLINT Have just received a quantity of glue, of a superior quality, which they offer for sale on reasonable terms. They have also on hand a general assortment of both Mahogany and Cherry-tree Furniture, made in the best and most fashionable manner. Likewise, an elegant assortment of Gilt, Fancy, Bamboo and Fanback chairs, to be disposed of on accommodating terms. N.B. Two Journeymen that are workmen, one a Cabinetmaker and the other a Chairmaker will meet with good encouragement by applying as above." On April 12, 1812 in the *Connecticut Courant* they announced, "the copartnership of Wells & Flint, is this day dissolved by mutual consent. All persons having open accounts with said firm are requested to call on Erastus Flint who is authorized to settle the same."

WERNER, John M., *Charleston, S. C.*
Listed in 1819 directory as cabinetmaker on Pinckney St.

WESSELS, John, *New York City*
Listed as chairmaker when made a freeman in 1750. Still working in 1773, when he was a witness to a will.

WEST, Abby, *New London, Conn.*
Advertised in *New London Gazette*, Feb. 22, 1807, as chairmaker. Another advertisement in the *Gazette*, Oct. 8, 1828, announced a sale of his chairs, West having died.

WEST, Samuel, *Baltimore, Md.*
Listed in directories during 1810–18 as cabinetmaker.

WEST, Thomas, *New London, Conn.*
Probably a relative of Abby. Advertised "Windsor Chairs, etc." in *New London Gazette* on April 26, 1815, March 26, 1823, and Feb. 27, 1828.

WEST, Thomas and David S., *New London, Conn.*
Advertised in *Connecticut Gazette*, April 22, 1807: "THOMAS and DAVID S. WEST Have entered into partnership, inform those who may please to favor them with their custom, that they can be supplied with Chairs and Settees of various fashions, at the new shop, opposite the Methodist meeting house, where no other branch of business will be attended to, therefore it is hoped general satisfaction will be given."

WEST, William, *Boston, Mass.*
Listed as chairmaker in 1800.

WEYMAN, Edward, *Philadelphia, Pa.; Charleston, S. C.*
Known as an upholsterer at the "Sign of the Royal Bed," at corner of Chestnut and Second streets, Philadelphia. In October 1755 moved to Charleston, taking his sign with him, and setting up a shop on Elliott St. By 1757 located on Tradd St. In 1764 was established on Queen St. in partnership with John Carne under the firm name of Weyman & Carne. Weyman advertised on Dec. 2, 1766 "That he still continued the Cabinet and Chair Work business for which purpose he has furnished himself with good workmen." It is probable that he himself was not a cabinetmaker. (*Antiques*, May 1933; Burton; Downs, No. 73)

WHARTON & DAVIES, *New York City*
In 1817 advertised "fancy chairs" both painted and in curly maple, side chairs, armchairs, rocking chairs, settees, and sofas.

WHEATON, William E., *Manchester, Mass.*
Married Sarah Augusta Edwards, March 18, 1844, at which time listed as cabinetmaker.

WHEELER, Josiah, *Boston, Mass.*
Listed as cabinetmaker in 1799.

WHIDDEN, Michael, *Portsmouth, N. H.*
Working as cabinetmaker during 1738–68. First of several generations of cabinetmakers. (*American Collector*, June 1937)

WHIPPLE, John, *Salem, Mass.*
Married Mary Hitchings, Jan. 8, 1826. Working as cabinetmaker for Kimball & Sargent at 199 Essex St. in 1837. *See* entry for Israel Fellows.

WHITCOMB, J. L., *Lowell, Mass.*
Listed only in 1833 as cabinetmaker.

WHITE, Alexander, *Salem, Mass.*
Married Nancy P. Holman, Jan. 26, 1826. Working as cabinetmaker for Kimball & Sargent at 199 Essex St. in 1837. Disappears from directories in 1842.

WHITE, Andrew, *Annapolis, Md.*
Advertised as cabinetmaker in 1761.

WHITE, Charles, *Charleston, S. C.*
Listed in directory for 1807 as cabinetmaker at 36 Broad St.

WHITE, Daniel, *Lowell, Mass.*
Listed in directory for 1832 as cabinetmaker.

WHITE, George, *Charleston, S. C.*
Listed in 1813 directory as cabinetmaker at 120 Church St.; in 1816 listed at same address but as joiner.

WHITE, Gottlieb, *Charleston, S. C.*
Born 1762 in Germany; died December 1822. Listed in directories during 1809–19 at 36 Broad St. (Burton)

WHITE, John, *Boston, Mass.*
On tax list of 1687 as joiner.

WHITE, Joseph, *Antiqua, N. H.*
Died circa 1718. Made a will in 1718 in which he left most of his estate to his brother Samuel; both were listed as joiners. (*American Collector*, June 1937)

WHITE, Peter R., *Baltimore, Md.*
Listed in directories during 1810–20 as cabinetmaker.

WHITE, Samuel, *Portsmouth, N. H.*
Brother of Joseph White (*q.v.*). Listed in Joseph's will of 1718 as joiner.

WHITELOCK, George, *Wilmington, Del.*
Born Jan. 8, 1780; died June 24, 1833. Possibly served his apprenticeship in Philadelphia. Had shop at 137 Market St., adjoining Town Hall; lived at 145 King St. Cabinet- and chairmaker. His label—found on several pieces of furniture—appears on the inside of each end door of a kidney-shaped sideboard of mahogany with satinwood inlay, standing on four tapering legs, made about 1800. This was included in the exhibition of furniture at Wilmington in 1950. It showed that his work ranks in every way with that of Philadelphia cabinetmakers of his time. (*Antiquarian*, Jan. 1930; *Antiques*, Aug. 1950)

WHITING, Jonathan, *Boston, Mass.*
Listed as cabinetmaker in 1807.

WHITNEY, Jedidiah, *Charleston, S. C.*
Listed in directories during 1813–19 as cabinetmaker at 1 St. Philip St. In 1819, however, he is listed as carpenter.

WHITNEY, Thomas, *Lexington, Ky.*
Listed in directory for 1806 as cabinetmaker on Main St. (Whitley)

WHITNEY & BROWN, *Boston, Mass.*
In 1829 advertised that they made "Fancy Chairs, at the Sign of the Large Chair, 57 Cornhill."

WHITTEMORE, John, *Charlestown, Mass.*
Born 1662. Notice of his death in Cambridge in 1702 listed him as a turner and his age as forty.

WHITTEMORE, Joseph, *Charlestown, Mass.*
Born 1688; died 1740. Probably son of John. Turner.

WHITTEMORE, Joseph, *Charlestown, Mass.*
Born 1713; died 1762. Turner. Undoubtedly the third generation of a family engaged in wood turning.

WHITTIER, Daniel, *Lowell, Mass.*
Listed as cabinetmaker in 1837.

WIGHTMAN, Richard, *Boston, Mass.*
Listed in directory for 1820 as cabinetmaker at 126 Orange St.

WIGNERON, Charles, *Newport, R. I.*
The Aaron Lopez account book (at Newport Historical Society) records the following for 1767:

Cr. Charles Wigneron
By 6 maple tea tables at £18 per agreement. Old Tenor £108

WILD, Edward, *Boston, Mass.*
Working as cabinetmaker in 1730.

WILKINSON, Robert, *Baltimore, Md.*
Listed in directory for 1799 as cabinetmaker.

WILKINSON, Thomas, *Boston, Mass.*
Listed as chairmaker on Winter St. in 1796.

WILKINSON & SMITH, *Baltimore, Md.*
Scharf wrote that "On Sunday December 4th (1783) Baltimore Town witnessed such a scene as to threaten at one time the destruction of a greater part of it. About four o'clock in the afternoon a fire broke out in a frame building on the west side of Light street, occupied as a shop by Dr. Goodwin. The flames immediately caught the frame buildings of Messrs. WILKINSON & SMITH's cabinet and manufactory on the south side, and Mr. Hawkins' two three-story brick houses. On the north they communicated to the 'magnificent structure,' the Baltimore Academy, and the Methodist meeting house."

WILL, Mathew, *Charleston, S. C.*
Listed in 1801 directory as cabinetmaker at 205 Meeting St. In 1802 in partnership with William Marlin (*sic*). In 1806 at 41 Trott St. (Burton)

WILLARD, Henry, *Boston, Mass.*
Cabinetmaker at Boston Neck in 1802.

WILLARD, Jonathan, *Providence, R. I.*
Directory of 1828 lists him as cabinetmaker at 115 South Main St.

WILLARD, Josiah, *Boston, Mass.*
Listed in directory for 1801 as chairmaker.

WILLETT, Marinus (Colonel), *New York City*
Born in 1740 in Jamaica, L. I.; died 1830. Great-grandson of Thomas Willett, first mayor of New York. Advertised in New York papers during 1773–74: "MARINUS WILLETT removed his Vendue store to the house lately occupied by Weldron & Cornell next door to Abraham Lott's Esq. Treas. Every article in the . . . CABINET or CHAIRWAY may be had on the shortest notice and executed in the best manner by Willet and Peasey, at the said Vendue store, at the sign of the Clothes press near the new Oswego market, at the upper end of Maiden-Lane, who will take dry goods in pay.

"N.B. There is on hand at either of the above places an assortment of choice mahogany furniture."

So far as is known no furniture of Willett's is in existence.

A tablet on the corner of Broad and Beaver streets, New York City, pictures Willett on June 6, 1775, seizing the wagons of the British regiment embarking to reinforce the British Army at Boston.

WILLIAMS, Ichabod, *Elizabeth, N. J.*
Working in the last years of the 1700s. Used a printed label. Made inlaid case furniture. (*Catalogue*, State Museum, Trenton, N. J., 1953)

WILLIAMS, Jacob, *Baltimore, Md.*
Listed in directories from 1800 to 1810 as cabinetmaker.

WILLIAMS, John, *Boston, Mass.*
Came from Ireland in 1715. Listed as joiner.

WILLIAMS, John and James, *Baltimore, Md.*
Cabinet- and chairmakers at 68 South St., 1833. (Varley)

WILLIAMS, Jonathan, *Newport, R. I.*
Chairmaker in 1823 at corner of Washington Square and Clarke St. (Richardson)

WILLIAMS, Moses, *Preston, Conn.*
His will, dated March 25, 1803, left his "grandson Samuel Tallman joiner's shop, land it stood on, all the tools in shop." (*Probate Wills of Norwich*)

WILLIAMS, Philip, *Annapolis, Md.*
Advertised as cabinetmaker in 1769.

WILLIAMS, Thomas Russell, *Salem, Mass.*
Baptized March 30, 1783. Married Ruth Abbot, June 22, 1806. Member of Williams & Adams on Brown St. in 1804. (*See* entries for Benjamin and Nehemiah Adams.) In *Antiques*, August 1940, is pictured an inlaid mahogany tambour secretary with the following label:

CABINET WORK
of all kinds
Made and Warranted by
THOMAS R. WILLIAMS
Brown Street, Salem
North Side of Washington Square

WILLIS, William, *Charlestown, Mass.*
Notice of arrival in Charlestown in 1663 listed him as joiner.

WILLISTON, Samuel P., *Salem, Mass.*
Listed as cabinetmaker from 1830 until 1846, after which he turned the shop at

52 Endicott St. into a variety store. Later on he followed various occupations.

WILLMONTON, Samuel, *Manchester, Mass.*
Born May 15, 1807. Married Sarah Morgan, Nov. 21, 1831, at which time called a cabinetmaker.

WILSON, Jesse, *Providence, R. I.*
Listed in directory for 1824 as cabinetmaker working over 6 North Water St., residing at 130 Main St.

WILSON, John, *Charleston, S. C.*
Advertised in *City Gazette and Daily Advertiser*, March 18, 1790, that he had "Some very elegant mahogany furniture for sale, consisting of breakfast and dining Tables, bedsteads, a very elegant commode chest of Drawers" at the sign of the "Cradle and Coffin," 217 Meeting St. Disappears from directory after 1807. (Burton)

WILSON, John, *Madison, Ind.*
A widower with six children who arrived in Philadelphia in 1808 from Ireland. Learned the trade of woodcarving and became a cabinetmaker. In 1818 moved to the Western Reserve and married a girl from Lexington, Ky. In 1821 made a cherry bureau desk in the Sheraton style, a sideboard, and a side table. The desk is illustrated and Wilson's story told in *Antiques*, October 1945.

WILSON, Joseph, *Baltimore, Md.*
Listed in directories during 1807–20 as cabinetmaker.

WILSON, Nathaniel, *Charlestown, Mass.*
Born 1661. Notice of death in 1733 listed him as joiner.

WILSON, Robert, *Lexington, Ky.*
Working in 1818 as cabinetmaker. (Whitley)

WILSON, Thomas, *Baltimore, Md.*
Listed in directories from 1800 to 1802 as cabinetmaker.

WILSON, William, *Charlestown, Mass.*

Baptized 1660. Listed as chairmaker when married in 1679 in Boston.

WILT, Jacob, *Baltimore, Md.*

Listed in directory for 1804 as cabinetmaker.

WINSLOW, Kenelm, *Plymouth and Marshfield, Mass.*

Born in Droitwich, Worcestershire, England, in 1599. He was a brother of Governor Edward Winslow of Plymouth, who came to America on the *Mayflower* in 1620. Kenelm came on a different ship, also called the *Mayflower*, which left London in March 1629 and arrived in Salem on May 15, with many Puritans for the Bay Colony and a few passengers for Plymouth. He was listed as "coffin maker," a term synonymous in the days of the Old Colony with cabinetmaker. From Salem he went down to Plymouth and in 1634 married Mrs. Ellen (Newton) Adams. She had come from London on the *Anne* in 1623 and circa 1625 had married John Adams. He arrived at Plymouth on the *Fortune* in 1620, and died in 1633, one year before her marriage to Winslow. Winslow died in Salem in 1672, Ellen in 1681.

It is thought that John Alden and Winslow both worked at cabinetmaking, either in individual shops, or, as is more likely, together. In 1632 Alden had moved to Duxbury and in 1641 Winslow had moved to Marshfield, thus both were near to each other and close to Plymouth.

There have been attributed to these two men, either working alone or together, some half dozen oaken court cupboards and twice as many chests made during the years 1650–70.

The chests are oak and pine, framed, of the stiles and rail construction, some with arched panels, some with multi-angled panels, all with serrated molding. Each chest in the group has two drawers at the bottom, placed end to end. The feet at times are square, at other times turned. Split spindles, turtlebacks, and satellites are used in their decoration. One small chest, illustrated in *Antiques*, October 1954, is of pine with the exception of some oak in the drawer linings. It is constructed of molded boards with bootjack ends. This chest has the serrated molding, a painted cedar graining, and scratched geometric decoration. It was exhibited at the Harvard Tercentenary Exhibition and a date of circa 1675 was given to it, obviously a bit late if Winslow had anything to do with its construction, since he died in 1672. At the Detroit Institute of Arts there is a dower chest of oak and pine attributed to Winslow or Alden, or both, made about 1660. Another is in Pilgrim Hall, Plymouth, Mass. This has diamond-shaped panels with five turtlebacks applied to the center of each. The moldings are serrated, and a pair of long split spindles is applied to the end stiles and to those between the three panels. Short spindles in pairs are applied to the stiles at the end of each drawer and to the space between. Another chest similar to the one in Pilgrim Hall, although bearing a label in a handwriting obviously much later in date and showing evidence of having been tampered with by some owner, is at the Stone House, Guilford, Conn. This was owned by the Hall family of Yarmouthport, Mass., for more than a century prior to 1885 and was at one time on exhibition at the Wadsworth Atheneum, Hartford, Conn.

Closely related to the chests is a small group of some half dozen court cupboards attributed to Plymouth about 1650–70. One of these is the Prince-Howes at the Wadsworth Atheneum. (PLATE I) History traces its origin directly to Plymouth. Thomas Prince (in some records spelled Prence) arrived in Plymouth in 1665 and lived there until his death in 1673. In his will he left this cupboard— of the press variety—to his wife Mary Howes, whom he had married in 1667 as his fourth wife. Mary left Plymouth shortly after her husband's death for Cape Cod, taking the cupboard with her.

There it was discovered in an old house at Dennis long years later. A second cupboard in this group, known as the Tracy Cupboard, was for some time on exhibition at the Fleming Museum, University of Vermont, but has now been returned to its owner in the West. A third is in the American Wing of the Metropolitan Museum of Art, New York City.

All the cupboards in this group are made of oak in two sections. Each section has four panels in the back; these panels, the bottoms and backs of the drawers, the interior of the cabinet, and the upper outside panels are of pine. They have a carved serrated molding running across the top and repeated between the drawers of the lower section, and they depend upon the use of spindles and turtlebacks, or bosses, for ornamentation. The moldings applied to the panels and drawers are of cedar. The heavy serrated, or toothed, molding between the drawers and on the upper section is of oak. The heavy posts of the upper section, the split spindles and bosses, the channel moldings, and the drawer panels are painted a greenish-black. While the toothed points of the serrated moldings are in the greenish-black, the spaces between the points are red. Apparently the cedar moldings were originally red.

It is thought probable that the Governor Edward Winslow Chair, made about 1635 and owned by the Pilgrim Society at Plymouth, could have been the work of Kenelm. At the Metropolitan Museum of Art there is the Plymouth Chair, which shows the same type of serration about the seat and across the lower edge of the cresting, indicating the same makers as those for the Plymouth cupboards and chests. At Pilgrim Hall, Plymouth, there is a table believed to have been used by Governor Edward Winslow in his council chamber. It is eight feet long with a single gate at each end. The turnings are early. Could this have been made by Kenelm Winslow? or John Alden? (*Antiques*, Jan. 1930; Bradford; Willison)

WISWALL, Oliver, *Boston, Mass.*
Cabinetmaker on Hawkins St. in 1789.

WOHLFAHRT, Johann Jacob, *Salem, N. C.*
Moravian cabinetmaker. In 1773 apprenticed to Andreas Broesing, joiner, and in 1775 to Frederick Beck, master joiner. Working as late as 1790. (Fries, *Records of the Moravians in North Carolina*)

WOLTZ, George, *Hagerstown, Md.*
Born 1744 in York, Pa.; died 1812 in Hagerstown, Md. His grandfather, F. R. Woltz (1696–1782), came to America from Switzerland in 1731 and settled in the German section of Pennsylvania. It is not known when George began cabinetmaking. The years 1785–1812 seem to have been his most productive. Although he is said to have worked in walnut and cherry, no cherry pieces have been identified. For a short time he advertised that he made chairs and spinning wheels. He is believed to have taught as many as fifty apprentices. Downs says that Woltz "made clock cases and chests of drawers with fluted corners in the Philadelphia style." (*Antiques*, March 1939)

WOOD, Thomas, *Charlestown, Mass.*
Born 1707. On the list of those who suffered losses in the fire of 1775, Wood's loss estimated at £4000.

WOOD, Thomas, *Charlestown, Mass.*
Born 1743; died 1814. Son of Thomas. Joiner.

WOODBRIDGE, John, *Newburyport, Mass.*
Died 1715. Notice of death listed him as joiner.

WOODBURY, Larkin, *Beverly, Mass.*
Born March 6, 1794; died after 1848. Married Louisa T. Lee on Nov. 5, 1822 and Emily Story Goldsmith on Nov. 4, 1848. Listed as cabinetmaker.

WOODILL, John Anthony, *Charleston, S. C.*

Died 1805. Joined his father-in-law, John Watson, in 1798 under name of Watson & Woodill. Listed in 1801 directory on Lynch's Lane.

WOODIN, Thomas, *Charleston, S. C.*

Died July 26, 1774. Advertised Sept. 7, 1767 in *South Carolina Gazette; and Country Journal*: "THOMAS WOODIN Carver and Cabinet Maker teaches Drawing in all its Branches . . . AND has to sell on the most reasonable terms some curious mahogany work, viz. Desks and Book-Cases with glass doors, Ladies Dressing-Tables, with all the useful apparatus; Chinese Bamboo Tea-Tables, and Kitchen Stands, &c." He lived at house of Mr. Dandridge on White Point (now White Point Gardens) at the foot of Dr. Murray's bridge, next door to Mr. Morris, the painter. (Burton)

WOODRUFF, George, *New York City*

Working from 1808 to 1816. Constructed furniture similar to the Sheraton-influenced work of Phyfe. (*American Collector*, Jan. 1938).

WOODWELL, John, *Newbury, Mass.*

Born Jan. 25, 1802 in Newburyport; died April 6, 1836 in Newbury. Cabinetmaker.

WORTHINGTON, William, Jr., *Georgetown, Va.*

Advertised in 1812 as cabinetmaker.

YEOMANS, John, *Suffield, Conn.*

Land records of 1725 list him as joiner.

YOUNG, Stephen and Moses, *New York City*

Brothers who began their partnership at 73 Broad St. in 1804, resided at 28 Marketfield St. Stephen continued in the cabinetmaking business, later moving to North Moore St., while Moses opened a mahogany yard. After 1835 Stephen is no longer listed in the New York Directory, and Moses is not listed after 1840. They worked in the style of Duncan Phyfe and may have been apprentices in his shop. A drop-leaf table in Phyfe style bears the label "Stephen and Moses Young's Cabinet & Chair Ware-House, Broad Street, 79, New York."

There seem to have been other members of this family who worked as cabinetmakers: James, listed in the directories for 1801–2 with a shop at 6 Reed St.; Paoli, who was working between 1812 and 1822; Samuel, listed as chairmaker in 1832; and Joseph, at 139 Reed St. during 1821–25. (*American Collector*, Jan. 1938)

YOUNKER, Francis, *Baltimore, Md.*

Listed as cabinetmaker in directories during 1810–20.

ZIVELY, William, *Salem, N. C.*

Moravian cabinetmaker working about 1797. (Fries, *Records of the Moravians in North Carolina*)

GLOSSARY

ACANTHUS: A leaf ornament based upon the foliage of the *Acanthus spinosus*. The basis of all foliage ornament in classic Greek and Roman decoration. Popular with certain American cabinetmakers for carved decoration, particularly Duncan Phyfe and others of his day.

APRON: A strip forming a structural part of furniture. In tables, it is the piece that connects the legs just under the top; in chairs, the piece beneath the seat; and in case furniture, the piece along the base. Sometimes called skirt.

ARM SUPPORT: The upright supporting the front end of a chair arm. It may be either an extension of the foreleg or a separate piece extended from the seat rail.

ASTRAGAL: A small semicircular or convex molding sometimes decorated with beads.

BALL FOOT: Ball-shaped base adjoining slender ankle of furniture leg. Chiefly found on seventeenth-century furniture.

BALUSTER: A small turned column, usually with a square base and cap, supporting a rail. Sometimes used in chair backs.

BALUSTER TURNING: A column-shaped turning characteristic of the Elizabethan and Jacobean periods.

BANDING: A decorative inlay or strip of veneer, usually of a different wood or material than the surface to which it is applied to give contrast in color or grain. Used around the front of drawers, on the edge of tables, and so on.

BANISTER: A baluster.

BANISTER-BACK: Pertaining to a chair with balusters, or banisters, usually split turnings, running vertically between upper and lower rails. Flat side of turnings usually toward the front.

BAROQUE: An architectural style of Italian origin also applied to furniture design. The Renaissance carried this style everywhere during the years 1550-1750. In essence the baroque style made use of large curves, broken scrolls, twisted columns, distorted and broken pediments, and oversized moldings. In its later years, there was much use of painted, gilded, and polychromed surfaces with inlays and marquetry.

BEAD: A small rounded convex molding or half round molding, either continuous or broken into small beadlike embossments.

BEADING: A small molding with beadlike design.

BELLFLOWER or HUSK ORNAMENT: Conventionalized form of a bell-shaped flower, often carved, painted, or inlaid; generally in a series forming a chain or pendant.

BEVEL: A sloping edge, of various angles. *See* also chamfer.

BLOCK FOOT: Square, vertical-sided base of a straight, untapered leg.

BLOCK FRONT: A type found on case furniture in which drawer fronts and doors display panels, the center one usually concave or sunken, those at either side convex or raised. *See* entry for John Goddard.

BOMBÉ: Pertaining to the bulging contour of case furniture. In America bombé furniture was principally made in and around Boston, Mass.

BONNET TOP: A term applied to scroll-top pieces of furniture, such as secretary, highboy, and chest-on-chest, in which the top is partly covered by an extension backwards of the scrolls. Also called hooded top.

BOSS: An ornamental round or oval protuberance. Also called egg or turtleback,

239

See entries for Allis, Belding, Dennis, and Winslow.

BOW FRONT: Convex-shaped front. Characteristic of some eighteenth-century furniture.

BOW TOP: Continuously curved top rail of a chair. Found in certain Windsors.

BRACKET CORNICE: Uppermost molding with projecting supports—brackets or modillions—at regular intervals. A feature of Elizabethan and Jacobean furniture.

BRACKET FOOT: A base used on the legs of case furniture; the corner edge straight, the inner edge curved. In the French bracket foot, both edges curved.

BROKEN PEDIMENT: Triangular-shaped pediment over windows, doors, cabinets, etc., with peak cut away and lines at each side straight or curved in swan-neck or deep scrolls.

BULBOUS: Pertaining to a turning resembling a bulb. Characteristic of turned work in sixteenth- and seventeenth-century English furniture.

BUN FOOT: A flattened bun-shaped base with narrow ankle above. The English used the term synonymously with ball foot.

CABRIOLE LEG: One shaped in a double curve, the upper part swelling out, the lower swinging in, the foot again flaring out. The knee may be plain or carved. Used with various types of feet.

CANT: An inclined surface, as in a chamfered or beveled edge.

CARTOUCHE: Ornamental scroll-shaped form enclosing a surface often painted or carved.

CHAMFER: The surface formed by the beveled cutting away of a corner or molding.

CHANNELING: Grooving or fluting used as a decorative accent on furniture.

CLAW-AND-BALL FOOT: Leg base carved to represent a bird's claw clasped around a ball. In America used extensively during Chippendale period.

CLUB FOOT: Leg base shaped like a club, with thick flat bottom. Also called Dutch foot, or pad.

COCKBEADING: A rounded molding projecting beyond an edge or surface, particularly used around case furniture drawers.

CRESTING: An ornamental top piece, usually of a chair, sofa, or mirror.

CROSS RAIL: Horizontal bar or rail in chair back.

CYMA CURVE: Simple double reversed curve similar to letter S.

DENTILS: Equally spaced rectangular blocks resembling teeth often used beneath a cornice molding.

DIAPER WORK: Surface decoration consisting of regular repeats of a design to form diagonal patterns.

DOVETAIL: Tenon shaped like dove's spread tail or reversed wedge, fitting into corresponding mortise and forming a joint. Used for joining boards at ends.

DOWEL: Headless wooden pin used to join two pieces of wood together in cabinetwork.

DRAKE FOOT: A Dutch or club foot whose sides form points or toes, usually three in number. In America, generally found on furniture constructed in the neighborhood of the Delaware River.

DRAPERY: Carved or painted drapery forms used as decoration.

DUTCH FOOT: *See* club foot and pad foot.

ESCUTCHEON: In cabinetwork, a brass or ivory fitting for keyhole or a back plate for handle or pull.

FESTOON: Loops of flowers, drapery, etc., painted or carved, used as furniture decoration.

FIDDLE-BACK: Pertaining to chair in which the back has a vertical central splat shaped like a vase or fiddle. Usually found in Queen Anne chair or its adaptations. Used in later chairs of American Empire and early Victorian styles.

FINIAL: Vertical ornament, usually of wood or brass, placed vertically to accentuate a point or the ending of a structural feature such as a post or pediment.

FLEMISH SCROLL: A baroque scroll formed of two C scrolls, one carved in the opposite direction to the other to resemble the letter S.

FLUTING: A series of hollow, rounded grooves or channels used on pilasters, legs, etc. Opposite of reeding.

FOLIATED: Having leaves or foils.

FRETWORK: Ornamental geometric pattern made of straight lines or bars usually joined at right angles; similar to lattice-

THE CABINETMAKERS OF AMERICA

work. Sometimes applied on a solid background; again carved on solid background in low relief. Used in Chinese Chippendale style of furniture and in Gothic designs.

GADROON: An ornamental edge consisting of a series of reeds or flutes in a rounded molding. Common in Tudor-Elizabethan and Jacobean woodwork. Used by some cabinetmakers in the Chippendale period.

GALLERY: Ornamental railing of wood or metal along edge of table, desk, etc.

GESSO: Plaster material used for raised decoration. Often gilded.

GOTHIC: Pertaining to the Middle Ages —twelfth to sixteenth century. Applied to architecture and furniture styles. The Gothic revival in England took place in the late eighteenth century, in America in the early nineteenth.

GOUGE CARVING: Somewhat primitive form of decorative carving done with a chisel or gouge.

GUILLOCHE: An ornament composed of curved, interlacing lines or bands.

HOODED TOP: Pertaining to those pieces of scroll-top case furniture such as chests-on-chests, highboys and secretaries, in which the top is partly covered by an extension backwards of the scrolls. Also known as bonnet top.

HOOP-BACK: Pertaining usually to a Windsor chair, in which the top rail is made of a bent piece of wood that runs in a continuous curve from one side of the seat to the other. Synonymous with bow-back.

INCISED ORNAMENT: Carved or engraved decoration.

INLAYING: A decorative process in which contrasting material is set into a grooved surface.

JACOBEAN: Pertaining to the Stuart period, immediately following the Tudor-Elizabethan—1603-88.

KETTLE FRONT: See Bombé.

KNEE: The upper convex curve or bulge of a cabriole leg.

LADDER-BACK: Pertaining to a chair with horizontal slats or rails resembling rungs of a ladder.

LAMINATE: To build up layer upon layer, each successive layer laid across the grain of the one below. This method was used in the construction of furniture by John Henry Belter.

LOZENGE: Conventional decorative diamond-shaped motif.

LUNETTE: Crescent-shaped or semicircular ornament.

MARLBOROUGH LEG: Heavy straight-grooved furniture leg used on some pieces in Chippendale style.

MARQUETRY: Inlay of various kinds of woods and veneers to form a design.

MEDALLION: Decorative frame—oval, round, square, or octagonal—enclosing a painted or carved decorative figure or ornament.

MITRE JOINT: The joint of two pieces of wood at an angle of 90 degrees so that the line of joining bisects the angle; also the joint formed in a molding where its line of direction changes.

MODILLIONS: In furniture, the projecting brackets or large molded dentils under the cornice of an entablature. Usually embellished with carving.

MOLDING: a shaped linear trim to outline cornices and other surfaces to secure a decorative effect; concave or raised continous strips of wood used as decoration or to hide joints.

MORTISE: A hole, gap, or the like, in a piece of wood designed to receive the tenon of another piece. Used in joining.

MOUNT: A piece of decorative hardware or metal ornament used on furniture.

NECKING: Any small molding or collar around the upper part of a pillar or column.

OGEE: A molding shaped in a double cyma curve with the convex sides meeting in a point; that is, a double continuous curve, concave below, passing into convex above. S-shaped in profile.

ONION FOOT: Leg base of oval shape.

ORMOLU: Gilded bronze used in the decoration of furniture. Term originally given to a coating of ground gold applied to alloys of copper and zinc. Ormolu mountings characteristic of eighteenth-century furniture. Used in America in late eighteenth and early nineteenth centuries by such cabinetmakers as Phyfe, Lannuier, and their contemporaries.

OVOLO: A rounded, convex molding.

OXBOW: Pertaining to cabinet furniture with a front having a compound curve, the central curve being concave, that at either end convex. The reverse of serpentine.

OYSTERING: A veneer showing cross-sectional grain in irregular concentric rings similar to the design on oyster shells.

PAD FOOT: End of a cabriole leg flaring into flat pad shape. Also called Dutch or club foot.

PATERA: An ornament resembling a shallow dish; small circular or elliptical carved ornament applied on pediments, doors, legs of furniture. When carved with a rose, called rosette.

PATINA: The surface color or appearance of wood resulting from polishing or wear.

PAW FOOT: Carved paw of animal used with cabriole leg.

PEDESTAL: Molded base supporting chest of drawers, cupboard, table, column, etc.

PENDANT: A hanging ornament or drop.

PILASTER: Slightly projecting pillar, usually with molded or ornamental base and cap. Often used as corner posts on case furniture.

QUARTERED: Pertaining to a log sawed into quarters, each quarter then cut into boards.

RAIL: Horizontal member in the frame of of cabinetwork or paneling.

RAKE: Angle or slant, as of chair legs or chair back.

RECESSED STRETCHER: A stretcher set back from the front so that it joins the two side stretchers as in some tables, chairs, etc.

REEDING: Semicircular molded projections. Opposite of fluting.

RIBBAND-BACK: Pertaining to back with a ribbon-like motif used in certain Chippendale chairs.

ROCOCO: A style of architecture and ornamentation chiefly developed under Louis XIV and Louis XV. Florid, making use of ornate curves, shells, etc., but much less robust than baroque.

ROSETTE: A round or foliated ornament or disk; a rose-shaped patera.

SALTIRE: An arrangement of stretchers in X form.

SCALLOP SHELL: Decorative motif popular for carving: concave semicircular shell, with ridges radiating from small ornamental base. Often used by the Goddards and Townsends on their block-front furniture.

SCRATCH CARVING: Crude carving done on early pieces with a V chisel.

SCROLL: Spiral form used in ornamentation.

SCROLL FOOT: Base of leg carved in the form of a scroll. This scroll may turn forward or backward; when it turns forward, the base is called a Flemish scroll foot, when it turns backward, the base is called an English scroll foot.

SCRUTOIRE: An enclosed writing cabinet; a desk.

SEAT RAIL: Member of the frame of a chair, settee, or bench on which the seat is built.

SERPENTINE: Pertaining to cabinet furniture with a front having a compound curve, the central curve being convex and that at either end concave. Opposite of oxbow.

SERRATED: Having sawtooth ornamentation. *See* entry for Winslow.

SLATS: Horizontal rails in a chair back.

SNAKE FOOT: End of a cabriole leg flaring into snake's head.

SPADE FOOT: A rectangular base resembling a spade at the end of a tapered leg.

SPANISH FOOT: Convex, ribbed, and spreading base of leg, sometimes slightly scrolled or turned under.

SPINDLE: A small turned pillar used in the structure or decoration of furniture; plain, or with ornamental turnings. Split spindles were used extensively on Jacobean furniture. *See* entries for Alden, Allis, Belding, Dennis, Disbrowe, Winslow. It is generally believed that split spindles were produced by gluing two pieces of wood together with a piece of paper between. These were turned as one spindle, then soaked until they separated, producing two half spindles.

SPIRAL TURNING: Twisted turned work found in chair and table legs of the seventeenth century.

SPLAT: Broad, flat upright support in middle of chair back.

SPLAY: Spread outward.

SQUAB: A loose cushion for chair or couch.

STILE: In furniture or paneling, one of the two outer vertical pieces in the frame.

STRAPWORK: Carved ornamentation imitating plaited straps, used especially in the Tudor-Elizabethan and Jacobean periods. *See* entry for Dennis.

STRETCHER: A brace between the legs of a chair, table, or other piece of furniture.

SUNBURST: Round design with rays issuing from center.

SUNRISE: Design for carving or inlay in which the design was less than a complete circle, with rays issuing from the center of the base.

SWELL FRONT: Convexly curved front.

TAMBOUR: A flexible sliding door or cover made by gluing thin strips of wood to a linen backing.

TAPER: To become smaller toward one end. Characteristic of some eighteenth-century furniture legs such as Hepplewhite.

TENON: A projection at the end of a piece of wood that fits into a hole (mortise) in the piece to which it is joined.

TOP RAIL: The top member of a chair back, sofa, or settee.

TURNING: A shape formed by woodworking tool.

TRACERY: In Chippendale furniture, applied fretwork.

TRIPOD TABLE: One with the top mounted on a center pedestal supported by three legs.

TRUMPET LEG: Sometimes pear-shaped, or combined with inverted-cup turning and bun foot. Popular on pieces of William and Mary period.

VENEER: A thin layer or layers of rare or beautiful wood glued together crosswise upon solid background. Used to gain an effect of wood grain not provided by the wood it covers.

WAINSCOT: In wainscot chairs, panelwork.

WATER LEAF: Carved detail resembling a lengthened laurel leaf. Used on Hepplewhite and Sheraton furniture. *See* entry for Hook.

BIBLIOGRAPHY

It would be neither desirable nor feasible to list every book, newspaper, record, and pamphlet studied. When any of the references below are repeatedly mentioned in the text they are abbreviated there. Any publication containing data relating to one cabinetmaker only has been listed in his biographical sketch.

Abstracts of Wills, Vols. I-VIII. At New-York Historical Society, New York City.

Adams, Sherman Wolcott. The History of Ancient Wethersfield, Connecticut, *ed.* Henry R. Stiles. New York: Grafton Press, 1904. 2 vols.

Alden, John E. Rhode Island Imprints. 1949. At the Newport Historical Society there are 327 of the volumes listed by Alden, many of great interest to the student of cabinetmakers.

Allen, Francis Olcott, *ed.* The History of Enfield, Connecticut. Lancaster, Pa.: Wickersham Printing Co., 1900. 3 vols.

American Collector. Publication containing many authoritative contributions.

Antiques, 1922-56. Magazine foremost in publishing information regarding cabinetmakers and their productions as it becomes available. Its contribution to our knowledge of southern cabinetmakers invaluable.

Baltimore Furniture, The Work of Baltimore and Annapolis Cabinetmakers from 1760 to 1810. Baltimore Museum of Art, 1947. Baltimore: John D. Lucas Printing Co.

Barber, John Warner. Connecticut Historical Collections. New Haven: Durrie and Peck, 1836.

Barbour Collection of Connecticut Vital Records. Presented to the Connecticut State Library by General Lucius A. Barbour and his son Lucius Barnes Barbour, late Examiner of Public Records. Contains copies of the entries of births, marriages, and deaths in the original town records of every town in the state—up to about 1850—where the records had not previously been published. The 139 volumes listed under names of the towns.

Bayles, Richard Mather, *ed.* History of Windham County, Conn. W. W. Preston & Co., 1889.

Belknap, H. W. Artists and Craftsmen of Essex County, Massachusetts. Privately printed, 1927. Most of data compiled from Currier, Felt, and Perley (*q.v.*).

Bentley, (The Rev.) William. Diary, 1784-1819. Salem: 1905-14. 4 vols.

Berkley, Henry J. "A Register of the Cabinetmakers and Allied Trades in Maryland as Shown by Newspapers and Directories, 1746-1812," Maryland Historical Magazine, March 1930.

Bishop, Henry Fitch. Historical Sketch of Lisbon, Connecticut, from 1786 to 1900. New York: H. F. Bishop, 1903.

Bissell, Charles S. Antique Furniture in Suffield, Connecticut. Hartford: Case, Lockwood & Brainard, 1956.

Blake, E. V. History of Newburyport, Massachusetts. 1845.

Bordley, James J. Maryland Furniture. Typewritten manuscript at Maryland Historical Society, Baltimore.

Bradford, William. Bradford's History of Plimouth Plantation. From the original manuscript. Boston: Wright and Potter Printing Co., 1898.

Brigham, Clarence S. History and Bibliography of American Newspapers 1690-1820. 1947. 20 vols. Copies of old newspapers may be found in several collections. The New York Public Library, the New-York Historical Society, the Yale University Library, and the American Antiquarian Society at Worcester, Mass., all have large numbers of old newspapers. In every capital city there is usually a collection of the state newspapers in the state library and the local historical societies have excellent collections. Newspapers began much earlier than the city directories and contain interesting advertisements and other notices. The *New York Gazette* began in 1725; the first newspaper in Maryland was published in Annapolis in 1745.

Burghers and Freemen of New York, 1701-1775. New-York Historical Society, New York City. Records of shopkeepers and tradesmen in colonial New York, all of whom were required to take the oath of loyalty to the English King, to pay fees and taxes, and to stand watch.

Burton, E. Milby. Charleston Furniture, 1700-1825. Charleston (S. C.) Museum, 1955.

Camp, David Nelson. History of New Britain, with Sketches of Farmington and Berlin, Connecticut, 1640-1889. New Britain: W. B. Thomson & Co., 1889.

Carpenter, Ralph E., Jr. The Arts and Crafts of Newport, Rhode Island, 1640-1820. Preservation Society of Newport County, 1954.

Catalogue, The Work of Baltimore and Annapolis Cabinetmakers. Exhibition at Baltimore Museum of Art, 1947.

Catalogue, Exhibition of Furniture. At Historical Society of Fine Arts, Wilmington, Del., 1950.

Catalogue, Girl Scouts Exhibition. New York, September 1939.

Catalogue, Three Centuries of Connecticut Furniture, 1635-1935. Exhibition at Wadsworth Atheneum, Hartford, 1935.

Centennial of the Social Circle in Concord, 1782-1882. Cambridge: Riverside Press, 1882.

Cescinsky, Herbert, and Hunter, George

Leland. English and American Furniture. Garden City: Garden City Publishing Co., 1929.

Chapin, (The Rev.) Alonzo B. Glastenbury for Two Hundred Years. Hartford: Case, Tiffany & Co., 1853.

Coffin, Joshua. Sketch of the History of Newbury, Newburyport and West Newbury from 1635 to 1845. 1845.

Collections of the Connecticut Historical Society, Hartford. Vol. 14: Original Distribution of the Lands in Hartford among the Settlers, 1639.

Comstock, Helen. "Furniture of Virginia, North Carolina, Georgia and Kentucky," Antiques, January 1952.

Cornelius, Charles Over. Furniture Masterpieces of Duncan Phyfe. Doubleday, Page & Co., 1922.

Cothren, William. History of Ancient Woodbury, Connecticut. Waterbury: William R. Seeley, 1871. 3 vols.

Cousins, Frank, and Riley, Philip M. The Woodcarver of Salem—Salem McIntire. Boston: Little, Brown & Co., 1919.

Crofut, Florence S. Marcy. Guide to the History and the Historic Sites of Connecticut. New Haven: Yale University Press, 1937.

Currier, J. J. History of Newburyport, Massachusetts, 1764-1909. 1906-9. 2 vols.

Dearborn, John J. A History of Salisbury, N. H. Manchester, 1890.

Directories. Sources of much information. Compiled by cities and all towns of any size. Did not appear as early as newspapers. First Maryland Directory appeared in Baltimore in 1796; that of New York City in 1786.

Documents Relative to the Colonial History of the State of New York. Albany: Weed, Parsons & Co., 1853-87. 15 vols.

Dow, George Francis. The Arts and Crafts in New England, 1704-1775. Topsfield, Mass.: Wayside Press, 1927.

Downing, Antoinette F., and Scully, Vincent J., Jr. The Architectural Heritage of Newport, R. I. Cambridge: Harvard University Press, 1952.

Downs, Joseph. American Furniture, Queen Anne and Chippendale Periods. New York City: Macmillan Co., 1952.

Dyer, Walter A. Early American Craftsmen. New York: Century Co., 1915.

Elfe, Thomas. Account Book, 1768-1775. At Charleston, S. C., Library Society.

Erving, Henry Wood. The Hartford Chest. Pamphlet published by Tercentenary Commission, State of Connecticut, 1935.

Essex Institute, Salem, Mass. Collections. Invaluable data on cabinetmakers and their works, including the Curwen Papers, 1652-1899, the Elias Hasket Derby Papers, 1776-90, the Samuel McIntire Papers, the Sanderson Papers, and many others that relate to the industrial and economic history of Salem.

Felt, Joseph B. History of Ipswich, Essex and Hamilton. Cambridge: Charles Folson, 1834.

Fraser, Esther Stevens. "Painted Furniture in America," Antiques, June and September 1924, January 1925. "Pennsylvania Bride Boxes and Dower Chests," Antiques, July and August 1925, September 1926, February, April, and June 1927.

Fries, Adelaide L. The Road to Salem. University of North Carolina Press, 1945.

———, ed. Records of the Moravians in North Carolina. University of North Carolina Press, 1943. 2 vols.

Green, Mason Arnold. Springfield, Massachusetts, 1636-1886, History of Town and City. Boston: Rockwell and Churchill, 1888.

Guild, Lurell Van Arsdale. The Geography of American Antiques. New York: Doubleday, Page & Co., 1927.

Halsey, R. T. H., and Cornelius, Charles Over. Handbook of the American Wing. Metropolitan Museum of Art, New York City, 1932.

Hayden, Arthur, and Stowe, Charles Messer. The Furniture Designs of Chippendale, Hepplewhite and Sheraton. New York City: Robert McBride and Co., 1938.

Hinckley, F. Lewis. A Directory of Antique Furniture. New York: Crown Publishers, Inc., 1953.

Hipkiss, Edwin J. Eighteenth Century American Arts; the M. and M. Karolik Collection, Museum of Fine Arts, Boston, Massachusetts.

Hornor, William MacPherson, Jr. The Blue Book, Philadelphia Furniture, William Penn to George Washington. Privately printed, Philadelphia, 1935.

Jameson, (The Rev.) E. O., ed. History of Medway, Massachusetts. 1886.

Judd, Sylvester. History of Hadley and Hatfield. Collections of papers bound into volumes at Forbes Library, Northampton, Mass.

Kettell, Russell Hawes. Early American Rooms, 1650-1858. Portland, Me.: Southworth-Anthoensen Press, 1936.

———. The Pine Furniture of New England. New York: Doubleday & Co., 1929.

Killikelly, Sarah H. The History of Pittsburgh, Its Rise and Progress. Pittsburgh: B. C. & Gordon Montgomery Co., 1906.

Kimball, Fiske. Mr. Samuel McIntire, Carver, the Architect of Salem. Published by the Essex Institute, Salem, 1940.

Little, T. W. Brief of Title, Thomas Dennis, Land, Genealogy of Colonel Thomas Dennis, His Forebears, and Descendants. Typewritten history, at Connecticut State Library, Hartford.

Lockwood, Luke Vincent. Colonial Furniture in America. New York: Charles Scribner's Sons, 1913. 2 vols.

Love, William DeLoss. The Colonial History of Hartford, Gathered from the Original Records. Hartford: 1914.

Luther, Clair Franklin. The Hadley Chest. Hartford: Case, Lockwood & Brainar Co., 1935.

Lyon, Irving Whitall. Colonial Furniture of New England, 3d ed. Boston: Houghton Mifflin, 1925.

Mason, George Champlin. Reminiscences of Newport, 1884.

Massachusetts Historical Society Collections. At the Society Headquarters, Boston.

Mechanics Festival and Historical Sketches. Providence: 1860.

Miller, Edgar G., Jr. The Standard Book of American Antique Furniture. New York: Greystone Press, 1950.

Minutes of the City of New York Common Council, 1675-1776. New York: Dodd, Mead & Co., 1905.

Moore, Mabel Roberts. Hitchcock Chairs. Pamphlet published by Tercentenary Commission, State of Connecticut, 1935.

Morse, Frances Clary. Furniture of the Olden Time. New York: Macmillan Co., 1917.

New Haven (Colony) Records of the Colony of New Haven. Hartford: Case, Tiffany & Co., 1857-58. 2 vols.

New Haven Town Records, 1659-1684, ed. Franklin Bowditch Dexter. New Haven: printed for the New Haven Colony Historical Society, 1917-19. 2 vols. Ancient Town Records.

Nutting, Wallace. Furniture Treasury, 2d ed. Framingham, Mass.: Old America Co., 1928. 3 vols.

Offutt, Eleanor Hume. "Cabinetmakers of Kentucky," Antiques, February 1954.

Orcutt, Samuel. A History of the Old Town of Stratford and the City of Bridgeport, Connecticut. Published under the auspices of the Fairfield County Historical Society. New Haven: Tuttle, Morehouse and Taylor, 1886. 2 parts.

———. History of the Towns of New Milford and Bridgewater, Connecticut, 1703-1882. Hartford: Case, Lockwood and Brainard Co., 1882.

Ormsbee, Thomas. Field Guide to Early American Furniture. Boston: Little, Brown & Co., 1951.

Perley, Sidney. The History of Salem, Massachusetts. Privately printed, Salem, 1924-28. Vol. 1 covers the years 1626-37; Vol. 2, 1638-70; Vol. 3, 1671-1716.

———. Salem in 1700. Privately printed. Salem.

Richardson, George H. Scrapbooks. At Newport Historical Society.

Rockwell, George Lounsbury. History of Ridgefield, Connecticut. Privately printed, 1927.

Rose, Jennie Haskell. "Pre-Revolutionary Cabinetmakers of Charlestown," Antiques, April and May 1933.

Rose-Troup, Frances. The Massachusetts Bay Company and Its Predecessors. New York: Grafton Press, 1930.

Sawyer, Timothy T. Old Charlestown. Boston: J. H. West Co., 1902.

Scharf, Thomas G. Chronicles of Baltimore. 1874.

Shattuck, Lemuel. History of the Town of Concord. Russell, Odiorne & Co., 1835.

Sheldon, Hezekiah Spencer. Documentary History of Suffield, in the Colony and Province of the Massachusetts Bay in New England, 1660-1749. Springfield, Mass.: Clark W. Bryant Co., 1879.

Smith, Ralph Dunning. The History of Guilford, Connecticut, from Its First Settlement in 1639. Albany: J. Munsell, 1877.

Stackpole, Everett S. History of Winthrop, Maine. 1925.

Steiner, Bernard Christian. A History of the Plantation of Menunkatuck and of the Original Town of Guilford, Connecticut, Comprising the Present Towns of Guilford and Madison. Written largely from the Manuscripts of R. D. Smyth. Privately printed, Baltimore, 1897.

Stiles, Henry R. The History and Genealogies of Ancient Windsor, Connecticut, revised ed. Hartford: Case, Lockwood and Brainard Co., 1891-92. 2 vols.

Susswein, Rita. "Pre-Revolutionary Furniture Makers of New York City," Antiques, January 1934.

Swan, Mabel Munson. Samuel McIntire, Carver, and the Sandersons, Early Salem Cabinetmakers. Essex Institute, Salem, Mass., 1934.

Thompson, J. R. History of Stratford, New Hampshire, 1773-1925. Concord: Rumford Press, 1925.

Townsend-Goddard. Metropolitan Museum of Art Studies, 1928, Part 1.

Varley, Charles. View of Baltimore. Samuel Young, 1833.

Walpole Society. The Arts and Crafts in Philadelphia, Maryland and South Carolina. Vol. 1 (1721-85), 1929; Vol. 2 (1786-1800), 1932.

Waters, Thomas Franklin. Ipswich in the Massachusetts Bay Colony. Ipswich Historical Society, 1917.

Weeks, John M. History of Salisbury, Vermont. 1860.

White, Alain Campbell. The History of the Town of Litchfield, Connecticut, 1720-1920. Compiled for the Litchfield Historical Society. Printed by the Litchfield Enquirer, 1920.

Whitley, Edna. Register of Kentucky Cabinetmakers. Kentucky Historical Society, 1951.

Willison, George F. Saints and Strangers. New York: Reynal & Hitchcock, 1945.

Woodhouse, Samuel. "Benjamin Randolph of Philadelphia," Antiques, May 1927.

Wyman, Thomas B. The Genealogies and Estates of Charlestown, in the County of Middlesex . . . Mass. Boston: D. Clapp & Son, 1879. 2 vols.